BLOOD FOR THE GHOSTS

BLOOD FOR THE GHOSTS

Classical Influences in the Nineteenth and Twentieth Centuries

Hugh Lloyd-Jones

Regius Professor of Greek
in the University of Oxford

The Johns Hopkins University Press

Baltimore, Maryland

First published in
Great Britain in 1982 by
Gerald Duckworth & Co. Ltd.
The Old Piano Factory
43 Gloucester Crescent, London NW1

© 1982 by Hugh Lloyd-Jones

First published in the
United States of America in 1983 by
The Johns Hopkins University Press
Baltimore, Maryland 21218

Library of Congress Catalog Card Number 82-49061

ISBN 0-8018-3017-6

Photoset by
E.B. Photosetting Ltd., Speke, Liverpool
Printed and bound in Great Britain by
Robert Hartnoll Ltd., Bodmin, Cornwall

'We know that ghosts cannot speak until they have drunk blood; and the spirits which we evoke demand the blood of our hearts. We give it to them gladly; but if they then abide our question, something from us has entered into them; something alien, that must be cast out in the name of truth!'

Wilamowitz, *Greek Historical Writing*, Oxford, 1908

TO MARY

Contents

Preface

We have unfortunately no exact equivalent for the German term *Nachlebenstudien*: 'the survival of the classics' will not do, for it suggests the study of the way in which classical texts and monuments survived the wreck of antiquity, whereas the term properly denotes the continuing life of the classics and the effect which they have continued to exercise upon the world. In the domain of art history and the history of the Renaissance, such studies were domesticated in England by the migration of the Warburg Institute from Hamburg in the thirties. But in that of ancient literature they have been little practised by English scholars, although eminent men from the Continent like Rudolf Pfeiffer and Arnaldo Momigliano have published important contributions to these studies in the English language. *Nachlebenstudien* often overlap with the history of scholarship, but they are not identical with it; often they are less concerned with scholars than with creative writers and other artists.

The studies contained in this book are to a great extent concerned with the period since the middle of the eighteenth century, when the Greeks came to be studied directly and no longer through Roman eyes to a greater extent than they had been before. The decline of belief in Christianity now led people to examine the pre-Christian stages of their own civilization with special care, for ancient thought and society might furnish models that might be of use in the reconstruction of our own.

At this time early Greek religion began to seem increasingly worthy of respect. Now that not even Christians maintained the truth of everything asserted in their sacred texts, now that even believers were prepared to defend the Christian myths as myths, Greek religion could no longer be disposed of by arguing that belief in its divinities was impossible. It could be seen that the gods stood for the forces that controlled the universe and that belief in them might pose less awkward problems than supernatural claims made on behalf of persons located in historical times. In that religion the gods showed no special concern for men, and on the surface it might be held to account more easily for the character of the world as we know it than a religion which by postulating a benevolent divinity obliges itself to confront the problem of evil. Greek religion has interested some of the most influential thinkers of the period in question, and has often influenced their work.

Much of what has been written about the influence of Greek literature in modern times has been concerned with the detection of direct echoes, or with modern works which make use of Greek decor but have little intrinsic relationship with Greek models. This is of small interest compared with the influence exerted by certain general characteristics of Greek literature upon those who have been able to apprehend them. The most effective use of it in modern times has been made by those who, like Goethe and Schiller, have insisted that in the best Greek writing detail always stands in close relation to the general themes which pervade the work; classicism in the best sense is the best antidote against the pedantic naturalism and wearisome accumulation of unnecessary detail that is the most tedious feature of most modern writing. Matthew Arnold in his lectures *On Translating Homer* showed English readers how Greek literature may be made use of in a creative imitation that has nothing to do with mere copying.

The enthusiasm for classical studies created by the German classicism of the great period led directly to the intensive study of ancient civilisation as a whole which marked the nineteenth century. This development inaugurated a great age of scholarship; but when scholars turned their backs on the classicism of the age of Goethe, rejecting it as an unrealistic idealisation, they also abandoned its humanistic purposes. Much learned work became dry and cumbersome, so that a hostile reaction set in. The tendency was accentuated by the separation between life and art that was prompted by Romanticism. Writers and artists, eager to protect their art from contamination by the sordid reality of the post-industrial world, marked it off as a distinct preserve, and so fatally cut it off from its roots in contemporary reality. Scholarship shared the fate of art and literature; the trend is seen in an extreme form in the career of Housman.

Nietzsche in the early seventies signalled the danger, but for many years his warning was disregarded; only after 1914 did the rift between scholarship and humanism become generally apparent. In the late twenties and early thirties a group of German scholars tried to deal with it by proclaiming the existence of what they called a 'third humanism' which was to reconcile the two; this movement petered out miserably with the coming of National Socialism, but in any case the crisis was hardly to be dealt with by such a method. It came, indeed, from the intensification of a problem which is implicit in the very nature of scholarship. On the one hand, ancient languages and philosophy can be mastered only by hard work. If scholarship were not an exact and rigorous discipline, its educational value would be small; and though classical studies are by no means the only ones that provide a useful intellectual training, their ability to do so contributes greatly to their value. On the other hand, learning exists for people, and not people for the sake of learning; we study antiquity in order to use it for our own purposes. A work of art or literature is indeed a historical document, which needs to be studied in its historical context; but it is a document that came into existence for a special purpose, and its historical and social significance cannot be properly appreciated unless its artistic purpose and character are borne in mind.

Awareness of the problem has in recent times often taken the form, especially in America, of hostility to the exact disciplines of scholarship. But though learning requires a great deal of drudgery, a scholar capable of exact detailed work need not be dry, and a would-be literary critic or humanist's work is not made admirable by the mere proclamation of a literary purpose. I have lately read a review of a number of books about Virgil's *Georgics*. One of these books is by a dunce altogether incapable of understanding the poet's words. The other is by a would-be literary scholar honoured in his own country; he is able to construe the text, but his book is as useless as the other, for it is written with a woolly imprecision and a humourless flatness that disqualify him as an interpreter of Virgil almost as much as ignorance of Latin disqualifies his companion in misfortune. The truth is that the interpretation of ancient literature is not an easy business; Napoleon said that the greatest crime is to practise a profession of which one is not the master. One must be both a competent linguist and technician and have a sympathetic understanding of literature, history and philosophy.

But apart from this perennial problem, classical studies in our time are faced with many difficulties that arise from the nature of the society that we live in. Learning languages requires time and effort. It is done most easily in childhood, when the memory is at its best and the mind is not yet ripe for more exacting kinds of study; but in our time sentimentalists, especially in America but increasingly in Europe also, wish to prevent children from being made to work. Such people are commonly contemptuous of memory and anything that may be done to train it; but when the Greeks called memory the mother of the Muses, they were only expressing the obvious truth that all learning and intelligence depend upon it. In our time power has been given to the uneducated, who are hostile to all education, but especially to education which is not vocational; the new social studies resemble the old divinity in aiming to strengthen rather than eradicate people's prejudices, and they are hostile to studies of a different kind. Against all these antagonists, civilised people must be prepared to fight.

Several of the essays in this book, like the inaugural lecture reprinted at the beginning, are concerned with scholars I have known. After I had given the lecture, a colleague of unimpeachable respectability reminded me of Housman's remark (*Collected Papers* iii 1152) that 'smoke ascending from domestic altars draws in a current of cold air from abroad'. I understand his attitude; but I am not sorry to have described the aims and methods of some distinguished scholars who have lived in recent times, and in particular to have pointed out how much classical education in England owes to the eminent men who came to this country as refugees from Hitler's persecution. Classical scholarship is and always has been a collective and an international enterprise, and it will be sad for us if the close connection with scholars abroad which these men helped us to establish is ever allowed to lapse.

The lecture on Dean Gaisford, given in honour of Lord Dacre of Glanton, and the Jane Ellen Harrison Lecture on Gilbert Murray have not appeared in print before; the essay on Goethe will soon appear as the introduction to a reprint of Humphry Trevelyan's *Goethe and the Greeks* and the obituary notices of Rudolf Pfeiffer and Sir Denys Page in the *Proceedings of the British Academy*, vol. lxv. All the other pieces have appeared previously, and I wish to thank the publishers and editors who have printed them for permission to reprint. I owe a special debt to Professor Mary Lefkowitz, to Professor Rudolf Kassel, to Mr Colin Haycraft and to Mr John Gross, Editor of the *Times Literary Supplement*, without whose encouragement many of these essays would not have been written.

Oxford, 1982   H.Ll-J.

1

Greek Studies in Modern Oxford

'A Greek Professor, especially if he brings to the task, as I do, little
enough of solid performance in scholarship, must feel it to be his first
duty to understand his predecessors.' Those words were spoken by
Professor Donald Robertson in his inaugural lecture at Cambridge
more than thirty years ago; and they have served me as a starting-
point in composing mine. A new Professor is expected to praise his
immediate predecessor, and to give some account of his own
conception of his duties. I can most easily speak of Professor Dodds
within the framework of a short account of Greek studies here from
the beginning of the nineteenth century; and if I must explain my
notion of the duties of the Professor, I should prefer to do so by giving
my own view of the achievements of my predecessors, a method which
will also give me the welcome opportunity of acknowledging my debt
to those scholars who have helped me most. No praise of a man's
scholarship is worth anything unless it comes from a scholar who is at
least his equal; and I am not so impertinent as to suppose that
anything I say about them can much gratify the eminent men of
whom I wish to speak. What I shall say of them will be said not in the
hope of pleasing them, but to show how a pupil and follower of theirs
views their achievement and interprets their example. Little of what I
have to say of the past will be new to the more senior members of my
audience; but I hope it may have some interest for the younger ones. I
remember as an undergraduate becoming gradually aware that the
history of Greek studies here in modern times had been an unusually
distinguished one; but since no general account was available, it took
me some time to piece together any sort of picture. Greek studies in
Oxford have flourished incomparably more during the present
century than during any other; and perhaps there is no harm in
someone drawing attention to this fact in public. When I have spoken
of the past, it will be easy to pass on to a word about the present and
about the future.

* Inaugural Lecture, Oxford, 1961.

If you will bear with a little pious antiquarianism, I may mention that three previous Professors have belonged to Corpus Christi College, and that seven have been what are called in Christ Church gremial members of the House. I seem to be the first to have been Fellow of a Cambridge college; that college is Jesus, which like Christ Church can now claim that its members hold both the Greek Chairs established by King Henry VIII in 1546. Nine Greek Professors at Cambridge have been at Westminster School; I am the seventh at Oxford to have been there. Had I not gone to Westminster, I should almost certainly have studied modern history; but I had as Headmaster a great teacher of the classics, a man who combined to an extraordinary degree exact scholarship with the power to make his pupils enjoy the subject – J.T. Christie, later Principal of Jesus College, Oxford.

From 1711 the Chair was held for an entire century, with one interruption of four years, by men educated at Westminster and Christ Church. If these men had other qualifications, they have left no proof of them in print. But at the end of that period Westminster and Christ Church offered a candidate who was beyond question the best Greek scholar yet produced by Oxford – Peter Elmsley. He was not appointed. Another Christ Church man was in the field, inferior to Elmsley in critical acumen, but in weight of learning even his superior. Dean Jackson gave his powerful support to Thomas Gaisford; and Lord Grenville's letter offering the Chair led him to draft the characteristic answer, 'My Lord, I have received yours and accede to the proposal.'

In intellectual distinction Gaisford cannot be compared with Elmsley; but in a much longer life his contribution to learning was to prove hardly less substantial. He edited a whole succession of classical authors, grammarians, lexicographers, and fathers of the Church; some of these works were little more than reprints, but others offered greatly improved texts, and all, but in particular the editions of the ancient metricians and lexicographers, were of real value to learning. As a Delegate of the Press for many years Gaisford did further service to Greek studies; Wilhelm Dindorf's edition of the scholia on Homer and Henry Fynes-Clinton's massive contributions to ancient chronology are only two of the many learned works which Gaisford persuaded the Delegates to accept and aided by his own enormous erudition. His correspondence with Fynes-Clinton, preserved in the library of Christ Church, shows a first-hand acquaintance with the ancient authors, pagan and Christian, that must rouse envy and admiration in scholars working now, when so much time has to be sacrificed to the study of secondary authorities. Gaisford's scholarship, like his character, belonged to an age that had vanished long before his death in 1854; solid, massive, and rugged, it had about it few of the qualities bestowed by Venus and the Graces. His vast folios, closely packed with small print and containing few comments not strictly relevant to the constitution of the text, belong to an eighteenth-century world in which the editor felt no need to concern himself with archaeology, philology, or comparative religion, or even with textual criticism in the sense now given to the term. Nor was Gaisford concerned to interpret the classics by any other means than by providing texts. During his long tenure of the Chair, it is doubtful if it ever occurred to him that he might give lectures; if the suggestion was ever made, we may be sure that he rejected it with indignation.

Gaisford lived on until the time when the first University Commission made radical changes in the old Oxford; he lived on into a time in which it must have seemed to him that Greek learning in England, if not already dead, was dying fast. The new preoccupation of the academic body with the instruction of the young and with the issuing of diplomas was, as we all know, an excellent thing; but we should not imagine that it brought immediate benefit to classical learning. On the contrary, the old kind of scholarship, represented on the one hand by chalcenteric editors of many texts like Gaisford and on the other by acute textual critics in a limited field like Porson and Elmsley, died away, and for a time no other took its place. We all remember Housman's famous allusion, inspired by a remark of Wilamowitz, to the disastrous year 1825, which consigned Dobree and Elmsley to the grave and Blomfield to the bishopric of Chester. If anyone suspects that Housman was exaggerating, let him examine the books on classical subjects bought by some college library here or in Cambridge between, say, 1820 and 1840, and see if he does not find evidence of a sharp decline in standards.

One of the few Oxford scholars who felt and resented this decline was John Conington, who had been a favourite pupil of Thomas Arnold at Rugby; his edition of Aeschylus' *Choephori*, published in 1857, is still valuable to scholars. Conington could appreciate the greatness of Gottfried Hermann, in those days the greatest living master of the Greek language; but he was no more aware than most of his colleagues of the immense widening of the whole conception of classical studies that had been accomplished by men like Boeckh, Welcker, and Karl Otfried Müller, men who insisted that the interpreter of Greek literature must concern himself not only with linguistic scholarship, but with many other disciplines that play an essential part in the study of antiquity as a whole.

Conington's *Choephori* marks him out as the best Greek scholar in

Oxford at the death of Gaisford; it is doubtful whether any of his work in Latin was its equal. But a year before Gaisford's death Conington had been chosen to fill the newly instituted Corpus Chair of Latin. Lord Palmerston's first choice as the new Greek Professor was the new Dean of Christ Church, Henry George Liddell, who had deserved well of Greek scholarship as a partner in the invaluable lexicon which was to go into seven editions during his own lifetime. But Liddell preferred not to combine the Chair with the onerous responsibilities of the Dean; Scott too was now Head of his College. Palmerston next had the fascinating idea of appointing an eminent archaeologist, the discoverer of the ancient Cnidus and Halicarnassus; but Sir Charles Newton could hardly have been expected to throw up his position at the British Museum in return for the £40 that was then the Professor's annual stipend. So the choice fell upon the celebrated Benjamin Jowett, who retained the Chair after becoming Master of Balliol in 1870 and held it until his death in 1893.

The place of this eminent man in the literary and social history of his time is, of course, assured; it would be none the less so had he never held the office of Greek Professor. To anyone who holds that the first duties of a Professor are to be a good scholar and to promote good scholarship in others, Jowett's appointment must seem a disaster. Jowett was a great teacher; he had a magnetic influence over the young; but we think of him as tutor and as Master, never as Professor. The young Housman wrote home that he had absented himself from Jowett's lectures in disgust at the Professor's gross ignorance of Greek. Here we must make allowance for a juvenile excess of rigour; but any page of the original edition of Jowett's famous translation of Plato will supply some evidence in favour of Housman's stern judgment. Even if one could forgive Jowett's deficiencies as a scholar and his reluctance to take action to amend them, what can we say of his openly expressed aversion to research, of his opposition to every scheme calculated to advance sound learning in the University, of his not only failing to perform what are usually held to be the duties of a Professor, but actually coming forward as the main adversary of the interests he might have been expected to protect? Yet it is impossible to ignore the distinctive contribution to the traditions of the Chair made by this remarkable man. The *Plato* and the *Thucydides* are defective in point of scholarship; but as literature they have great merits, and they reached, and still reach, a wide public. Jowett did take the revolutionary step of lecturing to undergraduates; even Housman might agree that something in the way of professorial lectures was better than nothing. Jowett was the first Greek Professor in modern times to interpret the classics to undergraduates, and the first to interpret them to the educated general reader. I am not persuaded that these facts tend to his discredit.

Jowett stood for the principle that all else in Oxford should be subordinated to the task of educating the young. The then equally revolutionary view that the main purpose of the University should be the pursuit of learning was championed in nineteenth-century Oxford by Mark Pattison.[1] He deserves perhaps a greater share than any other man of the credit for bringing Oxford education into line with the great movement which had originated in the Germany of F.A. Wolf and Wilhelm von Humboldt and ended by revolutionising all the universities of Europe. Too many people know Pattison simply as the author of posthumous memoirs which they suppose to shed a lurid light on university life, and which they mistakenly imagine to resemble modern fictional treatments of the subject; in fact, Pattison is many times more entertaining. In these memoirs he, like all writers with a real flair for autobiography, clearly exposes his own weaknesses; these are morbid egoism, utter lack of humour, and acute self-consciousness. But they give an astonishingly vivid picture of a mind which came to be deeply influenced by a desire for learning; and those who sympathise with that desire may find that the book exercises a powerful stimulus upon them. The life of Casaubon and the two volumes of collected essays testify to Pattison's enormously wide reading; yet the great life of Scaliger was never finished. His writings on the history of scholarship can scarcely be said to describe the work of scholars; rather, they describe the escape of scholars from the doubts and perplexities engendered by religion into the haven of the life of learning. Like the life of Milton, the life of Casaubon is really a concealed autobiography. But Pattison's writings constitute a protreptic towards scholarship that has rare power; they make one realise what he, during his life, did for his friends and pupils. Almost every serious scholar in the Oxford of his day benefited from his friendship and encouragement; and every proposal in the interest of learning had his support. Contempt and indifference towards science, so characteristic of Jowett and his circle, was utterly alien to Pattison, who never relaxed his efforts to assist Sir Ray Lankester and others to restore to science the place it had occupied in the Oxford of Wren, Hooke, and Wilkins. Pattison made ceaseless war upon the provincialism that is the besetting curse of university life. Like Jowett, he had his contacts with the literary and political world of London;

[1] See John Sparrow, *Mark Pattison and the Idea of a University* (1967).

but unlike Jowett, he kept in touch with continental scholarship, and formed with the distinguished scholar Jacob Bernays a friendship that had lasting consequences.

One unfortunate effect of Jowett's retention of the Chair after becoming Master was to exclude a Balliol man who was a far better scholar than himself, his own biographer, Lewis Campbell. Campbell would have made an admirable Professor; his edition of Sophocles is on a smaller scale than Jebb's, but he was certainly not Jebb's inferior in critical acuteness. Jowett was eventually succeeded by Ingram Bywater, who had been one of Pattison's circle, and was now fifty-three years of age. Bywater had achieved what Pattison had imagined, and had stored with immense knowledge, particularly of Greek philosophy and of the early period of modern scholarship, a mind of great precision, subtlety, and penetration. We may regret that in his later years his increasing pre-occupation with book-collecting reduced his output; the great edition of Diogenes Laertius was never finished. But his achievements are still substantial; no English scholar of his time except Jebb, Campbell, and Munro can be compared with him. Before he was thirty he had made his name by discovering portions of Aristotle's lost *Protrepticus* embedded in Iamblichus; at thirty-seven, following in the track of Pattison's friend Bernays, he published a collection of the fragments of Heraclitus that was to have a decisive influence upon Hermann Diels in his great undertaking of editing all the fragments of the philosophers before Socrates. He did masterly work upon the text of several prose writers, but most particularly Aristotle; and his commentary on the *Poetics* is, within the limits he imposed, a work of singular perfection.

'You must not expect from me,' said Bywater to Charles Cannan of the Clarendon Press, 'anything about fine art, for I don't think Aristotle said anything about it. I have looked it up in the dictionaries, and I see that the term is much later.' The early friend of Pater was certainly not indifferent to the thing denoted by that term; but he was too sensitive to the danger of reading into Aristotle ideas not earlier than Winckelmann to venture upon any discussion of modern theories of art and poetry. But the story indicates a restriction of scope which though admirable from one point of view might from another seem regrettable. 'Bywater', writes his biographer, 'did not apply Aristotle's dicta to later compositions, or form general canons of criticism by their aid.' In this he acted wisely; but his readers might still have welcomed some explanation of the differences of approach that make it unprofitable to confound Aristotelian with modern conceptions in such a way, and some account of how modern treatments of the subject differ from that of Aristotle. Bywater's notion of how a commentator or a lecturer should expound his text was one that the undergraduate or the general reader might find disagreeably austere. Not that he failed to make a deep impression upon his pupils and his colleagues, particularly through the medium of the Oxford Aristotelian Society; we think in particular of his early influence upon the Aristotelian studies of Sir David Ross. The late Dr Chapman drew an attractive portrait of Bywater in his essay called 'The Portrait of a Scholar'. One may suspect that he has somewhat softened the astringency of his formidable subject. Someone once suggested to Bywater that Heads of Houses should be chosen by means of an examination. 'That would mean no change,' he answered, 'provided you chose those who came at the bottom of the list.' That must be dated after 1870, when Jowett was elected to the Mastership of Balliol.

During the early years of the century there had come to be marked dissatisfaction among the young with the strictly textual exposition of the school of Bywater. Nothing could have done more to allay this discontent than the choice of Bywater's successor. I knew Gilbert Murray only in old age; but even then he still knew much Greek poetry by heart, and one could not hear him talk of it without being fired by his enjoyment of the subject. What impact his teaching made when he was younger can be seen from the essays published with his unfinished autobiography,[2] and in particular from that of Mrs Henderson. Murray's approach to the study of the classics was radically different from his predecessor's. When he studied a Greek play, he tried to visualise its performance; he tried to get behind the words of the text to the beliefs and attitudes that were active in its writer's mind. 'In dealing with Greek literature,' he said in his inaugural lecture of 1909, 'as with every other, in order to understand we must also feel.'

This attitude of Murray's marked a revolution; it was to this attitude that he owed much of the extraordinary effect which he made upon his contemporaries. But is it not owing to this attitude that much of his work has now become unfashionable? We cannot deny that the famous translations, which once made Euripides a living force in the London theatre, employ a language and versification alien to us, and as it seems to us, alien to the originals: nor that to his interpretation of Greek thought and literature, Murray now seems to have brought with him too much of his contemporary world. The danger of doing that is one which must be boldly faced by anyone who attempts the desperate undertaking of trying not merely to construe

---

[2] *An Unfinished Autobiography* (1960).

ancient texts, but to get an insight into the minds of those that wrote them. It is easy enough to see where one's predecessors have failed by importing modern ideas and preconceptions; it is never possible to be sure one is not committing the same offence oneself. The kind of interpretation which Murray attempted is for this reason inordinately difficult, perhaps even more difficult than emending a corrupt text or reconstituting a lost work from fragments; work like his can seldom hope to escape modification in the course of time. Wilamowitz said that a scholar should be resigned to the transitory life of his productions, and that was certainly the attitude of his friend and pupil, Gilbert Murray. Yet much that Murray has done will retain its value, and the influence of his work will long survive. In the field of linguistic scholarship, his Euripides has remained the best edition for more than half a century, and many things in it reveal the exquisite feeling for Greek that we know from his memorable versions. Let anyone who doubts it compare his text of the *Heracles* with that published by Wilamowitz with his famous commentary. But above all he will be remembered as the interpreter of Greek civilisation to his contemporaries, and as a scholar who never ceased to try to penetrate behind the written word to the thoughts and beliefs of the world from which it came.

Murray's tenure of the Chair was marked by important new developments in Greek studies here, in all of which he took an active interest. Grenfell and Hunt continued to publish at regular intervals volumes of the papyri they had brought from Oxyrhynchus, incomparably the most important of the great papyrus finds. Apart from the extension of our knowledge of Byzantine law, administration, and social life in Egypt from Ptolemaic until late Roman times, the additions to the remnant of Greek literature that we possess and to our understanding of what we had before have exercised a fertilising influence on every branch of the study of the subject. The new papyri containing Lesbian poetry stimulated Mr Lobel to produce his masterly editions of Sappho and Alcaeus. It had been customary, as in some places it still is, to 'restore' mutilated fragments of these authors with insufficient regard both to the amount of space in the manuscript left to be filled and to the linguistic and metrical practice attested by the existing texts. In the introductions to these two books Mr Lobel made a rigorous examination of Sapphic and Alcaic usage; and on this foundation offered a text that set new standards of objectivity, exactitude and critical acuteness. He later succeeded Hunt as principal editor of the literary texts in the Oxyrhynchus series; and from the first provided other editors of papyrus texts with an incomparable model of what ought to be their practice. Immense patience and skill in piecing together innumerable scraps, some of them minute; exhaustive knowledge of the remains of Greek literature and of ancient scholarship; unfailing sobriety and constant refusal to argue beyond the evidence; almost inhuman accuracy and the sharpest faculty of observation have enabled him to produce work of a perfection hardly equalled by any other editor of Greek texts who has produced so much, all of it elegantly and concisely expressed and unencumbered by superfluous parade of an acquaintance with secondary sources.

It is not quite true that Mr Lobel has done no teaching; can he not claim as a pupil our present Chancellor?[3] But we do not think of him as a teacher; when in wartime he was pressed into service to mark a collection paper, he is said to have inquired whether koppa or digamma signified the lower mark. The main labour of his life has been spent upon an object whose value for our entire comprehension of Greek literature is not easy to exaggerate; and he has done infinite service not only to his professional colleagues, but to many who could scarcely spell the name of Oxyrhynchus.

The years that have seen the publication of Mr Lobel's work on papyri have seen also the appearance of the long series of books and articles in which Sir John Beazley transformed our whole understanding of Greek vase-painting. That one is studying the classics in a university which contains these two men is a thought in which even those most hostile to the cult of personalities may take satisfaction.

Apart from Pattison and his friends, classical scholars in nineteenth-century Oxford had singularly little interest in what went on abroad. Gilbert Murray was utterly free from their insularity. As a young man he wrote to Wilamowitz and went to study under him;[4] and neither of the great wars in any way weakened his sense of classical scholarship as a collective European enterprise. When Hitler's persecution of the Jews drove out from Germany many of the foremost classical scholars, Murray at once set to work to help them; and it was largely due to him that Oxford had the great good fortune to secure the services of a number of these distinguished men. One may doubt whether even Berlin at the turn of the last century could boast of the presence of so many classical scholars of the first order as could Oxford at the time of the Second World War. The great archaeologist Paul Jacobsthal became the colleague of Sir John

[3] The Rt Hon. Harold Macmillan.
[4] In fact Murray only expressed his *intention* of going; the anecdote describes what happened to one of his pupils, but was misunderstood; see W.M. Calder and E.C. Kopff, *CP*72 (1977) 33-4.

Beazley. Felix Jacoby continued here his gigantic task of editing, with an exhaustive commentary, the fragments of the Greek historians. Rudolf Pfeiffer was able to work together with Mr Lobel upon the unpublished fragments of Callimachus from Oxyrhynchus, and to complete his great edition of this poet with its masterly commentary upon the fragments. Paul Maas, to whom I must acknowledge a special debt of gratitude, was here to place his unique mastery in the textual criticism and metric of Greek and Byzantine literature at the disposal of the Clarendon Press and of any serious student who sought his help. As Corpus Professor of Latin, Oxford obtained the services of Eduard Fraenkel, whose vast learning in both Greek and Latin is equalled only by his determination to assist his colleagues and his pupils in any way he can. To him everyone who has made a serious study of the classics here during the last quarter of the century must acknowledge a debt; and future generations also will feel gratitude to the interpreter of Horace and the author of the massive commentary on the *Agamemnon*, whose great stores of learning have benefited and will continue to benefit every genuine student of Greek poetry. No one has done more to bring it home to us that a man cannot become learned without reading books, or to remind us that we must hold hard to the conception of classical studies as a unity which Professor Fraenkel's own teacher, Wilamowitz, so splendidly maintained. Another great service done us by these distinguished men is to have made us more closely in touch with Continental scholarship; through them, we have formed connexions with foreign scholars that we greatly value.

I doubt if the teaching given by Oxford classical tutors has ever been more skilful or more conscientious than it was during the period of Murray's tenure of the Chair; yet the great sacrifices which Oxford asks of her tutors did not prevent several of these men from making important contributions to Greek scholarship. J.U. Powell produced an excellent edition of the fragments of Alexandrian poetry; and Sir Arthur Pickard-Cambridge put on a firm basis our knowledge of the antiquities of the Attic theatre, clearing the ground of many wild speculations in the process. I think with affection as well as admiration of John Dewar Denniston, whose friendship and encouragement meant much to me, as it did to many others. To be taught to write Greek by a man with his intimate knowledge of the texts, prose as well as verse, was a remarkable experience, particularly since he taught the subject with a zest, gaiety and humour that are seldom combined with so much learning. His *Greek Particles* must be considered one of the greatest contributions to our knowledge of the Greek language made during the century: it shows not only the learning, assiduity and lightness of touch of its author, but also the quality he praised in Jebb, his exceptional feeling for Greek.

I cannot forbear to mention two other scholars who were college tutors during Murray's tenure of the Chair. Over and above his achievements in other fields, Sir Maurice Bowra then made, as he is still making, important contributions to the study of Greek poetry; and he, more than any other, has been Murray's successor as an interpreter of Greek literature to the educated public of today. During Murray's last years as Professor, Denys Page began in Oxford his brilliant career as an editor and interpreter of the Greek poets. To his help and encouragement, first here at Christ Church, then in Cambridge, and ever since, I owe more than I can say. But every student of Greek literature must be grateful for the great contribution to our understanding of Homer, of tragedy, of early lyric and of all Greek poetry from the beginnings to the Byzantine age made by his deep learning, his penetrating intelligence and his splendid eloquence.

At the time of his appointment to succeed Murray, Professor Dodds was mainly known as an authority upon Neoplatonism, and as the author of a critical edition of the *Elements of Theology* of Proclus which had moved a great scholar to write that he knew no better edition of a classical text. Some people may have assumed that the new Professor had more in common with Bywater than with Murray. But that would not have been a safe assumption. Dodds had been Murray's pupil; and Murray's influence may be seen throughout his work. He had already published two articles that mark a new stage in the understanding of Euripides' thought; and in his inaugural lecture of 1936 he advocated a view of scholarship more akin to Murray's than to Bywater's. That lecture was a warning against allowing the humane element in Greek studies to be submerged by the preoccupation of scholars with the technique of their profession.

> We should not make it a complaint against a Bywater [he said] that he devoted his great powers to editing the *Poetics* for his fellow scholars instead of expounding Greek literature to England at large. But if the learned world as a whole decides to leave wide surveys to the journalist, it will promote that fatal divorce between academic and popular thinking which must end by peopling the one camp with dead truths and the other with sentimental illusions.

The works published by Professor Dodds since the delivery of that lecture are not altogether of the kind its hearers might have been led to expect. None is directed solely to the general reader, and only one can be read by those ignorant of Greek. But all are of a kind calculated to advance even the general public's understanding of antiquity; and the one book suitable for the Greekless reader is one of singular attractiveness and singular importance. We may take as a guiding thread through the development of his work his awareness, in the first instance probably derived from Murray, of the importance of understanding the irrational factors present from first to last in Greek thought but previously neglected by most modern scholars. Early in his career Professor Dodds had demonstrated from the texts that Euripides, far from being a rationalist as Verrall glibly termed him, deserves far more the epithet of irrationalist, as one who showed men in the grip of irrational forces which left them helpless. His masterly commentary on the *Bacchae* displays a command of the technique of scholarship which many who have given their whole lives to the acquisition of such technique in dealing with poetical texts may look upon with hopeless envy. Yet the most remarkable feature of the book is its introduction; where besides a full account of the religious phenomena that throw light on the action of the play, we find a judicious and sympathetic explanation of the poet's purpose that makes the most eloquent and tasteful advocacy of those who argue that Euripides was 'for' or 'against' Dionysus seem shallow and immature.

In his Sather Lectures delivered in 1949 and published two years later, Professor Dodds surveys a selection of Greek interpretations of irrational behaviour from Homer to the Hellenistic age. Great learning is applied with unfailing skill and judgement to obtain answers to problems that lie at the heart of the understanding of the ancient world. What led to the collapse of the rational elements in Greek thought before the astral determinism of Babylon and the other Oriental mystery cults? The question is not only important for the understanding of antiquity, but has a relevance to our modern situation. The topic is surveyed with an erudition and an exactitude worthy of Bywater; the choice of topic and the manner of presentation make us think of Murray.

Professor Dodds's latest major work, the edition with commentary of Plato's *Gorgias*, shows the same perfect balance between the elements of scholarship personified by his two predecessors. He has devoted to the establishment of the text a minute care which the superficial observer might find surprising in the scholar who twenty-five years ago exalted humanism at the expense of technique. But once again the splendid technical equipment of the author is focused upon an object whose understanding must tell us more not only about ancient civilisation, but about our own. No dialogue of Plato is occupied with questions more relevant to the problems of today than this. As Dodds shows in a fascinating appendix, the arguments of Socrates' chief antagonist not only anticipate, but have actually influenced those of Nietzsche, whose irrationalising tendencies typify an important element in the intellectual world of our contemporaries.

I shall make only a brief mention of other aspects of Professor Dodds's work; of his great good sense and patience in the conduct of faculty business; of his unvarying kindness to pupils and colleagues; of his lectures, with their remarkable combination of thoroughness and eloquence. Like Murray, Dodds has a memorable voice; when I first heard him lecture, during my schooldays, I rightly guessed that like Murray he had written poetry. Another poet described him in last year's Creweian Oration as the wisest man whom he had known; and Professor Auden's judgment will have found an echo in the minds of many of his hearers.

The record of Greek studies in modern Oxford does not seem to me one to be ashamed of; and yet it would be idle to deny that at the present moment classical education seems to be more than usually under attack. To some extent, these attacks proceed from that general hostility towards humane studies, which in some quarters, as one would expect, is never relaxed; but to the voices that come from these quarters are now added those of a number of more or less respectable advocates of the claims of science to an increased share of talent and of the rewards of talent. But these are not the only critics of classical education and of its present-day professional exponents: there are others who sympathise with our aims but who disapprove of the manner in which we are trying to achieve them.

Critics of the first type start by echoing Disraeli and contending that in modern England we have not one culture but two, the traditional culture and the new scientific culture. Each is ignorant of and hostile towards the other; but in particular, the traditionalists have never accepted the industrial revolution. They have shut their eyes to the obvious truth that it has improved conditions for the working classes, and must therefore be a good thing; several famous writers, but most often Ruskin and D.H. Lawrence, are said to typify this attitude. Too much talent is still being wasted on the obsolete and unproductive arts subjects, and that at a time when we desperately need more scientists and technicians in order to keep up with Russia and America. In particular, it is dangerous that politicians and administrators in a scientific age should remain ignorant of scientific matters.

To talk about two cultures seems to me both wrong and dangerous. If we are to go on using the word 'culture' in the usual way, it would seem that we had not two cultures, but one; only that this one had now become so rich and so extensive that it had become difficult for people to be equally familiar with more than a few of its different aspects. No word is more useful to the educational publicist wanting to whip up his hearers into a state of indignation than the word 'specialisation'. That specialisation involves great dangers, especially in a modern society, anyone can see; but it is equally obvious that some measure of specialisation is absolutely indispensable, particularly in a society like our own. Much as I should like to, I find it impossible to follow the work of some of my own colleagues within my own subject; how then can I expect to be ready at a moment's notice to repeat the Second Law of Thermodynamics? In fact, I believe that scientists and humanists are much better disposed to one another and much more alive to the value of one another's work than they were some thirty years ago, when most of the more prominent advocates of the 'two cultures' theory were young. This seems to me especially true of Oxford; which in view of previous history is a remarkable circumstance. Since the time of Pattison Oxford has always contained a number of humanists who protested against the attitude towards science so characteristic of Jowett and his circle. But the attitude of Jowett was still common until times well within living memory. Every reader of Sir Roy Harrod's memoir of the late Lord Cherwell will remember the comic but appalling description of how at a meeting during the twenties a number of elderly Greats philosophers tried to explain to Einstein certain logical considerations which completely ruled out of account his theory of relativity. That scene would be impossible today; and the credit for the change of attitude belongs largely to the school of logical analysis. No intelligent person who had studied in a school dominated from the end of the war until the other day by that great teacher and great philosopher, the late John Austin, could possibly retain the attitude towards science imputed by certain elderly scientists to the representatives of 'the traditional culture'.

But if men trained in the humane studies are not hostile to science, are they not dangerously ignorant of scientific matters? I am not convinced that ignorance of science in politicians or administrators is as great a danger as is commonly supposed. In order to decide on a basis of exact knowledge between the views of Cherwell and the views of Tizard, Sir Winston Churchill would have needed to be an equally distinguished scientist himself. Perhaps Sir Winston should not have been in charge at all; perhaps the main political and administrative posts should be reserved for scientists. But this arrangement would involve certain political difficulties; and since we are notoriously short of eminent scientists, they have many other things to do. There is this further difficulty, that not all men of first-rate ability are capable of profiting by a scientific or mathematical training. Some, with the best will in the world, simply do not find it interesting. Better an able arts man than an incompetent technologist; a large mass of indifferent recruits would only make life more difficult for such important people as the Cavendish Professor of Physics at Cambridge, who has lately complained that good scientists are being diverted from research by having to waste their valuable time in teaching. Most of us 'traditionalists' enjoy teaching, and will be glad to be allowed to go on trying to help those whose potentialities will be best developed by the education that we have to offer.

I believe that most enemies of 'the traditional culture' hate it because they have somehow identified it with an element in the modern English character which was accurately diagnosed by Matthew Arnold, one which has caused moments of despair to most intelligent people in the England of today; a stubborn self-complacency and an obstinate resistance to any kind of change. Contemporary literature is full of indignation against this quality; though it is rare for the writer to make an accurate diagnosis of the object that provokes his anger. Usually he identifies it with a political party, a social class, an academic subject, or a group of subjects; but a moment's reflection is enough to show that it is found in all parties, all classes and all branches of study. It is against this self-complacency, and against the philistinism and provincialism that go hand in hand with it, that all educators have to fight. It is no use saying that we need more administrators who have done this or that subject. The unexciting truth is, that we need more administrators, and indeed more people in all professions, who have lively and enterprising minds; and such people are just as likely to be found among arts graduates as among scientists.

But this kind of criticism is not the most important that we must consider. Its exaggerations are too obvious, and the prejudices that have given rise to them are too apparent. Humanistic education will always be available for many people, if only because there will always be many people who demand it; we have to inquire whether we are doing the best we can to satisfy their demand. Professional scholars have three different duties; one to their subject, one to their pupils, and one to the general public. Are classical scholars in England, and in particular here in Oxford, carrying out those duties?

We have lately been charged with neglecting our duty to the general reader; and among our critics are some who deserve to be listened to with respect. Popular interest in our subject, they point out, is very great, as the demand for translations and interpretative books attests;

comparatively few such books, they complain, are the work of professional scholars. There is some truth in this; but there are notable exceptions, and there are various extenuating circumstances. Most of what is good in the popular works now appearing has originated in the work of professional scholars. The middleman who does the useful work of conveying to the wider public ideas derived from learned sources is doing a useful piece of work; but if he then boasts of the superiority of 'amateurs' over 'professionals', we shall hardly take him seriously. But ought we to leave this work to middlemen? Should we not present our results to the general reader in a palatable form? In theory this is obviously desirable; but it is not always possible. The mass of material, both primary and secondary, which the scholar must control, is nowadays so great, the difficulties of the subject are so various and so acute, that the scholar is more desperate than ever for what to him is the most precious of all commodities, time. Most of us have to devote much of our time to teaching, especially if we happen to be in Oxford; nor should we resent that obligation. None the less, I must admit to feeling some sympathy with this complaint. We could make our subject more real to our pupils if we had been quicker to replace the critical view of Greek literature adopted during the late nineteenth century with a fresh and independent viewpoint of our own. Nothing dates so quickly as literary criticism; and that makes scholars like Housman doubt the very possibility of applying it to ancient literature. We can see where our predecessors read into ancient texts the thought of their own time: if we try to replace their critical outlook with a new one of our own, will not our work seem to our successors as uncongenial as we now find that of our predecessors? A good edition of Manilius will retain much of its value fifty years later; a book like *Five Stages of Greek Religion* will be largely out of date. Does that mean that Housman was right to dismiss Murray as one who could have been a good scholar, but preferred to be an indifferent man of letters? My answer would be, a thousand times no. I say no not simply because the impact of Murray's work on his contemporaries seems to me to justify his attempt, although to modern scholars that attempt seems unsuccessful; I say no because I believe in the possibility of understanding ancient thought, at least in some degree, without importing modern prejudices. If we carefully control every statement we make about an ancient theory or belief by reference to the evidence, if we are constantly on the watch against importing Christian or other modern preconceptions into antiquity, it seems to me that we have a slender chance of getting at the truth. Most likely we shall fail; at best, we may get at that fraction of the truth which it is possible for our generation to apprehend. But the attempt is worth while, as a few books like Dodds's *Greeks and the Irrational* seem to me to show. Murray and Dodds have both made it, and I shall do anything I can to follow them.

I have spoken of our duty to the general reader; what of our duty to our pupils? We know that all Oxford inaugural lectures are haunted by the ghost of Sir Charles Firth; who in his own suggested some changes in the syllabus, and was cut by all his colleagues for his whole tenure of the Chair. I must defy this ghost; for so many people think that Honour Moderations in its present state is unsatisfactory that I feel obliged to say something on the subject. Verse composition is now optional; but it seems that some tutors still devote most of their teaching time to composition. Many undergraduates are unable to cope with the large amount of translation, both from prepared books and unprepared, that is demanded. The essays written in the examination are on the whole poor; many candidates seem to have had little practice in writing them. More disturbing still is the low standard of much of the work done upon the special books and special subjects, the part of the examination best calculated to bring out the candidates' critical sense. Far too many simply try to reproduce what they have taken down at lectures.

Certainly the amount of work demanded is more than most of the present candidates are able or willing to perform; the men are coming up not only less well prepared, but also less prepared for hard work. But we could hardly reduce the syllabus much without serious loss, unless some changes were made in the final examination also. The amount of composition required could scarcely be cut down much further. It is true that the old type of Mods. tutor grossly exaggerated the importance of this exercise, making it an end in itself instead of a useful instrument of elementary training; and that much harm was done by the excessive fuss made about the University Scholarships. But I should strongly resist any attempt to abolish this requirement. Throughout his career Wilamowitz insisted on its value, and never ceased to try to persuade his countrymen to copy us in this respect. But it is still true that in the past tutors have spent far too much time in teaching composition. Ever since I started teaching, I have given less and less teaching time to this work. I have never found that this made the slightest difference to the quality of my pupils' versions, and I believe that the experience of many others who have done as I have done has been the same.

Can we much reduce the amount of translation done in Mods.? We must continue to demand a good deal; the importance of enabling our pupils to read the texts quickly is very great. But we can improve the quality of their work by giving them practice in translation; just as we can improve the quality of their essays by making them write more essays. It would be easier to instil a critical approach to textual criticism if undergraduates more often had the opportunity to hear the views of more than one mature scholar on the problems presented by their special books. To some extent this can be managed by discussion of such problems with their tutors; but teaching time is limited, and not every tutor can cope with every book in the syllabus. If we were to reduce the large number of special books and subjects between which the candidates may choose, it would be possible to arrange for each to be dealt with by two lectures, or by a class in addition to a lecture. These suggestions for the use of teaching time are not inventions of my own; they are only what many tutors have been doing for some years now. I believe that they can take us much of the way towards the solution of our main problems; but not all the way. We are finding it desperately hard to teach our pupils all that we must teach them within the space of five terms. It is possible that the degree of Bachelor of Philosophy, now that the syllabus has been revised, will do something to ease the strain. But the time may be approaching when we shall have to ask ourselves whether the total separation of the linguistic and literary from the historical and philosophical studies of our course can remain permanent.[5]

Finally, what of our third duty, that towards our subject? Oxford is privileged to have men of great ability to teach the classics; are they given full opportunity to contribute what they can to the advance of knowledge? I feel the strongest hostility to Jowett's view that everything in Oxford should be subordinated to teaching; but almost equally averse to the notion that everything should be subordinated to research, even if that word is being used in its good and not its sinister sense. The truth is that in a great university teaching and research should be intimately connected. Hardly anyone can be a first-rate teacher at the university level unless he has an active interest in his subject; hardly anyone can be a first-rate scholar unless he periodically subjects his notions to the test of expressing them in print. That college tutors should be active researchers is therefore a prime need of the colleges themselves. At present it is hard for classical tutors to do much research because most of them are desperately overworked. They do not complain; they would not suggest, like the eminent Cambridge physicist I have mentioned, that schoolmasters

[5] A distinguished scholar, reviewing this lecture in a periodical published behind the Iron Curtain, approved of my suggestions for changes in the curriculum, but felt certain that they would never be adopted. They had in fact been adopted before his review was published.

should be called in to take the burden from their shoulders. But if there were more of them, they could discharge their threefold duty far more effectively; and it would take only a fraction of the vast sums now being made available for science to lighten considerably the heavy burden that falls upon them.

Even as things are, college tutors continue to make a substantial contribution to scholarship. This year should see the publication of a commentary on a Greek play which everyone who has the slightest knowledge of its author's work knows is certain to prove one of the most notable of modern times.[6] If our teaching burden could be lightened, we could increase our output; but if we younger scholars are to prove anything like worthy successors to our eminent seniors, if Oxford is to keep her place as a great European centre of classical scholarship, we shall need to prosecute our studies with both zest and confidence. Scholarship has to steer a middle course between slovenly fertility and sterile perfectionism. Of the two, the former is the greater danger: but at present we in Oxford are more threatened by the latter. We are too easily daunted by the immense mass of secondary authorities upon our subject; we are too easily inhibited by authoritative sermonisings about method. The secondary authorities are important, and we ought to know our way about them; but there are moments when it is good to bear in mind that what matters most is intimate acquaintance with the ancient authors. In some matters it makes sense to talk of method, and then one must find out what the method is; but in others talk of method is merely the refuge of second-rate minds looking for a mechanical procedure that they think will automatically produce results. There are countless problems which no method applied *a priori* has a chance of solving; and here an empirical approach offers the only prospect of success. In the remarkable talk he gave on the wireless on the hundredth anniversary of the birth of Housman, D.R. Shackleton Bailey singled out the quality in Housman's work which had made the reading of the *Manilius* one of the most memorable intellectual experiences of his life. He found it in Housman's 'unremitting, passionate zeal to see each one of the innumerable problems in his text not as others had seen it or as he might have preferred it to appear, but exactly as it was'. If we can do our utmost to cultivate and keep alive that zeal, we shall have some hope of fulfilling not altogether inadequately the intimidating responsibilities that devolve upon us.

[6] W.S. Barrett (ed.), *Euripides: Hippolytos* (1964).

2

Goethe

Goethe's relationship to the Greeks is a very well-worn subject, particularly in Germany. German classical scholars have written much about it, some of it excellent; Rudolf Pfeiffer and Karl Reinhardt[1] come to mind. But others have lapsed into sentimental adulation, which has stimulated an adverse reaction. Humphry Trevelyan's book gives a full account of the facts, and discusses them with calm and sober intelligence; it continues to be indispensable. In 1949, eight years after its publication, Ernst Grumach brought out the two splendid volumes of his *Goethe und die Antike*,[2] in which Goethe's writings and recorded utterances about each ancient author and each topic relating to the study of antiquity are arranged under the appropriate headings.

In 1807 a new classical periodical, the *Museum der Altertumswissenschaft*, was dedicated to 'Goethe, dem Kenner und Darsteller des griechischen Geistes'.[3] The person responsible for the dedication was Friedrich August Wolf, the leading Greek scholar of the time, and the view of Goethe's Hellenism which it implies was widely held throughout the nineteenth century and has never been without defenders. But even during Goethe's own lifetime it did not go unopposed. In 1817 the Romantic poet Ludwig Tieck wrote that Goethe's reverence for antiquity was 'an empty superstition for a

[1] The relevant literature is enormous; I have been content to cite in the notes several studies by classical scholars which have appeared since Trevelyan's book first appeared in 1941 which supplement it in a useful way. In particular I would name the articles on Goethe by Karl Reinhardt included in *Tradition und Geist*, 1960, and cited below; Rudolf Pfeiffer, 'Goethe und der griechische Geist', *Deutsche Vierteljahrsschrift für Literaturwissenschaft und Geistesgeschichte* 12 (1934) 283f. = *Ausgewählte Schriften* (1960) 235f.; Albin Lesky, 'Goethe der Hellene', *Almanach der Universität Innsbruck* (1949) = *Jahrbuch des Goethe-Vereins* 67 (1963) 39f. = *Gesammelte Schriften* (1966) 629f.; Wolfgang Schadewaldt, *Nachwort* to GA (see n.2) ii 971f., reprinted in *Goethestudien* (1963).

[2] Ernst Grumach, *Goethe und die Antike* (2 vols.) (1949): this is subsequently referred to as *GA*.

[3] *GA* ii 946.

lifeless phantom with no substance',[4] and that opinion was shared by many of his contemporaries. In 1888, the last year of his activity, Nietzsche wrote that 'Goethe did not understand the Greeks':[5] this pronouncement, seemingly based on a crude equation of Goethe's attitude with that of Winckelmann, has found many echoes since. In 1935 Miss E.M. Butler, afterwards Schroeder Professor of German at Cambridge, argued in a book called *The Tyranny of Greece over Germany* that the admiration felt for Greek cultures by German writers, from Lessing to George, was an unmitigated disaster. This work seems to have been written in a fit of emotional disturbance caused by the National Socialists' coming to power; but it has interest as an extreme example of a widespread tendency.

Goethe's relationship to Greek art and literature is a matter of considerable importance, not only for the understanding of his own life and works, but for the history of European culture. Whatever we may feel about the nature of his Hellenism, we can hardly deny that he, more than any other individual, was responsible for the immense energy devoted to classical studies by Germany during the nineteenth century. At different times he took great pains in order to obtain the kind of acquaintance with Greek art and literature that his purposes required, and considering the number and the nature of his preoccupations, the knowledge of it which he ended by possessing must be thought very considerable. He had a high regard for scholarship; he employed a good scholar, Friedrich Wilhelm Riemer, as his indispensable assistant; and he made effective use of his friendship with scholars of the highest rank, like Friedrich August Wolf and Gottfried Hermann. But we must be on our guard against the tendency of professors to claim him as one of themselves. His interest in antiquity was above all practical, designed to serve his own purposes; in this respect, as in every other, the needs of the immediate moment, what the Greeks called *kairos*, counted for much in his life.[6] There was always an ambiguity in his feelings about scholarship, and he remained in the best sense of the words an amateur, a dilettante.

At the start of his career, classical studies were less highly regarded than at any time since the Renaissance. The wars of religion had inflicted severe damage upon them, as upon other branches of culture; the seventeenth century, despite notable achievements, had been on

---

[4] 18.12.1817, to K.W.F. Solger.
[5] In the section of *Götzen-Dämmerung* called 'Was ich den Alten verdanke', s.4 (in *Kritische Gesamtausgabe*, ed. G. Colli and M. Montinari, VI, 3 (1969) 153). See Erich Heller, 'Nietzsche and Goethe', in *The Disinherited Mind* (1952; 3rd edn., 1971) 91f.
[6] See Schadewaldt, op. cit. (in n.1 above), ad init.

the whole a period of decline. It was then that the leading spirits of the French Enlightenment decided that they could now dispense with the aid of the ancient classics, which had helped their forebears to emerge from medieval darkness, but which had now been left behind in the advance towards illumination.

No country had suffered more from the wars of religion than Germany; and there the standing of classical studies sank particularly low. Early in the eighteenth century, prevailing trends were hostile to antiquity. Rationalists agreed with the French that it was out of date; pietists disapproved of it because it had been unchristian. Greek studies were particularly backward; since the Renaissance, despite certain notable exceptions, most people had seen the Greeks through Roman spectacles. Of course many people had some acquaintance with classical mythology, usually derived from such compilations as the moralising and euhemerising handbook of Goethe's great-uncle, Johann Michael von Loën. Also, the French faction that had defended antiquity in the Battle of the Books had a not uninfluential German representative in Johann Christoph Gottsched, the disciple of Boileau; but the only literary products of this tendency were the facile Anacereontics of such writers as Gleim and Götz and the rococo Hellenism of the early Wieland.

However, signs of a new tendency could be discerned. J.M. Gesner in Göttingen and J.F. Christ in Leipzig put new life into classical teaching in their respective universities. The influence of Fénelon's *Télémaque*, using a Homeric subject to inculcate the newly fashionable virtues of simplicity and sincerity, could be seen in Germany. In a treatise published in 1740 the Swiss writer Johann Jacob Breitinger defended Homer against the strictures of Charles Perrault. Klopstock and Lessing both derived inspiration from the ancients; Lessing's studies of ancient drama combined with his own plays to loosen the hold of French dramatic theorising. In 1755, when Goethe was six, Winckelmann[7] brought out his *Gedanken über die Nachahmung der Griechen in der Malerei und Bildhauerkunst*; eight years later came his great history of ancient art. The public was beginning to tire of the baroque and the rococo, and Winckelmann's *Gedanken* met with an immediate success.

The boy Goethe picked up ancient mythology rapidly, both from books and from puppet-shows with titles like *Die Tragödie der rasenden Erzzauberin Medea*; he learned Latin well enough to delight in Ovid's *Metamorphoses*, and made a start in Greek. But among the various languages with which he played about, Greek was the one he knew

---

[7] Cf. Rudolf Pfeiffer, *History of Classical Scholarship*, ii (1976), 167f.

least well; in the novel consisting of letters from six or seven brothers and sisters supposed to be written from different places and in different languages which he wrote when he was twelve or thirteen,[8] Greek is used only in an occasional postscript added by the brother who writes Latin. It is a great deal more significant that at this age he read all of Racine and most of Corneille. After his illness in 1764, his study of philosophy in the condensed version of J.J. Brucker's history of the subject gave him a general acquaintance with the views of the principal Greek thinkers: and by the use of similar compendia he tried to obtain a notion of the main outlines of Greek history. This made him aware of the deficiency of his linguistic knowledge; and when the time came for him to attend the university, he wished to study classical philology at Göttingen. In 1763 Christian Gottlob Heyne had taken up an appointment there, and no man living would have been better capable of giving Goethe the kind of training that he felt he needed. But Goethe's father insisted that he go to Leipzig to study law.

There were at Leipzig several people would could have helped Goethe greatly, if he had made a serious effort to pursue his Greek studies. But in what on the face of it seem the somewhat desultory intellectual activities of this period in his life Greek had little part; the disappointment of an encounter with some modern Greeks who proved unable to give him the assistance he had hoped for may have discouraged him. But one experience of this time proved important in this connection. The school of art directed by Adam Friedrich Oeser, who had taught Winckelmann, contained a few casts of Greek statues, and Oeser drew Goethe's attention to the casts of ancient gems contained in the *Daktyliothek* of Philipp Daniel Lippert, which offered one of the few means of getting some notion of ancient art then readily available. Goethe was at all times deeply sensible to visual impressions; small objects of art were scarcely less fascinating to him that large ones, and he took special pleasure in the study of gems and coins. Oeser also introduced him to the works of Winckelmann. The great history of art, which had appeared in 1763, he did not read until he was in Rome in 1786; but he read at Leipzig, probably in 1766, Lessing's *Laokoon*, Winckelmann's essay on the imitation of the Greeks in painting and sculpture, and the two essays published to supplement that work during the following year. The effect of this may not have been immediate, for in 1768 he visited Dresden without seeing the collection of antiquities; but in 1769, after his return home

[8] Goethe's own dating is corrected by Hanna Fischer-Lamberg, *Der junge Goethe* i (1963) 451.

from Leipzig, he made an expedition to Mannheim to see the Elector's collection of casts, and a letter written at the time shows that the experience made a deep impression.

Trevelyan has rightly pointed out that what impressed Goethe at this time was not Winckelmann's aesthetic theory but his picture of the Greeks as a people devoted to physical and intellectual beauty and free from the constraints imposed by a society such as that which Goethe himself lived in. It was now that he formed the opinion which he never had occasion to revise, that the Greeks had been the people who, beyond all others, had lived in accordance with Nature. Winckelmann's celebrated notion that the essence of Greek art lay in 'noble simplicity and quiet greatness' did not at this time appeal to him. One of the casts that he had seen in Mannheim was of the Laocoon group, and Goethe took a lively interest in the celebrated controversy which it occasioned. Winckelmann had praised the sculptors for making Laocoon merely moan in his agony, and not scream as he does according to Virgil; Lessing had defended Virgil, pointing out that plastic art had different principles from literary art, and that Greek writers had been as ready as Virgil to represent the vocal expression of physical agony. Sculptors, on the other hand, Lessing thought, moderated that expression in order that their statues should be beautiful. The youth Goethe was greatly struck by Lessing's treatise; but he refused to accept this theory. The Greeks, whose art was based so firmly upon Nature, could not have watered down the expression of strong emotion so as to give beauty to their statues; and Goethe suggested that Laocoon does not scream only because he cannot do so, the attitude in which he is portrayed rendering it impossible. Whatever may be thought about this ingenious solution of the problem, it is remarkable that even at the age of twenty Goethe asserted his conception of the Greeks as living and creating in accordance with Nature in such a characteristic fashion.

The encounter with Herder in Strasburg during the winter of 1770-71, so decisive in many ways, brought about a marked change in his attitude towards the Greeks. Herder's assertion of the rights of natural feeling against the intellectualism of the Enlightenment implied that the poetry of unsophisticated ages, epic, folksongs and ballads, scorned by the sophisticated admirers of Voltaire, in fact possessed a special value. The Goethe of the *Sturm und Drang* period admired Ossian; he admired Shakespeare far more; but a yet more important author in his eyes was Homer, upon whom he flung himself with altogether fresh enthusiasm. Wood's essay on Homer's original genius, which fell into his hands at this time, confirmed him in the impression that Homer above all other poets wrote in accordance with the dictates of Nature. Using the Latin version by Samuel Clarke that was reprinted in Ernesti's edition, he worked hard to understand the Greek, laying the foundations of what was to become a close acquaintance with the poems. In a letter of 1771,[9] he claims to be able to read Homer almost without the aid of a translation; Homer was probably the only Greek author with whom he attained this degree of familiarity.

At this time Goethe also read a little Plato and Xenophon, and formed the design of writing a play about the death of Socrates; but this, like so many of his projects, came to nothing. He also read Anacreon, Theocritus and Pindar, who all figure in his *Wanderers Sturmlied*, where he contrasts the two former with the latter; but he can have had little notion of the real character of any of these authors. 'Anacreon' at that time meant not the real lyric and elegiac poet of the sixth century B.C., but the Anacreontic poems of later ages, from the Hellenistic to the Byzantine, which had naturally been dear to the age of the rococo. I am inclined to question Trevelyan's view that Goethe will have found Theocritus relatively easy; at any rate, neither the praise of him in *Wanderers Sturmlied* nor any subsequent mention of him by Goethe suggests a very close acquaintance. Like most readers of the seventeenth and eighteenth centuries, Goethe thought of Pindar as a rude giant with no respect for rules: that derives from the account of Pindar given by Horace in the second ode of the fourth book, not from the real author, then most imperfectly understood, even by scholars. The short lines in which *Wanderers Sturmlied* is written derive from the short lines in which it was customary to print the text of Pindar before Boeckh worked out the correct division of the periods in his edition of 1811-21; and the passage about Pindar might have been written without knowledge of Pindar's actual work. In 1772 Goethe worked hard at Pindar, doubtless using a translation. He made a translation of the fifth Olympian ode,[10] ironically enough a poem whose Pindaric authorship has been questioned since ancient times and is rejected by most modern scholars; his ignorance of the principle of metrical responsion between strophe and antistrophe does not prevent it from being a fine piece of work, since Goethe followed the words of the original, which are not irregular or 'dithyrambic' in the modern sense.

How much acquaintance with Greek tragedy lies behind the

---

[9] 6.(?). 1771, to J.D. Salzmann (*GA* i 118).

[10] *GA* i 227-8. On 'Goethes Pindar-Erlebnis', see O. Regenbogen, *Griechische Gegenwart* (1942) = *Kleine Schriften* (1961) 520f.; F. Zucker, 'Die Bedeutung Pindars für Goethes Leben und Dichtung', *Das Altertum* (1955) 171f.

reference to it in the address on Shakespeare's birthday given by Goethe in 1771 is not easy to determine. But definite evidence of his knowledge of at least one tragedy is contained in the delightful short satire 'Götter, Helden und Wieland' of 1773. Its marked resemblance to a dialogue of Lucian may be due to indirect influence; but it is worth remembering that Lucian had been the favourite author of Rektor Albrecht who taught Goethe Hebrew when he was a boy.[11] In this work Goethe ridicules what he thought the unsympathetic and patronising treatment of the Greeks in Wieland's *Alceste* and in the letters relating to it which Wieland had published in the *Teutscher Merkur*. The rococo habit of using Greece to provide a trivial kind of décor is amusingly made fun of; but even more interestingly Goethe protests against an attitude to the legend which is still common among readers. For Wieland, as for many moderns, Admetus' acceptance of his wife's sacrifice of her life in order to save his appeared intolerable. To Goethe it seemed perfectly natural; and though Euripides' attitude is doubtful in that he certainly allows the rightness of Admetus' conduct to seem questionable in the scene in which he reproaches his parents for not having been willing to make the sacrifice, there can be little doubt that the inventors of the original legend saw the matter as Goethe did.[12] Goethe would have had little sympathy with modern attempts to show by invoking a supposed irony or other unconvincing devices that Admetus is being blamed for an attitude which to him seemed natural; and we find here a signal instance of his natural sympathy with Greek modes of thought, even when they are surprising or shocking to Christian or humanitarian sentiment.

Goethe makes a colossal Hercules of boundless vital energy ridicule Wieland for having represented him as 'eine wohlgestalteter Mann mittlerer Grösse'; and his Hercules is typical of the figures from Greek mythology whom he uses as symbols during his period of *Sturm und Drang*. Prometheus stands for the creative power of the arts, Ganymede for inspiration, Dionysus, under the name of Bromius, for the universal vitalising power; Apollo, Mercury and Minerva also figure in the poetry of his 'Titanic' phase, interspersed with such figures from German and other mythology that served his purpose.

---

[11] See Paul Friedländer, 'Aristophanes in Deutschland', *Die Antike* 8 (1932) 236 = *Studien zur antiken Literatur und Kunst* (1969) 537, who seems to me slightly to exaggerate Aristophanic influence on the work. On Rektor Albrecht, see *GA* i 314-15. For Lucian's influence on Wieland, see Christopher Robinson, *Lucian and his Influence in Europe* (1979) 157f.

[12] See Kurt von Fritz, *Antike und Abendland*, 5 (1956) 53f. = *Antike und moderne Tragödie* (1962) 295f.

Goethe was still far removed from the classicism of his later life, in which Greek influences, as well as Greek images, were effective; at this time such Germanic characters as Götz von Berlichingen, the buffoon Hanswurst and Dr Faustus, originally a popular sixteenth-century caricature of a Renaissance humanist, might equally well lend themselves to his requirements.

In a letter to Herder of 1772[13] Goethe quoted from Pindar's eighth Nemean ode the saying that one should be content not to miss the mark in any of one's actions, but should have strength to master one's powerful longings. These words well describe the use he made of the Greeks during his first Weimar period, between his move to that place in 1775 and his departure to Italy in 1786. In his mind they stood for the self-discipline that could help him to shake off the strains that had troubled him during his period of *Sturm und Drang*. In the *Triumph der Empfindsamkeit*, written during the winter of 1777-78, Goethe ridiculed the sentimental affectation of the age, which his own *Werther* could hardly have been denied to have encouraged; the facile invocation of the Greeks which often accompanied this tendency does not escape his mockery. Into this satire Goethe 'criminally' (*freventlich*), as he put it, worked a poem of great power and beauty, his *Proserpina*. Trevelyan must be right in saying that the upper world for which Proserpina longs must stand for Goethe's ideal conception of Greece as a place whose inhabitants lived according to Nature, enjoying the repose and self-control which during this phase of his career meant so much to him. These qualities, fostered by the influence of Charlotte von Stein, are all-important in his *Iphigenie*, the prose version of which was begun in February of 1779. How much Greek tragedy he had read when he composed it is disputed. Scholars have claimed to find allusions to many Greek plays, and he may have known some or all of these from the *Théâtre des Grecs* of the Abbé Brumoy (1730) or from the *Das tragische Theater der Griechen* of J.J. Steinbrüchel (1763). But the only two whose influence can be demonstrated are the *Iphigenia in Tauris* of Euripides and the *Philoctetes* of Sophocles; the depiction of Iphigenia's dilemma owes something to that of the dilemma of Neoptolemus. It is worth noting that on 23 March 1780 Goethe read aloud the *Helena* of Euripides to the Grand Duchess Anna Amalia: Musgrave's edition of the year before may have come into his hands. This play is in several ways akin to the *Iphigenia in Tauris*;[14] both describe the escape of a heroine from captivity in a barbarian country, productive of anxiety but ending happily, and both create a magical atmosphere and finish

[13] 10(?).7.1772 (*GA* i 226-7).
[14] On the resemblances, see Cesare Questa, *Il ratto dal serraglio* (1979) 14f.

in peace and reconciliation. Although in later life Goethe spoke unkindly of the *Helena*, I cannot help wondering whether he knew it when he wrote his *Iphigenie*; it surely had some influence on the Helen episode of Faust. Still, though *Iphigenie* has a Greek subject and derived inspiration from Greek models, it is far further from the world of Greek tragedy than some of Goethe's later works; it is more like French tragedy, except that the interior life of the characters receives more attention. These characters, with what Trevelyan calls 'their gentle nobility and unselfishness, their perfect consideration for each others' feelings' breathe the atmosphere of the world of Charlotte von Stein, whose influence was at that time doing so much to tame and restrain the passionate young poet of the period of *Sturm und Drang*.

A work that in some respects comes closer to the Greek world than *Iphigenie* is the prose drama *Elpenor*, begun in 1781, when Goethe's interest in Greek tragedy had been stimulated by the presence in Weimar of the Swiss translator J.C. Tobler, and taken in hand again and finally abandoned two years later. The plot is Goethe's own invention, but it is like the plot of a Greek tragedy; Goethe was acquainted with the Roman mythographer Hyginus, and one wonders if he knew the summary of the plot of Euripides' *Cresphontes* which it contains.[15] The work has a Greek setting, and the characters, with their passionate hates and loves, are liker to those of a Greek tragedy than the characters of *Iphigenie*; but this play also was to end in peace and reconciliation. Trevelyan believes that the real reason for Goethe's failure to finish it lay in the inconsistency which this involved; the morality of the gentle *Iphigenie* of the first Weimar period and that of the bitterly revengeful Electra of Greek tragedy were not easily to be reconciled.

Goethe had other Greek authors also in hand during the first Weimar period. During 1777-78 he read some Aristophanes, and even adapted the *Birds* for the purpose of a modern satire. But nothing in his writings suggests an intimate relationship with this author, over whom he once even fell asleep; Aristophanes is firmly rooted in his own time and place, and presents difficulties which the aids available to Goethe could hardly have enabled him to overcome.[16] It is strange to find him studying the Orphic hymns, which praise various gods and personified abstractions in high-flown poetic language. We now know them to date from about the end of the second century A.D., and

---

[15] *Hygini Fabulae*, ed. H.I. Rose (2nd edn, 1963) cxxxvii (pp. 100f.).

[16] See Wilhelm Süss, *Aristophanes und die Nachwelt* (1911) 116f. I prefer his brief treatment to the lengthier discussion of Friedländer, op. cit. (in n.11 above), 537f.

to contain much Stoic matter;[17] but before the nineteenth century they were held to be a product of early Greek religion. Part of their content derives ultimately from Plato; it has been remarked that the wonderful poem *Urworte: Orphisch* (1820), which expresses so much of Goethe's view of life and to which I will return later, is Platonic rather than Orphic. Herder and Tobler interested Goethe in the epigrams of the Greek Anthology, and this stimulated him to compose epigrams of his own in elegiac metre; the same period saw the beginning of his experiments with the German accentual hexameter. Meanwhile he was building up his collection of casts, and was thinking much of Greek art, and particularly sculpture; the writings of the German painter Raphael Mengs, whom he later knew in Rome, served as a surrogate for those of Winckelmann. The Mignon of *Wilhelm Meisters Lehrjahre*, on which Goethe was now working, longs, like Proserpina, for the South; the wish to obtain a direct acquaintance with Greek art must have been among the many factors which impelled Goethe to take off for Italy in 1786. But when he arrived there, Greek art was only one of the things that contributed to the deep satisfaction which the expedition caused him.

Goethe had little time for the relics of the Middle Ages; at Assisi he ignored St Francis, having eyes only for a temple of Minerva that is not especially remarkable. He was impressed by certain Roman relics, such as the amphitheatre at Verona, the Colosseum and the Pantheon, but finally came away with the impression that Roman art was largely derivative, and had not much to offer him. But about the art of the Renaissance he felt very differently; on his first visit to Rome he was overwhelmed by the Sistine Chapel, and he was deeply impressed by the art of Raphael, in which he recognised, not without reason, an affinity with the Greeks. Always markedly responsive to the beauties of Nature, he was enraptured by the Italian countryside, and he was fascinated by the warmth and openness of Italian life. The South of Italy in particular delighted him, and he felt that it preserved much of the character it had had in ancient times, when it was permeated by Greek influences.

In those days Greek art, even in Italy, was far more difficult to study than it is now. Many of the works which are now most admired had not then been discovered; for example, the remains of the shrine of Zeus at Olympia, the Parthenon, the temple of Aphaea in Aegina and that of Apollo at Bassae. Many of the works which were then most

---

[17] See R. Keydell, *Pauly-Wissowas Real-Encyclopädie der cl. Altertumswissenschaft* xviii (1942) 1321f.: the best edition of the hymns is by W. Quandt (2nd edn, 1955).

admired are now known to be of far later date than was then
supposed, or even to be Roman copies of lost originals. But Goethe
showed an astonishing capacity to make the most of what was then
available.

At the very beginning of his stay, he saw in the Maffei Museum in
Verona Greek reliefs that were later the subject of wonderful
descriptions in the account of his Italian journey that he published in
1816.[18] In the Veneto Palladio's work aroused his admiration, and
served him as an example of the creative imitation of ancient models
by a man of genius. In Padua he acquired a copy of Winckelmann's
history of ancient art, which he had not read before; now it served him
as an indispensable guide in all his study of the subject. Winckelmann
had performed the essential task of distinguishing the four main
periods of Greek art, the archaic, down to Phidias, the grand or lofty
period, when Phidias, Polyclitus, Scopas and Myron were at work, the
beautiful period, from Praxiteles to Lysippus and Apelles, and the
later period of imitation. Rome contained only two works believed to
date from Winckelmann's archaic period, to which Goethe believed
that he could add a third, the Minerva Giustiniani.[19] Goethe also felt
special admiration for the Apollo Belvedere and the Laocoon group;[20]
the former is probably of the fourth century B.C., but the latter seems
to be dated by a new discovery in the first century A.D. None the less,
enough was available to give Goethe the general impression of Greek
art which he needed, and to supply his imagination with a powerful
stimulus. He observed that the representation of the gods by Greek
artists seemed to conform to certain closely defined types, and since he
believed that the gods stood for the fundamental forces which create
and sustain the universe, he felt this fact to be specially significant.
His preoccupation with the idea of Nature and the need to follow it in
life and art had led him to embrace a kind of Platonism peculiar to
himself. Just as while in Sicily he was occupied with the notion of the
Urpflanze, the original form of vegetation, so during his last stay in
Rome he was occupied with that of the *Urmensch*, the essence common
to all humanity. The Greeks, he believed, had obtained an insight into
that essence, and the types that represented the major gods gave
expression to the different qualities that belonged to it. From studying
these Goethe believed he had deduced the norm which was the
common denominator of all the variations, and so attained a

[18] See G. Rodenwaldt, 'Goethes Besuch im Museum Maffeianum zu Verona', 102.
Winckelmannsprogramm der archäologischen Gesellschaft in Berlin (1962).
   [19] See *GA* 536f. and Max Wegner, *Goethes Anschauung der antiken Kunst* (1944) 48f.
   [20] See *GA* 529f. and 547f. and Wegner, op. cit., 57f. and 69f.

knowledge of the rules which the artists had followed in producing them. For some years after his return from Italy he worked with the assistance of his friend, the expert on art Heinrich Meyer, to confirm the truth of what he called his principle by the systematic examination of many works of art. Whether or not it had any basis in fact, Trevelyan is right to say that for Goethe it 'had all the power and depth of a religious revelation', and for many years it had a most potent effect on its discoverer.

Goethe's journey to Naples and Sicily gave him the chance to make the acquaintance of some remarkable specimens of Greek architecture of the classical period. Nothing in his travels is more remarkable than his account of his visit, in March of 1787, to the fifth-century temples at Paestum.[21] The 'squat, tapering column-masses, pressed close against one another' seemed to him at first 'oppressive, even terrifying'. 'Yet I quickly pulled myself together', he goes on, 'remembered the history of art, thought of the age which found such a style fitting, called to mind the austere school of sculpture, and in less than an hour I found myself at home.' I am not sure that Trevelyan is right to infer from the strictly factual character of Goethe's description of the fifth-century temple at Segesta that he was not greatly impressed by it; his account of the temples at Agrigento, where the so-called temple of Concord certainly aroused his admiration, is equally precise and unemotional. When he was leaving for Sicily, the Prince of Waldeck asked if on his return he would care to accompany him to Greece. Greece would certainly have been uncomfortable, and Goethe might not have been able to see many monuments of ancient art; yet when we think of some of the descriptions of it written by travellers of this period, we must regret that he declined the invitation.

In Karlsbad, just before his departure for Italy, he had *Iphigenie* in hand, reading the *Electra* of Sophocles with its problems in his mind. During his progress through Verona and the Veneto and his first stay in Rome he was occupied in translating it from prose into verse, at the same time studying Euripides, who he wrote helped him to understand that love of rhetoric and argument which was even stronger in the Greeks than in the Italians. His alterations, particularly the complete rewriting of the fourth act which he carried out in Venice, were designed to make the play more like a Greek tragedy, and laid greater stress on the dark history of the House of Atreus. While in Bologna he conceived the plan of another drama, *Iphigenia at Delphi*, which was designed to present a direct clash

[21] For the relevant extracts from the *Italienische Reise*, see *GA* i 454f. (Paestum), 455f. (Agrigento), 459f. (Segesta); cf. Wegner, op. cit., 9f., 10f. and 13f.

between the Iphigenia-morality and the Electra-morality. Iphigenia and Orestes, returning from Tauris, reach Delphi at the same time as Electra, who has gone there to dedicate the axe with which so much blood has been shed in the House of Atreus. Electra, believing that Iphigenia has sacrificed her brother but not knowing her to be her sister, is about to kill her with the axe when by a fortunate chance she discovers her identity. None of this play was ever written; Goethe was distracted by the excitements of arriving in Rome. By the time he was ready to return to writing poetry, the moment for the new Iphigenia was past; for he had acquired too much sympathy with the Electra-morality to be capable of executing a work in which the Iphigenia-morality was designed to triumph.

In 1786 Goethe came to know the young poet, novelist and scholar Karl Philipp Moritz,[22] known to English readers for his entertaining account of his travels in their country, who after an unhappy life had made a name with his autobiographical novel *Anton Reiser*, and had now taken refuge in Italy after an unhappy love-affair. Goethe took greatly to Moritz, and when he broke an arm, visited him daily and cared for him like a brother. Moritz helped him with the metrical problems posed by *Iphigenie*; his manner of sketching began to show Moritz' influence. After Goethe's return from Sicily the two men earnestly discussed together the questions treated in Moritz' book *Götterlehre, oder mythologische Dichtungen der Alten* which was published in 1791.[23] The greater part of the book consists of a clearly and elegantly written guide to Greek mythology; but the first thirty or so pages contain a general account of Greek religion that is of great interest. For Moritz the Greek gods stood for the forces that control the universe; Platonism with its world of eternal and immutable ideas was simply the old religion in a new form. The gods maintain order in the universe, treating men as beings of secondary importance, and punishing severely any offence against their honour. Men represent the gods as exalted beings, whose form expresses human qualities at their highest level; but since they are part of Nature, their essential attribute is not goodness, but power. We are assured by Christian Gottfried Körner[24] that Goethe played a considerable part in the working out of these opinions, and there is little doubt that they were

[22] See now Mark Boulby, *Karl Philipp Moritz: at the Fringe of Genius* (Toronto, 1980).

[23] The *Götterlehre* was reprinted in 1948 by Moritz Schauenburg, Lahr (Schwarzwald); there is an English translation (Oxford, 1832), from the fifth German edition entitled *The Mythology of the Greeks and Romans*; cf. Max Kommerell, *Lessing und Aristoteles* (1940) 258-62.

[24] See O. Gruppe, *Geschichte der klassischen Mythologie und Religionsgeschichte* (1921) 106.

shared by him. Before the end of his first stay in Rome, he had adopted this attitude to Greek religion, and before he left for Naples on 21 February 1787 he had lost all sympathy with the Iphigenia-morality of his first Weimar period. Moritz omits to point out that the early Greek gods are moral to this extent, that Zeus in his capacity as the protector of oaths, suppliants and strangers was held to regard men's crimes against each other as an offence against his privileges which he was bound in the long run to punish. But so far as it goes the view of ancient religion taken by Goethe and Moritz is correct and its working out at this particular moment in history is an event of great significance.

Goethe's new attitude to the Greek gods was reflected in the plan for a *Nausikaa*, which he conceived while in Palermo. The subject which he chose has an obvious relation to his own life; again and again he deserted, in obedience to his daimon, as he would put it, a woman whom he had loved and who loved him. At this time he was in the process of breaking away from the most important women in his career, Charlotte von Stein, and Trevelyan must be right in finding in the tragic nature of the plot, which was to culminate in Nausicaa's suicide, a reflection of Goethe's new awareness of the sombre side of the Greek attitude to life. Only 175 lines were written, for the luxuriant vegetation of the gardens of Palermo fatally distracted him in the direction of the search for the *Urpflanze*; they excite the keenest disappointment at his failure to finish the work. One magical couplet wonderfully conveys the beauty of the Sicilian sky:

Ein weisser Glanz ruht über Land und Meer,
Und duftend schwebt der Aether ohne Wolken.[25]

Although the 'model' of the *Römische Elegien*, so far as they have one, is the Roman elegists, and particularly Propertius, they are highly expressive of the change in Goethe's outlook that reflects his new attitude to Greece. Whether or not Faustina stands for a real person, Goethe's attitude to physical love had certainly undergone a modification during his stay in Italy; and that its effects were not merely temporary is shown by his action in 1788 in installing Christiane Vulpius as his mistress. Concubines, says an ancient Athenian orator, we have for the sake of our bodily health, unlike wives, whom we have for the procreation of children and hetairai, whom we have for pleasure; I think Goethe would have agreed with

---

[25] 'A white glow rests over land and sea, and the aether hovers fragrant with no clouds.'

him. His new paganism is also reflected in the *Venezianische Epigramme*, which contain his most uninhibitedly erotic verses and also his bitterest polemics.

The years between 1790 and 1793 were an unproductive period for Goethe; perhaps his absorption in the French Revolution was connected with a need for rest after the immense intellectual exertions of the preceding period. His interest in Greek things declines correspondingly; but in 1793 we find him studying Homer and then Plato, and working carefully through the collection of ancient gems lent him by Princess Gallitzin. He distracted himself from world affairs, as he put it, by composing the four thousand hexameters of *Reineke Fuchs*, a work which is free of Homeric allusions but in which Schiller rightly recognised an Homeric tone. In 1794 Goethe's Homeric studies were stimulated by the presence in Weimar of Johann Heinrich Voss, the author of the standard German translation of the two epics, and this time saw the composition of several fine pieces of translation of passages of Homer by Goethe himself. In August 1794 he again visited the cast gallery in Dresden, and with Meyer's aid continued his investigation of the ideal canons adopted by the Greek sculptors.

The utilisation of Greek art and literature played a vital part in the immensely fruitful interchanges between Goethe and Schiller which began during the summer of 1794. The famous letter written by Schiller to Goethe on 23 August of that year shows complete awareness of the central importance to Goethe of his conception of Nature and her laws, and of the use he made of the Greek world in order to gain an insight into their working. Having been born in the north of Europe, where he was not surrounded by an ideal Nature or an idealising art, Goethe had had to correct the world that had been forced upon his imagination in accordance with the pattern which his creative spirit had made for itself; this 'could be accomplished only with the aid of guiding principles', and these had been supplied by the study of Greek art and literature. In the essay *Über Anmut und Würde* which he had published in June 1793, Schiller had argued that man should seek balance between duty and inclination, spirit and matter, *Sittlichkeit* and *Sinnlichkeit*; he should not suppress his sensual instincts, or the higher morality that resided in the harmony between the two principles could never be achieved. This point of view coincided remarkably with that which Goethe had arrived at during his Italian sojourn. In this work and in the later essay *Über naive und sentimentale Dichtung*, Schiller adopts the same view of the Greeks as a people living close to Nature and in accordance with her laws to which Goethe had for so long subscribed. Whether or not one agrees with Schiller in regarding Goethe as a 'naive' poet, one who depicts Nature directly instead of reflecting on the difference between the world and the ideal, that is certainly the kind of poet Goethe wished to be.

The aesthetic theory which the two men worked out during their collaboration strongly insisted that a work of art should express in a clear and necessary way the essential determinants (*Bestimmungen*) of its subject; it must not lose itself in details which are not related or are only loosely related to those determinants. From this basic principle the two men deduced the specific character of the various literary genres, taking their departure from a careful examination of Aristotle's *Poetics*.[26] They had no objection to the mixing of genres, which Goethe obviously practised; *Wilhelm Meister* is and is not an epic work, *Reineke Fuchs* too has epic elements, *Hermann und Dorothea* has epic features but is in general an idyll. Schiller saw that the genres predominating in the literature of his own time were those of elegy, idyll and satire, which taken together apply to most of Goethe's poetry. But they used the classification in terms of genre to bring out the nature of the essential determinants in each particular case. Their aesthetic theorising was designed to help literature to deal with the crisis of their own time. Imaginative writers were faced with the problem of the separation between the private and the public spheres, between social production and private acquisition, between man as citizen and man as individual. Hellenism supplied a suitable ideal, since its productions revealed, in the words of Lukács,[27] a unity between 'the palpable and realistic expression of the particular and the clear grasp of the essential'. What Goethe and Schiller produced was not an aestheticism remote from actual life, nor a mere trifling with forms, but a serious attempt to save literature from a decline into the accurate observation of innumerable petty details. How great the danger was we can see by glancing at the literature of the nineteenth century, but still more easily by thinking of the writings of our own contemporaries.

But when Lukács describes the crisis of the time in purely political and economic terms, it seems to me that he fails to do full justice to the two poets' purposes in a way that illustrates the characteristic weakness of Marxian theorising about literature. In his view they were trying to enable bourgeois literature to cope with the situation created by the French Revolution; they wished to obtain for Germany without revolution the results which the revolution had obtained for France. Their firm insistence on the ideal of Greek antiquity demanded of the

---

[26] See *GA* ii 771f.

[27] G. Lukács, *Goethe and his Age*, tr. R. Anchor (1968; original edition, 1947).

rising bourgeoisie a degree of self-assurance and determination which in the long run it proved unable to live up to. But Goethe and Schiller did not see their problem as one created by politics or economics. They did see that writers of their time were faced with a crisis created by the decay of Christian belief; they felt that the collapse of Christianity left the educated man without a religion. Goethe often spoke and wrote of Christianity with violent distaste; at other times he treated it with a mixture of affection and contempt. Yet he was very far from being irreligious; he laid the strongest stress on the importance of what he called *Glaube*.[28] By that he did not mean belief in any creed; his real religion is seen in his belief in the essential excellence of Nature. That as he realised is closer to the religion of the ancient Greeks than it is to Christianity; the essential attribute of their gods was not moral goodness, but power. The Greeks, he wrote, describe terrible things, we describe terribly; 'only men able to exist for themselves alone', he thought, could confront such divinities as the Zeus and the Athena who were portrayed by Phidias.

In 1795 Friedrich August Wolf published his famous *Prolegomena ad Homerum*, in which he contended that the Homeric epics had no essential unity, but had been put together out of miscellaneous lays as late as the sixth century B.C. There had been no Homer, only a succession of Homeridae, 'sons of Homer': the Homeric poems were in a sense a joint production of the Greek people. Goethe's immediate reaction[29] was hostile; he would not part readily with his belief in the individual genius of the greatest of all poets. But after thinking the matter over carefully and discussing it with Wolf himself in May 1795, he changed his mind. Indeed, he found the theory well suited to his purpose; for though he could scarcely hope to rival Homer, if there was really no Homer, but only a plurality of Homeridae, surely he too might become one of them.[30]

The idyll *Alexis und Dora*, written in 1796, is a love story set in a scene of unspoiled Nature: it was a rehearsal for a far more ambitious work. Goethe began *Hermann und Dorothea* on 11 September 1796, and completed six of its nine books during the following nine days; he astonished Schiller by turning out 150 hexameters a day. The poem deals with a subject from contemporary life, and has been called an idyll rather than an epic; it has something in common with the epyllia, 'little epics' written by Hellenistic poets. But it is a creative imitation of Homer in the best sense of the term: Homer supplies one

[28] The point is well brought out by Heller, op. cit. (in n.5 above), 96f.
[29] See *GA* i 144f.
[30] See the verses at *GA* i 146.

of the elements combined in order to create a new and original masterpiece. There are few Homeric reminiscences; what is Homeric is not only the directness and 'naiveté' of the description of the world and the movement of the action, but the firm concentration on the essentials of the plot and the close relation of each of the details to the purpose of the whole.

An interesting problem is posed by the poem on the unbinding of Prometheus which Goethe planned as early as April 1795, and of which twenty-three lines written in 1797 are all that we have. We know nothing of the plot; but Goethe's attitude to Greek religion suggests that it was very different from that of Shelley's poem on the same subject, in which Prometheus overcomes Zeus and takes over the government of the universe. As in the case of the lost *Prometheus Unbound* of Aeschylus, it is likelier that any concessions which Zeus may have made to Prometheus did not greatly affect the workings of a power which firmly kept men in a subordinate position and did not feel itself bound by the morality they had evolved.

The fragments of this work consist mainly of two choral passages; but there are also two lines of dialogue, not in ordinary German iambic pentameters, but in the remarkable imitation of the Greek iambic trimeter which Goethe used for part of the Helen episode of *Faust* and Schiller for the Montgomery scene of *Die Jungfrau von Orleans*. Karl Reinhardt[31] has shown that Goethe derived this metre from the translation of Aeschylus' *Agamemnon* by Wilhelm von Humboldt, which was not published until 1816, but an early draft of part of which was in Goethe's hands in 1797, a year when he was much occupied with Aeschylus. The rather stiff trimeters of the inventor of the metre altogether lack the marvellous ease and lightness with which Goethe was able to write in it.

Goethe now turned to a highly ambitious work upon an Homeric subject, nothing less than a continuation of the *Iliad*. He prepared himself for the writing of the *Achilleis* by a sustained course of Greek literature – Homer, tragedy, Aristophanes, minor works attributed to Homer, Herodotus, Thucydides, Plutarch; the opening lines of his poem deliberately continue the closing lines of the *Iliad* as Voss translates them. He made a careful study of every ancient treatment of the story of Achilles, and spared no effort to make the outward form of the work as Homeric as was possible. Yet if it has an affinity with any Greek poetry, it is with tragedy rather than with epic; and Goethe knew just as well as Schiller did that the whole plan of the work was

[31] See his 'Sprachliches zu Schillers Jungfrau', *Akzente* 2 (1955), 206f. = *Tradition und Geist* (1960) 366f.

unhomeric. The notion of an Achilles who is suffering from the very modern disease of weariness of life – *Weltschmerz* – is far from Homer; so is the romantic passion for Polyxena. Karl Reinhardt[32] has shown in detail how closely the *Achilleis* is related to Goethe's personal life and how typical it is of its own period; Goethe became increasingly aware of this. Like Schiller he was coming more and more to realise that his own time was so different from that of the ancient Greeks that his dream of being able to write as they had written was impossible. He finally abandoned the *Achilleis* before coming to the end of the first book, and with Schiller's encouragement decided to recreate Greece while at the same moment lamenting that Greece could not be recreated. So he came back to *Faust*, leaving the six hundred and fifty lines of the *Achilleis* as a fragment of tantalising beauty.

Faust had been begun and planned in its main outlines as early as 1775; in Rome Goethe had altered the plan and had written at least some sections of the first part. In June 1797 he resumed work on it; even as late as 1800, the Helen episode was to be on the lines of a Greek tragedy, with a chorus that sang of Helen's ancestry. September of that year saw the composition of the Helen fragment, 265 lines long. Goethe told Schiller that for a time he was tempted to separate this work from *Faust* and to complete his *Helen* as an independent tragedy; and though he decided against this course of action, he felt so much out of sympathy with the modern world that was to play its part in the romantic section of the work that he seems not to have completed the Helen episode before 1825. It was originally intended to give expression to the delight in action and creation that Goethe had attained to as a result of his Italian experience. This could not be conveyed without the tragic sense of the impossibility of permanently possessing such delight, and for the moment Goethe thought that this would have been too painful.

From September 1800, when he was working on his Helen episode, the tide of Goethe's Hellenism, to all appearances, was receding. He ceased to work intensively at Greek literature; his occupation with Greek art became desultory. True, his productions in the Weimar theatre, for some of which masks were employed, reflected his preoccupation with the notion that Greek drama is concerned with types rather than individuals. In his play *Die Natürliche Tochter*, produced in 1803, and set in contemporary France, all the characters except the heroine are denoted only by their titles or the names of

---

[32] 'Tod und Held in Goethes Achilleis', *Beiträge zur geistigen Überlieferung* (1947) 224f. = *Von Werken und Formen* (1948) 31f. = *Tradition und Geist* (1960) 283f.; cf. O. Regenbogen, op. cit. in n.9 above, *Kl. Schr.*, 495f.

their professions; but that is not an especially Hellenic feature. The essay on Winckelmann, published in 1805, marks in a sense his farewell to the active pursuit of creative imitation of Greek poetry; modern man, Goethe wrote, was too far separated from Nature by his social conditions and the state of his religion to be capable of attaining that balanced coordination of all faculties which had marked the Greeks during their greatest period. Their 'unverwüstliche Gesundheit' depended on a pagan outlook which was fundamentally opposed to the Christian view of life; it is clear that this had more importance in Goethe's eyes than the contemporary political or economic situation.

The last period of his life, from about 1805, is often referred to as his period of *Weltliteratur*, a term which owes its currency to him. He never relaxed his opposition to German romanticism, to which he applied one of his strongest terms of condemnation, the word 'unhealthy'; but he was not unkind to romantics in other countries, and he could now take a sympathetic interest in the Christian mysticism of Zacharias Werner, lend a sympathetic ear to the plea of Sulpiz Boisserée that he should support the movement for the completion of Cologne Cathedral, and make a protracted study of Near-Eastern poetry at the time of the *West-Östlicher Divan* and of Chinese poetry at that of the *Chinesisch-Deutsche Jahres- und Tageszeiten*.

At the same time, Trevelyan is right to say that 'Greece remained to the end his foremost, in a sense his only, love'; he was now making use of other cultures with the aid of the methods he had learned by his study of the Greeks. In 1817 the sculptures from Aegina in Munich and the frieze from Bassae and the Elgin Marbles in London all became accessible at almost the same time. At first Goethe thought of travelling to England to inspect the Elgin Marbles; in the end he contented himself with ordering a cast of a horse's head from the east pediment, and later ordering a painter to make lifesize drawings of the entire frieze, which he exhibited in his house in Weimar. The following year he finished off and published his essays on Myron's famous sculpture of a cow and on the pictures described by Philostratus. In the former,[33] he argues that the cow is that shown on the coins of Dyrrhachium, and warns against accepting the claim of the many Greek epigrams on the subject that its main merit was its naturalism; the latter[34] was originally meant as an introduction to a volume of etchings representing the pictures described by the sophist of the third century A.D. He followed with close interest the

[33] *GA* ii 515.
[34] *GA* ii 882f.

controversies excited by the interpretation of mythology and the ambitious theory of symbolism put forward by the Heidelberg professor Friedrich Creuzer, sharing the healthy scepticism of the great Leipzig Hellenist Gottfried Hermann. The attempt of Creuzer to derive all Indo-Germanic mythologies from a single source provoked these amusing verses:

> Auf ewig hab' ich sie vertrieben,
> Vielköpfige Götter trifft mein Bann,
> So Wischnu, Rama, Brahma, Schiven,
> Sogar den Affen Hannemann.
> Nun soll am Nil ich mir gefallen,
> Hundköpfige Götter heissen gross.
> O war' ich doch aus meinen Hallen
> Auch Isis und Osiris los![35]

Until almost the end of his life, Homer was seldom far from his thoughts. In 1820-21 he revised and finally published the digest of the *Iliad* he had made for his own use in 1798,[36] and so had occasion to reread Wolf's *Prolegomena*. His admiration for the author's learning and acuteness remained unaltered, but he found that even as his understanding followed Wolf's arguments, a strong conviction of the essential unity of both poems came over his mind.[37] Six years later this change of opinion found expression in verse:

> Scharfsinnig habt ihr, wie ihr seid,
> Von aller Verehrung uns befreit,
> Und wir bekannten überfrei,
> Dass Ilias nur ein Flickwerk sei.
> Mög' unser Abfall niemand kränken;
> Denn Jugend weiss uns zu entzünden,
> Dass wir ihn lieber als Ganzes denken,
> Als Ganzes freudig ihn empfinden.[38]

[35] 'For ever I have expelled them; many-headed gods come under my prohibition; thus Vishnu, Rama, Brahma, Shiva, even the monkey Hanuman. Now I am supposed to take pleasure in the Nile; dog-headed gods have a great name! If I could only clear out Isis and Osiris also from my halls!'

[36] *GA* i 174f.

[37] *GA* i 172f.

[38] 'With the acuteness that belongs to you you have freed us from all obligation to show respect, and we admitted in excessive freedom that the Iliad was merely something patched together. May our defection give no one pain! For young men have the power to inflame us, so that we prefer to think of Homer as a whole, and to delight in apprehending him as a whole.'

The tragedians, particularly Euripides,[39] also occupied Goethe during this period, partly because of the stimulus afforded by his friendship with Gottfried Hermann, whose gifts of books and articles sometimes provoked interesting reactions. Hermann's study of the tragic tetralogy of 1819 led Goethe to bring out four years later a brief essay[40] in which he insisted that there was nothing unsuitable in a poet's intercalating lighter entertainment amid serious matter, exemplifying this from the satyr-play which combined with three tragedies to make a tetralogy; the Euripidean satyr-play *The Cyclops* is the subject of one of his unfinished essays.[41] In 1821 Hermann sent him his paper on the fragments of Euripides' lost tragedy *Phaethon* which had been discovered in a palimpsest found among manuscripts that had belonged to Clairmont College, a Jesuit institution near Paris. The myth of Phaethon, the mortal offspring of the Sungod, who insists on being allowed to drive his father's chariot and after a brilliant beginning comes to grief, had fascinated Goethe ever since he had read it as a boy in Ovid's *Metamorphoses*; he already owned several copies of works of art that represented it. Hermann's present stimulated Goethe into writing a German reconstruction of the play, incorporating a translation of the verses of the original that survived in the palimpsest and in quotations, and based upon a serious scholarly investigation, as the accompanying notes clearly show.[42] Goethe had the assistance of two trained Greek scholars in Karl Göttling, who supplied him with a literal prose translation of the fragments, and Friedrich Wilhelm Riemer, his usual helper in such matters; but he himself was clearly the director of the enterprise. The scholarly part of it was conducted with much tact and skill, as even a reader equipped with the excellent modern edition of James Diggle,[43] incorporating the new fragment published from a Berlin papyrus in 1907, is well placed to see; and the translation of the actual fragments is one of the finest modern renderings of any Greek poetry, so that one keenly regrets that Goethe did not know the wonderful chorus starting with a description of the nightingale's song at dawn which is contained in the Berlin papyrus.

Goethe also devoted an interesting essay to the speech of Dio Chrysostom which contrasts the treatment of the legend of Philoctetes

---

[39] See in general Uwe Petersen, *Goethe und Euripides: Untersuchungen zur Euripides-Rezeption in der Goethezeit* (1974).

[40] *GA* i 249f.; cf. Petersen, op. cit., 167f.

[41] *GA* i 299.

[42] *GA* i 276f.; cf. 292f.

[43] J. Diggle, *Euripides, Phaethon* (Cambridge, 1970).

by each of the three great tragedians;[44] and he made a masterly
version of that part of the final scene of Euripides' *Bacchae*[45] in which
Cadmus awakens his daughter Agaue to a realisation of the fearful act
she has committed under the influence of Dionysiac intoxication.
During the last year of his life he was gratified by Heimann's
dedication to him of his edition of the *Iphigenia in Aulis*; he read not
only that play but the *Ion*, and in a letter to Göttling defended
Euripides against the low estimate of him made popular by A.W.
Schlegel in his famous lectures on the Greek tragedians.[46] As
Euripides' greatest work Goethe singled out the *Bacchae*. 'Kann man
die Macht der Gottheit vortrefflicher und die Verblendung der
Menschen geistreicher darstellen', he wrote, 'als es hier geschehen
ist?'[47] He remarked that it is interesting to compare this ancient
depiction of a suffering god with Christian descriptions of the agony of
Christ, and indeed the twelfth-century author of the *Christus Patiens*
used extracts from the *Bacchae* to construct a cento which described
that subject.[48]

Goethe in his talks with Eckermann made remarks about Sophocles
that are of much interest:[49] he was far from sharing Hegel's opinion
that Creon in the *Antigone* represents the point of view of the state, and
therefore has some degree of reason on his side. In 1831 he heartily
enjoyed Paul-Louis Courier's new translation of Longus' *Daphnis and
Chloe*, a work of which he had entertained a high opinion since reading
Amyot's version in 1807.[50] Goethe retained enough of the eighteenth-
century admiration for a simple life in proximity to Nature to find this
author's somewhat artificial naiveté appealing.

Goethe's preoccupation with the Greeks reached its climax and
found its summing-up in the final version of the episode of Helen and
in the *Klassische Walpurgisnacht*[51] written in order to lead up to it in
1825. The whole business of the conjuring-up of Helen to amuse the
frivolous Emperor and his courtiers is introduced almost casually, and

[44] *GA* i 251f.

[45] *GA* i 288f.

[46] *GA* i 297-8.

[47] 'Could there be a finer depiction of the power of the divinity or a more intelligent
portrayal of the blindness of men than we find here?'

[48] For recent discussion and bibliography, see Innocenza Giudice Rizzo, *Siculorum
Gymnasium* 29 (1977) 1f.

[49] *GA* v 261f.

[50] *GA* i 316f.

[51] See Karl Reinhardt, 'Die klassische Walpurgisnacht; Entstehung und
Bedeutung', *Antike und Abendland* 1 (1945) 133f. = *Von Werken und Formen* (1948) 348f.
= *Tradition und Geist* (1960) 309f.; cf. Paul Friedländer, 'Mythen und Landschaft im
zweiten Teil des Faust' (1953) = *Studien zur antiken Literatur und Kunst* (1969) 572f.

the suggestion is treated deprecatingly by Mephistopheles. Then comes the moving and perplexing episode of the descent to the mysterious deities called the Mothers, held by Mephistopheles to be necessary before the conjuration can be managed. Goethe told Eckermann that he had learned of the existence of the Mothers from a puzzling reference in Plutarch's life of Marcellus (ch. 20);[52] nothing is known of them from any other source, but for Goethe they are mysterious female spirits of Nature and life. As Trevelyan says, one must be cautious about the exact significance of the episode; but it serves to emphasise the danger and difficulty of the enterprise of evoking Helen, and it suggests an awareness of the dark and mysterious side of Greek religion not easily explained by the popular and superficial view of Goethe's Hellenism.

Goethe never quite forgot the rococo Greece of his early years, which he had come to view with an amused indulgence; and it makes a last appearance in the *Klassische Walpurgisnacht*, where the strange monsters, horrors and supernatural beings of various kinds that proliferate in Greek mythology parade for our amusement. At the same time they help to strengthen our impression of the uncanny and irrational elements in Greek religion, and to remind us of the important truth that the whole calling-up of Helen is not a matter-of-fact episode, but part of a magical phantasmagoria. After the monsters, the appearance of the wise centaur Chiron and other more exalted figures bring us nearer to heroic Greece.

Now comes the Helen episode,[53] revised and expanded from the Helen fragment of 1800. Helen had been sent on ahead from Troy by Menelaus, and has reached Sparta. She is presented as a dignified and noble figure; the strictly Greek form of trimeter that Goethe had taken over from Humboldt is here used with an uncanny skill. The metamorphosis of Mephistopheles into the sinister Phorkyas conveys yet one more reminder that Goethe was not unalive to the grotesque elements in Greek belief. When Faust presents himself to offer Helen a refuge from the danger that seems to menace her, he speaks in rhyming couplets; Helen, noticing the difference between these and her own trimeters, asks Faust to teach her this new trick, and he does so by setting up lines for her to finish with an obvious rhyme. In the most natural way in the world, Goethe has presented a successful takeover bid in terms of metre. Faust transports Helen to his castle,

[52] *GA* ii 858-9.

[53] See Karl Reinhardt's lecture 'Goethe and Antiquity: the Helen Episode of Goethe's Faust', *Goethe and the Modern Age* (Chicago, 1950) 38f. = *Tradition und Geist*, 274f. (in English).

and for a time their life is unhampered by the sinister elemental forces which surround her; then with the loss of their son Euphorion, a figure reminiscent of Phaethon, and with Helen's disappearance, leaving nothing but her robe, these elements close in once more, and the episode ends with a Dionysiac orgy like that described by Aeschylus in a wonderful fragment from his lost trilogy about Orpheus (fr. 71 Mette).

To grasp the significance of the Helen episode, we must remember that it is magical; Helen vanishes, and only her robe is left. Goethe was aware that he could not revive the conditions in which the Greeks had lived and worked; his creative imitation of their art could only help him to bring off a dazzling but momentary feat of illusion. None the less, Faust will continue his struggle towards higher forms of existence, profoundly affected by the experience he has undergone.

Trevelyan observes that Goethe used his study of the Greeks to obtain the grasp of southern European culture which he needed in order to correct the bias given to him by his northern origin; he used them, one may add, to strike a balance between the Titanism of his period of *Sturm und Drang* and the resigned attitude of his first Weimar period. He was able to do so effectively because his notion of the Greeks was closely linked with the conception of humanity which formed part of the idea of Nature, highly characteristic of the eighteenth century but at the same time peculiar to Goethe himself, which was central to his whole way of thinking. Still more important than his search for the original plant, the original colour, the original phenomenon was his search for the original man; and he found the original man, the qualities in virtue of which a man is human, to be exemplified in the Greeks.

Such an attitude, Trevelyan writes, would be impossible nowadays, for the value of civilisations outside Europe is now well known even to Europeans, and indeed it became known to Goethe himself during the final phase of his career. Many modern critics would add that the intensive study of ancient civilisation which has been carried out since Goethe's time has shown that he idealised the Greeks to an unreasonable degree. There were undoubtedly naive classicisers who excessively idealised the Greeks and their society: Rousseau's belief in the essential goodness of human nature and Herder's belief in the essential excellence of the cultures of individual peoples led directly to such an attitude. Winckelmann might without grave injustice be accused of having idealised the Greeks, and the tendency was widespread till well into the nineteenth century. One such idealiser was Marx. 'The Greeks were natural children', he wrote, 'the attraction Greek art has for us does not stand in contradiction to the undeveloped stage of society on which it grew. It is, rather, its result; it is inextricably bound up, rather, with the fact that the immature social conditions under which it arose, and under which alone it could arise, can never return.'[54] Once the dictatorship of the proletariat has been established, the state will wither away, and mankind will return to the beautiful simplicity of its historic childhood; the naiveté of this opinion must be connected with the sentimental view of the Greeks which its author shared with many of his contemporaries.

But on close examination Goethe's attitude to the Greeks proves to reveal a high degree of realism. In theory, he told Riemer in 1813,[55] the Greeks strongly believed in freedom; but the freedom which each believed in was his own, for inside each Greek there was a tyrant who needed only the opportunity to emerge, and true despotism arose from the desire for freedom. He warned people against allowing their admiration for Greek art and science to lead them to regard the actions of the Greeks and their behaviour to others as exemplary,[56] and he remarked that the claims of society upon the individual had been far more imperious in ancient Greece than they were in his own time.[57] His writings show no trace of the belief, common among naive classicisers, that the ancient Greeks were more moral in the modern humanitarian sense than the men of his own time. Writing to Fritz von Stein from Rome in 1787, he expressed the fear that with the victory of humanitarianism the world would become one large hospital in which some human beings would nurse others.[58]

Goethe was concerned to fill the gap left by the collapse of Christianity, to which he greatly preferred the religion of the Greeks. In that religion the gods stood for the forces which control the universe; as Thales put it, everything was full of gods, for the gods corresponded with that Nature in which Goethe so passionately believed. Greek religion put man and his claims in the place which the operations of Nature in the world assigns him, a place in which he is wholly subordinated to the immortal gods. But from Homer's time on the Greeks believed in a kind of kinship between gods and men; Goethe nowhere, so far as I know, quotes the opening of Pindar's sixth Nemean ode. 'The race of gods and the race of men are one', but it

---

[54] See p. 146f.

[55] *GA* i 63.

[56] *GA* i 62.

[57] 18.11. 1806, to Riemer (*GA* i 63).

[58] 8.6.1787, cited by Schadewaldt, op. cit. (in n.1), 1045. 'Nicht als paradiesisches Unschuldsvolk eines Menschenfrühlings, nicht als ein Volk schönen Junglingen, sondern als fest in der Wirklichkeit stehende tüchtige und gesunde Menschen sieht Goethe die Griechen': Richard Harder, *Die Antike* 9 (1933) 30 = *Kl. Schr.* (1960) 460.

expresses one of his most cherished beliefs. The highest element in man seemed to him divine, and the more a man felt himself to be a man, the more like he was to the immortal gods. Following Rudolf Pfeiffer,[59] we may take the poem of 1820, *Urworte: Orphisch* as a guide to his world outlook. Men and gods alike are subject to the rule of necessity; the gods are immortal, but human fate is bounded by death. Each man has his individual nature, his daimon; Goethe would have agreed with Heraclitus that character is a man's daimon. Man's life is subject to the operations of *Tyche*, not blind chance, but a factor which the gods control; it remains inscrutable to man himself. Man is also subject to the urges comprehended under the name of *Eros*, not merely love – though like the Greeks Goethe thought of love as a dangerous and terrifying force – but all deep longings and ambitions. A man's judgement might be taken from him by *Ate*, delusion or infatuation, a kind of godsent madness; that danger he must resist by cultivating *Sophrosyne*, not so much 'moderation' as safe thinking, discretion, resignation to the limits imposed upon humanity dictated by saving common sense. *Sophrosyne* was closely linked with what he called 'die göttliche Scheu'; that has been equated with *Aidos*, reverence or respect, but it is even closer to what Plato in the Laws called 'divine fear', *theios phobos*.[60] This quality is linked with the capacity to wonder or admire, *to thaumazein*, in a wonderful passage of Goethe's *Farbenlehre*.

The outcome of man's efforts was decided by *Ananke*, necessity or compulsion, but what gave him strength to bear up against that knowledge was *Elpis*, Hope. So far Goethe's outlook seems virtually identical with the religious outlook of the early Greeks; but when we come to *Elpis*, we find an important difference between the two. For the Greeks Hope is an ambiguous concept; sometimes it is the chief consolation given to mortals for all the limitations imposed by their condition, but at other times it is a dangerous delusion. Goethe's conception of Hope was closely linked with his belief in a basic affinity between Man and Nature, his belief in the essential goodness of the universe. For all its peculiarity, his idea of Nature was typical of the age in which he lived; in the last resort, the eighteenth-century idea of a benevolent Nature, held as it might be by deists and atheists, was nothing but the residue of the faith in a benevolent God implanted by long centuries of Christianity. The Greeks were a good deal less

---

[59] Op. cit, in n.1 above, 242f.

[60] *Laws* 671 D; see the first chapter of Edgar Wind's *Art and Anarchy* (1960) and also his article in *Zeitschrift für Asthetik und allgemeine Kunstwissenschaft* 26 (1932) 349f. = *The Eloquence of Symbols* (1981) 1f.

confident of the interest taken by the gods in man. Their attitude to life was a tragic attitude; the *Iliad* is in one sense of the word a tragedy, and it was from the *Iliad* that the great tragedians got their inspiration. It has often been observed that Goethe drew back when he approached the neighbourhood of tragedy.[61] Iphigenia is not really capable of slaughtering her brother; Faust strikes a bargain with the devil, but we know from the start that for all his remorse over poor Gretchen he is never going to have to pay the devil's bill. Just as much as Rousseau, with whose rejection of the doctrine of original sin he surely sympathised, Goethe shrank from believing in the finality of evil; with that qualification, he had more sympathy with Christianity than is immediately apparent, as the end of *Faust*, for all its ironies, clearly shows. Soon after the end of the last world war, Karl Jaspers remarked that in their present situation Germans were turning to Shakespeare, to the Bible, to Aeschylus rather than to Goethe.[62] Goethe himself once said that he thought he had achieved something as a poet, but that compared with Aeschylus or Sophocles he was nothing; he was not given to indulgence in false modesty, and it is likely that he believed what he was saying. If these poets have access to a dimension in which Goethe never moves, it is because their religion gave them a tragic vision of the world which Goethe lacked; his attitude, like that of the early Greeks in so many ways, differs from theirs in this vital particular.

For Goethe self-perfection and self-cultivation, *Bildung* and *Kultur*, ranked as the highest human activities. Carelessly interpreted, that might give the impression that he was dedicated to an idle and selfish form of aestheticism; and before the end of the nineteenth century his name had often been invoked by believers in such doctrines. Nothing could be more unjust than this; Goethe believed that the aim of self-perfection was to acquire excellence, *arete*, *virtus*, *virtù*, which was displayed in action. For him piety was only a means to an end; the goal of human effort was not peace in paradise but effective work.[63] 'Des echten Mannes Feier ist die Tat'; both Wilhelm Meister and Faust are and become *praktikoi*, men of action. In particular, the artist must act; by action he imposes a law upon the formless

---

[61] See in particular Erich Heller, op. cit. (in n.5), 'Goethe and the Avoidance of Tragedy', p.37f. and George Steiner, *The Death of Tragedy* (1961) 166f. 'So sind denn seine Dramen, einschliesslich des *Faust*, des *Egmont* und des *Tasso*, auch alle keine Tragödien, obwohl diese Werke in gewisser Weise zeigen, dass Goethe fähig gewesen wäre, Tragödien zu schreiben, wenn er sich dazu hätte bringen können': K. von Fritz, *Antike und moderne Tragodie* (1962) 472, n.47.

[62] K. Jaspers, *Unsere Zukunft und Goethe* (1948) 22, cited by Heller, op. cit., 41.

[63] See Pfeiffer, op. cit (in n.1), 248f.

succession of experiences, so that they acquire a shape that gives them permanence; thus man can exercise a creative power which is akin to the divine creative power visible in Nature. 'If I can go on working to the very end', Goethe said to Eckermann when he was eighty, 'Nature is obliged to assign to me another form of being when my present form of being is no longer able to contain my spirit.'[64] A Greek would have smiled grimly at these words, which to him would have seemed arrant hybris; how can any man oblige Nature, or the gods, to grant him anything? Goethe would have recognised that the remark issued from the German, not the Greek, side of his nature; yet it illustrates the place occupied by Hope, *Elpis*, in an attitude to life which for all the strength of the Germanic element in the creator of *Faust* must be acknowledged to have strong affinities with Greek thinking.

---

[64] 4.2.1829; see Walter Kaufmann, 'Goethe's Faith and Faust's Redemption', in *From Shakespeare to Existentialism* (1959) 61f.

3

Humboldt 1

Mark Pattison took Joseph Scaliger, who died in 1609, to have been the last man to be acquainted with virtually the whole body of knowledge available in his time; others have claimed this for Leibniz. But a century later, when knowledge had enormously increased, the brothers Wilhelm and Alexander von Humboldt covered between them almost the entire territory. Wilhelm's new biographer thinks that Alexander, the scientist and explorer, is the more famous; but for those interested in the humanities Wilhelm is a most important figure.

His career falls into three sections. First, after an elaborate education and a brilliant start to his career in government service, he left that service to devote eleven years to self-perfection; during that period he made himself into a proficient classical scholar and produced a series of writings about politics, culture and education that had great effect. Second, in a political and diplomatic career that lasted from 1802 to 1819, he played an important part in the Prussian resistance to Napoleon and in the debates of the Congress of Vienna; Talleyrand thought him one of the three or four most distinguished statesmen with whom he had had contact. During this period he reorganized the German school and university system in such a way that they became the models for advanced education everywhere; he took the leading part in founding the University of Berlin, which set the pattern for the universities of the world. He also found time to produce valuable written works, dealing for the most part with the philosophy of history. Third, between his retirement from the Government in 1819 and his death in 1835 he made an incomparable contribution to linguistics; apart from detailed investigations of the Basque, Sanskrit, Chinese, Malayan and Indonesian languages, he produced theoretical discussions of the subject whose influence has been enormous, and is not exhausted even now. 'The play of intelligence', writes George Steiner of this work, 'the delicacy of particular notation, the great front of argument which Humboldt

* A review of *Wilhelm von Humboldt: A Biography vol. i: 1767-1808* (1978), by Paul R. Sweet in *The Times Literary Supplement*, 20 October 1978.

exhibits give his writings on language, incomplete though they are, a unique stature.'[1] Steiner classes Humboldt with Plato, Vico, Coleridge, Saussure and Roman Jakobson as one of the very few who have said anything about language that is both new and comprehensive.

Humboldt had a most varied and interesting life, which brought him into contact not only with politicians and diplomats but with many of the most eminent writers and scholars of his time. He was intimate with both Goethe and Schiller, as the exchange of some remarkable letters testifies, and with other famous writers; he could discuss the classics with Christian Gottlob Heyne, F.A. Wolf and Hermann virtually on equal terms; he was at home in political and literary circles in Paris, Rome and Madrid. His extensive correspondence is of great interest; the letters between him and his remarkable wife alone fill seven volumes.

Between 1903 and 1936 the Berlin Academy brought out seventeen volumes of Humboldt's collected writings; yet in 1936 Rudolf Pfeiffer[2] wrote that he was less read than his importance might lead one to expect. It is not that Humboldt's writing is obscure or dull, for it has the lucidity of much pre-Hegelian German. But Pfeiffer is right in saying that it lacks charm; he seldom, except in the letters and the official memoirs, ventures a memorable phrase, and the high level of generality which, despite his mastery of details, much of his discourse maintains, strains the attention of the reader. Access to his writings is easier than when Pfeiffer wrote, for in 1963 Marianne Cowan published a selection from it in English translation under the title of *Humanist Without Portfolio*, and the following year Walter Flemmer brought out an excellent selection of the original texts in Goldmann's Gelbe Taschenbücher. But the comparative opaqueness of his writing makes the need for a comprehensive study of him all the greater; and through the German literature about him is extensive, there has been no such work since Rudolf Haym's biography of 1856. In English, there is nothing at all adequate. Since Haym's day great quantities of relevant material have accumulated, and Paul Sweet's work fills a very real need.

Its author is very well acquainted with the material; he writes not, perhaps, incisively, but clearly and pleasingly; and he shows a sane and solid judgment. He is no classical scholar, as we learn on page 22, when he calls Aristodemus and Euthydemus 'Aristodem' and 'Euthydem', because he has learnt of their existence from Humboldt's

---

[1] *After Babel* (1975), 79.
[2] *Ausgewählte Schriften* (1965), 257.

juvenile collection of texts of Plato and Xenophon bearing on providence and immortality; rather a high proportion of the rare errors in this beautifully produced book occurs in classical names and quotations. Astonishingly, he does not mention that during Humboldt's Roman period his children's tutor was F.G. Welcker, later to become famous as a scholar. But so far this deficiency has handicapped him less than one might expect, and he has produced a learned, enjoyable and useful book.

Born in 1767, two years before his brother Alexander, of a rich and aristocratic Prussian family, Wilhelm lost his father at the age of eleven, and was brought up by tutors chosen by his mother, an intelligent but chilly lady of Huguenot descent. The tutors were well chosen, and the two gifted boys made phenomenally rapid progress. In Berlin they moved in lively intellectual society, largely Jewish; the beautiful and intelligent Henriette Herz and Moses Mendelssohn's gifted daughter Brendel Veit, later the wife of Friedrich Schlegel, were among their friends. A short stay at the University of Göttingen brought them into contact with Heyne, at that time the leading classical scholar in the country. Heyne's fame has been unfairly eclipsed by that of his pupil F.A. Wolf, who rebelled against his master, but as F. Klingner[3] has pointed out, Heyne was the first to entertain the comprehensive notion of the study of the ancient world which was to become general during the nineteenth century. In Heyne's hands that study was directed to a humanistic end; but at the same time he insisted on proper attention to detail, and his influence must have helped to protect Humboldt against an excess of theorizing.

At twenty-four Humboldt entered government service, and in one year was thought to have gone as far as the ordinary competent official might have gone in six. Then upon becoming engaged to the brilliant and beautiful Caroline von Dacheröden he asked to be relieved of his official duties, and devoted the next eleven years, from 1791 to 1802, to the endeavour to perfect himself. The concept of *Bildung*, the systematic 'formation' of one's character and intellect, was then popular among German intellectuals, as W.H. Bruford's studies help to show; and at all times Humboldt felt an urge to stand aside and reflect on life in general. In particular he wished to improve his grasp of Greek antiquity, whose study he thought to be the instrument of education that could help him most. In 1792 he made friends with F.A. Wolf (b.1759), who had been a professor at Halle since 1783 and

[3] *Studien zur gr. u. röm. Literatur* (1964), 701f. *Christian Gottlob Heyne 1729-1812*, the catalogue of an exhibition held in Göttingen to mark the 250th anniversary of his birth in 1979, contains valuable material.

was to publish his famous contribution to the Homeric Question in
1795: the two men's influence upon each other was profound. In 1794
the Humboldts moved to Jena, where Wilhelm spent three years in
daily contact with Schiller and saw much of Goethe. The period
between 1798 and 1801 was spent chiefly in Paris, where he met
Bonaparte and made friends with Sieyès and Mme de Stael, and made
two excursions into Spain which were to have notable results.

Humboldt started by subscribing to the general attitudes of the
German Enlightenment as they had been developed by Leibniz and
by Moses Mendelssohn. In later years he made a careful examination
of the works of Kant, as some of his linguistic writings show, but on
the whole he remained faithful to his early principles. He did not
reject religion, but felt it to be a matter for the individual, so that he
was strongly opposed to the enforcement of Lutheranism by the
Prussian state; some critics have complained that his humanism
lacked a religious element. Arriving in Paris soon after the fall of the
Bastille in 1789, he sympathized with many aspects of the Revolution
in its early stages; but in the thoughts on constitutions which the new
French constitution stimulated him to write down in 1791-92 we find
a distrust of the operations of 'mere reason' and a respect for organic
development that recalls Burke. His essay on the limits of state
activity, written in 1792, was withheld from publication by its author,
partly because of new developments in France and partly because of
the appearance of a German version of Burke's *Reflections*; it was not
published until 1851, but then powerfully influenced Mill's *Essay on
Liberty*. Humboldt, with his strong belief in the right of the individual
to develop his own nature without interference, wished to restrict the
powers of the state to those required for the maintenance of security;
as Matthew Arnold noticed, he wished to use state action to enable
the individual to manage without the state, and Professor Sweet is
right to say that some elements in his theory would be acceptable even
to socialists and anarchists. Later, when he reformed the Prussian
educational system, Humboldt was to show himself ready to use state
power without restraint to carry out his own purposes.

Other writings of this time are concerned with *Bildung*, which
Humboldt saw as a development of human powers (*Kräfte*) designed
to save man from becoming alienated from his inner self; seizing on
his concept of 'alienation' as an anticipation of Marx, Marxist critics
seem to have failed to notice that Humboldt must have got it from
Rousseau. Like Rousseau he is concerned to avoid the dry and frigid
rationality of many of the *philosophes*; he attaches much importance to
what he calls *Sinnlichkeit*, a term combining the associations of
sensitivity with some of those of *sensuality*. His insistence that the

ancient Greeks were conspicuous for this quality is one of the features that separates his view of them from that of Winckelmann, who had died in the year before his birth.

This point is firmly made in what Humboldt modestly called a 'sketch' concerning the study of antiquity, which was sent to Goethe and Wolf early in 1793; it was not published until 1896, but had no small influence on Wolf's general account of antiquity (*Darstellung des Altertums*), a work which itself had a great effect. The ideas which it contains were to be developed further in two important productions of the years 1806/07, as we shall see presently. During the early 1790s Humboldt worked hard at Greek, taking great pains with some translations from Pindar and Aeschylus. His translation of the *Agamemnon* of Aeschylus, though not published until 1816, was begun in 1796, and Goethe was in possession of an early draft in 1799; Karl Reinhardt has shown the part played by Humboldt in the genesis of the wonderful imitation of the Greek iambic trimeter used by Goethe in the Helen episode of the second part of *Faust* and imitated by Schiller in the Montgomery episode of the *Jungfrau von Orleans*.[4]

During his Jena period Humboldt was also occupied with his design for the foundation of a science of 'comparative anthropology' which on the basis of an exact study of the different characteristics of the various races and nations would explore the different ways in which they might develop. Despite Humboldt's overriding admiration for Greek culture, the new science was to do this without giving the preference to one form of development over others. Humboldt's ideal was not static but dynamic, and he wished modern men to use the Greeks, not to copy them. He saw character as the outward manifestation of powers, activities or vital forces (*Kräfte*), and the new discipline was designed to help men to develop these in the ways considered most desirable. He produced a fragment of a treatise on comparative anthropology, and also a fragment of a study on the eighteenth century designed to be carried out by the methods of that discipline; both break off at the point where real difficulty arises, the point where the method is about to be applied to the positive treatment of the material. It was only many years later, after Humboldt's retirement from public life in 1819, that he made real headway with his great design, and then he did so by means of his investigations of linguistics. This work took its origins from his visits to Spain, where he became fascinated by the Basque people and their language, perhaps the only non-Indo-European tongue still spoken in a European country; later he made them the subject of a study which

---

[4] *Tradition und Geist* (1960), 366f.

though now superseded in certain details remains of the first importance.

While Humboldt was in Paris Goethe brought out *Hermann und Dorothea*. Goethe was not then the celebrity he became later; but Humboldt at once recognised the full greatness of the poem, and explained it in a critical study that not only contains much excellent matter about epic poetry in general but remains a notable example of the felicitous application of the expressive theory of aesthetics. Professor Sweet justly remarks that Humboldt goes so far in asserting the autonomy of the poet's imagination in the domain of art that he comes near to anticipating the aesthetics of Baudelaire and the French Symbolists.

In 1802 Humboldt returned to government service, and by great good fortune the post of Prussian envoy in Rome happened to be available for him. Rome made the most profound impression upon him; he found her to be as supreme among cities as Homer is among poets; and she is the subject of the most memorable of his few poems. After finishing his study of the Basques he returned to the subject of the Greeks, and in the fragment called 'Latium and Hellas: Reflections on Classical Antiquity' resumed the theme of the earlier 'sketch' of 1793. The same subject is handled in a fragment on the Greek character in its ideal aspects designed as part of a projected history of the decline and fall of the Greek city-states. Humboldt studied the Greeks not for information but for inspiration; and this work with its Gibbonian title was meant to encourage the Germans to save themselves by their own efforts from meeting at the hands of Napoleon the same fate which the Greek states had met at those of Philip of Macedon.

In these two pieces Humboldt worked out further, under the influence of Schelling, his explanation of the superiority of Greek culture. Only the Greeks, he argued, were able to create an art capable of doing justice to the ideal element in reality, which they did by virtue of an affinity between nature and the Greek artist's mind; they were enabled to unite the earthly with the divine by reason of their deep longing for the ideal, their *Sehnsucht*. When Humboldt says that no other language except German has the notion I suppose he is thinking of the Greek *pothos*. Modern man made the mistake of aiming at reality itself, whereas the Greeks aimed at reality through art, and since reality in itself was unattainable, the Greeks were more successful. Humboldt was hardly less aware than Nietzsche, who in several respects went back to his ideas, of the delicate tension on which the perfect equilibrium of the greatest Greek art depended. His reason for attaching such importance to the study of Greek culture at its greatest was the need to understand and if possible emulate the *Sehnsucht* that had inspired it.

This work did not prevent Humboldt from discharging his diplomatic duties with notable success. He established excellent relations with the all-powerful Cardinal Consalvi; he sweetened with exquisite tact the somewhat bitter pill of the King of Prussia's refusal to make any concessions to the Pope; and he maintained just the right non-committal attitude towards the over-riding issue of a possible concordat between the papacy and the whole of Germany. In 1806 he was raised to the dignity of Minister Plenipotentiary; but during the same year the disaster of Jena reduced his duties to those of an observer, and before long his own financial interests urgently required his presence in Berlin. In October, 1808, he left Rome, never again to see Italy; but he was soon to assume even more important responsibilities, and to discharge them with triumphant success. It is to this point in his career that Professor Sweet's first volume brings us; one eagerly looks forward to the second volume.[5]

---

[5] See Chapter 4.

4

Humboldt 2

The first volume of this admirable biography, reviewed by me in the *TLS* of 20 October 1978, ended at the point when its subject left Rome in October 1808 after six years as Prussian envoy to the Holy See. The second consists of four long chapters. The first covers the years between 1808 and 1810, including the period of eighteen months during which Humboldt carried out his epoch-making reform of Prussian education; the second the years between 1810 and 1815, which he spent first as Prussian Minister to Austria and then as Hardenberg's colleague as delegate at the Congress of Vienna; the third the final phase of his political career, including his brief spell as Prussian Minister in London and ending with his fall from power at the end of 1819; and the fourth the period between then and his death in 1835, marked by his later studies in the philosophy of history and the greater part of his vast contribution to the study of language.

Humboldt might have seemed a strange choice to head the section of the Ministry of the Interior that was responsible for education and ecclesiastical affairs. He was not known to be religious, he had never been to school, and he had only spent a brief time at a university. But nothing interested him more than education, and he had spent many years upon his own. When he took over, elementary education in Prussia was in a poor state, especially in the country districts, where the post of schoolmaster was often entrusted to a retired soldier, cobbler or tailor. J.E. von Massow, who had been in charge of education from 1798 to 1807, thought that the education of the lower orders should be such as to fit them for the station in life to which they had been called. Humboldt, with his eighteenth-century belief in the dignity of all beings as such, insisted that all should have the same basic primary education; he supported the introduction of Pestalozzi's methods, though he attached more importance than Pestalozzi to the study of the Bible. He established the humanistic gymnasium as the

* A review of *Wilhelm von Humboldt: A Biography, vol. ii: 1808-1835* (1980), by Paul R. Sweet in *The Times Literary Supplement*, 24 October 1980.

basic institution leading to the university, resisting the powerful advocates of vocational training in secondary education. Humboldt was not opposed to the idea of technical and business schools, and avoided excessive emphasis on language study; he made philosophy, mathematics and history the central subjects; but he firmly separated vocational training from that humanistic education which could promote what he called *Bildung*, self-formation. The gymnasium has often been reproached with being 'elitist'; but if it often became so after Humboldt's time, that was not his fault, since he was a convinced believer in meritocracy, and did all he could to promote equality of opportunity.

Massow had been in favour of letting the Prussian universities disappear, preferring to encourage institutions of the type of that École Polytechnique which was so successful in contemporary France. Humboldt believed that the state existed for the sake of the individual, and that none of its duties were more important than that of promoting individual *Bildung*. Professors were not there to serve the students, but both were there to serve knowledge (*Wissenschaft*); together they were to form a community of scholars. He took great pains to provide the new University of Berlin with professors of the highest quality; Schleiermacher, Fichte, F.A. Wolf and the lawyer Theodor Schmalz were already in Berlin and could provide a nucleus, and several young men who later had brilliant careers were appointed; Savigny, aged 31, and Boeckh, aged 25, were chosen, and Bopp came later, on Humboldt's recommendation. The university was closely linked with the Prussian Academy, which had hitherto failed to realise the hopes of its founder, Leibniz, but whose great days now began. Humboldt carefully avoided the mistake of not allowing scholars enough freedom; he knew that some people preferred to be on their own, and thought everyone should be allowed to work in his own way. He tried hard to get the king to invest the university with a large endowment; but this was refused, for the authorities did not wish it to become too independent. In spite of this the newly founded university at once became a model for the universities of Europe, just as the university of Leiden had after its foundation two centuries before. Advocates of real learning in England, like Mark Pattison, looked to it for inspiration, just as reformers of secondary education, like Matthew Arnold, looked to the Humboldtian gymnasium.

Hardenberg's accession to power in 1810 was a misfortune for Humboldt, who throughout a long and varied relationship was to stand in Hardenberg's shadow. The Chancellor's immediate solution of the problem he presented was to send him to Vienna, a less congenial post than Rome, and one where a difficult task awaited him. At the very start, enemies circulated the rumour that he was closely linked with the activists of the Prussian *Tugendbund*, who were agitating for a renewed revolt against Napoleon. Humboldt felt indeed much sympathy with Gneisenau and his supporters, but he was fully aware of the inadvisability of any action for the time being. The marriage of Marie Louise had given Austria a kind of special relationship with France, and until as late as August 1813 Metternich continued to be extremely cautious. It is true that Henry Kissinger in *A World Restored* has assured us that from 1811 Metternich had secretly worked for the downfall of Napoleon; here as usual Kissinger follows Wilhelm Oncken in his work of 1884-86,[1] but Sweet points out that even Srbik in his admiring biography of Metternich thought that Oncken went too far in this respect. Soon after Metternich replaced Stadion in 1810, Humboldt saw that he was likely to retain power, and acted accordingly. He handled the complicated situation with great tact and flexibility, explaining Austria's difficulties to his own government and waiting till May 1813 before putting real pressure upon Metternich. But he was the life and soul of the movement to rise against Napoleon, and in the last stages he fought with all his strength until Austria declared war on the eleventh of August.

At this time Hardenberg was in poor health, and there seemed to be a real possibility that Humboldt might replace him; but his single-minded determination and not unconscious intellectual superiority made him enemies. When Stein made his proposals for the reorganisation of Germany, Humboldt defended the smaller German states; he felt that Germany's strength was cultural, not political, and thought they helped to preserve cultural values. During the Congress of Chatillon and later he strongly upheld Prussian claims against Metternich. He got his way over the preliminary organisation of the Congress of Vienna, but not over the eventual decisions. Talleyrand saw with great clarity that Prussia was the power most likely to be a danger to France in the future, and set himself to oppose her. But though Prussia failed to get the whole of Saxony she was richly compensated in Westphalia and the Rhineland, territories that were destined to turn out more valuable. Similarly at the Second Peace of Paris Humboldt failed in his struggle against Russia and England, who wished to impose moderate terms on France, but Prussia now added the Saar basin to the Ruhr, largely through his efforts.

After the successful conclusion of the war, the change of atmosphere

---

[1] In an interesting note on p.255, Sweet points out that though Kissinger gives the impression that the only part of Oncken's book that is valuable is the documents, his own debt to this writer seems to be very considerable.

that could be felt everywhere in Europe could be felt in Prussia also. A reactionary trend set in, and it was not favourable to Humboldt's interests. His earlier memorandum advocating the removal of all disabilities placed upon the Jews had not been fully accepted by Hardenberg in his edict of emancipation of 1812, and after 1815 the law was administered in reactionary fashion. In his youth Humboldt and his wife Caroline had much frequented the company of Jews; but now his son-in-law Colonel von Hedemann belonged to the Christian German Dining Club, where 'no Jews, no French, and no Philistines were tolerated', Caroline said unkind things about the Jews, though she still saw them, and Humboldt himself ceased to see them. This was a sign of the times. Reactionary counsellors like Prince von Sayn-Wittgenstein and the clergyman Ancillon became influential; the trend towards absolutism was unmistakable. Humboldt had a long struggle to obtain the royal donation to which his services entitled him; the economic situation, it is true, was bad, but other less deserving people had been given more.

In 1817-18 Hardenberg got rid of him by sending him as Minister to London. Though he delighted in the Elgin Marbles and discussed the temple of Bassas with Sir Charles Cockerell, Egyptian hieroglyphics with Thomas Young and Sanskrit with Charles Wilkins, he had less time for cultural activities than might have been expected. But he got on well with the Prince Regent, who sang to him at dinner, entertained him at the Brighton Pavilion, amid architecture as different as possible from that of Tegel, and later as king had him painted by Sir Thomas Lawrence; he gratified his own monarch by defending the interests of his brother-in-law the Duke of Cumberland, the wickedest of all Queen Victoria's wicked uncles; and, most important of all, he negotiated a loan to the Prussian Government by the London Rothschilds, thus making friends, to his own later advantage, with the powerful financier Christian von Rother. But when after his return to Berlin in 1818 Hardenberg offered him a choice between four posts, he turned them all down, wishing only to be a member of the *Staatsrat*, where he would certainly have been a nuisance to the government; his friendship with Stein can have done nothing to lighten Hardenberg's suspicions. Pressed to accept ministerial office in February 1819, he took up his duties only in June, because of diplomatic duties at the Frankfurt headquarters of the *Bund*. Soon afterwards he was put out by the arrest of certain liberals, including his friend, the eminent Greek scholar F.G. Welcker, and also by the Government's shelving of the question of a new constitution; the passing of the reactionary Karlsbad Decrees in late September made his position virtually intolerable. That issue, together with his strong dislike of Hardenberg's system of personal government as Chancellor, provoked the act of defiance which led to his dismissal on the last day of 1819.

With complete equanimity Humboldt retired to Tegel and occupied himself with learned work. After Hardenberg's death in 1822, Job von Witzleben tried to get him made Chancellor; but prejudice against him, particularly in the narrow mind of Frederick William III, was still too strong. The thought that he might well have been appointed to that office remains one of the fascinating might-have-beens of history; Sweet quotes Hajo Holborn as having written that Humboldt's programme 'might have paved the road towards the progressive acceptance of the rising middle and lower classes into an integrated political community'. Greek poets and historians liked to point to a particular event which seemed to start a chain of happenings leading to disaster as a 'beginning of evil'; in this sense, Humboldt's dismissal might be regarded as the 'beginning of evil' from which the at first triumphant but later disastrous course of Prussian history started.

Sweet is surely right to contest the view that Humboldt really wanted nothing better than to retire from politics and live the life of a scholar. He was by no means unambitious; but he refused to compromise, and having staked his career upon a single throw and lost, he accepted the result with a good grace. Unlike thorough-going politicians such as Metternich and Bismarck, he had abundant resources for living happily in private life. In 1830, after his successful chairmanship of the committee set up to establish the new Berlin Museum, he enjoyed a partial return to favour, and was awarded the Order of the Black Eagle. He was appointed to the *Staatsrat*, and very soon justified Hardenberg's reluctance to admit him to that body by making himslf such a nuisance to the government that it was compelled to suspend the sittings.

Humboldt took pleasure in the Silesian estate of Ottmachau, which had been conferred upon him by the king; he purchased another estate Hadmersleben near Magdeburg; and Caroline had her own Burg Örner, in Hanover, which she preferred. But his own favourite residence was Schloss Tegel, just outside Berlin, which after the alterations which he employed Schinkel to carry out expressed and still expresses his elegant austerity with singular fidelity. Here he housed his impressive collections of ancient sculpture, mostly acquired in Rome, and modern works by artists like Thorwaldsen and Rauch; and Sweet justly remarks that Tegel has the same symbolic significance with regard to Humboldt that Monticello has with regard to Thomas Jefferson.

Humboldt's disappearance from public life was disastrous for Germany, and perhaps for Europe; but in one way it was most fortunate, for the literary work which his leisure enabled him to carry out was of singular importance. He followed up his earlier important studies in historiography of 1814 and 1818 with the treatise *Über die Aufgabe des Geschichtschreibers*: his insistence that it is the historian's task to discover the ideas that lie behind the facts had great influence on historical writing of the nineteenth century, and has been invoked in recent times to warn historians not to lose their central purpose in a mass of details.

But Humboldt's work on the philosophy of history was far less important that his contribution to linguistics. He learned an immense variety of languages, and did valuable work on Ancient Egyptian, Chinese and Sanskrit. In studying this last, he was greatly attracted by the Bhagavad-Gita, and particularly by its message that the motive must be in the deed, and not in the event; in a review of his edition of the work Hegel declined to share his high estimate of its value. He did valuable work on Amerindian languages, and Sweet has interesting information about the contacts with the American linguists John Pickering and Peter Du Ponceau which he owed to George Bancroft. From 1827 he was increasingly occupied with the languages of South-East Asia, Indonesia and Polynesia, and between 1830 and 1835 appeared his monumental study of Kawi, the hieratic and poetic language of Java, with its famous book-length introduction *Über die Verschiedenheiten des menschlichen Sprachbaues und ihren Einfluss auf die geistige Entwicklung des Menschengeschlechts*.

Sweet has made good use of a considerable part of the extensive modern literature about Humboldt's linguistics; but he is not familiar with it all, as a glance at the extensive bibliography given by Anna Morpurgo Davies in *Current Trends in Linguistics*, vol. 13 (1975) will show, and in some places he has over-simplified complicated questions. He tells us that Humboldt took over from F. Schlegel the distinction between agglutinative and inflecting languages, but held that the latter had developed from the former. But Gertrud Pätsch has shown that Humboldt expressed different views about linguistic classification at different times, and never came to any firm conclusion on the subject. He conceived of language as being, in Aristotelian terms, not an *ergon*, a finished product, but an *energeia*, a creative activity. The form of language is the unvarying factor that underlies each linguistic act; and each language has its inner form, in virtue of which it has its particular world outlook. Humboldt thought that classification should depend upon the inner form; but sometimes he identified this with the organic principle which serves to differentiate the various languages, and at other times with the general form of thought.

Humboldt is often referred to as a precursor of the linguistic relativism of modern theorists like Sapir and Whorf, and he certainly believed that each language embodied a different way of looking at the world. But as Sweet says there is also a universalist element in his thinking. He did not believe that differences between languages had anything to do with race, but did think that advanced types of linguistic morphology went with higher stages of cultural development. Just as language could facilitate thinking, it could also hinder it; and Humboldt thought some languages more satisfactory than others in this respect. He thought each language had its own intrinsic value, but he preferred the Indo-European languages, and in particular Ancient Greek. Often disregarded or belittled by the positivistic linguists of the nineteenth century, his work with its great wealth of fertile general ideas is now receiving much attention.

Language did not monopolise his energies during his last years. In 1830 he brought out an admirable study of Schiller's intellectual development, and also a highly interesting review of the new volume of Goethe's *Italienische Reise*. He wrote a considerable quantity of poetry, as well as many letters full of general reflections upon life to his friend Charlotte Diede; a selection of these letters, published after his death, seems to have owed much of its great popularity to qualities not especially typical of Humboldt's usual self. Humboldt's marriage was beyond all doubt successful, and the rich, clever and attractive Caroline was not only his wife but his best friend. But her positive and independent character was not responsive to a side of his nature which required a woman to be obedient and indeed submissive, and this requirement had to be fulfilled by Charlotte Diede and her predecessor Johanna Motherby.

An enemy once called Humboldt 'cold and clear as the December sun', causing Caroline to begin her next letter 'Liebe klare, kalte Dezembersonne'. But Humboldt himself wrote:

Hell wie Dezembersonne sie mich nannten
weil sie in mir nicht an Gefühle glaubten;
die mir so oft des Lebens Ruhe raubten,
die innre Stürme sie in mir nicht kannten.[2]

---

[2] ' "Bright as the December sun", they called me, because they believed I had no feelings; they knew nothing of the inner storms which so often robbed me of my life's repose.'

The cool rationality of his outward demeanour masked, indeed, a passionate temperament. He was certainly not without ambition, but he refused to compromise with persons or principles that he disapproved of; and having staked his career upon a struggle against them and lost, he could retire into private life with perfect contentment and produce a great quantity of work of striking learning and originality. For him the study of language was a means of studying man. People have complained that he was interested in man only, and lacked a religious sense; but he was true at all times to an eighteenth-century conception of human nature that did not altogether lack a religious element.

The second volume has the same general characteristics as its predecessor. Professor Sweet is an expert on diplomatic history, and not surprisingly his account of Humboldt's diplomatic activities is particularly good. But he has taken great pains over Humboldt's cultural and literary activities also, and a reader interested in any aspect of this extraordinary man must be grateful to him for a notable achievement.

5

Coleridge

'This book proposes, in effect, a new method of literary criticism, or, at any rate, a mutation of existing practice among English-speaking critics.' These are the words which the author of '*Kubla Khan' and the Fall of Jerusalem* begins her introduction. 'The intention', she continues, 'is to explore the possibilities of a literary criticism which can absorb and bring to bear on literature the work of other disciplines.' Invoking Lukács and Sartre, as well as Lucien Goldmann and (with certain reservations) Roland Barthes, E.S. Shaffer pleads for the recognition of the critic's duty to consider the whole milieu of a work of art. She applies this principle by examining the effect on chosen writers of the higher criticism of the Bible as it developed in Germany during the second half of the eighteenth and the first half of the nineteenth century. The first four chapters of her learned and intelligent book are concerned, more or less, with Coleridge; the fourth contains an admirable study of Hölderlin's great poem 'Patmos'; the fifth is concerned with Browning's 'A Death in the Desert' and the sixth with George Eliot's *Daniel Deronda*.

Through the radical Fellow of Jesus, William Friend, Coleridge came into contact as an undergraduate with the Unitarian group centring upon Joseph Priestley whose members were the first Englishmen to become alive to the importance of the new critical movement. He profited from the close acquaintance with German literature and criticism of Thomas Beddoes and his friends in Bristol; and Dr Shaffer shows that well before his visit to Germany in 1798-9 he had studied the Latin commentary on the Book of Revelation of the Göttingen theologian Johann Gottfried Eichhorn. Eichhorn had attended the seminars of Christian Gottlob Heyne, the great scholar to whom rightly belongs much of the credit for the institution of the seminar and the development of modern methods in classical scholarship which was for long assigned en bloc to Friedrich August

* A review of '*Kubla Khan' and the Fall of Jerusalem* by E.S. Shaffer in *The Times Literary Supplement*, 6 February 1976.

Wolf. Heyne was a notable pioneer in the critical study of mythology, the first to regard myths as 'philosophemes about the cosmos'.

From his twentieth year Coleridge meditated the writing of an epic poem on the destruction of Jerusalem by the Romans in A.D. 70, a plan that seems to have been dearer to his heart than any of the other numerous projects which he never realised. Dr Shaffer cogently argues that in forming this plan Coleridge was actuated by the wish to contribute to the creation of a new Christian apologetic, based on the acceptance of the findings of the higher criticism and on the frank recognition that the foundation legend of Christianity was a myth like other myths and, like them, one with a symbolic value. Together with historical matter derived for the most part from Josephus, Coleridge planned to make abundant use of the Book of Revelation, which in Eichhorn's opinion presented an imaginative picture of the capture and destruction of the city. The Apocalypse was popular with the poets of the time, eager for relief from the rationalism of the Enlightenment, and often influenced their depictions of visionary experience. Many of them gave their work an oriental colouring, not vague and indeterminate but detailed and specific, and several described a primitive paradise or Eden, for example, Klopstock in his *Messias* and Salomon Gessner in *Der Tod Adams*.

With great ingenuity Dr Shaffer detects similar elements in a poem Coleridge actually did write, 'Kubla Khan'. Deprecating the 'jocose antiquarianism' with which J. Livingston Lowes explained the composition of the poem in terms of an associative theory of subconscious composition, she rejects not only that theory but the account of the poem's sources that accompanies it. Here she is in harmony with the view of the late Humphry House, who wrote that 'were it not for Livingston Lowes, it would hardly still be necessary to point out the poem's essential unity and the relation between its two parts'. She is able to throw light on Coleridge by a sensitive analysis of Hölderlin's poem 'Patmos', written at that stage of his career when Christian as well as Greek mythology entered into his design. Dr Shaffer argues that he shared with Coleridge the concept of a divine revelation conveyed to the community through the seer or poet, bringing salvation to the former, though dangerous to the latter. Coleridge, she thinks, believed in a Platonic revelation common to all religions and thought to have been contained also in the ancient Mysteries, such as those of Eleusis, Samothrace, and the cults of Isis and of Dionysus; scholars were less aware of the differences between these than they have now become. Coleridge located his Christian version in the Apocalypse, regarding Christianity as the summation of all revelations communicated in myth. 'Kubla Khan', in Dr Shaffer's view, is the image of the symbolic process of human gnosis. This seems probable enough, though in the poem the poet seems more concerned with the process of the revelation than with what will be revealed.

Dr Shaffer observes that English interest in the higher criticism, very marked in the 1780s and 1790s, fell off as soon as the threat from revolutionary France made the public wary of what were considered radical opinions. Not till the 1820s did interest revive, among the Noetics at Oriel. Dr Shaffer mentions the translation of Niebuhr's history of Rome by Connop Thirlwall and Julius Hare, the two volumes of which appeared in 1828 and 1832 (more details are given by A. Momigliano in his article 'G.C. Lewis, Niebuhr e la critica dei fonti', in *Contributo alla Storia degli Studi Classici*, 1955). George Eliot's translation of Strauss's *Leben Jesu* appeared not in 1835, as an unfortunate slip makes Dr Shaffer appear to say, but in 1846; and the wider public was not fully alerted to the issues at stake before the controversy that followed the publication of *Essays and Reviews* in 1859.

From Coleridge and Hölderlin Dr Shaffer passes to Browning, whose poem 'A Death in the Desert' appeared in the volume *Dramatis Personae* in 1864. Renan's *Vie de Jesus* had come out in French the year before, and Dr Shaffer argues that Browning must have read it before his poem reached its final form.

In the poem the dying John confesses that he was not really present at the Crucifixion; and Dr Shaffer thinks Browning was aware of the doubts cast by Renan on the claim of the author of the Fourth Gospel to have been present at the events which he describes. Browning, she rightly remarks, was not attacking the higher criticism, as has been asserted; in his poem the falsity of John's claim causes deep remorse to John himself, but cannot impair the genuineness of his revelation or the validity of the myth which forms its content. Dr Shaffer finds here a defence of Christianity based on the recognition of the mythical nature of its evidences and a concept of the special vulnerability of the human being through whom the revelation is communicated, just as she has found these things in Coleridge and in Hölderlin.

In the sixth chapter Dr Shaffer employs her 'new method of literary criticism' in a defence of *Daniel Deronda* against the strictures of F.R. Leavis in *The Great Tradition* and of Henry James in the 'Conversation' about that novel which first appeared in 1876 and which Dr Leavis helpfully reprints in an appendix to his book. She records George Eliot's enthusiastic reaction to a suggestion by Frederic Harrison, the champion of Positivism, that she should write a novel that embodied the positivist ideal of society; she explains the significance for the novelist's literary work of her translations of Strauss, Spinoza and

Feuerbach; and she sets out to show the working of the influence of these and other contemporary thinkers in *Daniel Deronda* itself. She sees the book as a 'cosmopolitan religious epic', designed 'to join East and West in a new synthesis' and resting on Strauss's mythological view of history and Feuerbach's translation of Christian theology into the terms of secular thinking.

Dr Shaffer's account of these and other intellectual influences on the novel is illuminating; but not every reader will share her feeling that as soon as these have been explained the impression, so commonly found, that the book is an artistic failure will be removed. 'A thorough appreciation of Feuerbach', she tells us, 'extirpates Leavis's double error about George Eliot, his contempt for the basis of her art in the emotional life and his incomprehension of the level at which her emotional life moulded it.' In fact her exposition of the theories on which George Eliot wished to act makes it easier to understand the reasons for the failure of the last half of the novel. The verdict not only of James and Leavis but of the common reader has been that the first part, which Dr Leavis calls *Gwendolen Harleth*, is as fine a piece of writing as anything the author ever did, and gives pleasure of an order not equalled even by the best parts of *Middlemarch*. Then the smugly virtuous and altogether unreal Jews, cosseted by the author as Angela Davis might be by the hostess at a radically chic party, start to exude a repellent ink, as of a cuttlefish, over the living, interesting characters, and suffuse the whole second part of the book with a distasteful quality. Dr Shaffer pleads that Deronda is not held up as a mirror of perfection, but is himself exposed to the ironic vision with which the author regards Gwendolen and the other gentile characters; she speaks of his 'ardent hypocrisy and tender cruelty'. But even if we regard this as a correct statement of George Eliot's intention, we cannot feel that that intention has been adequately executed.

The priggishness and dullness of the Jewish characters obliges the reader to regard them from a standpoint different from that of the author, who looks on them with a tolerance manifestly denied to Gwendolen, not to mention Grandcourt. Henry James's character Constantius remarks that one element in George Eliot is spontaneous, but another is artificial. The moral lesson is driven home with merciless didacticism; the incidents of the plot, and some of the qualities given to the characters, seem to be rigged in its interest. It is one of the tragedies of literature that the writer of genius who had the power to create the marvellous Gwendolen, one of the most perfectly realised women in English fiction, had to pursue her in the name of morality with all the hostility of an ugly, dowdy, provincial, nonconformist female for another female lacking all these qualities. Continental theories, assiduously mastered, supply the basis for a very English puritanism. Dr Shaffer blames the critics' failure to praise the book as she would wish upon their ignorance of these theories; she may not take kindly to the suggestion that for a novelist, as for a critic, a close acquaintance with the whole culture of a period is not always an unmixed blessing. Comprehensive learning and a zest for the history of ideas makes this book not only a useful contribution to learning but an exhilarating piece of reading. But unless these qualities are combined with a sensitive appreciation of purely literary values, their application, though it may throw light on literature, hardly constitutes 'a new method of literary criticism'.

6

Gaisford

Thomas Gaisford was born at Iford Manor in Wiltshire in 1779 and educated at a private school near Winchester. He came up to Christ Church in 1797, and was made Student by Dean Jackson in 1800. For a time he served as a tutor, and had Peel among his pupils, and from 1809 to 1811 he examined in the recently established Honour Schools; but in the words of a not unsympathetic obituary notice 'he never allowed the instruction of his pupils to interfere with his pursuit of his own studies'. In 1812 the Regius Chair of Greek was vacated by the promotion of the Dean's brother, William Jackson, to the episcopal throne of Oxford. It might have been expected that another Christ Church man, Peter Elmsley,[1] six years older than Gaisford and already eminent in scholarship, would have been preferred; less brilliant than Porson, he was more systematic, and beyond doubt his intellectual gifts were greater than those of Gaisford. But Elmsley was a Whig and an Edinburgh reviewer; though he was on friendly terms with Gaisford, he was not congenial to all at Christ Church. Cyril

---

* One of a series of lectures given in the Library of Christ Church to mark the completion of twenty years as Regius Professor of Modern History by H.R. Trevor-Roper, now Lord Dacre of Glanton; it was delivered on 7 November 1977.

In general, see H.R. Luard in *DNB* xx (1899), s.v.; Sir John Sandys, *History of Classical Scholarship* iii (1908), 395f.; H.L. Thompson, *Christ Church* (1900), 193f.; W. Tuckwell, *Reminiscences of Oxford*, 2nd ed. (1907), 122f.; E.G.W. Bill and J.F.A. Mason, *Christ Church and Reform, 1850-1867* (1970); E.G.W. Bill, *University Reform in Nineteenth-Century Oxford: A Study of Henry Halford Vaughan, 1811-1885* (1973); W.R. Ward, *Victorian Oxford* (1965). Mr Harry Carter kindly informed me regarding Gaisford's work for the Clarendon Press; Mr I.G. Philip allowed me to read an early draft of the chapter on the Bodleian Library which he is preparing for the volume of the forthcoming *History of the University of Oxford* which is being prepared under the direction of Mr T.H. Aston which covers the period 1689-1800; and Mr Richard Jenkyns, who is a relative of Gaisford's second wife, supplied personal details.

[1] Interesting correspondence of Elmsley, some of it relevant to Gaisford, is published and discussed by N. Horsfall, 'Classical Studies in England, 1810-1825', in *Greek, Roman and Byzantine Studies* 15 (1974), 449f.

Jackson, who from his retirement at Felpham still exercised great influence, gave his support to Gaisford, and he was appointed. In his day the notion that professors ought to lecture was not quite a novelty; nearly fifty years before the Regius Professor of Modern History at Cambridge, the poet Thomas Gray, had been grievously shocked by a rumour that the requirement to do so might be enforced.[2] Gaisford never lectured, and his failure to do so was complained of; yet as we shall see presently he discharged other duties of the chair with great conscientiousness.

The story goes that the first draft of Gaisford's answer to Lord Palmerston's letter offering the chair ran 'My Lord, I have received your letter and accede to its contents', but that this was fortunately shown to Jackson, who made Gaisford substitute a letter of his own dictation. Gaisford's marked deficiency in urbanity and sociability seems to have been accompanied by a remarkable persuasive power. He married a wife whose personal attractions contrasted strongly with his own, and who was moreover a niece of Dr Van Mildert, Canon of Christ Church and later Bishop of Durham; when she died, he replaced her with a sister of Dr Jenkyns, Master of Balliol. In 1823 he was made Canon of Llandaff and Worcester; in 1829, after rejecting the Bishopric of Oxford as a post liable to interfere with his studies, he received the Golden Stall at Durham; and two years later Van Mildert arranged for him to exchange this with Samuel Smith for the Deanery of Christ Church. This office he held from 1831 until his death in 1855, continuing to hold the chair of Greek.

It has been written that 'it is Gaisford's misfortune to be remembered chiefly as a butt of some largely apocryphal anecdotes'.[3] Indeed the mention of his name reminds many people that he is said to have ended a sermon in the Cathedral with the words: 'And in conclusion, let me urge upon you the value of the study of the ancient tongues, which not only refines the intellect and elevates above the common herd, but also leads not infrequently to positions of considerable emolument.' People also remember that when he received a letter beginning 'The Dean of Oriel presents his compliments to the Dean of Christ Church', Gaisford is said to have remarked, 'Oh yes – Alexander the coppersmith to Alexander the Great.' We are told that when Gaisford said to his pretty daughter 'You can't turn down Jelf; he knows more about γε than any man in Oxford', Miss Gaisford is said to have replied that she fancied she knew something about μέν. But just as all the best Spoonerisms are

[2] See R.W. Ketton-Cremer, *Thomas Gray: a Biography* (1955), 231f.
[3] Bill and Mason, op. cit., 6.

said, on the best authority, to have been made up by W.L. Courtney, so all the best Gaisford stories may well have been made up by Osborne Gordon.

I shall try presently to show why no person tolerably familiar with the history of the Bodleian Library or of the Clarendon Press, not to mention that of classical scholarship, in Gaisford's time can accept the judgment I have just quoted. But what can be said of his record as Dean of Christ Church? 'A splendid scholar, but a bad Dean' was Gladstone's verdict.[4] Under Jackson, who was Dean from 1783 to 1809, Christ Church had flourished as it never has before or since. Cyril Jackson was one of those rare human beings who without apparent effort both command allegiance and inspire affection, and combined genuine enthusiasm for education and learning with an unusual power of influencing others, both in Oxford and outside. No Dean has cut a more important figure either in the university or in the greater world; witness his masterly management of the Duke of Portland's election to be Chancellor, his contribution to the bringing down of Addington's administration, his delivery in avoiding by resignation the awkward issue posed by the candidature for succession to the Duke of Lord Grenville, a Christ Church man with strong support inside the college who happened to support Catholic Emancipation. At the same time Jackson was active in the support of scholarship and learning, both in the college and in the university. He took a leading part in the institution of the Honour Schools, and was at the centre of the movement to revitalise the Bodleian Library and the Clarendon Press; no person played a greater part in the revival of Oxford during the last quarter of the eighteenth century. Jackson took full advantage of the college's freedom from the restriction of places on the foundation to founder's kin or to natives of particular districts that hampered other institutions, for he and many of the Canons were conscientious in the exercise of the right to nominate to Studentships; and as tutors were recruited from the Students, Christ Church then had the best tutors in the university. In his time and for long afterwards, Christ Church educated many men who were later to hold great power and influence, Canning, Peel and Gladstone among them; and thanks largely to him they received as good an education as England at the time was capable of providing.

After Jackson's retirement in 1809, the splendid machine which he had set in motion continued for some years to function. But neither of his two immediate successors was worthy of the post, and their inertia contributed to the decline that was to follow. Jackson had hoped to be

[4] John Morley, *Life of Gladstone* (1903) i, 49.

succeeded by William Carey, later Bishop of St Asaph, a man still remembered with gratitude by present and past Westminster Scholars of the House. But instead Lord Liverpool got the place for his old tutor Charles Henry Hall; and it was after fifteen years of him and seven of the equally unmemorable 'Presence of Mind' Smith that Gaisford took over.

Beyond doubt Gaisford did his best to remedy the decline of discipline that had set in under Hall and Smith, and tried hard to enforce by strictness the rule of industry that Jackson had maintained by firmness tempered by affability. Collections in Hall were a terrifying ordeal. 'Of course,' Ruskin[5] writes, 'the collective quantity of Greek possessed by all the undergraduate heads in hall was to him infinitesimal. Scornful at once and vindictive, thunderous always, more sullen and threatening as the day went on, he stalked with baleful emanation of Gorgonian cold from dais to door, and door to dais, of the majestic torture chamber, vast as the great council hall of Venice, but degraded now by the mean terrors, swallow-like under the eaves, of doleful creatures who had no counsel in them, except how to hide their crib in time, at each fateful Abbot's transit.' But this severity could not arrest the falling standard. A year before Gaisford became Dean, the old oral examinations in the schools had been replaced by written tests; translation became less important, composition and philosophy more so. Other colleges, like Oriel and Balliol, were now free to elect fellows from the whole university by open competition, and their tuition benefitted. The decline of Westminster School adversely affected Christ Church. Gaisford himself and some of the canons nominated Students for the best reasons, but others failed to follow their example; the quality of tuition declined, so that the more ambitious undergraduates broke the rule against hiring tutors from outside the college. Gaisford became suspicious of the value of the Honour Schools, and discouraged Christ Church men from reading for them. During his first four years as Dean, Christ Church had obtained twenty-eight First Classes; ten years later between 1841 and 1845 it obtained only six. It must be admitted that even Jackson might have had difficulty in obtaining industrious behaviour from the Christ Church undergraduates of the period of Gaisford's rule. The records of undergraduate dissipation contained in the chapter of W.G. Hiscock's *Christ Church Miscellany* that is called 'The Dark Age' hardly support the notion that between Waterloo and the Crimea the sons of the nobility and gentry advanced in industry and responsibility.

[5] Ruskin, *Praeterita*, ch. 11.

Gaisford was not personally a snob, but his extreme conservatism made him slow to take account of changing social conditions. In those days the dons did not dine in Hall, and the High Table was occupied by the noblemen and gentlemen commoners while the other undergraduates sat below. Gaisford was careful to maintain distinctions of rank and wealth. He saw the promise of William Stubbs,[6] whose name he playfully latinised to 'Stobaeus' after the anthologist; but he would allow no one who had been a servitor to become a Student, and so Stubbs and other valuable men were lost to Christ Church. In justice I should add that this policy saved the college from having to retain T.E. Brown, and so adding to the consciousness of having reared Martin Tupper a measure of responsibility for the poem that begins 'A garden is a lovesome thing, God wot'.

People who feel that a great Dean must be able to point to physical changes in the college made under his rule may observe with disapproval that under Gaisford hardly any such change occurred; even the repair of the steps and parapet wall of Tom Quad carried out under Sir Francis Chantrey at a cost of £2,000 was largely undone later. The college was saving up to remedy the known inadequacy of the Chaplains' Buildings; action was finally taken during the sixties, under the Ruskinian guidance of Dean Liddell, with the results we know. Perhaps we should commend Gaisford for his thrift; but if he had seen what eventually occurred, he would surely have regretted that nothing had been done before the Neo-Gothic style had prevailed over the Neo-Classical.

Gaisford served continuously on the Hebdomadal Council, where he did all he could to avert change. He did not care for University Reform. When the first University Commission sent a circular to heads of houses, he returned no answer, and he wrote to Liddell, who was one of the commissioners: 'I feel, in common with almost everyone both at Oxford and Cambridge, that it is a measure which can be productive of no good, and may eventually breed discord and disunion, and destroy the independence of those bodies.' There is no need to ask what Gaisford would have thought of the Christ Church, Oxford Act of 1867, through which the Dean and Canons ceased to be the governing body of the college. Throughout his reign the strength of the movement for reform was growing, and Gaisford's influence outside the walls of his own college was in no way comparable with that of John Fell or Cyril Jackson. He failed to prevent the election as

---

[6] See *The Letters of William Stubbs*, ed. W.H. Hutton (1904), 18.

Chancellor of the Duke of Wellington, a candidate unacceptable to Christ Church by reason of the famous quarrel after Lord Charles Wellesley was sent down for breaking open a gate; he failed in a most uncollegiate attempt to throw a crumb of comfort to professors by giving them some measure of control over the revised examinations. In the Bodleian and in the Press, as we shall see presently, the story was very different.

Gaisford's best friends admitted that his behaviour to others stood in startling contrast with that of the great Dean who gave him his first promotion and whose work he attempted to continue. 'You will never be a gentleman,' Jackson is supposed to have said to him, 'but you may succeed as a scholar'; the dubious anecdote crudely underlines a real difference. 'He was blunt and outspoken,' writes a sympathetic critic, H.L. Thompson, 'but perhaps a little lacking in suavity of manner'; in the language of the radical academic gossip William Tuckwell this becomes 'a rough and surly man.' Thompson's claim that Gaisford had 'a kind and generous heart' did not impress another academic radical, Goldwin Smith.[7] 'The Dean,' he wrote in his autobiography, 'was called the Athenian blacksmith, and both parts of the nickname were deserved ... For his manners, his friends could only say that his heart was good; which, as an autopsy was not possible, could give little satisfaction to those who suffered from his rudeness'. Even his eventual successor, Liddell, a man strongly bound to Gaisford by their common love of scholarship, referred to him in letters written home as an undergraduate as 'The Old Bear', and later in a letter to Sir Henry Acland called him 'a man unreasonable in all things except philology, and bookselling, and the management of libraries'.[8] To Ruskin,[9] who came up in 1840, he appeared as 'the stern captain, who with rounded brow and glittering dark eye, led in his old thunderous Latin the responses of the morning prayer'. 'The Dean,' Ruskin wrote, 'though venerable to me from the first, in his evident honesty, self-respect, and real power of a rough kind, was yet in his general aspect too much like the sign of the Red Pig which I afterwards saw set up in pudding raisins, with black currants for eyes, by an imaginative grocer in Chartres fair; and in the total bodily and ghostly presence of him was only a rotundly progressive terror, or sternly enthroned and niched Anathema.' Looking at the portrait by

[7] Goldwin Smith, *Reminiscences* (1910), 50.

[8] H.L. Thompson, *Henry George Liddell, D.D., Dean of Christ Church, Oxford: A Memoir* (1899), 18; C.E. Mallett, *A History of the University of Oxford* (1927) iii, 219 (citing a letter of Liddell to Sir Henry Acland written in February 1852).

[9] Op. cit. (in n. 5).

Pickersgill which now hangs in the vestibule of the Hall,[10] one can imagine the effect of an expression of displeasure upon that composed but formidable countenance. The authentic flavour of Gaisford seems to be conveyed by a notice in the Upper Library, very neatly printed:

ORDERED

That the Porter do not permit any persons into the Library, except upon the ordinary footing of Strangers.

All members of the College must observe the regulations made by the Chapter respecting the keys of the Library.

Undergraduates, who may be indulged with permission of entrance during Library hours, are to consider the indulgence personal, and are not to introduce their friends without express leave.

One seems to find here the same hand as in the famous notice still standing at the Rose Lane entrance to the Meadow, which instructs the Keepers and Constables to keep out 'all beggars, all persons in ragged or very dirty clothes, persons of improper character or who are not decent in appearance or behaviour and to prevent indecent, rude or disorderly conduct of every description'.[11]

Yet few if any Oxford residents of Gaisford's time made a larger contribution to scholarship than he. Both as administrator and as editor he gave a powerful impetus to the renewed activity of the Bodleian and the Press; and his published works, amounting to more than fifty volumes, constitute a massive achievement in both classical and patristic studies. The nature of his work is not easy to explain, even to a specialised audience; for it cannot be properly described without some account of the conditions, very different from ours, in which he operated and without the rehearsal of many details that must make for dryness. Gaisford struck up a curious friendship with 'old Hancock', the porter at Canterbury Gate, whom he used to call 'the Archbishop of Canterbury'; and on one occasion Hancock presumed to invite the Dean and some visitors to take tea in the subterranean recesses of his domain beneath the Lodge. I do not believe the invitation was accepted, and it will not surprise me if some readers decline the invitation to accompany me into some of the underground boiler-rooms of classical scholarship which the nature of

[10] It is reproduced by Sandys (op. cit. on p. 83), and in the catalogue mentioned on p. 92 below (cf. n. 16).

[11] A photograph of the notice will be found in Christopher Hobhouse, *Oxford* (1st edn., 1939; 5th. ed., with supplement by Marcus Dick, 1952, still one of the best guidebooks to Oxford).

my subject now compels me to extend to them.

Gaisford's work can be understood only against the background of the European scholarship of his time.[12] The first renascence of classical literature started in the thirteenth century, and reached its climax in Italy during the fifteenth and in France during the sixteenth century. But before the seventeenth century was over a second revival got under way, principally in Holland and in England; this reached its peak in Germany during the century after Waterloo, and since 1914 has been running down under the impact of the wars of our own time. The original renascence did far more for Latin than for Greek. Latin was the *lingua franca* of educated persons in the west, Greek an exotic luxury; during the early centuries of the revival, only an isolated genius like Politian went far in Greek scholarship. In the sixteenth century the French, despairing of rivalling Italy in Latin, took up Greek studies with brilliant success. Still, even as late as the middle of the eighteenth century few people read Greek with genuine understanding, 'Greek, sir,' said Johnson, 'is like lace; a man gets as much of it as he can.'

The scholars of the second revival were less concerned and more concerned with literature than their predecessors. They inherited the task of redressing the balance between Greek and Latin; for as the eighteenth century proceeded a new and insistent demand for Greek developed. France, it is true, decided that she could now manage without the classics; the Battle of the Books marked the abdication from the front rank in classical studies portended a century before, when Scaliger had left for Holland and Casaubon for England. But in Germany the appetite for Greek grew rapidly; this was the age of Lessing, Winckelmann and Goethe. Till now Europe had been content to look at Greece through Roman spectacles; now for the first time it made a sustained effort to see the ancient Greeks directly, an effort in which professional scholars acted as the agents of the culture as a whole.

The new age demanded texts of the chief literary authors which were sufficiently purged of the corruptions and interpolations that infested most of the manuscripts surviving from the middle ages to be readily understood by modern readers. It also needed tolerable texts of other writers, of less literary merit but useful for historical or linguistic reasons or as aids to the understanding of literary texts. The urgent task of purifying the latter made it necessary to produce adequate editions of the grammars, dictionaries and commentaries

---

[12] See Wilamowitz, *History of Classical Scholarship*, tr. Alan Harris (forthcoming); R. Pfeiffer, *History of Classical Scholarship* ii (1976), chs. 10-14.

surviving from antiquity, many of which contained quotations or explanations useful for this purpose. Scholars with a fine feeling for style and language naturally tended to specialise in editing or emending the literary writers; others, often less acute and sensitive but sometimes more capable of arduous labour, took on the heavy burden of editing texts of the other sort, which because of their great extent and their many difficulties had been neglected by the scholars of earlier generations. Of course some people were active in both kinds of work, as was the great scholar Bentley (1662-1742), who at the start of this period did more than any man to shape the more refined tools which the scholarship of the new age demanded; but most according to their temperament and aptitudes tended to one side or to the other. Most English scholars tended to the literary side; in Gaisford's time Porson (1759-1808), Elmsley, and other members of what is not quite accurately called the school of Porson took the same direction. Not that England loomed quite as large as local pride sometimes imagines; the Leipzig professor Gottfried Hermann (1772-1848), working on a far larger scale than any of his English contemporaries, did more than any man to bring about a radical change in the quality of the texts not only of the tragedians but also of the epic and lyric poets.

When I speak of a second revival, I do not mean to imply that the scholars of the period were impelled by the same spirit that actuated the great writers who drew inspiration from antiquity. The bewigged professors of eighteenth-century Germany and Holland were not poets or aesthetes, and did not resemble them. Hermann was an admirer of Kant, whose rigorous logic he applied to the problems of scholarship; Goethe, though he much admired his work, was somewhat repelled by the element of dryness it contained. Most of the scholars who took in hand the heavy labour of editing the drier and more extensive authors were Dutch or German. In Holland Hemsterhuis, the learned contemporary of Bentley, edited the encyclopedia of Pollux and the voluminous works of Lucian. Ruhnken took on the Platonic lexicon of Timaeus and Valckenaer the grammatical treatise of Ammonius; the latter has only just been superseded, the former remains in use. In the next generation, Wyttenbach edited the whole of Plutarch; thanks to the revival of activity in the Clarendon Press dating from the time of Jackson, this work bore the Oxford imprint. In Germany university professors like Fabricius, Gesner and Ernesti carried on the same tradition; different as they were from the humanists of the new age, their labours supplied these with indispensable material. Few people now turn to their works, except as monuments of the history of scholarship; yet without them the vast edifice of learning that was to be erected during the nineteenth century could hardly have come into being.

The improvement of transport and the development of photography have made it hard for modern scholars even to imagine the difficulties which their predecessors had to cope with. Even if the difficulties of an editor's task had been better understood than they were before the nineteenth century, few editors could have acted on their understanding; for manuscripts were scattered over Europe, and were often locked away in libraries whose owners, whether lay or clerical, did not readily grant access. Nor did the scholars of that time possess the aids that we now take for granted; men like Gaisford worked with no Thesaurus, no Liddell and Scott, no Pauly-Wissowa, and with special lexica to authors far fewer and less reliable than those we now have. This state of affairs had certain compensations; few modern scholars have the intimate acquaintance with texts, including those of authors not familiar to the ordinary reader, displayed by Gaisford in the correspondence with Henry Fynes Clinton, the great authority on ancient chronology, now in the Library of Christ Church.

The way in which scholars like Gaisford edited texts was not the modern way. It has now long been realised that the scientific editing of a text surviving from before the age of printing is a historical investigation, one that involves systematically collecting the various witnesses, determining their relationship with each other and their value in the reconstitution of the original, and where necessary having recourse to conjectural emendation. This method was made generally known by Karl Lachmann's famous edition of Lucretius, published in 1850, and is popularly known as the method of Lachmann, although it is now known that the main credit for its working out over a period of twenty years or so belongs to others.[13] Early editors proceeded differently. The renaissance scholars responsible for the first printed editions of most texts used whatever manuscript might come to hand; even when more than one were available, they often used one only. They had no means, other than the superficial, of determining a manuscript's age, let alone its quality; palaeographical science was rudimentary before the seventeenth century. Later editors would often assemble several manuscripts, using either originals or collations, and present their readers with a selection of variant readings. Gradually editors learned how to tell early manuscripts from late ones; they tended to assume that early ones were better, which they are often but by no means always. In the early period many scholars emended in

---

[13] S. Timpanaro, *La genesi del metodo del Lachmann* (1963); in general see E.J. Kenney, *The Classical Text*, Sather Classical Lectures (1974), vol. 44.

excess, often imposing norms of style and grammar that the writers they emended never aimed at. Reacting against this tendency, some scholars swung over to an opposite extreme; some editors offered an exact diplomatic transcript of what they held to be the best authority, putting emendations, if they made any, in an apparatus criticus below the text. Often an editor would reprint a text from a predecessor, leaving manuscript variations as well as emendations in the apparatus, even in places where the vulgate text made nonsense. This kind of editing survived in some cases till well into the nineteenth century.

Unlike most of the English scholars of his time, Gaisford concentrated not on the purification of the texts of literary authors, but on the provision of the necessary aids, not shrinking from the labour involved by the editing of extensive works. In this he chose a task well suited to his powers, for his strength lay in unremitting industry and in solid judgment rather than in sensitivity to style or flair for divination. He began modestly enough[14] with a series of school editions of Euripides, followed by revisions of other men's editions of Euripides and Cicero that contained little of his own. His more ambitious editorial work took its origin from the desire to communicate to the learned world what was available in the Bodleian.

The Bodleian had possessed important Greek and Latin manuscripts since the time of Laud, who not only presented some himself, but also encouraged William Herbert, Earl of Pembroke, to buy and give to the university the great collection of Giacomo Barocci.[15] In 1698 the university bought the manuscripts purchased by Edward Bernard when the library of Nicholas Heinsius was sold at Leyden; Bentley during his stay here made good use of these treasures. In general the eighteenth century in Oxford was a bad period for the acquisition of manuscripts, as it was for that of books. But towards the end of it there was a resurgence of activity. William Scott, later Lord Stowell, persuaded the university to spend more on books, and there was a systematic attempt to improve the collection of early printed books by purchase from the Pirelli and Crevenna libraries. In the year of Gaisford's first publication, 1805, the university bought for £1,025 the great collection of manuscripts, collations and learned correspondence of the Dutch scholar, J.P. D'Orville, including, to name only what would most appeal to Gaisford, the splendid Euclid written for Arethas in A.D. 888. A year later Gaisford brought out a

---

[14] See Luard, art. cit. (on p. 83) for a list of Gaisford's writings.

[15] See Edmund Craster, *A History of the Bodleian Library, 1845-1945* (1952), on the Pirelli and Crevenna Sales, see I.G. Philip, *Transaction of the Cambridge Bibliographical Society* 7, 1979, 369f.

catalogue of this collection; it was the first such catalogue available to readers, who till then had had to rely on the old lists of 1697-98. In 1809 the university paid £1,000 for the collection of the former Librarian of Cambridge University, Edward Daniel Clarke, including the unique manuscript of Plato from the Monastery of St John on Patmos; once more Gaisford rapidly brought out a catalogue of the new acquisitions, which he followed up in 1820 with a transcription of the Plato. By far the most important consequence of his appointment to succeed William Jackson in the chair of Greek in 1812 was that he became a Curator of the Bodleian, and remained one till his death forty-three years later. In 1817 the university paid £5,444 for the great collection assembled by the Venetian priest Matteo Luigi Canonici; this includes the Juvenal, copied in about 1200, which contains thirty-six lines not found in any other manuscript, and the fourteenth-century Catullus which is probably the earliest surviving manuscript of that author. In 1820 the university acquired the library of the Veronese collector Giovanni Saibante; this includes the eleventh-century codex of Arrian's *Epictetus* from which all the other extant manuscripts derive. In 1824 Gaisford travelled to the Hague for the sale of Gerard Meerman's collection, including precious classical manuscripts from the library of Clermont College, the Jesuit institution near Paris. Although Sir Thomas Phillipps was the most successful bidder, Gaisford returned with spoils of great value, including the fifth-century codex of Eusebius' version of St Jerome's Chronicle whose importance no one realised till Mommsen came to Oxford in 1888. Individual items, too, were often bid for; in 1814 Oxford missed the Towneley Homer, but in 1817 it acquired a fifteenth-century Suidas and in 1820 the Codex Ebnerianus of the New Testament. In all this activity Gaisford was the prime mover; and it was at his instigation that H.O. Coxe began the systematic catalogue of Greek manuscripts that we still use, as brought up to date by Mr Nigel Wilson. 'At work on MS II,' writes Coxe in his diary. 'Just as the Dean came in, found it to be Psellus. The Dean nudged me and chuckled.' The other Curators were of little consequence; 'the control of the Library,' wrote Sir Edmund Craster, ' ... was in fact left in the hands of Dr Pusey and Dr Gaisford. The latter in particular, with his enthusiasm for Greek manuscripts and his knowledge of book values, was the real ruler.' The organisers of the splendid exhibition of Greek and Latin manuscripts of 1975 rightly chose as frontispiece to its catalogue[16] Atkinson's mezzotint of Pickergill's portrait of the

---

[16] R.W. Hunt and others, *The Survival of Ancient Literature* (1975); for specimens of more Greek manuscripts in the Bodleian, see Nigel Wilson, *Medieval Greek Bookhands*, published by the Medieval Academy of America in 1972.

Dean. Gaisford seems to have taken as keen an interest in the purchase of books as in that of manuscripts; the lean years of the nineteenth century are those which lie between his death in 1855 and Ingram Bywater's election as a Curator in 1884.

The two Bodleian catalogues of 1806 and 1809 were followed in 1810 by a more ambitious publication; the first edition of the most important ancient work on Greek metre to appear since 1726 and the first competent edition since 1553.[17] The first printed edition of Hephaestion had been a Juntine printed at Florence in 1526; the one manuscript used belongs to the third of the three classes into which the manuscripts of this author are nowadays divided. In 1553 the work was edited by Adrianus Turnebus, Reader in Greek at Paris, probably the most competent person to perform the task then living. He used at least two manuscripts, one of the second and one of the third class, and also improved the text by emendation. One of his manuscripts contained the ancient scholia, in a disturbed order, which Turnebus tried to remedy by guesswork. Much remained to be done; but nothing was done before 1726 and then the man who did it was the vain and foolish Dutchman, J.C. de Pauw. He added little except new errors; even the misprint in the title in Turnebus' edition was faithfully reproduced. Gaisford used three manuscripts of the first class, two in the Bodleian and one in Cambridge, besides two of the third class from the British Museum. He gave a text closely based upon Turnebus, very occasionally using his new witnesses to make improvements; he was also able to print some scholia not previously known. The next editor, R. Westphal in 1867, had no new manuscript material; but he saw the superiority of the first class of the manuscripts and based his text upon them, making almost many conjectures, some of them rash but many of them right. During the eighties the foundations of the modern text were laid by Hoeschelmann and Studemund, who found important witnesses in Vienna and Milan and divided the manuscripts into their three classes; the edition of M. Consbruch (1906) makes Gaisford's seem antediluvian. Still, Gaisford had made available to scholars a useful work not easily obtainable, and had made the first improvement in its text since 1553. Although his work was in no way comparable with what Bentley or Reiske would have effected with the same materials, for an Oxford scholar of his day it was a creditable performance. It amounts to far less than had already been achieved by Elmsley, who two years later was passed over in Gaisford's favour for the chair of Greek. Yet that Elmsley would have made as much as Gaisford, in the

---

[17] See M. Consbruch, *Hephaestionis Enchiridion* (1906), pref., esp. pp. xxivf.

Oxford of the time, of the advantages the chair offered cannot, I think, be taken for granted.

Gaisford's editions of literary authors are less numerous and less important than his texts of works of secondary rank, such as dictionaries, encyclopaedias and anthologies, and than the editions of patristic texts which formed a large portion of his output during the latter part of his career. The *Poetae Graeci Minores* of 1814, in three volumes, pretends to be no more than a revision of Winterton's collection of 1635, and the very modest claims made in its preface are borne out by the absence of any effort to improve the text by emendation. But in the cases of Hesiod and Theocritus Gaisford could offer new manuscript material from the collations left to the Bodleian by J. St Amand in 1755 and from those made in Paris by F.J. Bast, the editor of Gregory of Corinth, which on his death in 1811 had passed to the Clarendon Press and since 1885 have been in the Bodleian.[18] Both these texts were edited with scholia; although the leading modern expert on the subject[19] is right to call the edition of the Hesiod scholia 'wretched', it has still not been entirely superseded. Gaisford's *Herodotus* of 1824 is almost entirely derivative, though he recollated a valuable Cambridge manuscript and provided English notes to accompany the Latin notes of various hands. His edition of the Laurentian scholia on Sophocles, and later of the poet's text, had the merit of giving to the public Elmsley's collations and the part of the edition he had finished. Six years after Gaisford's edition had appeared in 1824, Hermann[20] drew attention to the great importance of the new material. But for the emendation and elucidation of the difficult text, Gaisford had done little.

More important among his works is the two-volume edition of Aristotle's *Rhetoric* which appeared in 1820.[21] This difficult text had been edited in 1584 by the great Italian scholar, Petrus Victorius, who had collated many manuscripts in Florence and in other places. He imparts their readings only sparingly; but he shows himself aware that there is value in the tenth-century manuscript in Paris known as A, now known to be our best witness for the text. Apart from an elegant Latin version of the first two books published in 1585 by Marcus Antonius Muretus, who championed against the cautious Victorius the claims of a properly judicious emendation,[22] nothing

---

[18] See Craster, op. cit. (in n.15), 94 and 193.

[19] M.L. West, *Hesiod: Theogony* (1966), 103.

[20] In the preface to the second edition of the Erfurdt-Hermann *Antigone* of 1830.

[21] See R. Kassel, *Der Text der Aristotelischen Rhetorik* (1971), 104f.

[22] Dr Carlotta Griffiths has discussed their controversy in a paper of great interest which I hope will soon be published.

further had been done to improve the text. Finding little material in Oxford – though Balliol provided a text of the scholia and the Bodleian a copy of the medieval Latin version – Gaisford obtained collations of five manuscripts in Paris. Four were of little value, but the fifth was A. Gaisford made more use of it than Victorius had done, while admitting in his preface that he might have made more. Yet he prints a text based on Buhle's unoriginal edition of 1791, and to the confusion of his reader notes variants as they differ from Sylburg's text of 1584. In 1831, only eleven years after Gaisford, the work was edited by Immanuel Bekker (1786-1871), a scholar whose unremitting concentration on the multiple editing of texts makes it natural to compare his work with that of his English contemporary. Bekker with his usual palaeographical flair made a far better selection of Paris manuscripts to report, and he went beyond Gaisford in his use of A. But over and above the advantage given him by the godsent opportunity of being in Paris when the conquests of Napoleon had concentrated innumerable manuscripts in that place, Bekker was no mean textual critic. He did far more by emendation than Gaisford for the authors whom he edited, most notably for Plato, but also for Aristotle.

Gaisford's most impressive achievements lie in his editions of voluminous secondary authors – the vast anthology compiled during the fifth century of our era by John Stobaeus, the huge tenth-century encyclopaedia once known by the name of its supposed author Suidas, but which it is now fashionable to call the Suda (a Byzantine word for a kind of fortress), the numerous ancient collections of Greek proverbs, the Latin writers upon metre, the ninth-century commentary of Choeroboscus upon the fifth-century grammatical treatise of Theodosius, with the same author's commentary on the Psalms, the immense dictionary called the *Etymologicum Magnum*.

For his *Suidas* Gaisford used better collations of the Paris manuscripts than had been available to Bentley's friend Ludolf Kuster in 1700, and he added useful notes; but he took over too much from the old editors, and left many difficulties unexplained.[23] Still, he showed sound judgment in the constitution of the text, and the next German editor, G. Bernhardy, failed to improve on his performance.

Gaisford did about as well in editing the third and fourth books of the anthology of Stobaeus, those containing the extracts from Greek literature. Their manuscript tradition differs from that of the first two books, which contain extracts from scientific and philosophical

---

[23] See Ada Adler, *Suidas* i (1928), xii.

writings.[24] Modern editors divide the witnesses into three groups. Editors before Gaisford had used only a member of the first group, with the exception of Hugo Grotius, who in a brilliant treatment of the poetic extracts only, published in 1623, had used a Paris codex belonging to the second. Gaisford had a collation of this manuscript, and recognised its value; but he exaggerated its merits, and failed to cope adequately with the difficulties it presented. In 1855-57 the same books were edited by the great scholar August Meineke, like Gaisford a busy man; he was the headmaster of an important Gymnasium in Berlin. Meineke brought no new manuscript information, but with his gifts of divination he improved the text in countless places; he had the penetrating critical intelligence which Gaisford lacked. The first half of Stobaeus Gaisford edited near the end of his career, when his powers were beginning to decline.[25] His collation of the Codex Augustanus was of little value, and in the way of emendation he had virtually nothing to show.

We possess many different Byzantine collections of Greek proverbs, all ultimately dependent on a corpus of five collections made from literary texts during late antiquity. Most of these belong to what is now called the vulgar recension; our knowledge of the earlier form of the work dates only from 1868, when Emanuel Miller published a codex from Mount Athos which had found its way to Paris. The immense task of sorting out the complicated relationships between the various collections was then taken in hand by Otto Crusius and his pupils;[26] but they died without completing it, and it is not yet finished. Before Crusius scholars were content to publish separately the many lists of proverbs arranged under the successive letters of the alphabet and often overlapping with each other without attempting to investigate their relationships. Gaisford published one new list from a codex in the Meerman collection and another from one of Bast's collations, and used material in the Bodleian and in the British Museum to improve the text of some lists already published. The two-volume Göttingen edition of 1839-51, which we still use, offers more material than Gaisford's, but does not entirely supersede it.

The modest aim of Gaisford's edition of the Latin metrical writers,[27] as he explains in the preface, is to improve the text a little

[24] See O. Hense, Stobaeus iii (1894), lxiv.

[25] See C. Wachsmuth, Stobaeus i (1884), p. xxv.

[26] The pages of Crusius and his pupils dealing with the paroemiographers are reprinted in a third volume attached to the reprint of the Göttingen edition of Leutsch and Schneidewin in 1961; cf. L. Cohn in R.-E. iii (1899), 2364f.

[27] See the prefaces to the separate works in H. Keil, Grammatici Latini vi (1874).

with the aid of some new manuscript material. He mentions few conjectures, whether by himself or others; yet for forty years his edition was the best available. He was the first to publish a complete text of Choeroboscus on the canons of Theodosius from the only manuscript that has it all; but here the collation made for him by an agent engaged by Miller let him down badly.[28] The same writer's commentary on the Psalms must still be read in Gaisford's edition in the same volume.[29]

A far larger and more important text for which we still have to turn to Gaisford is the most extensive of the ancient dictionaries known as Etymologica, the so-called *Etymologicum Magnum* (1848). The works exist in various versions and in various manuscripts, and the task of clearing up their complicated relationships was taken in hand only at the end of the last century by the great scholar Richard Reitzenstein.[30] The *Magnum* had been edited from a now lost but certainly inadequate manuscript by Callierges in 1499; Sylburg in 1594 had been able to supplement this only with a Vatican codex of a much shorter version of the work. Gaisford used not only a Bodleian manuscript from the D'Orville collection, but collations of a Venice and a Paris manuscript. 'It is easy,' wrote Reitzenstein, 'to find fault with Gaisford's edition; the perversity, the apparatus related not to his own text but to that of Sylburg, the awkward long-windedness of the annotation, the constant failure to distinguish between a source and a parallel – all this easily affects one's attitude towards the greatness of the concrete achievement, the careful demonstration of a large number of borrowings and the generally sound justification of the transmitted text.' Gaisford's unwillingness to emend is generously put down by Reitzenstein to a fear of correcting the source rather than the work he is editing; but some might find here what the modern editor of Stobaeus, Otto Hense, calls Gaisford's 'timidity or weakness of judgment'.[31] Yet the praise of Reitzenstein, a man uniquely qualified to judge, means much.

Gaisford's career as a patristic scholar began as late as 1839 with an edition of the *Graecarum affectuum curatio* of the fifth-century bishop Theodoret; he was the first to employ two out of the eight among the twenty-seven extant manuscripts selected by the modern editor Raeder for the constitution of the text, one in the Bodleian and one in

---

[28] See A. Hilgard, *Theodosii Canones, etc.,* ii (1894), p. cxxivf. For the date of Choeroboscus see W. Bühler, *Byz. Zeitschr.* 69 (1976), 397f.

[29] *Choerobosci Dict. in Theodosii Canones et Epimerismi in Psalmos* (1842).

[30] See Reitzenstein, *Geschichte der griechischen Etymologika* (1897), 222f.

[31] Op. cit. (in n. 24).

Paris.[32] In 1842 he published from the unique manuscript in Vienna the so-called *Eclogae Propheticae* of the church historian and apologist Eusebius, the contemporary and panegyrist of Constantine the Great. The work consists of the last four and only surviving books of an apologetic work in nine books that forms a general elementary introduction to Christianity.[33] The text has not been edited since Gaisford, and the next editor will find much to do; for even a cursory glance shows that much improvement could be effected by conjecture.

The three-volume edition of the Septuagint which Gaisford published in 1848 contained some new manuscript material, but its importance hardly survived the fundamental researches which Tischendorff began a few years later. In 1843 he brought out a two-volume edition of the fifteen books of Eusebius' *Praeparatio Evangelica*, a work valuable to classical scholars as well as theologians for the numerous quotations it contains.[34] R. Stephanus in 1543 had used two Paris manuscripts, Vigerus in 1628 had added a third; but Gaisford could offer two better Parisini, two manuscripts in Florence and two in Venice. But despite his detailed apparatus he was content to reproduce the vulgate text, and his notes contain little in the way of emendation. Diels in his edition of the Greek doxographers speaks of this edition with impatience: 'ex Gaisfordii indigesta mole ... quanta perversitate Eusebii illa editio confusa sit, nolo conqueri.'[35] Yet here too Gaisford had improved upon his predecessors. His edition of the surviving half of the second instalment of Eusebius' vast work, the ten books of the *Demonstratio Evangelica*, belongs to his last years, when his powers were failing.[36] R. Stephanus had used only a Paris manuscript of small value, and Gaisford had a good collation of a twelfth-century Parisinus, besides a manuscript belonging to St John's College; but apart from the usual failure to improve the text by emendation, he made many errors in transcription.

The same faults attend the edition of the polemical works of Eusebius against Hierocles and Marcellus, published in the same year. The unique manuscript of Hierocles, Paris. 451, was not available, and Gaisford used a collation of a copy of it in Venice. For the Marcellus,[37] Richard Montagu in 1628 had only a copy of the unique manuscript;

---

[32] See P. Canivet, *Thérapeutique des Maladies Helléniques* i (1958), 73f.

[33] See E. Schwartz, *R.-E.* vi (1909), 1386 = *Griechische Geschichtsschreiber* (1959), 518.

[34] See K. Mras, *Eusebios, Werke* viii, *Praeparatio Evangelica* i (1954), lxiiif.

[35] H. Diels, *Doxographi Graeci*, 2nd ed. (1929), 43; cf. 159.

[36] See C.A. Heikel, *Eusebios, Werke* vi, *Demonstratio Evangelica* (1913), xxvi.

[37] See *Eusebios, Werke* iv, *Contra Marcellum*, ed. E. Klostermann, rev. G.C. Hansen, 2nd ed, (1972), xxiv.

Gaisford had the manuscript itself, but failed to make the best use of it. For his last work, his edition of Theodoret's church history, Gaisford had two important Bodleian manuscripts, A (twelfth century) and B (eleventh century), but failed to draw the important distinction between the two hands that wrote the former, and failed to appreciate the latter at its true value.[38]

The evidence I have assembled, almost entirely at second hand, may help to form a judgment upon Gaisford's achievement as an editor of texts. In critical intelligence he does not rank high; whether through over-caution, incapacity or a blend of both, he failed to improve the texts he edited by emendation, comparing unfavourably in this respect with the contemporary editors of multiple Greek texts, Immanuel Bekker and Wilhelm Dindorf. He relied largely on collations by others, who sometimes let him down; in dealing with the manuscripts which he personally collated, he maintained accuracy, but lacked the palaeographical skill of Bekker. Yet no one can fail to feel awe before his immense industry; had he been slaving in a garret to support a large family, he could hardly have worked harder. He made available many important texts not previously easy for scholars to obtain, and in doing so published much manuscript information not previously available. Though he lacked flair, he possessed good sense; and scholars have reason to be grateful for his massive contribution.

That contribution is not restricted to his editorial labours or his work for the Bodleian. The Clarendon Press owes him much; for though he was not interested in typography or in Press administration; he promoted many of its learned publications, and in doing so developed important connections with scholarship abroad. Since 1795 the Press had been bringing out successive volumes of the great edition of Plutarch by Daniel Wyttenbach.[39] After the disastrous fire in that great scholar's library Gaisford visited him in Holland, helped him to rearrange his papers and to finish off his work, and after his death completed its valuable index. Wyttenbach had recommended F. Creuzer of Heidelberg as the editor of a complete *Plotinus*, a difficult, voluminous and important author not published since Perna's editio princeps of 1580. The edition by Creuzer and G.H. Moser came out in 1835; it has many errors, and not all of us will agree with the latest editors that its reluctance to emend makes it by far the best edition;[40] yet in its day it was a pioneering work.

[38] Theodoret, *Kirchengeschichte*, ed. L. Parmentier, rev. F. Scheidweiler, 2nd ed. (1954), xxi.
[39] *Plutarchi Opera* (1795-1830).
[40] P. Henry and H.-R. Schwyzer, *Plotini Opera* i (1959), xxvi.

Gaisford's son recorded that on a visit to Leipzig they called at a suburban house whose door was opened by a shabby figure whom they took to be the famulus. When the Dean gave his name, this person rushed forward and embraced him. He was Wilhelm Dindorf, the only man to ever make a fortune out of editing classical texts, described by Wilamowitz as 'dexterrimus ille editionum caupo'.[41] That verdict is too harsh. Dindorf sometimes worked too fast, and the quality of his works is variable; but he knew Greek well and unlike Gaisford could emend effectively. Well might he embrace his patron; for while Gaisford dealt with bulky and prosaic authors, Dindorf under his auspices edited for the Press the masterpieces of Greek literature and their scholia – Homer, the scholia on the Odyssey, the Venice scholia on the Iliad, the Greek dramatists, with scholia and notes, Demosthenes with same, the scholia on Aeschines and Isocrates, the lexicon of Harpocration, the works of the most cultivated of the early fathers, Clement of Alexandria. At the same time the Press brought out Bekker's edition of the whole of Aristotle.

Gaisford also encouraged native scholars. He assisted J.A. Cramer, a Christ Church man who was Principal of New Inn Hall, Regius Professor of Modern History and Dean of Norwich, with the valuable series of publications of ancient works of scholarship called *Anecdota Oxoniensia* and *Anecdota Parisina*. I have already spoken of the active help which he gave to another Christ Church scholar, Henry Fynes Clinton, with his two great works on Greek and Roman chronology. He took an active interest, from its inception in 1834, in the Greek lexicon of two young Students of Christ Church, Henry George Liddell and Robert Scott.[42] If Gaisford knew a man to be a true scholar, he was capable of surprising kindness. He called upon the young Max Müller,[43] and in spite of having been assailed by the revolting Scotch terriers Müller kept to prove his Anglophilia, gave a sympathetic ear to his plea that the Press should publish an Icelandic dictionary. When asked if he would place Müller's name on the books of Christ Church, Gaisford established that there were precedents for the admission of a German in the cases of one Wernerus and one Nitzschius, so that all was well.

Gaisford was a man of the eighteenth century who lived far into the nineteenth. Both as Dean and as scholar, he did his utmost to

---

[41] Wilamowitz, *Aeschyli Fabulae* (1914), xiii.

[42] See Thompson, op. cit. (in n. 8 above), 67: 'The Dean encourages the project very much', writes Liddell to Vaughan at the outset, 'and has given us a number of valuable hints.'

[43] See Nirad C. Chaudhuri, *Scholar Extraordinary: the Life of Professor the Rt. Hon. Friedrich Max Müller, P.C.* (174), 94-5.

continue the work of his great predecessor, Cyril Jackson, and the revival of education in Oxford which Jackson had promoted. His abilities, as he well knew, fell far short of Jackson's; his industry and devotion to duty knew no limits. He was well aware of the decline of education in the college, and did his best to arrest it, often by an alarming severity not tempered, like that of Jackson, by urbanity and geniality. He put his faith in the college exercises, not in the university examinations. From the point of view of younger men, like Jowett and even Liddell, this was deplorable; but to a scholar of the old school like Gaisford, the new dispensation appeared in a different light. 'Our own great age of scholarship,' Housman was to write in 1903,[44] 'begun in 1691 by Bentley's *Epistola ad Millium*, was ended (in 1825) by the successive strokes of doom which consigned Dobree and Elmsley to the grave and Blomfield to the bishopric of Chester'. In Germany the expansion of classical education and its use as an instrument for the education of a new governing class was accompanied by an intensification of its scientific thoroughness; but in this country the corresponding process meant that the energies of the ablest scholars were almost totally absorbed in teaching and in the production of superficial textbooks for the use of students. The best classical work done in England during this period was in ancient history and philosophy, not in ancient literature, and for the most part it was done outside the universities; the Oxford and Cambridge of the time can no more point to a greater name in ancient history and in Platonic and Aristotelian studies than Grote than they can point to a greater name in philosophy than Mill. Gaisford was succeeded in the chair of Greek by Jowett, who retained the post until his death in 1893. His translations of Plato and Thucydides served an educational purpose of a kind, and are tolerable specimens of nineteenth-century mandarin prose; but they are not works of high scholarship, and the time lately spent by a committee of learned men in removing the howlers from the *Plato* might have been better spent in making a new version. Jowett not only failed to promote research, but tried to impede those who did. In the Bodleian he supported the disastrous regime of Nicholson; whatever one may think of him as Master, he was not a good Professor. Yet he epitomised the spirit of his time; and when Mark Pattison tried to get a new benefaction used to buy books for the Bodleian, Jowett managed to get it spent on building the Examination Schools. Asked to suggest a motto for the new building, Ingram

[44] A.E. Housman, *M. Manilii Astronomicon Liber Primus*, 2nd ed. (1937), xlii = *Selected Prose*, ed. John Carter (1961), 41 (cf. Wilamowitz, *Euripides, Herakles*, 2nd ed. (1899), 227).

Bywater suggested 'Multi pertransibunt et *non* augebitur scientia'.[45]
Gaisford, of course, never lectured, and in his later years seemed to a
young and active scholar like John Conington to be failing to carry out
his professorial duties.[46] It is hard, though, to refuse all sympathy to
his attitude to the learning of the examination schools and its
purveyors. One may doubt if even a Jackson could have made the
Christ Church undergraduates of his time work as the contemporaries
of Canning, Peel and Gladstone had worked; no individual could have
reversed a trend conditioned by the general state of the nobility and
gentry at the time. But in the face of the prevailing tendencies
Gaisford stuck to what he thought was right with courage and
determination. Not everybody living now will deny all sympathy to his
attitude towards reform. The work of the First Commission did
indeed guide us along a path that has led to the loss of our
independence; and not all of us are persuaded that the world would be
a better place if nineteenth-century Christ Church had become more
like Balliol.[47]

When Gaisford died, a sum of money raised for a memorial was
spent on an object most characteristic of the time but most
inappropriate to him, the establishment of prizes for Greek verse and
prose composition. These prizes had a distinguished history; in fiction
the most notable winner is Sir Max Beerbohm's Duke of Dorset, in life
Sir John Beazley with his famous account of a visit to the Zoo as
Herodotus might have described it. But now the ablest
undergraduates are no longer interested, so that we have been
compelled to find another use for the money; part goes towards a prize
for composition in the Schools, part towards an annual lecture. It
might be argued that this form of commemoration of a Professor who
never lectured is equally unsuitable. But a lectureship can serve to
maintain our links with scholars everywhere, and to promote sound
learning; and these are objects which Gaisford had very much at
heart.

---

[45] See W.W. Jackson, *Ingram Bywater: the Memoir of an Oxford Scholar*, 1840-1914, 2nd
ed. (1917), 70f.

[46] Mark Pattison, *Memoirs* (1885), 248, speaks of Conington's 'sarcasms against
the Greek professor', which must mean Gaisford, since Pattison is evidently speaking
of a time before Conington's election to the Corpus Chair of Latin in 1854.

[47] See above, p. 85. Gaisford wrote of the Oxford Bill: 'I think it not merely
inexpedient, but unjust and tyrannical' (see Bill and Mason, op. cit. (p. 83 above), 38).

7

Grote

It was lucky for George Grote that he left Charterhouse at fifteen and a half, in 1809, to go into his father's bank. In the Oxford or Cambridge of that time he would have had little encouragement to study history or philosophy; but in London he met Bentham and James Mill, and became a convinced Utilitarian; he read Niebuhr on Roman history and Schleiermacher on Plato. Apart from being a successful banker, he sat for nine years in the House of Commons as member for the City of London; he took an important part in the foundation and later in the government of London University and University College; he produced an important and original book on Plato, and left unfinished the first critical study of Aristotle's work attempted in modern times; and he wrote a history of Greece which remained for many years the best in any European language. The influence of this book, both at home and on the Continent, was immense. 'Grote is the Athanasius of Greek history in England,' wrote an Oxford historian of the old school in a book published in 1948. At that date the remark was absurd, for hardly anyone in England had read Grote for years. But in about 1890, when this particular historian's mind attained its final perfection, it was still true.

Many people have criticised Grote for being unable to see Greek history except in terms of his own political and philosophical convictions. True, he was too quick to identify the oligarchs and democrats of ancient Athens with the political parties of his own time, and his dislike for despotism led him to give insufficient credit to Philip and Alexander for their achievements in uniting Greece and in attempting to reconcile Greeks with Orientals. Like all his contemporaries and many of his successors, Grote studied political history without enough regard for social structure. The difference between 'oligarchs' and 'democrats' in an ancient city state seems less radical when we remember how many of its inhabitants were slaves or resident aliens and thus without political rights; and in any ancient state, however democratic, the rich and noble could exert great

* A review of *George Grote* by M.L. Clarke in the *New Statesman*, 15 June 1962.

influence. Grote was not properly aware of the difficulty of governing an empire while maintaining a democracy of the fifth-century Athenian kind. He was free enough from anti-imperialist bias to regret the collapse of the Athenian empire, but did he realise that if it had continued its rulers might have been less like Pericles than like those Diadochi of whom he had such a low opinion?

But Grote's partisanship went together with great learning and great honesty. Like Clarendon and Gibbon, he benefited from his experience of politics. His very bias lends his historical writing a vigour which is often absent from the work of more dispassionate authors, just as his definite philosophical attitude lends force to his criticism of ancient philosophy. It may seem strange that this convinced Utilitarian should have devoted a large book to Plato, and should have treated him with so much sympathy. But Plato had a critical and rationalising, besides a dogmatic and idealistic side, and this appealed strongly to Grote, as it did to Grote's master, James Mill. A great philosopher often needs to be saved from those disciples who choose to emphasize only that part of his teaching which is opposed to reason. Grote's remarkable study anticipates much that is valuable in modern criticisms of Plato's authoritarian side; but his sound learning saves him, at least to some extent, from the failure of some modern critics to see Plato in the context of his own time, and his good sense saves him from the hysterical exaggeration into which some of the ablest of them have fallen.

Professor Clarke is right not to claim too much for Grote. He acknowledges that the learning of the *History* is now superseded, and that its style, though clear and vigorous, is not distinguished enough to make the book a classic. But Grote will always have an honoured place in the history of scholarship. 'He was determined', writes Arnaldo Momigliano in a memorable lecture,[1] 'to understand and respect evidence from whatever part it came; he recognised freedom of speech, tolerance, and compromise as the conditions of civilisation; he respected sentiment, but admired reason.'

The personal life of the historian was not eventful, and offers few such relieving episodes as his passion (shared by Mrs Grote) for the dancer Fanny Elssler, his passion (not shared by Mrs Grote) for the sculptress Susan Durant, and his long and valiant efforts to make it impossible for a clergyman to hold a philosophical chair at University College. But the author of this excellent book is a lively writer as well as a good scholar, and he is always readable.

---

[1] 'George Grote and the study of Greek History', London, 1952 in *Contributo alla Storia degli Studi Classici* (1955), 213f.

8

Leopardi

Sebastiano Timpanaro is at once the most distinguished classical scholar now working in Italy, a leading authority on Leopardi, and a Marxian theorist of striking originality, who can be read and admired even by the enemies of Marxism. Like all the best Italian classical scholars of his time, he was a pupil of Giorgio Pasquali (1887-1952), who after studying in Göttingen under Wilamowitz and Eduard Schwartz taught many Italians how to make the best use of German scholarship while remaining unmistakably themselves. Shunning the *mondo cane* of the Italian universities, Timpanaro works in the office of a great publishing house. His brilliant study of the nineteenth-century development of the study of the history of a text is known to English classical scholars, partly through its influence on E.J. Kenney's excellent book *The Classical Text*; but so far the only works of his available in English are his books *Materialism* and *The Freudian Slip*. In the latter he deals amusingly and devastatingly with *The Psychopathology of Everyday Life*, showing how many of the mistakes there explained by far-fetched theories may be accounted for less excitingly but more plausibly by considerations familiar to anyone acquainted with the elements of textual criticism. In the former he castigates those up-to-date Marxists who like to titivate their Marxism with an admixture of anthropological structuralism or Chomskyan linguistics. He likes to regard Marxism as the legitimate descendant of eighteenth-century rationalism; unfortunately this is not its only ancestor. When Timpanaro remarks that those who mix their Marx with Chomsky are letting in Kant by the back door, one may retort that so long as Marx himself is part of Marxism, Hegel is comfortably seated in the parlour.

After starting his career with valuable work on the difficult and important early Roman poet Ennius, Timpanaro published in 1955 the first edition of the brilliant study of Leopardi's classical

* A review of *La filologia di Giacomo Leopardi* (2nd edn, 1977), by Sebastiano Timpanaro in *The Times Literary Supplement*, 13 October 1978.

scholarship now made available in a revised form. The new edition
takes account of much good work done in the meantime, most of it by
Timpanaro himself or under the stimulus of his book. The reader is
greatly assisted by being able to use the excellent edition of much of
Leopardi's scholarly work brought out by Timpanaro in collaboration
with Giuseppe Pacella in 1969, and the work is valuably supplemented
by the two chapters about Leopardi in his *Classicismo e illuminismo nell'
ottocento italiano* of 1965.

Though Foscolo and Pascoli made use of scholarship in their
poetry, neither was a scholar in the same sense as Leopardi. Isolated
in Recanati, Leopardi had to work in very difficult conditions. His
father's library lacked many of the leading Greek authors; it lacked,
for instance, Pindar, the three great tragedians – except for a
sixteenth-century edition of three plays of Sophocles –, Aristophanes,
Herodotus, Thucydides and Xenophon. But an exceptional gift for
scholarship asserted itself very early in the poet's life; self-taught in
Greek, he made himself the best Italian Hellenist since Petrus
Victorius in the sixteenth century. If he had never written a line of
poetry, this achievement would deserve a place in the history of
scholarship. As he was not only a great poet, but also a thinker, if not
exactly a philosopher, of singular honesty, acuteness and originality,
one cannot help wondering what effect the very great amount of time
and trouble which he devoted to classical and patristic studies had
upon his own formation.

The task Timpanaro set himself was not easy, since much of
Leopardi's scholarly work remained unpublished in his lifetime – not
all of it has been published even now – and part of it appeared without
the proofs being corrected and in a form which the author might not
have approved. Timpanaro has not only mastered the resulting
difficulties, but has described the nature of Leopardi's achievement in
relation to the conditions of his time with great clarity and exactitude.
In doing so, he has drawn a picture of the intellectual life of the
period, or rather of a certain section of that life, which is both
fascinating and illuminating; he has also – especially if this book is
studied in conjunction with his study of classicism and illuminism –
made an important contribution to the understanding of Leopardi's
thought.

At first sight Leopardi's scholarly work seems to have nothing
whatever to do with poetry. Most of it was done on prose authors of
the post-classical period; most of it is austerely textual. Leopardi
made some admirable emendations; but they were made by means of
close attention to the authors' language and style rather than by a
startling gift of divination; they are more like the work of Elmsley than

the work of Porson. The juvenilia are works of compilation: only the *History of Astronomy*, written at fifteen, shows the hand of the future poet. Notes on the third-century Christian chronographer and encyclopedist Julius Africanus show a grasp of the principles of textual criticism amazing in so young an author. During the period of the 'literary conversion', Leopardi made as stylistic exercises several translations from the classics, and the notes which he appended to them contain some serious contributions to knowledge.

In 1815 Angelo Mai published the first of his remarkable discoveries in the Ambrosian and Vatican Libraries, the letters of Marcus Aurelius's tutor Fronto. Leopardi at once produced a translation, accompanied by an impressive letter of dedication and by an introduction and notes of value; soon after, he did the same for the excerpts from Dionysius of Halicarnassus's Roman history which Mai discovered. The friendly correspondence with Mai which ensued was one of the factors which encouraged Leopardi to come to stay with relations in Rome in 1822-23, hoping to find suitable employment, preferably in the Vatican library, of which Mai was now the prefect.

Timpanaro brilliantly describes the intellectual world of the Italy of the Restoration, and particularly the world of Rome; we recognise another facet of the Italy we know from Stendhal. In Germany a heroic age of scholarship was in full swing; the great linguistic and textual school of Hermann was rivalled and balanced by the great historical epigraphical and archaeological school of Boeckh and Otfried Müller. But almost none of the new learning had made its way across the Alps. Such literary scholarship as there was was of the old Jesuit-humanistic kind, which preserved the forms of humanism without its content; useful antiquarian work was done, but it was antiquarian and not historical. Archaeology in Rome counted infinitely more than literary studies; any stone, Leopardi remarked, meant more than any book.

In such an atmosphere, Leopardi's scholarship failed to make the impression it deserved. Mai rewarded him for his brilliant work on the subjects of two more of his discoveries, the *Chronicle* of Eusebius and the *De republica* of Cicero, and for the splendid poem addressed to him on the occasion of the latter, by appropriating his unpublished conjectures without acknowledgement.

The Cardinal seems to have been actuated not by hostility to an unbeliever, but by simple professional jealousy; others, however, had observed tendencies in Leopardi's thinking which his refusal to take minor orders seemed to confirm. At that time the Prussian Minister in Rome was the greatest living Roman historian, B.G. Niebuhr, and he at once perceived Leopardi's exceptional qualities. When Niebuhr left

Rome he let it be known that the personal favour he would most appreciate would be Leopardi's appointment to a suitable post; but his request fell upon deaf ears. In May of 1823 Leopardi was obliged to give up his Roman hopes and to return to the depressing atmosphere of Recanati.

A plan for him to translate the whole of Plato came to nothing; it had been conceived by an uncle who wished his nephew to make Plato available as a defender of the faith, which was not what Leopardi wanted. A plan for a complete edition of Cicero likewise foundered; Leopardi knew better than the publisher what such a work involved, and the editorship was transferred to the poet's enemy, Niccolò Tommaseo. But until 1827 Leopardi continued to produce valuable notes upon the texts of ancient authors. As one might expect, his reading during the period of the *Operette morali* included much Hellenistic philosophy, and the intellectual diary contained in the *Zibaldone* helps us to understand something of its effect upon his thought. But during the last ten years of the poet's life, when the resigned mood of his middle period had yielded to a new 'titanic' defiance of the antagonistic universe, he ceased from scholarly activity, handing over all his classical papers to the Swiss scholar Louis de Sinner. This was partly due to his declining health, and in particular to failing eyesight; but it was also the effect of an increasing preoccupation with his poetry.

The *Zibaldone* helps us to understand the importance for the formation of Leopardi's style of the exact study of language which his scholarship helped to promote. His verse has a clarity and simplicity which has a real affinity with that of the ancients. But classical antiquity was also an element in his intellectual background, as Timpanaro had demonstrated in the two chapters devoted to Leopardi in his *Classicismo e illuminismo nell' ottocento italiano*. In Italy the habit of seeing Leopardi as a romantic has long been out of fashion. The postwar reaction against the reduction of Leopardi to an 'idyllic' poet by Croce, who disliked and therefore chose to ignore his intellectual background, reached its furthest point in the *Leopardi progressivo* of Cesare Luporini. While fully approving the stress laid by Luporini on the importance of the rationalism which Leopardi derived from the Enlightenment, Timpanaro firmly declines to see him as a kind of proto-Marxist, or as a believer in any form of 'the idea of progress'. He clearly shows that Leopardi's belief that the whole nature of the universe was necessarily adverse to human aspirations left no room for the idea that society might be readjusted in a way that rescued man from the consequences of this condition.

From the start the tendency to a belief in progress which Leopardi's sympathy with eighteenth-century illuminism might have been expected to promote was offset by an attitude of titanic defiance of a hostile universe, which seems to have originated from the influence of Alfieri. In this first phase Leopardi thought of Nature as a kindly mother who conceals from her children the real nature of their condition; later he would come to think of her as a cruel stepmother who had condemned them knowingly to a miserable existence. At the beginning of his career Leopardi's attitude to the ancient world derived in its essentials from Rousseau. Antiquity exemplified a healthy but primitive way of thinking, sustained by noble illusions; with the coming of Christianity, degeneration had set in.

About 1823 Leopardi became aware that the view of the human condition taken by the early Greeks was in general anything but optimistic; and this discovery not only served to increase his respect for ancient thinking, but helped to confirm him in the belief that man's unhappiness was due not to any particular social or political conditions, but to the basic circumstances of his position in the universe. Hellenistic philosophy made a substantial contribution to the philosophy of resignation which Leopardi worked out between 1823 and 1827, the period of the *Operette morali*.

During his last ten years, Leopardi returned to his earlier mood of defiance, against the background of a view of the universe still blacker than that of his earlier phases, and without the Alfierian rhetoric visible in the first period of his work. This was the period of his life in which he devoted least attention to the writings of the ancients; yet the influence of ancient pessimism upon his thought can still be seen.

9

Gladstone

One day when my wife was shopping in Oxford, a bearded scarecrow thrust into her hand a most peculiar leaflet (*Students Stand Up!* by Moses David, London, 1974). It is published by an organisation calling itself the Children of God, and though the incident it describes purports to take place in England, its language has a markedly transatlantic flavour. The author with two fellow-students is assigned because of unusual scholastic achievements to do research on the Greek classic, Homer's *Odyssey,* and the professor tells them that it is far superior to such foolish fallacies as the Bible. The author leaps to his feet and under total inspiration in the power of the Spirit lectures the professor 'like they do in the House of Commons, with the eloquence of an orator'. 'What has Homer done for humanity?', he askes, 'What future can he offer us other than one peopled with nightmarish maniacal monstrosities and unutterably cruel, selfish and demonic deities ...? For despite the Greek culture's love of youth and beauty, art, philosophy and literary masterpieces, its fiendish religion carries both they and Homer to a ghoulish grave.'

This estimate of Homer is not without precedent in the writings of the Fathers of the Church. But it is lucky for its authors that they offered it to an Oxford public too late for it to come to the notice of the subject of this article. In the value he attached to the Bible Gladstone would have agreed strongly with its author. But it was his firm opinion that the next most valuable human writings were the Homeric poems; and the pamphleteer would have exposed himself to a rebuke whose severity no modern parliamentarian could hope to equal.

Throughout his long career Gladstone gave an astonishing amount of precious time to the intensive study of this favourite author. With his usual scrupulous regard for truth he wrote to contradict the

* First published in *The Times Literary Supplement,* 3 January 1975, 17ff, this paper was written for one of the seminars on Gladstone organized by Dr H.C.G. Matthew, Editor-in-Chief of the Gladstone Diary, and was read at Oxford on 7 November 1974. I am grateful to Dr Matthew for much assistance.

assertion that he read some Homer before starting work each morning; his occupation would hardly have allowed it. But when asked late in life how often he had read through the *Iliad* and the *Odyssey*, he paused for reflection and then answered that he thought he must have done so about thirty times.[1] During what even by Victorian standards must be thought an exceptionally busy life, he found time to publish four books about Homer, one of them in three stout volumes, and the series of his Homeric articles extends over some fifty years. It takes but little knowledge of his character to know that he would never have devoted so much time and care to work which he regarded merely as the recreation of his leisure; and indeed he made perfectly explicit his conviction that in expounding the Homeric poems he was discharging an educational duty of the first importance.

Gladstone's Homeric studies, like his religion, were a side of his activities into which his official biographer found it hard to enter with proper sympathy and understanding.[2] Their importance to Gladstone is clearly recognised by his most recent biographer, Sir Philip Magnus. He writes that they throw more light on Gladstone than on Homer,[3] and there is truth in this. One may read through several accounts of Homeric studies in the nineteenth century without finding mention of Gladstone's name,[4] and one can see why. He was not, and never claimed to be, a researcher; he made no new factual discovery and initiated no new critical approach. Many of his opinions have been rendered obsolete by increased factual knowledge; but that he has in common with the most eminent Homerists among his contemporaries. What may have done more to deter scholars from taking account of his contribution is that it contains an element of marked eccentricity, strangely reminiscent of the doctrines of the British Israelites.[5] An interesting essay has been devoted to Gladstone's Homeric Studies by the late Sir John Myres (1869-1954), who was at one time Wykeham Professor of Ancient History at Oxford. This was first published in 1958;[6] but it is based on a lecture given as early as 1907 to inaugurate Myres's tenure of a Chair of Ancient History founded at Liverpool in Gladstone's honour. Myres had literally sat at Gladstone's feet when he addressed the Oxford Union Society in 1891,[7] and he treats his

[1] John Morley, *The Life of William Ewart Gladstone* ii, 423.

[2] See Morley, op. cit, iii, 543f.

[3] Philip Magnus, *Gladstone* (1954, paperback edition 1963), 123.

[4] His name is absent even from the detailed account given by E. Drerup in *Das Homerproblem in der Gegenwart* (1921).

[5] Mark Pattison, *Essays* ii, 166, compared Gladstone's work on Homer with Warburton's *Divine Legation*.

[6] Sir John Myres, *Homer and his Critics*, edited by Dorothea Gray (1958), 94f.

[7] See T.J. Dunbabin, *Proceedings of the British Academy* 41 (1955), 350.

Homeric studies sympathetically. He deals admirably with Gladstone's efforts to show that the facts of archaeology confirmed his belief in the reality of Homer's world; but he says little of Gladstone's interpretation of the Homeric poems themselves and of the religion they describe, which seems to me a more interesting topic.

As a boy at Eton Gladstone threw himself into the study of Greek and Latin with the same zest which he devoted to many other activities of the place.[8] The Christ Church of his day retained something of the quality it had under Dean Jackson, who made even the *jeunesse dorée* study hard, and many even among gentleman commoners were considered reading men. Gladstone took full advantage of what Christ Church and its tutors offered. He twice competed for the blue riband of translation from and into Greek and Latin, the Ireland Scholarship, but was both times disappointed. On the second of these occasions the scholarship went to a boy still at Shrewsbury, who had matriculated prematurely and was therefore technically eligible to compete; the examiners remarked that his answers to the questions were more concisely written than those of some of the other candidates.[9] A copy of Gladstone's Latin verses which Morley has preserved[10] is certainly superior to anything an undergraduate today could manage; but at that time there must have been several who were capable of equalling it.

Gladstone obtained his First in Classics by a comfortable margin, more easily than he did his First in mathematics. Later he complained that the curriculum was too narrow, and its concentration upon composition and translation must have been little to the liking of one whose interest always lay more in the matter of literature than in its manner. In short, Gladstone was a very good but not an outstandingly successful student. Like several of the ablest of his contemporaries, he attached great importance to modern languages, and worked systematically to master them. His Italian was particularly good; his German, acquired chiefly in order to gain access to the latest theological literature, was to prove useful when he came to work on Homer.

A strong belief in the value of a classical education was of course far from rare in the England of the early nineteenth century. What distinguished Gladstone from others was that he thought the study of Homer far more important than that of any other ancient author. This is evident not only from his writings but from the concern he showed

[8] See Morley, op. cit., 26f.

[9] See Morley, op. cit., 61f. On Christ Church in Gladstone's time, see Myres, op. cit., 96f.

[10] Op. cit., 63, n.1.

at the time of the first University Commission, when he still represented the University in Parliament, that the time allotted to the study of this author should be increased.[11] Such an attitude towards Homer was general among the Greeks themselves throughout antiquity; the manuscripts of Homer recovered from the sands of Egypt outnumber those of all other Greek authors put together. It may be found among Greeks even today; and the fact reminds one that unlike some modern admirers of ancient culture Gladstone showed strong sympathy with his Greek contemporaries. In 1850 he attacked Palmerston for sending gunboats to Greece in the cause of Don Pacifico; during his mission to the Ionian Islands in 1858-9 he angered British officials by his sympathy for everything Greek; in 1869 he was a member of the Government that made over the islands to Greece, and in 1881 he would willingly have done the same with Cyprus,[12] and so saved us the embarrassments of the present time. The view that the Turks were basically very decent fellows was not shared by Gladstone. In 1876 he wrote that 'the Turks are, upon the whole, since the black day when they first entered Europe the one great anti-human species of humanity'; in 1894 he called the Turk 'the great assassin'; and in the last year of his life he told Sir Edward Hamilton that he would be perfectly content to stand alone, against the entire world, in defence of the principle that the nations of Europe were a community designed by God to uphold the highest standards of civilisation.[13]

Matthew Arnold's view that the two sources of our culture are Hebraism and Hellenism assumed a concrete form in Gladstone's mind. God had made a double revelation of himself through the Jews and through the Greeks. The historic books of the Old Testament contained the basic truths of a correct theology; but 'they were not intended to present, and did not present, a picture of human society or of our culture drawn at large'. 'Their aim', he wrote, 'is to exhibit it in a master-relation, and to do this with effect they do it, to a great extent, exclusively.'[14]

The Homeric poems, on the other hand, present a picture of human society and of human nature; they show human nature in the most admirable form which it is capable of assuming without the assistance

---

[11] See Morley, op. cit., 498f; Myres, op. cit., 98f.

[12] See letter no 403 in Agatha Ramm, *The Correspondence of Mr Gladstone with Lord Granville, 1874-1884.*

[13] In his pamphlet *The Bulgarian Horrors and the Question of the East*; see Magnus, op. cit., 242, 430, 428.

[14] The quotations are from the essay on 'The Place of Homer in Education and in History', in *Oxford Essays* (1858), 5.

of divine revelation. In an extraordinary passage near the end of the second volume of his main Homeric work Gladstone blames the Jews for having kept the divine revelation to themselves; 'they have not supplied the Christian ages', he writes, 'with laws and institutions, arts and sciences, with the chief models of greatness in genius or in character'.

The whole character of Gladstone's work on Homer was determined by this fundamental conviction, and he showed how much importance he attached to it by choosing to explain it in the valedictory address as Lord Rector of Edinburgh University which he gave in 1865.[15] Once it is understood, the reasons for his attitudes to all the principal Homeric problems become clear. It required him to insist that the world Homer depicted was not imaginary but real; and with every means at his disposal he set himself to persuade others that this was so. In defiance of the prevailing trend of belief in the multiple authorship of the poems, he believed in a personal and individual Homer, and held that he must have lived only a generation or so after the events which he described.

No critic has insisted more strongly than Gladstone on the poetic excellence of Homer; but he believed that over and above their poetry the epics contained a vast quantity of precious information, about human society and human life, and this he set himself to extract and illustrate in detail. He fully described the political and social world depicted in the poems; but what interested him most was their religion. He took this to be a real religion, not a divine apparatus invented for literary purposes; and he set himself to show how the plots of both poems were enacted against the background it provided. His belief that Homer presented human nature at the highest level which it could by its own unaided powers attain to lead him to study the characters of the poems and to show how the poet had drawn their individual qualities.

The long series of Gladstone's Homeric publications begins in 1847 with his detailed examination of the extreme analytical theory put forward by the famous German scholar, Karl Lachmann.[16] In 1858 he published the three stout volumes of *Studies on Homer and the Homeric*

[15] *Studies on Homer and the Homeric Age* (1858) ii, 530. The whole final chapter of the second volume, which is entitled 'The office of the Homeric Poems in relation to the early Books of Holy Scripture', is relevant in this connexion; the valedictory Rectorial Address 'On the Place of Ancient Greece in the Providential Order of the World', given at Edinburgh on November 3 1865, is printed in *Rectorial Addresses* delivered before the University of Edinburgh, 1859-1899, ed. Archibald Stodard-Walker (1900), 25f.

[16] *Quarterly Review* 162, 181f.

Age, which in spite of all subsequent modifications of his views contain the essential results of his Homeric studies and remain the fundamental text for their appreciation. In 1869 he condensed their contents, with some additions, into an attractive volume called *Juventus Mundi*; and in 1876 the apparent confirmation of his belief in the reality of Homer's world by the sensational discoveries of Schliemann, together with new information about Egypt, led him to publish his *Homeric Synchronism: an Enquiry into the Time and Place of Homer*. In the same year appeared an excellent small volume called *Homer*, written for the series of History and Literature Primers edited for Macmillans by the historian J.R. Green; and in 1890 he resumed and amplified his views in a brief work called *Landmarks of Homeric Study*; these last two books should be read by anyone who imagines that Gladstone could not write concisely. He also published many articles about Homeric and early Near Eastern topics, several of which were incorporated into the books which followed them. The latest seems to be the paper on 'The Ancient East and Greece' which he delivered at the Ninth Congress of Orientalists in 1892.[17]

Gladstone's first Homeric publication, his review of Lachmann, maintains a strongly unitarian position. Myres (page 106) finds it 'at first sight remarkable that a scholar with so exact and minute a knowledge of the Homeric text should have held so tenaciously to the belief in a personal Homer'; but though such an unqualified belief as Gladstone's is no commoner now than it was in his time, belief in a 'monumental composer' who may even be referred to as Homer is widely held even today.

Lachmann thought the epics had been stitched together from eighteen independent lays, much as during the nineteenth century itself the Finnish national epic known as the *Kalevala* had been stitched together out of independent poems by the scholar Lönnroth. Few people would deny that Gladstone's criticism of this extreme analytic attitude was most effective; again and again he shows up Lachmann's objections to the countless inconsistencies which he discovers in the poems as captious and insubstantial.

But it must be remembered that Lachmann's extreme position was by no means typical of the Homeric analysis of the time. Far more influential was the so-called nucleus theory worked out by the great scholar Gottfried Hermann between 1832 and 1840,[18] expounded to the English, in a somewhat modified form, by Grote in his *History of Greece*, whose first edition appeared in 1846, and accepted in one form

[17] See *Proceedings of the Ninth Congress of Orientalists* (1893), 1f.
[18] See Drerup, op. cit., in n.6 above, 15f; cf. E.R. Dodds in *Fifty Years (And Twelve) of Classical Scholarship*, ed. M. Platnauer (1962), 2f.

or other not only by most German scholars of the time but also by most English scholars, including Sir Richard Jebb and Walter Leaf.

According to this theory an original *Iliad* and *Odyssey* by Homer were gradually expanded by later poets till they reached their present size soon before they were finally written down during the sixth century B.C. Gladstone was not utterly opposed to this theory, since it was not entirely inconsistent with his conviction that Homer described a real world. But he maintained that many of the alleged inconsistencies objected to by critics less radical than Lachmann were less damaging than they supposed; and he reposed excessive trust upon the general argument that the prestige of the Homeric epics must have been so enormous from the start as to protect them against alteration and interpolation of the kind assumed.

At the present time belief in a poet who may be called Homer is gaining ground, though it is very different from the belief maintained by Gladstone. There is a growing tendency for scholars who accept Milman Parry's proof that the Homeric tradition was for many centuries an oral tradition to place Homer at the end of it, and to believe that he may have had the aid of writing.[19] Holders of this kind of view may sympathise with much of Gladstone's polemic against the analysts, but they do not share his belief in a Homer living soon after the events which he described.

In defence of this belief, Gladstone insisted that the poet had historical aims, and pointed to many passages in the poems which seemed to support his claim; but he realised that these might be set down to a poetical contrivance, and did all he could to explain and illustrate the supposed historical content of the epics. He made himself acquainted with the latest developments in the archaeology not only of the Mediterranean but of the Middle East; and he plunged, not with very fortunate results, into the speculations upon early history based on etymological and other linguistic considerations to which the new science of comparative linguistics had given rise. The greater part of the first volume of his *Studies on Homer* is given over to an attempt to show that the various names applied by Homer to the Greeks are used with exactitude and correspond to real historical distinctions, an attempt which even the scholarship of his own time could show to be too sanguine. Nowadays, with further information from Oriental sources, the problem can be shown to be infinitely more complicated than it seemed a hundred years ago.

Just a hundred years ago the process that has revolutionised the

---

[19] See for example Adam Parry's introduction to Milman Parry, *The Making of Homeric Verse* (1971) or Albin Lesky's chapter on the Homeric Question in *A History of Greek Literature*, 2nd edn., English version (1966), 32f.

problem of the historicity of Homer began when Schliemann published the first of his books about his excavations on the site of Troy.[20] No one showed greater interest in Schliemann and his discoveries than Gladstone, who met him first in 1874, wrote a preface to the book about Mycenae that he brought out in 1876, and in the same year tried in his *Homeric Synchronism* to show how Schliemann's discoveries had vindicated his own attitude. Gladstone shared Schliemann's belief that the second city on the site of Hissarlik must be Priam's Troy, and that the tombs found at Mycenae must be those of the Atreidae.[21] As early as 1871, the three volumes of Buchholz's *Homerische Realien* had seemed to him to prove beyond dispute the reality of Homer's world. How much more certain were Schliemann's discoveries bound to seem to make it, especially when they were taken in conjunction with new evidence from Egypt which seemed to confirm the accuracy of what Homer tells us about that country![22] Gladstone was not an archaeologist, and could not appreciate the chronological difficulties which made against Schliemann's original naive assumptions, starting with the awkward fact that what Schliemann took to be the Troy of Priam was shown by the pottery on the two sites to be considerably earlier than what he took to be the Mycenae of Agamemnon. Gladstone stood by Schliemann when critical opinion turned against him, and in 1883, when he was ill and melancholy, found time while in office to write him a remarkable letter of consolation.[23]

It is sad that Schliemann's feelings towards Gladstone underwent a change; in 1885 he was so indignant over the failure to relieve Khartoum that he considered whether or not to destroy the signed photograph which his friend had given him. He could not bring himself to do this, but compromised by leading his family in procession to consign it to the lavatory.[24] I learnt this fact from the original German text of Emil Ludwig's life of Schliemann; I could not find it in the English translation.

A century after Schliemann's discoveries and three-quarters of a century after those of Evans, the innocent belief that Homer records Mycenaean history and portrays Mycenaean life cannot be accepted. Not many Mycenaean objects or practices can be identified with any certainty in the Homeric poems, and even fewer Mycenaean formulas

---

[20] H. Schliemann, *Trojanische Alterthümer* (1874), translated into English as *Troy and its Remains* (1875). There is a good account of Schliemann's work in Myres, op. cit. in n.8 above, 123f.

[21] See Myres, op.cit., 117f.

[22] See Myres, op.cit., 115.

[23] See Emil Ludwig, *Schliemann* (1930), 305. .

[24] Op.cit., 334.

can be held with any confidence to be embedded in their language.[25] The Mycenaean world presented in the Linear B tablets is a world of sober bureaucratic inventories of animals and products, not at all like the world presented in the epics. Homer's language, with its strong Ionic element, suggests to us, as it did to many of Gladstone's own contemporaries, that the poems came into being after the Dorian invasion and the emigration of the Greeks, who settled in the Aegean islands and in Asia Minor, or at the very least that they underwent many alterations during this period.

Many modern scholars believe in a great poet who may be called Homer, but most of these place him late in the tradition, usually in the eighth century. How far his account of the Trojan War may correspond with reality is still the subject of debate; and the debate is likely to continue. In 1959 Sir Denys Page[26] argue ' persuasively in the first chapter of his Sather Lectures that Troy VII A, Priam's Troy, was destroyed by a coalition that included the Achchijawa, identified by him and others with the Achaeans, dwellers in an island or a coastal city, identified by him with Rhodes. Since then some Orientalists have argued that the letter of the Hittite king on which the theory rests was really written a century earlier than has been thought, too early for it to be relevant to Troy VII A.[27]

In 1964 M.I. Finley[28] could argue with much cogency that Homer can tell us no more about the historical siege of Troy than the *Nibelungenlied* can tell us about Theodoric or the *Chanson de Roland* about Charlemagne. We know that Troy VII A was sacked during the Mycenaean period; we know that Mycenae really was, as Homer says, rich in gold; we know that the Mycenaeans were active on the far side of the Aegean during the relevant period. Some scholars think that the Catalogue of Ships in the second book of the *Iliad* preserves a great deal of information about Mycenaean Greece; others are less sanguine. We know little more, though we may and many of us do, guess a great deal.[29]

Yet in one sense Gladstone's insistence on the reality of Homer's world may be seen not to have been misplaced. Even if Homer's picture of the Mycenaean period is no more than an imaginative reconstruction of the past, containing only a few genuine survivals of

[25] There is a careful assessment in G.S. Kirk's *The Songs of Homer* (1962); cf. chs 8 and 14 of the abbreviated version *Homer and the Epic* (1965).

[26] *History and the Homeric Iliad* (paperback, reprinted 1972), ch.1.

[27] See O.R. Gurney in *Cambridge Ancient History* 3 II i (1973), 678.

[28] *Journal of Hellenic Studies* 84 (1964), 1f.; in the same number, his sceptical views are replied to by J.L. Caskey, Sir Denys Page and G.S. Kirk.

[29] Page in the fourth chapter of the work quoted in n.28 is sanguine; Finley, op. cit., 7f, is much less so.

authentic detail, Homer has preserved many details of the world known to him. In the *Iliad* such details are contained for the most part in the similes. But in the *Odyssey*, or at least in those parts of the *Odyssey* which are set in Ithaca, we find a detailed description of a world which cannot be invented; that is the basic assumption of a book like M.I. Finley's *World of Odysseus*,[30] and it seems unlikely to be wrong. In this respect, Gladstone's belief in the truth of Homer's picture of society would be upheld by a majority of modern scholars. The detailed account of the Homeric polity and of Homeric kingship which stands at the beginning of the third volume of *Studies on Homer* contains much that is acceptable as well as interesting.

Most of the second volume of the *Studies* is devoted to the subject of Homeric religion, in which Gladstone took a special interest. As early as 1837, he had scandalised the zealous Evangelical, Lord Ashley, by suggesting in the course of a speech in the House of Commons on the subject of Church Rates that the old pagan gods 'served a necessary purpose in their day, and foreshadowed at some points the teaching of the gospels'.[31] Of course Gladstone was well aware that Homer's religion is not like Judaism or Christianity; he is shocked by the Olympian gods' 'libertinism', by their cruelty and selfishness, by the lowness of the standard of their taste and feeling and by their moral inferiority to men.[32] At the same time he is led by a careful examination of the texts to claim that 'the championship of duty and the avenging of crime upon earth' are a concern to the Olympians. In the case of the *Odyssey* it is obvious enough that, in Gladstone's words, 'the Providence of the poem is on the side of virtue'[33] but even in the *Iliad* Gladstone recognises that the eventual fall of Troy is demanded by divine justice, and he is fully aware of the bearing of Homeric religion both on social ties and on political relations. He knows as well as Professor Adkins that the Greek word commonly translated by 'good' is not used in Homer in a moral sense; but he understands better than Professor Adkins that the Homeric word corresponding to 'good' or 'righteous' is the word commonly translated by 'just'.[34] Someone who has been forced by the prevalence of ingenious modern theories about Homer's defective morality to reassert all this must regard Gladstone's treatment of the subject with respect.

But it was Gladstone's recognition that Homer's religion contains

---

[30] Second edition (1956); paperback, (1962), cf. *Proc. Class. Ass.* 71 (1974), 13f.

[31] See Magnus, op. cit., 34-5.

[32] See *Studies on Homer* ii, 334f.

[33] Op. cit., 387.

[34] See op. cit., 421f.

elements of truth that led him to the most startling of his opinions.[35] These elements, he felt sure, must proceed ultimately from divine relevation. The Greek gods, he concluded, could not derive, as many scholars then thought they did, from worship of the heavenly bodies. Gladstone considered but rejected the theory, which had found adherents since antiquity[36] that the Greeks had borrowed, perhaps indirectly, from the Jews. Rather, he contended, the true theology learnt by Adam and Eve in Eden had been handed down by them to their descendants, but gradually corrupted in the course of time. To traces of this remote ancestry the Homeric religion owed the elements of theological truth which it preserved. The trinity of Jupiter, Neptune and Pluto, as Gladstone calls them, was a distant echo of the true trinity of Father, Son and Holy Ghost; aspects of the Redeemer might be discerned in the figure of Apollo; a defaced counterpart of the divine Logos was present in the shape of Minerva; Latona, as mother of Apollo, 'appeared to represent the tradition of the woman from whom the Redeemer was to descend'; and in the Titans and Giants on the one hand and the goddess Ate on the other Gladstone detects elements of the Evil One.[37] It is not surprising that drier and less enthusiastic minds, like that of Jowett, found this part of Gladstone's theory somewhat startling.

Gladstone's sympathetic understanding of Homer's religion is not affected by his theory of its origin; it helped him to describe the plot of the *Iliad* in a way that in an age when some readers have to be persuaded that the *Iliad* has a plot arouses admiration.[38] Despite the severity of Gladstone's moral standards, the natural sympathy with the heroic temperament which is everywhere in evidence helps him to do full justice to Achilles in his dispute with Agamemnon. Gladstone acknowledges that Achilles' rejection of the embassy sent by Agamemnon with an offer of compensation in the ninth book 'remains amenable to severe censure on the score of excess';[39] but he considers that Agamemnon's offer was radically defective, because it was not accompanied by an apology of the kind afterwards uttered by the king in Book Nineteen.

Gladstone's remark seems relevant to a passage where recent

[35] The most detailed exposition of the theory in question may be found in the third volume of *Studies on Homer*.

[36] Clement of Alexandria believed this: see H. Chadwick, *Early Christian Thought and the Classical Tradition* (1966), 43, with n.52 on p.141.

[37] The most startling series of propositions of this nature will be found at *Studies on Homer* ii, 43f.

[38] The plot of the *Iliad* is treated at *Studies on Homer* iii, 366f.

[39] Loc. cit., 377.

scholarship has found a grave inconsistency which seems to provide evidence for multiple authorship. Near the beginning of the sixteenth book, Achilles tells Patroclus that instead of triumphing the Trojans would now be piling the ditches high with their dead, if Agamemnon's feelings towards him were kindly.[40] Sir Denys Page complains[41] that Agamemnon has already made Achilles a handsome offer of compensation; how then can he claim that the king's feelings towards him are not kindly? But if Gladstone is right, no inconsistency exists; Agamemnon may have offered compensation, but he has not taken the right measures to soothe Achilles' wounded pride. At the end of this section of the book Gladstone considers the outline of the plot 'in relation to the Providential Government of the World and the administration of retributive justice'.[42] He finds that in the *Iliad* as in the *Odyssey* the justice of the gods is upheld at every stage and that in the end 'the authority of the providential order is reestablished'.[43]

In our own time not all scholars are willing to admit that characterisation exists in the heroic poems; the German theory that Homer lacks the concept of a unified self, and that his characters are at the mercy of whatever chance impulse a god may put into their minds, is widely regarded with respect.[44]

Gladstone would have had no use for it. He devotes some admirable pages to Homer's characterisation, illustrating his views from the treatment of Hector, Helen and Paris.[45] He describes Hector's martial valour with its admixture of boastfulness, and the strong sense of responsibility and the gentleness in domestic life that stand in contrast with his martial valour.

We may indeed complain that he writes of Homer's characters with a kind of chivalrous courtesy, Christian in its colouring, that sometimes blinds him to the merciless objectivity with which the truths of nature are presented by the poet. Deeply moved by Helen's self-reproaches in her talks with Hector and with Paris, Gladstone goes so far as to suggest that here Paganism 'comes nearest to the penitential tone and the profound self-abasement that belongs to Christianity'.[46] In spite of all his experience in handling fallen women, one sees that Helen would have got round him as easily as she does Hector or Priam. Despite those humble words, the goddess Aphrodite still finds it easy enough to force Helen to stop rebuking Paris and

---

[40] *Il.* 16, 71-3.   [41] Op. cit., (in n.26), 309f.

[42] *Studies on Homer* iii, 392.

[43] Op. cit., iii, 394; with this section, compare ii, 373f.

[44] On this theory, see my book *The Justice of Zeus* (1971), 9f.

[45] *Studies on Homer* iii, 555f.

[46] Op. cit., iii, 580-1.

to climb into bed with him; in Homer a god may prompt human actions, but without lifting responsibility from the shoulders of the human actor.

Gladstone's chapters on Homer and his successors in epic poetry and on the treatment of Homeric characters by later authors[47] are excellent examples of what we now call comparative literary study. He thought much harm had been done through the habit of regarding Homer through Roman spectacles, and the severity of some of his remarks about Virgil might have satisfied even Robert Graves. He was extremely well acquainted with Ariosto, Boiardo and Tasso, and most effectively contrasts their epic poetry with Homer's. The later treatment of epic characters served to confirm him in the view that Greek literature degenerated after Homer, which he argued for with much persuasiveness.

After this survey of the Homeric work, let us look back and consider its main features. The chief contention of this paper is that the whole of Gladstone's works proceeds from his initial certainty that the Homeric poems contain a picture of mankind and of its political and social life given us in order to supplement the revelation of true religion imparted by the scriptures. Gladstone's attempts, to which he devoted such enormous labour, to use the concrete data of archaeology and of Middle Eastern records to support his views have not withstood the course of time; the same is true of other attempts of the same nature made at the time that rested upon sounder reasoning. But his contention that Homer's world was real must in a certain measure correspond with truth; the whole body of knowledge built up in the century since Schliemann published his first results makes this certain. In the same way Gladstone's belief in the existence of a great poet called Homer may be vindicated, though in a more complicated way than he imagined.

But the part of Gladstone's work that was concerned with concrete fact is the least admirable. Gladstone was a great man, but he was no great scholar and would not have been even if he had spent his life in universities. I do not mean simply that he was not a scholar of the kind Germans call 'ein Philologe'.[48] Again and again he uses arguments

---

[47] Op. cit., iii, 500f.; 590f.

[48] Dr Matthew draws my attention to a letter written by Marx to Engels in 1858, soon after the publication of *Studies on Homer* (*Gesamtausgabe* ii, 336). 'Hast du in der *Times* die Kritik über Gladstones Buch über Homer gesehen? Es ist manches Amusante dadrinnen (in der Kritik). Ein Werk wie das von G. ist übrigens characteristisch fur die Unfähigkeit der Engländer, in Philologie etwas zu machen.' Marx had every right to an opinion on the subject; he had an excellent classical training, and kept up all his life the habit of reading Greek authors in the original; he much admired Aeschylus, especially his *Prometheus*.

that fall short of being proofs, concealing their weakness from himself as well as others by the siren charm and forcible persuasiveness of his lofty rhetoric.[49] That he lacked humour I would not dare to say; he certainly did not lack fantasy or gaiety;[50] yet there were grave limits to his sense of proportion. Fed upon the startling truths guaranteed to us by the authority of scripture, his imagination led him to embrace eccentric theories, sometimes recalling the oddest aberrations of seventeenth-century enthusiasts.

The part of his Homeric work which is most admirable is his literary appreciation of the poems, together with his account of the religious, political and social side of the Homeric world. Though he is not a very good scholar, he is a very good writer. Often rising to eloquence but never sinking to obscurity, his style is a powerful and flexible instrument. What qualified him especially well to interpret Homer is the sympathetic understanding of everything heroic which allows him to enter into the state of mind of Homer's characters and to grasp the essential nature of their morals and religion. This part of his work seems to me well worth reading for its own sake, even today.

Gladstone's peculiar view of the place of Homer in the scheme of things leads him to adopt one opinion which seems to me of special interest. Like most ancient Greeks, he thinks Homer far the most important ancient author; and he believes that the Homeric poems contain all the most important elements of Greek culture, which after them did not make progress but declined. This is a very different theory from that which shows culture gradually ascending from the

[49] Macaulay's masterly characterisation of the thirty-year-old Gladstone in his review of *The State in its Relations with the Church* (1839; see *Historical Essays*, Oxford edition 337-8) serves equally well to describe the Gladstone of *Studies on Homer* and even of the later Homeric works: 'Mr Gladstone seems to us to be, in many respects, exceedingly well qualified for philosophical investigation. His mind is of large grasp; nor is he deficient in dialectical skill. But he does not give his intellect fair play. There is no want of light, but a great want of what Bacon would have called dry light. Whatever Mr Gladstone sees is refracted and distorted by a false medium of passions and prejudices. His style bears a remarkable analogy to his mode of thinking, and indeed exercises a great influence on his mode of thinking. His rhetoric, though often good of its kind, darkens and perplexes the logic which it should illustrate. Half his acuteness and diligence, with a barren imagination and a scanty vocabulary, would have saved him from almost all his mistakes. He has one gift most dangerous to a speculator, a vast command of a kind of language, grave and majestic, but of vague and uncertain import; of a kind of language which affects us much in the same way in which the lofty diction of the Chorus of Clouds affected the simple-hearted Athenian (Aristophanes, *Clouds* 364). When propositions have been established, and nothing remains but to amplify and decorate them, this dim magnificence may be in place. But if it is admitted into demonstration, it is very much worse than absolute nonsense ...'

[50] See Morley, op. cit., i, 188.

splendid but primitive beginnings supposed to be shown by Homer to a climax in the profundities of Plato. Those modern theorists who prefer to present a cultural pattern synchronically rather than diachronically will feel that there is something to be said for Gladstone's picture; and so will others who have doubts about the kind of intellectual history that finds everywhere a linear development of a sort ultimately to be traced back to the influence of Darwin.

Darwin, whose *Origin of Species* came out a year after *Studies on Homer*, was one of those whose work had paved the way for the kind of criticism of religious orthodoxy Gladstone hoped to undermine. His theory of a double revelation enabled him to enlist Hellenism as well as Hebraism in the service of the Christian picture of the world, as we see clearly if we consider it in relation to the Christian apologetic that culminated in the book he published in 1890 under the title *The Impregnable Rock of Holy Scripture*. We can hardly fail to notice what is absurd about the theory, yet not without warming to the nobility and generosity that are mingled with the absurdity.

Sir Philip Magnus is surely right to think that Gladstone's Homeric studies throw an interesting light upon his personality. Ever since Christianity became the official religion of the Roman Empire, people in authority have felt, consciously or subconsciously, that it offered them little guidance in dealing with the problems with which their authority confronted them. Gladstone's complaint that Jewish religion did nothing to instruct mankind in politics or government seems to show that he was aware of this deficiency. But his love of epic poetry, and of Homer in particular, lay close to the deepest roots of Gladstone's personality.

His wife told Morley that anyone who wrote her husband's life must remember that there were two sides to his nature, one impetuous, irrestrainable, uncontrollable, the other an iron self-mastery achieved through the natural strength of his character and through constant wrestling in prayer. To these two sides the Homeric poems and the Bible corresponded. It is recorded[51] that one day at Hawarden Gladstone was playing in a parlour-game in which each player had to say on what day in past or future he would choose to live, and chose at once a day in ancient Greece. A pious person present said that he would choose the day of Pentecost, and Gladstone somewhat shamefacedly altered his selection to a day with Christ. Anyone searching for a clue that may serve to unwind some, at least, of the endless apparent complications and contradictions of his

---

[51] Sir E. Russell, *That Reminds Me* (1900), 123-4. Again I owe the reference to Dr Matthew.

extraordinary character might, I imagine, look for it in the not always easy coexistence of these disparate and sometimes conflicting elements.[52]

---

[52] Mr John Sparrow has drawn my attention to a striking indication of what very great importance Gladstone attached to his Homeric theories. Mrs Humphry Ward in *A Writer's Recollections*, 1918, 238, describes a conversation with Gladstone at Keble College, Oxford, on 9 April 1888, in these words: 'Wonderful old man! I see him still standing as I took leave of him, one hand leaning on the table beside him, his lined, pallid face and eagle eyes, framed in his noble white hair, shining amid the dusk of the room. "There are still two things left for me to do!," he said, finally in answer to some remark of mine. "One is to carry Home Rule; the other is to prove the intimate connection between the Hebrew and Olympian revelations!" '

10

Wagner

Wagner, said Thomas Mann[1] quoting Baudelaire as the chief example, is the composer who can convert the unmusical to music. One may discount the assertion of the embittered Nietzsche[2] that Wagner was not by instinct a musician; but he was far more than a musician. The leading notion of his musical theory was that music, poetry and the dance should be combined in the *Gesamtkunstwerk*, 'the combined work of art'. His verse must not be compared with the work of poets; it must be considered as a part of the complex of which it is an element. Yet in his way he is a considerable poet, not to be judged by his awful worst, as it appears, characteristically, in the opening scene of *Das Rheingold*.

In the history not merely of operatic but of theatrical production he is a great innovator and pioneer. No musician has read or written more. In a whole series of works, written during a great creative period in the late 1840s and early 1850s, he set out his theories about music; his collected works fill ten volumes.[3] Their style is often turgid, so that one is agreeably surprised to find his posthumously published autobiography, *Mein Leben* (printed only privately in Wagner's lifetime), so readable. His critical writings discuss not only music, but history, literature and philosophy; further explanations of Wagnerian principles were given by Nietzsche, while Nietzsche was still acting as Wagner's official prophet.[4]

Wagner stood at the centre of the general culture of his age; his

* This essay first appeared in the *Times Literary Supplement*, 9 January 1976.

[1] *Leiden und Grösse der Meister* (paperback edition, 1957), 233.

[2] In *Der Fall Wagner* (Kritische Gasemtausgabe, ed. Colli and Montinari, vi, 3, p.24.

[3] *Gesammelte Werke*, Leipzig, 1871-8 (4th ed., 1907); translated into English by W. Ashton Ellis as *Richard Wagner's Prose Works* (1829-9). These volumes do not contain *Mein Leben* (ed. M. Gregor-Dellin, 1969; English version, New York, 1911). A selection from the prose works in Ellis' version has been confusingly 'arranged' by A. Goldman and E. Sprinchhorn, *Wagner on Music and Drama* (1970).

[4] In *Die Geburt der Tragödie* (1872; see p. 133) and in *Richard Wagner in Bayreuth* (1876; ed. cit. in n.2 above, iv 1, 3f.

effect upon his contemporaries was profound; and his influence upon the later world has been enormous, although in England prejudice has till lately tended to obscure the fact. With the fall of Wagner's keen admirer and his daughter-in-law's protégé, Adolf Hitler, one might have expected that influence to be much reduced. In fact, Wagner is a great deal more popular outside Germany than he was thirty years ago. Perhaps all this may serve to explain why an unmusical person ventures to draw attention to an element in Wagner's work which in Germany has long been reckoned with, but which in this country seems entirely to have escaped notice. It is an element which is not without importance, though it is less considerable than Wagner himself and many of his admirers would have wished us to suppose.

'Of all the really great masters of the musical art,' says Wagner's son-in-law, Houston Stewart Chamberlain, in his biography, 'Wagner is the only one who enjoyed a thorough classical education.' He is going rather far, just as William Wallace is going rather far when he attempts to show that Wagner's claim to a knowledge of Greek literature was that of a pretentious ignoramus, and in doing so behaves like one himself.[5] The truth falls in between. Wagner, as Mann, echoing Nietzsche, has remarked, seemed born to be a dilettante. He acquired a smattering of many subjects; but he was adept at picking up just as much of each as he needed for his own purposes. At the Kreuzschule in Dresden, which he attended between the ages of nine and fourteen (1822-27), he showed great promise and learnt quickly.[6] An intelligent master, Karl Julius Sillig, marked the boy out as a future poet, and it was taken for granted that he would study classical philology; in particular, he enjoyed Greek history and Greek mythology.[7]

But when the family moved back to Leipzig in 1827, Wagner fell behind in his studies; on one occasion he was even moved down a class. This was because he had become too much absorbed in his musical studies to have time for other things. Wagner realised the danger, and at the age of seventeen engaged a private tutor to teach him Greek. The arrangement was a failure. Wagner's excuse is that the room in which they tried to read Sophocles together was near a tanner's yard, and the smell proved too much for his delicate nostrils. He failed to secure the firm grasp of the language which he was later to envy so much in others; and since after he had left school he was

[5] H.S. Chamberlain, *Richard Wagner*, tr. G. Ainslie Hight, 1900, 36; W. Wallace, *Wagner* (in the series The Masters of Music), 1925, 13f. and 283f.

[6] See C. von Westernhagen, *Richard Wagner*, 1956, 28-9; cf. Ernest Newman, *Life of Wagner* i, 56f.

[7] See *Mein Leben* i, 45f.

soon struggling to earn his living, it was long before the opportunity recurred.

During Wagner's stay in Paris (1839-42), one of the circle of German émigrés close to Heine which he frequented happened to be a classical scholar. This was Samuel Lehrs,[8] a brother of that Karl Lehrs who in Königsberg became one of the first Jews to obtain a chair of classical philology in a German university. Lehrs was a most amiable man, who was at the time scraping a living by editing texts for the French publisher Firmin Didot; a year after Wagner left Paris he died in great poverty. With his assistance Wagner renewed his efforts to learn Greek, and made an attempt to read Homer in the original. But in the end Lehrs told him that as things were, with his music in him, he would do better to learn what he needed without the aid of grammars and lexicons; to learn Greek thoroughly was difficult, and could not be done in one's spare time. This advice Wagner seems to have taken, and perhaps he acted wisely.

After 1843 when his appointment as Hofkapellmeister to the Saxon court at Dresden gave him means and leisure such as he had not before enjoyed, Wagner was able to advance his literary education. He was now able for the first time to build up a library, sadly forfeited to a creditor when his revolutionary activities forced him to take hurried leave. In the comfortable surroundings of his lodgings on the Ostra-Allee, with their view of the Zwinger, and later in the Marcolini Palace, he found time, in spite of his official duties and his great activity as composer and librettist, to read widely. A particularly happy time for him was the glorious summer of 1847, when he was finishing *Lohengrin*; it was then that he experienced a kind of revelation regarding Greek literature.[9]

He flung himself upon the famous translation of Aeschylus by Johann Gustav Droysen, the historian of the Hellenistic age.[10] Above all he admired the *Oresteia*, so much so that he later wrote in his autobiography that he had never subsequently been able to reconcile himself with modern literature. This reading, he added, had a decisive effect on his ideas about drama and about the theatre; and his own later writings show that what he said was true. He next read with almost equal enthusiasm Droysen's version of Aristophanes[11] and

---

[8] ibid., 181f.; for his advice to Wagner, see p. 221.

[9] ibid., 356.

[10] 1st ed., 1832; 2nd ed. (the one used by Wagner), 1841; revised edition by Walter Nestle in Kroners Taschenausgabe, no.152, 1939. For an excellent account of Droysen, see A. Momigliano, *History and Theory* 9 (1970), 139f. = *Quinto Contributo* (1975) i 109f.

[11] The three volumes appeared in 1835, 1837 and 1838.

went on to several dialogues of Plato; it was the *Symposium* which impressed him most. He read also the works of certain modern scholars; he names Niebuhr, Gibbon and the historical works of that same Droysen whose translations had so much delighted him. He next went on to the Germanic legends; but the impression made upon him by the Greek authors he had read by no means faded from his mind. The year after he wrote *Siegfrieds Tod*, the original version of *Gotterdämmerung*, and then in reverse order the books of the other operas of the *Ring*, which he finished during his stay in Zurich in 1851-2.

Wagner's classical reading continued into the Zurich period. In 1850 he re-read the *Odyssey* for the first time for many years, and records that he was deeply moved. He also continued to read the works of modern scholars. Classical studies in Germany had long before entered a phase distinct from the classicism of the age of Goethe, when modern readers had approached the ancients with an assumption of their direct accessibility unconditioned by the warnings of a developed historical sense. The new historicism insisted that the classics must be seen in their correct context, and used the data of epigraphy, archaeology and art history, besides the newly developed science of comparative linguistics, to explain the texts. Its main exponents in the field of classical antiquity were August Boeckh, Karl Otfried Müller and Friedrich Gottlieb Welcker; all of these writers Wagner at least dipped into. The Austrian poet Johann Nordmann met him at about this time, and wrote that he spoke of the ancients 'with an acumen that one might seek in vain in any professor'.

During the years of triumph after his acquisition of King Ludwig's patronage in 1864, Wagner never lost his enthusiasm for Greek literature. The eagerness with which he took up the twenty-four-year-old Nietzsche after their first meeting in 1868 shows how delighted he was to meet a qualified classical scholar who admired his work and sympathised with his aims. In *The Birth of Tragedy* (1872), Nietzsche made a sustained attempt to show that Wagnerian opera was a true rebirth of the tragic art. Originally the work consisted merely of what are now the first fifteen sections; then it was read aloud to Wagner and Cosima at Tribschen. They were polite, but could not conceal their disappointment that the book was not about Wagner. So the last ten sections, all about Wagner, came to be added; later Nietzsche came to regret their addition, and most readers would agree with him.

Wagner never lost his enthusiasm for Greek literature. Early in 1880, when he was staying in the Villa Angri near Naples, he arranged for the three plays of the *Oresteia* to be read on successive nights. Cosima wrote that she had never seen her husband so inspired and so transfigured, and twenty-five years later the Russian painter Paul von Joukovsky, who had been one of the company, wrote that the cry of 'Apollo! Apollo!' still resounded in his ears. Wagner wrote that he thought the *Oresteia* the most complete work of art from the aspect of religion, philosophy, poetry and art in general; characteristically he added, 'Seriously, it fits in with my work'.

All this, and particularly Wagner's own explicit testimonies, may encourage us to examine his work for traces of the impression which Greek literature, and particularly Greek tragedy, left upon his mind. We may start by noting certain points of detail, some of them interesting enough. But it is more important to ask what use Wagner made of Greek ideas; we will come to that later.

The early works up to and including *Rienzi*, were written in a style and manner alien from those of ancient literature, and we need not look there for its effect. Neither have *The Flying Dutchman* and *Tannhäuser*, works of the early 1840s, much ancient influence to show. Wagner himself has pointed out that both works show the influence of the *Odyssey*; but this influence is minimal. Senta is very different from Penelope, and apart from Heine's contribution, the legend of the Wandering Jew is far more relevant; and though Elisabeth may be said to stand to Venus as Penelope does to Calypso, the relation is hardly very significant. Wagner also drew attention to a Greek element in the plot of the ostensibly wholly medieval *Lohengrin*. Aeschylus wrote a lost play about the legend of Semele, who perished because she was foolish enough to insist that Zeus, her lover, should visit her in the manner in which he visited his immortal consort, Hera; but Wagner doubtless learned of her from Handel's opera. Wagner wished to minimise the Christian elements in the plot of the work; but in comparison with these the Greek element is superficial.

We have seen that Wagner greatly admired Aristophanes. *Die Meistersinger*, not completed until 1867 but sketched as early as 1845, resembles *The Frogs* in that both works deal with poetic rivalries and with the clash between different principles of poetic art. Wagner also greatly admired Plato's *Symposium*, and the figure of Hans Sachs has been thought to resemble Socrates. That the address of Hans Sachs at the end of the work was inspired by the conclusion of Aeschylus' *Eumenides* would have been a bold guess. But we have Wagner's own word for it that it was so, which may remind us that the processes by which an artist's mind works upon the material which it makes use of are not always to be discovered by the light of reason.

The plot of *Tristan* – Wagner wrote the poem in 1857 – has a surface resemblance to that of Euripides' *Hippolytus*; Tristan might be said to correspond with Hippolytus, Isolde with Phaedra, Brangäne with the nurse, Marke with Theseus. But again there is little significance in the likeness; apart from the detail that Isolde does love Tristan, and is not his stepmother, the treatment of their subjects by the two artists is so different that the influence, if any, is of little interest.

Parsifal seems, on the face of it, a very unGreek subject; but it is mildly interesting to note that one idea which it makes use of appears to have come to Wagner from a Greek source. The legends of the Grail seem not to contain the notion that the mysterious wound of Amfortas, or of whoever corresponds with him, can be healed only by the spear with which it was inflicted.[12] All three of the great Greek tragedians wrote plays upon a myth in which the same notion figured. The Greeks on their way to Troy landed by mistake in Mysia, in Asia Minor, whose king happened to be Telephus, a son of Heracles and a hero of the first order. He opposed their landing with success until he tripped over a vine tendril and was wounded by Achilles with his famous spear. The Greeks withdrew and returned home; and Telephus, having learned from an oracle that his wound could be cured only by the spear that had inflicted it, followed them and approached Achilles in disguise. He was detected and was in danger of his life; but he took refuge at an altar, and finally Achilles complied with his request and he in return piloted the Greeks to Troy. An allusion to the story in Goethe's *Tasso* (IV, 4)[13] may have brought it to Wagner's notice; he has invested it with a symbolic value highly expressive of his own conception of the redeeming power of love.

Far more interesting is the Greek element in the construction of the *Ring*. We have seen that Wagner began work upon the poems during the year after his Greek revelation of 1847. Several ancient Norse and German poems were made use of, but the main source is the Volsunga Saga, a late work, but based upon part of the Elder or Poetic Edda. There is no need to summarise its plot here; what is most important is to note that in the sources there is no link between the deaths of Siegfried and Brünnhilde and the Twilight of the Gods. Ragnarök, the day when the gods themselves will perish, does indeed figure in the sagas, but it is not precipitated by the curse upon the ring, and it does not come as Wotan's punishment for his pride and ambition in having built Valhalla.

The Volsunga Saga is of great interest, but it does not carry the

---

[12] See Jessie Weston, *The Legend of the Holy Grail* (1965).
[13] Professor Rudolf Kassel tells me that an opera *Telephus*, by K. Arnold, was produced in 1830, but he thinks it likeliest that Wagner knew of the story, as of other myths, from Gustav Schwab's popular work *Die schönsten Sagen des klassischen Altertums*, illustrated by Flaxman.

cosmic implications with which Wagner has invested it. Trilogies (or, if you count the loosely connected satyr-play which accompanied each, tetralogies) carrying the widest cosmic implications were composed by Aeschylus, an author whom, as we have seen, Wagner admired perhaps more than any other. Wagner expresses special admiration for the only surviving complete trilogy, the *Oresteia*; but so far as the plot of the *Ring* is concerned, more importance attaches to the *Prometheus Bound*.

This appears to be the sole surviving play of its trilogy; the reconstruction of the rest is, as it was in Wagner's time, a highly controversial topic. For our purposes it matters less how Aeschylus wrote his trilogy than how Droysen reconstructed it. He believed that the extant *Prometheus Bound* was the second play of the trilogy; the first, in his opinion, dealt with the theft of fire. It began soon after the beginning of time, and told of the original quarrel between Zeus, the new and ruthless master of the gods, who had lately dethroned his father, Kronos, and Prometheus, a god of the older generation and the special patron of mankind. Prometheus stole fire from Zeus to give it to men; the original title of what became *Das Rheingold* was *Der Raub* (The Theft).

At the start of the extant play, the fire-god, Hephaestus, acting on Zeus's orders, fixes Prometheus to a remote rock for an indefinite period of time. The prisoner is visited by a chorus composed of sea-nymphs, daughters of Ocean, who fly to him on wings to offer sympathy and comfort. Later comes their father, Ocean himself, riding on a winged bird. Prometheus comforts himself with the knowledge that he possesses a secret, told him by his mother the earth-goddess, who has the gift of prophecy, that will one day place Zeus in his power. One day Zeus will desire a female who is destined to bear a son mightier than his father; if Zeus begets a son by her, that son will serve him as he has served Kronos. Prometheus is now joined by Io, a mortal princess who is suffering grievously through being the object of Zeus's desire. Prometheus comforts her, and prophesies that it will be a descendant of hers who will finally release him. Finally Zeus on his throne high above hears Prometheus' threats and sends his herald Hermes to demand that he yield up his secret. When Prometheus refuses, a thunderstorm and earthquake follow, and he is swept down to Tartarus beneath the earth.

We have considerable fragments of the *Prometheus Unbound*, which Droysen took to be the third play of the trilogy; we do not know all the details of the plot. Prometheus was visited by Titans who had been released by Zeus, and who advised him in vain to give up his stubborn attitude and make his peace. Later came Heracles, the great hero whose father was Zeus and whose mother, Alcmena, was descended from Io. He shot the eagle sent daily to tear the liver of Prometheus; later, evidently through the mediation of Heracles, a settlement was reached. Prometheus told Zeus that the female destined to bear a dangerous son was the sea-nymph Thetis, later mother of Achilles; in return, Zeus released him. Men, whom Prometheus had rescued from annihilation by Zeus and had endowed with all the blessings of civilisation, must have received some advantage from the compact; perhaps Zeus granted them a share in Justice, hitherto reserved for himself and the gods alone.

The *Prometheus* was a favourite play of the Romantic age. English people will think first of its effect on Shelley; but it was also the favourite play of Marx, who wrote his doctoral dissertation on the atomism of Democritus and Epicurus, and unlike Wagner read Aeschylus in the original.[14] Let us first observe certain resemblances of detail between its plot and that of Wagner's *Ring*.

On the surface the character in Greek myth most like Brünnhilde is Athene; both are warrior maidens, the special favourites of their fathers. On the surface the character in Germanic myth most like Prometheus is Loge; both are fire-gods, both are cunning, both are alienated from the other gods. But consider now the points which Brünnhilde and Prometheus have in common. Each is the offspring of the earth-goddess who has the gift of prophecy. In Norse and German mythology there is no such goddess; Erda is a direct importation out of Aeschylus. In *Das Rheingold*, when she warns Wotan not to accept the ring, only the top half of her appears above the ground. Such appearances are a habit of Greek earth-goddesses which Wagner may easily have observed upon Greek vases.[15]

Both Brünnhilde and Prometheus defy the ruler of the gods, who in consequence orders a fire-god to secure them for an indefinite period of time. When Brünnhilde says, 'He bound me to the rock', (*Gotterdämmerung*, I, 3) this is truer of Prometheus than it is of her; when she speaks of an eagle tearing human flesh (near the end of the same scene), it is hard not to think her metaphor derived from Aeschylus. Each of the pair befriends and comforts a female, pursued by the great god; Brünnhilde is to be released by Sieglinde's son, Prometheus by Io's descendant. The scene in which Brünnhilde succours the pregnant and bereaved Sieglinde has been thought to show the influence of the scene in which Prometheus comforts the stricken Io.

The use Wagner has made of Prometheus in creating his version of

[14] See p. 143f.
[15] See E. Buschor, 'Feldmäuse', *Sitzungsberichte der Bayerischen Akademie* (1937).

Brünnhilde is of prime importance; for it is through the figure of
Brünnhilde, together with the innovation of making Wotan propagate
the Volsungs, so that the ring may be recovered, that the fate of
Siegfried is linked with that of Wotan. It is a vital part of the
machinery by which Wagner has imposed on the matter furnished by
the Nordic legends a form derived from that of an Aeschylean trilogy.
In the Volsunga Saga, the gods who correspond with Wotan and Loge
are taken prisoner by enemies, one of whose brothers Loge has killed.
To pay their ransom, they need gold, and steal it from the figure who
corresponds with Alberich. In Wagner, the gold is needed for the
building of Valhalla.

That change is vital, for it enables Wagner to make out of the
Nordic myths a story of crime and punishment like that of an
Aeschylean trilogy. In the *Oresteia*, the curse of Thyestes on the house
of Atreus, and in the Theban trilogy of Aeschylus, the curses of Pelops
on Laius and of Oedipus on his sons play an important part; so in the
Ring does the curse of Alberich. In the saga the Siegfried figure kills
the dragon simply because the Mime figure has persuaded him to do
so. In the *Ring*, Wotan knows that to get the gold and the ring away
from the dragon, he needs an innocent human hero. That is why he
generates Siegmund and Sieglinde, much as in the lost Greek epic
Cypria Zeus deliberately generated Helen so that men would fight over
her and so reduce the population of the earth.

It is interesting to note that in the saga Siegmund marries his sister,
but Sigurd, the Siegfried figure, is his son by a different wife. Wagner
was interested in incest, so we can see from his treatment of the myth
of Oedipus in *Oper und Drama*. In the sagas, the Siegfried figure rescues
a Valkyrie whom Wotan has imprisoned for giving victory to the
wrong man, we do not know to whom. They have a daughter, but
Brünnhilde herself suggests that Siegfried should marry Gutrune. In
the saga, it is the mother of Gunther and Gutrune who administers
the love-potion. Siegfried is killed by one of this woman's sons, but he
is not Hagen, neither is he connected in any way with Alberich.

In Aeschylus the threat that the lord of the gods will lose his power
is in the end averted. In the *Ring* it comes to pass; the day of Ragnarök
is realised. At the end of the *Prometheia*, the order of the world seems to
have been modified; at the end of the *Oresteia*, the terrifying Erinyes
are converted into spirits beneficent to Athens, where the rule of law is
now established. In the *Ring*, the downfall of the gods is to be followed
by the coming of a new world-order.

R.W. Gutman[16] has seen Aeschylean technique in the way in which
so many of the scenes of the *Ring* are occupied by a confrontation, in

16 *Richard Wagner: The Man, his Mind and his Music* (1968), 167.

Greek terminology an *agon*, between two characters. Even more Aeschylean is the way in which the guilt of Wotan and the curse of Alberich are used to link together the successive episodes of the tetralogy. There is a curious affinity between a musical device employed with great effect by Wagner and a certain feature of the art of Aeschylus. At the mention of the principal themes of the tetralogy – the ring, the curse, the giants, love, etc – the music impresses the fact upon the hearer by sounding the leitmotiv associated with the theme in question. Even if Wagner was not the inventor of the term *Leitmotif* he was surely the first to use it in such a subtle and pervasive fashion. Many scholars have remarked that Aeschylus, especially in his choruses, returns to certain pervading themes that run through the three plays of the *Oresteia*, often associating a particular theme with a particular image; none of them has illustrated the fact more tellingly (in *The Oresteia: A Study in Language and Structure*, 1971) than an American scholar, the late Anne Lebeck, whose early death cut short what would have been a brilliant career in scholarship. Without going so far as to propose that his use of leitmotiv was suggested to Wagner by his study of his favourite author, one may point to it as indicating that Nietzsche was not entirely mistaken in claiming that a peculiar affinity existed between Aeschylus and Wagner.

Another resemblance exists between the striking visual effects for which both dramatists are noted. In one of the most perceptive studies of Aeschylus in recent times, *Aischylos als Regisseur und Theologe* (1949), Karl Reinhardt has argued that the poet's use of such effects was dictated by the special requirements of his theology. Dramatic entrances from the air are a feature of the *Prometheus*; the daughters of Ocean enter either on a celestial omnibus or (more probably) each in her separate winged car; their father comes riding on a great bird. As early as *Lohengrin*, Wagner employed similar effects; the *Ring* is full of them. The thunderstorm and earthquake at the end of the *Prometheus* have their analogues in Wagner; so have the binding of Prometheus, the frenzied entry and exit of the demented Io, the first terrifying appearance of the Erinyes and the great trial scene upon the Hill of Ares.

Interesting as I find Wagner's use of Aeschylus in constructing the plot of the *Ring* and in imposing tetralogic form upon the matter of the Nordic myth, I am still more interested in trying to discover what may have been the Greek contribution to the actual thought reflected in Wagner's dramas, and to the attitude to human life which they exemplify. To do this one must first consider the series of detailed theoretical works in which Wagner between 1849 and 1851, in the middle of a great creative period, explained his revolutionary theory of music-drama to the public.[17] The first and shortest is *Die Kunst und die Revolution*, published in the autumn of 1849; for us it is the most important, for in fewer than forty pages it contains the whole essence of the theory later developed at much greater length. In December of the same year came *Das Kunstwerk der Zukunft* (135 pages) and in November 1851, *Oper und Drama* (over 200 pages); *Eine Mitteilung an meine Freunde* (114 pages), published at the end of 1851, is a reply to criticism which also contains theoretical remarks of great interest.

Die Kunst und die Revolution starts with the statement that no progress in modern art is possible without considering where that art stands in relation to the Greeks; it is only a link in the chain formed by the development which they began. There follows a brief sketch of Greek life and art which contains three assertions that lie at the root of Wagner's whole conception of the music-drama. First, Greek tragedy and comedy were not a mere entertainment, but part of a religious festival; they were attended not merely by the rich and leisured, but by a large cross-section of the citizen body. Secondly, its subject-matter was saga, which was the product of the people and which enshrined the people's ancestral wisdom. Myth was true for all time, so that the myths made use of by the tragedians were not irrelevant to the lives of their fellow citizens.

Thirdly, tragedy was not merely verbal, still less purely musical, but was a combined work of art (*Gesamtkunstwerk*) employing words, music and dance; all were the work not of the people, but of a single man, who also trained the actors and chorus and directed the performance.

From here Wagner goes on to sketch the historical process by which the different elements combined in the *Gesamtkunstwerk* had grown apart from one another, so that poetry, music and dance had each developed an independent existence. The process of decay had started with the Romans, of whose taste Wagner since his schooldays had entertained a low opinion. It was accentuated by Christianity, which taught men that their souls were at war with their bodies, and which justified the useless, dishonourable and miserable life they led on earth by pointing to the love of God. God had not created men, as the Greeks had erroneously imagined, for a happy life on earth, but had bound them in a horrible dungeon so as to reward the self-contempt which this induced in them with an eternal state of comfortable and inactive glory after death. Brought up to believe that the splendours of this world were the work of the devil, men were in no state to glorify

---

[17] There is a useful summary of Wagner's theories in the first chapter of Brian Magee's *Aspects of Wagner* (1968; paperback edition, 1972); longer accounts are given by Ernest Newman in *A Study of Wagner* (1899), ch. 5 and *Wagner as Man and Artist* (1925), 183f.

them in art. Christian art, continued the author of *Tannhaüser* and *Lohengrin* and future author of *Parsifal*, was no true art, for it could relate only to abstract spirit and the grace of God; all through the Middle Ages, the tension between church and state had inhibited the growth of any art that should deserve the name. The art of the period between the end of the Middle Ages and Wagner's own time gets even shorter shrift; true art, Wagner writes, is no less impossible under a despotism such as that of Louis XIV.

As for the art of Wagner's own contemporaries, most of it was a luxury product, made in order to please rich industrialists. True art would be the spontaneous product of the people and would cost nothing; this was twenty-six years before the opening of Bayreuth. The impotence of modern drama was exposed by its division into spoken drama on the one hand and opera on the other; true drama like Greek tragedy, would employ music, poetry and dance together. Greek art was conservative, for it gave expression to the conscience of the community; but modern art could express only the conscience of private persons, and must therefore be revolutionary. The process of decadence had severed the arts from one another, and they could be reunited only by revolution. The presiding deity of the new drama was to be Apollo, in the rather surprising company of Jesus; Jesus had shown that all men were equal and were brothers, while Apollo had invested them with strength and dignity. In the longer works that followed, the process of decadence was sketched in detail, and the nature of the new music-drama was more precisely specified.

Interested as we are in Wagner's relation to the Greeks, we must notice that his view of the history of art as forming a continuous chain of interdependent links was typical of the historicism of the time he lived in. No one should imagine that he intended to revive Greek tragedy; the historical sense developed by the scholars of his time made him fully aware that this would be impossible. His aim was to revive the true art of tragedy. Like the tragedy of the Greeks, his music-drama was to be part of a religious festival; it was to narrate myth, and it was to make use of poetry, music and the dance together. All three features were found in the picture of Greek tragedy drawn in Wagner's own time by Friedrich Gottlieb Welcker and Karl Otfried Müller.

Nowadays this picture strikes us as considerably idealised. Greek tragedy certainly began as part of a religious festival; but Dionysiac religion was very different from Christianity, and we may doubt whether the atmosphere in which it was enacted was permeated by the hushed awe which Wagner thought proper for a performance of *Parsifal*. Entertainment was part of its function, and an important part. The myths which it presented had been invented not by a mysterious collective entity, but like the dramas themselves by human individuals. Tragedy was indeed a combined work of art, but it bore a very different character from that of Wagner's music-drama.

Greek music in the classical age is an obscure subject, but it is clear that it was more like Middle-Eastern music of today than like modern symphonic music with its polyphonic orchestra. Music was in classical drama kept firmly in its place; never in any circumstances were the words to be permitted to be drowned by the accompaniment. The three famous Greek dramatists were great poets, whose verse, both lyric and dialogue, is incomparably richer than that of Wagner; his richness lies in the music. One function of the Greek chorus is to offer a kind of emotional commentary upon the action. In Wagnerian drama that is the function of the orchestra; Wagner thought that his own principle of fitting the accompaniment to the sense of the words reflected the close linking of word with melody and rhythm attested for Greek drama.

No composer has been more solicitous than Wagner that the orchestra should not drown the words; but such complex polyphony as his is far removed not only from the music but from the lyric verse used by the tragedians to comment on the action, and the emotions it arouses are far less subject to the discipline of reason. In Freudian terms, as Mann says, the voice of the singers spoke the language of the ego, while the music of the orchestra spoke the language of the id. Naturally such an orchestra could not be visible in the shape of a group of people in evening dress and holding instruments; so Wagner buried it below the stage and concealed the opening under the *Schalldeckel*. The *Festspielhaus* is an attempt to reproduce as far as possible the open-air theatre of the Greeks; what may strike an English person as its distressing resemblance to a nonconformist conventicle is purely accidental. Of course Wagner never imagined that he was reviving Greek tragedy. But the differences between his own *Gesamtkunstwerk* and the only other drama which he thought worthy of the name were greater than he seems to have realised.

Is Wagner to be numbered with those thinkers of his time who held Christianity to be a spent force and looked to Greek antiquity to help them provide a substitute? Nietzsche during his Wagnerian period certainly believed Wagner to be such a thinker, as he was himself; and the markedly anti-Christian tone of the passage from *Die Kunst and die Revolution* which I have summarised, and of other sections of his theoretical writings, seems to bear out his opinion. Wagner wrote in the heat of the situation arising out of the revolutions of 1848, when he was strongly influenced by his friendship with the socialist leader

August Röckel and by his reading of the revolutionary philosopher Ludwig Feuerbach. In his book *Das Wesen des Christentums* (1841), translated into English by the young George Eliot, Feuerbach had attacked the belief in a personal god as a mere projection of the believer's self and had advocated a pantheistic theory on Hegelian lines. It was the intoxication of this heady mixture that encouraged Wagner to sweep the whole of Christian art, not to mention art from the Renaissance to his own time, under the table.[18]

Wagner's socialism is manifest in the *Ring*, which Bernard Shaw, perhaps less than fully alive to certain of its other aspects, interpreted to an English public, not without truth, as a socialistic allegory. Wotan has sacrificed his honour for the sake of pomp and power; the old order has made a sordid bargain with industrialism, whose evils the picture of Alberich's Stalinist regime in Nibelheim powerfully presents. At the end of the work the old order is swept away, Siegfried has recovered the ring from the dragon, Brünnhilde has redeemed Siegfried by her love and has returned the ring to the Rhine-daughters, and her self-sacrifice has cleared the way for the coming of a new order to replace the old.

In fact, Wagner's attitude to Christianity, even in 1849 when he wrote *Die Kunst und die Revolution* was a good deal more complicated than the young Nietzsche realised. In October 1845 he had produced *Tannhäuser*; six years later he protested against those who found in it 'a specifically Christian tendency towards impotent pietism'. But without putting it in quite that way, one may wonder whether it is possible to avoid seeing *Tannhäuser*, and still more *Lohengrin*, if not as Christian works, at least as works containing certain Christian elements. Many people have maintained that the Christianising tendency that finally emerged, beyond all possibility of doubt, in *Parsifal*, produced in 1882, the year before Wagner's death, was due to Cosima's influence, supported by a growing conservatism fostered by the friendly relations between Bayreuth and the newly founded German Empire. Yet as early as 1862 Wagner had written to Bülow that of course his last work would be *Parsifal*.

As early as *The Flying Dutchman* we find in comparatively simple form Wagner's wholly characteristic and thoroughly romantic theme of redemption through love, usually of a woman for a man. For a time he was greatly attracted to the philosophy of Schopenhauer, and *Tristan* shows how his theory of redemption can be assimilated to the doctrines of that philosopher. Yet it has no essential relation to pagan

[18] On Feuerbach's influence on Wagner, see W.H. Hadow, *Richard Wagner* (1934), 130f.

religion or even to that oriental religion in which Schopenhauer took an interest, still less to any form of rationalism, but an obvious relation to Christianity and to medieval notions conditioned by Christianity. It forms the core of *Tristan*, it has great importance in the *Ring*; and it reaches its furthest development in *Parsifal*, with Kundry doubling the roles of Venus and Elisabeth.

Nietzsche in his *Birth of Tragedy* describes how in the tragedy of the Greeks – Sophocles is the author uppermost in his mind – the hero manifests his heroism by his courage in the face of a hostile and relentless universe, and finally establishes his heroic status in the very moment of annihilation. The hostile universe in question is not godless; but the gods who rule it are primarily concerned not with man and his wishes but with their own pleasure and their claim that men should render them due honour. The gods have certain favourites among mortals, and their rule maintains a kind of rough justice upon earth; but the complicated chains of crime and punishment which this involves remain for the most part inscrutable to human understanding.

In the world of the *Ring* we seem at first to be moving in such a universe. Siegmund and Sieglinde, and later Siegfried, are exposed to a hard and cruel world, with no protection from their divine progenitor; only thus are heroes made. Siegmund perishes not because he has done wrong, but because he has offended against the honour of a goddess, Fricka. Siegfried meets his end because of the curse upon the ring; the guilt which might have ensued upon his desertion of Brünnhilde in favour of Gutrune is eliminated by means of the love-potion. The cases of both Siegmund and Siegfried could be assimilated to those of Greek tragic heroes like Oedipus, Antigone, Hippolytus who are doomed for reasons among which personal guilt plays no part. Why, then, is it impossible to feel that Siegfried is tragic in the sense in which the Ajax or the Oedipus of Sophocles is tragic? It is because the notion of redemption through love has imported an element of sentimentality. George Steiner has well said in *The Death of Tragedy* (1961) that this is not tragedy, but 'near-tragedy'; 'near-tragedy', he writes, 'is precisely the compromise of an age which did not believe in the finality of evil. It represents the desire of the romantics to enjoy the privileges of grandeur and intense feeling associated with tragic drama without paying the full price'.[19]

In the finale of the *Ring*, Brünnhilde by her love redeems Siegfried, and when she returns the ring to the Rhine-daughters her love makes

---

[19] p. 166f. Steiner also remarks, with much truth, that Wagner has less in common with Aeschylus and Sophocles than with Alexandre Dumas fils and Victorien Sardou.

possible the coming of a new order which will make things better in the future. Just how the love of a woman for a man comes to be equated with the brotherly love which will make human life perfect in the socialist utopia is something which is not explored. In the *Prometheia* there is a possibility that Zeus may fall. But there is no assurance that if he does fall conditions will be better; he will be replaced not by Prometheus but by that formidable unknown quantity, the son whom Thetis would have born to Zeus. The figure of Wotan, who retains elements of nobility despite his sacrifice of essentials for the empty pomp of Valhalla, is to that extent a tragic figure. But in the *Ring* in general we find something profoundly alien to the spirit of an ancient tragedy.

Wagner was in a sense a Christian even when he wrote *The Flying Dutchman*; in his own time his kind of Christianity was still unorthodox, though no doubt many clergymen would sanction it today. He believed in the redemption of the world and of the individual by love; yet like a true follower of Rousseau, he was sure that man's natural impulses must be good. The doctrines of the Fall and of original sin were therefore uncongenial to him; so was the notion that reason should be used to discipline the emotions.

In our own time people often tell us that Greek tragedy reveals no belief in guilt or responsibility; and it is true that the meaning of these concepts in its world has often been dangerously oversimplified. But without some kind of belief in guilt and responsibility, tragedy is scarcely possible; even Goethe was too close to Rousseau to be capable of writing tragedy. Wagner, believing in the essential goodness of human feelings, is not a true tragedian. Nor is the theodicy of the *Ring* significantly like a Greek theodicy. The notion that the order of the universe can be replaced by an order that is not only new but morally superior is not paralleled in Greek thought. In ancient Scandinavia the day of Ragnarök finally arrived; the religion of Odin gave way to the religion of Christ. The end of *Götterdämmerung* is not so very different from the end of *Tannhäuser*, of *Lohengrin*, or of *Parsifal*.

Note:
Greek influence upon Wagner has often been written about in Germany, though in English I have found only P.C. Wilson's not wholly adequate Columbia University dissertation of 1919, 'Wagner's Drama and Greek Tragedy'. As early as 1907, Robert Petsch in the second Richard Wagner-Jahrbuch *drew attention to the use of the* Prometheus *in the plot of the* Ring; *his treatment has been amplified by later authors. Curt von Westernhagen's* Richard Wagner *(1956) contains a chapter (p. 132ff.) on the Germanic myths and Greek tragedy; I have searched the*

writings of the late Ernest Newman in vain for any indicating that he was aware of the significance of this element in Wagner's work. By far the most useful account of Greek influence upon Wagner is contained in three lectures by Wolfgang Schadewaldt, originally published in the Bayreuth programmes for Lohengrin *in 1962 and for* Die Meistersinger *in 1963 and 1964, and reprinted under the general title 'Richard Wagner und die Griechen' in the second volume of* Hellas und Hesperien *(Schadewaldt's collected shorter writings) in 1970 (ii, p.341ff.). My debt to Schadewaldt is considerable; his attitude is more reverential than mine, but my piece was not written for Bayreuth.*

11

Marx

'An exceedingly cultured Anglo-German gentleman'; that is how Marx in his later years appeared to his Russian visitor Maxim Kovalevsky. Marx was steeped in literature to an astonishing degree; he knew German, French, English, Italian, Spanish, Greek, Latin and a little Russian, and throughout his life read widely in these languages. In his theoretical writings, and also in his abundant journalism, Marx made extensive use of this wide literary knowledge; and so S.S. Prawer has made it the subject of a learned, useful and entertaining book. His acquaintance with Mark's writings, including his voluminous correspondence, is very close; he is familiar with the extensive literature that Marx made use of; and as one would expect of the brother of R. Prawer Jhabvala, he writes admirably.

As Professor Prawer remarks, Marx is too important to be left to the Marxists, to whose numbers, in his old age, after reading a young Frenchman's infuriatingly dogmatic exposition of what purported to be Marxian doctrine, he indignantly denied that he belonged. In our time no intelligent person would deny the vast historical importance of this writer or the greatness of his contribution to economics, sociology and historical studies in general. Not only the friends but the enemies of a powerful world religion are wise to make themselves acquainted with its prophet and its sacred texts, just as in the fifth century A.D. an intelligent Roman pagan might learn something of Jewish and Christian religion so as to understand Augustine.

A large literature, part of it valuable, has arisen on the basis of Marxism; not only in history, politics, economics and sociology, but in aesthetics and literary criticism, Marxism is a force that every educated reader has to reckon with. No one who remains ignorant of it can understand important literary critics like Lukács, Walter Benjamin or Lucien Goldmann. Enemies of Marxism, in particular, need to grasp the differences between the simplistic and positivistic doctrine of the eastern church, conditioned by the philosophical limitations of Lenin and other Russian interpreters, and sinking to its lowest level in the stuff put out under the names of Stalin and Mao,

* A review of *Karl Marx and World Literature* by S.S. Prawer in *The Times Literary Supplement*, 2 April 1977.

and the pretentious Hegelianising Marxism of the Frankfurt school and other western sects. Professor Prawer's book is not about Marxism, but it throws much light upon it, and especially upon Marxian aesthetics. It will be most valuable to future biographers of Marx.

Living in Trier, under the shadow of the Porta Nigra, Marx received as good an education as the Europe of his day could give. At school he acquired a firm grasp of both Greek and Latin, and throughout life kept up his acquaintance with both literatures. Shaw, never without a strain of cheap Voltairianism, sneered at Homer; Marx adored him, and in his family Homer was regularly read aloud. At school he read in the original Sophocles, Thucydides and Plato, Cicero, Virgil and Tacitus.

It may seem odd to find Marx translating Ovid, yet this interest persisted into later life; he preferred the poems of exile. In the questionnaire he filled up in 1865, Marx names Aeschylus, together with Shakespeare and Goethe, as one of his three favourite poets. Each year he read him through in Greek; on him, as on Goethe and Shelley, the *Prometheus* made a particularly strong impression.

But when Marx was young, classical studies in Germany were not a specialised academic discipline apart from others but an integral part of the literary and historical apparatus of the contemporary world. The young Marx read ancient literature as it had been read during the age of Goethe, with no doubts of its direct accessibility such as the growth of the historical sense was later to impart.

From boyhood, he also read widely in medieval and modern literature. From his father he learnt to know the writers of the Enlightenment; from his cultivated neighbour and future father-in-law, Baron von Westphalen, he learnt to know Shakespeare and the novels of Sir Walter Scott. Westphalen was Romantic in his tastes, and Marx, too, began as a Romantic; he wrote much Romantic verse of an alarming badness, at which in later life he and his wife were to laugh heartily. The mature Marx reacted violently against Romanticism, but we shall see that something of his early outlook continued to affect his attitude towards the ancient world.

At eighteen Marx studied for a year at the University of Bonn, where he attended courses given by the eminent Hellenists F.G. Welcker and A.W. von Schlegel. Then he moved to Berlin, where he concentrated on philosophy and finally became converted to Hegelianism. In 1841 he obtained his doctorate with a study of the difference between the atomistic natural philosophy of Democritus and that of his follower Epicurus. This was not published until 1927, when experts on the subject who were certainly not Marxists found it to contain much that was useful even at that date.

Marx used the tools of scholarship then at his disposal with impressive mastery; yet the motive force behind the thesis had been supplied by its author's recent conversion to the philosophy of Hegel. He thought the situation of Greek philosophy after Plato and Aristotle significantly like that of German philosophy in the post-Hegelian age. Hegel had completed the task of speculative metaphysics, and it remained for his successors to bring philosophy back into the real world and there to realise the ideal. Marx's strong sympathy with Epicurus and with his most eloquent disciple, Lucretius, comes out clearly in the thesis; he puts into the mouth of Philosophy personified the words of the Aeschylean Prometheus, 'In one word, I detest all the gods'. The thesis shows Marx as a fully-fledged Hegelian, but it also proves him to have been steeped in the aesthetics of the age of Winckelmann and Goethe. Marxian aesthetics developed out of this, and cannot be fully understood except with reference to it.

During the stay in Paris that began in 1843, Marx's mature philosophy took shape. He mastered the English political economists and the early nineteenth-century French political theorists; Engels later said that Marxism combined elements from English political economy, French political theory and German idealistic philosophy. After this time Marx made no systematic study of ancient philosophy, yet his earlier studies in that field did not cease to be important in his work. Any reader of his writings, and in particular of *Capital*, cannot fail to be struck by the warmth and frequency of his references to Aristotle. The author of *Capital* felt that he had much in common with the author of the *Politics*, and Marx calls Aristotle the founder of sociology.

Plato he mentions less often and less favourably, repelled, no doubt, by his theistic and idealistic philosophy of spirit. Yet through Hegel Marx had absorbed from Plato matter far more central to his own philosophy than anything derived from Aristotle. Plato's philosophy of ideas, it is true, is static; what makes Hegelian idealism suitable for Marx's purposes is its dynamism, the dialectical development of which spirit is made capable. Yet the one system is in the last resort an adaptation of the other; and the bold and ruthless manner in which Plato applies the surgeon's knife to society as he knew it in order to attain the justest possible commonwealth is far more akin to the spirit of Marx than is the caution and conservatism of Aristotle. When Marx called Aristotle the founder of sociology, how could he forget the eighth and ninth books of the *Republic*, which describe the degeneration of the ideal state through all the successive inferior constitutions till it reaches tyranny, the worst of all?

If the fifth-century sophist Protagoras was not the founder of sociology, it was surely Plato. When Sir Karl Popper prefixed the most powerful attack upon Marxism of our time with an onslaught upon Plato, he well knew what he was doing. The Hegelian notion that the study of history enables a philosopher to predict the course of history is grounded in Platonic idealism; and it is on that, in the last resort, that the allegedly scientific character of Marxian theory depends. Once you abolish the distinction between mind and matter, what name you give your single substance is not a question of the first importance. By calling his matter, Marx was able to cash in on the prestige of the physical sciences, never higher than during the 1840s when his system came into being. But his theory is above all else speculative and metaphysical; indeed, as Sir Isaiah Berlin remarked in the study which after nearly forty years still gleams like the golden bough through the murky forest of literature about Marx, in the strict sense of the word Marx is not a materialist at all. He took care to distinguish his own historical materialism from the 'vulgar materialism' advanced by mere empiricists.

In the introduction to his *Grundrisse*, written in 1857 but suppressed by Marx and not published till 1939, he comes to grips with the problem, somewhat awkward for a Hegelian, of the uneven relation between the development of material production and that of art and literature. No one can deny that he was right to insist that the conditions of production and distribution affect art and literature as they do other departments of life, nor did he himself overstress this economic influence upon culture in the crude way some of his followers have done. But for Marx the emergence of Greek art and literature, to which he attached the highest value, at a time when the general state of society was relatively primitive, constituted a serious problem; so did the case of Shakespeare. He was well aware that certain forms of great art are not even possible in an age of relatively high social development; epic poetry, in which Marx took the greatest pleasure, is an obvious instance.

The answer he gave to this question may surprise some of his modern followers. 'A man', he wrote,

> cannot become a child again, or he becomes childish. But does he not find joy in the child's naivety, and must he not strive to reproduce its truth at a higher stage? Does not the specific truth of each epoch come alive, in its true nature, in the nature of the child? Why should not the historic childhood of humanity, its most beautiful unfolding, exert an eternal attraction as a stage that will never return? There are illbred children and precocious children. Many of the peoples of antiquity belong in this category. The Greeks were natural children. The attraction Greek art has for us does not stand in contradiction to the undeveloped stage of society

on which it grew. It is, rather, its result; it is inextricably bound up, rather, with the fact that the immature social conditions under which it arose, and under which alone it could arise, can never return.

The notion of the Greeks as simple children of nature is characteristic of the naive classicism still prevalent in Marx's youth, and of a not especially sophisticated variety of that attitude. More than one critic has remarked, as Professor Prawer does, that such a view gravely underrates the maturity, complexity and profundity of Greek thinking.

In Marxian theory as a whole aesthetics play a most important part. The artist serves Marx as the type of the man whose work is a pleasure in itself. Modern industrial capitalism has taken the lives of most men horrifyingly far from this ideal; Marx aims to rectify, as far as possible, this state of affairs. When the dictatorship of the proletariat is realised, when only one class is left, when the state withers away, it would appear that the life of men will regain much of the beautiful simplicity of its historic childhood. One can hardly doubt that the roseate view of early Greece which Marx, like so many of his contemporaries had derived from his early education, helped to encourage the surprising optimism into which his prediction plunges when it reaches this important point.

Professor Prawer has chosen not to set out Marx's dealings with each author under the heading of that author's name, as Ernst Grumach did in his invaluable *Goethe und die Antike*, but to follow Marx through his career, showing how he used his literary knowledge in each of his successive writings. He guards most skilfully against the possibilities of boredom, often atoning by the vivacity of his own comments for a certain sameness in the subject-matter. If I have a criticism, it is that I find his tone a little too admiring. If we look closely at the material he presents, we find a reader of wide knowledge, vast energy and powerful sardonic wit; we do not find a reader of refined literary taste or of delicate aesthetic sensibility. A brief survey of the material will serve to make this clear.

It is interesting that Marx read *The City of God*; it is a pity he seems not to have recorded his impressions of a work that has some common features with his own. He knew Dante well, and often quotes him. He ransacks the *Inferno* for scatological abuse with which to pelt the miserable Herr Vogt; the fate of certain victims of poverty reminds him of that of Ugolino; and he movingly quotes the lines about the salty taste of the bread of exile and the bitterness of having to go up and down stairs which are not one's own. At the end of the preface to the *Grundrisse*, he declares his unwillingness to compromise in the form of a quotation from Dante so inappropriate that Professor Prawer is forced to adopt a translation which he knows to be inexact.

Marx was also familiar with Ariosto, Tasso and Boiardo. He once shocked Engels with a reference to Aretino. He knew Machiavelli's writings, including the *Histories* and *Mandragola*. He scolded Wilhelm Liebknecht for his ignorance of Spanish; *Don Quixote* was among his favourite books. He compares the Prussian press languishing under the censorship imposed by Frederick William IV to Sancho Panza deprived of all food by the court physician for fear a stomach upset might prevent the performance of his duties. But Marx's allusions to Cervantes are not always so felicitous; one wearies of his habit of comparing rival journalists or rival theorists with the knight of La Mancha or his squire. Besides Cervantes, Calderón, Lope de Vega and Tirso de Molina figure in his reading.

Sometimes Marx quotes Rabelais: often he quotes Molière; antagonists are compared with the familiar figures, Tartuffe, M de Porceaugnac, Georges Dandin. Corneille he quotes only from his criticism; Racine he read but seems not to have quoted; he seems not to mention La Fontaine or Mme de Sévigné. Voltaire and Rousseau played an important part in his life; his favourite prose writer was Diderot, especially on account of *Le neveu de Rameau*; and he enjoyed Beaumarchais.

The French Romantics he condemns, together with the other Romantics; he particularly detested Chateaubriand, who in his view 'combines in the most revolting way the aristocratic scepticism and Voltairianism of the eighteenth and the aristocratic sentimentalism and romanticism of the nineteenth century'. He quotes Hugo, but seemingly without affection; he rightly observes that Hugo's declamations against Napoleon III were not directed against the weakest points in his opponent's armour. Despite the difference between their political attitudes, Marx revelled in Balzac, often quoted him and seriously planned to write a book about him. As it is, his only published work on a literary topic was devoted to Eugène Sue's lurid bestseller *The Mysteries of Paris*, whose absurdities Marx has little difficulty in laying bare. We do not know that he read Stendhal or Flaubert; we do know that he often relaxed with a volume of Paul de Kock or Alexandre Dumas *père*.

Long before he came to England Marx, like many Germans of his time, had been addicted to the works of Shakespeare; as in the case of Balzac, the difference of political opinion did not disturb him. References to Shakespeare in his works abound, and many of these are not mechanical or conventional. Shylock and Timon are cited at length to illustrate the power of money, the former also in aid of Marx's known antipathy to Judaism. Thersites is quoted, not without sympathy; Bottom's play furnishes examples of people playing roles for which nature has not intended them. Marx more than once quotes the speech in which Cornwall denounces the disguised Kent as one who hides insolence under the guise of plain speaking, Professor Prawer remarks that he seems not to note that their speaker is one of the most odious characters in Shakespeare. Falstaff's and Dogberry's absurdities are claimed, in bitter tones, to illustrate the absurdities of various adversaries.

Late in life Marx was prepared to tackle Middle English to read *Piers Plowman*; he seems also to have read some Chaucer. Milton he mentions rarely, and then usually because he sold *Paradise Lost* for five pounds; perhaps Milton's Christianity prevented him from noticing how well he would have got on with Milton's Satan. Spenser he rails at for having taken part in the Elizabethan reduction of Ireland; Marx would never have been at home in Spenser's world. He mentions Dryden, but seems to care more for the author of *Hudibras*; Marx, who has been invoked by so many canting English puritans, delighted in the sharpest satire against English puritanism ever penned. He enjoyed Pope, especially, of course, the *Dunciad*, and Swift also after he had acquired his complete works in 1870. Defoe provided him with illustrations; he liked Fielding, and like so many Germans, he admired Sterne. He was totally incapable of appreciating Johnson.

Marx seldom quotes Scott, but certainly admired him greatly, *Old Mortality* being his favourite work. One of the few Americans he cites, along with Harriet Beecher Stowe, is Scott's imitator James Fenimore Cooper. He liked Byron, but not the other English Romantics, for all the congeniality of Shelley's politics.

He much admired Cobbett, though he shook his head over his economics; but the respect he began by feeling for Carlyle, one of the few English writers of the time familiar with German literature, waned as he became disgusted by Carlyle's admiration for Jean Paul and by the less pleasing aspects of his hero-worship. Marx did not share Carlyle's admiration for Frederick the Great, whom he used to speak of as 'der alte Sodomiter'.

Marx loved Dickens, not the sentimental creator of Little Nell and the Brothers Cheeryble but the savage depicter of bourgeois society, the Dickens of Pecksniff, Squeers, Bill Sikes and the Artful Dodger. Wishing to describe Gladstone's oratory to German readers, he thought of the Circumlocution Office in *Little Dorrit* and called it an 'um-die-Sache-herumschreibungs-burostil'. He read Thackeray; he preferred the Brontës to George Eliot; he read the novels of Disraeli and of Bulwer Lytton. He loathed Bentham, and also the poetic *Proverbial Philosophy* of Martin Tupper; 'neither Bentham nor Tupper', he wrote 'could have been manufactured except in England'.

Marx quotes from many German medieval texts – the Nibelungenlied, Hartman von der Aue, Wolfram von Eschenbach and others. To belabour the wretched journalist Karl Heinzen he invokes the 'Grobianische Literatur' of the Reformation period; 'no wonder', he writes, 'that booby literature should once again appear among the Germans'. He had little use for the pious poet Klopstock or the established critic Gottsched; he much admired Lessing, both as critic and as polemicist.

Like most cultivated Germans, Marx was steeped in Goethe. He often quoted *Faust*, usually the absurdities of the famulus Wagner or the sarcasms of Mephistopheles. *Reineke Fuchs* with its popular wisdom and its cyncism about politicians had a strong appeal for him. *Tasso* supplies him with the image of the silkworm for the poet who writes because he must and *Götz* with a stick with which to beat the unsuccessful tragedy of the hated Lassalle. In the *Communist Manifesto* he makes striking use of the *Sorcerer's Apprentice*; in the poem the magician returns to restore order, but in the Europe of the 1840s the *Hexenmeister* himself has lost control, 'Commodities are things, and cannot resist man', writes Marx in *Capital*, 'if they are not willing, he can use force' ('wenn sie nicht willig, kann er Gewalt brauchen'). Professor Prawer points out the allusion to Goethe's *Erl-King*, the ballad superbly translated by Sir Walter Scott; the demon whispers into the ear of the sick child:

> Ich liebe dich, mich reizt deine schöne Gestalt.
> Und bist du nicht willig, so brauch ich Gewalt.

Schiller's aesthetics are important for Marx, his poetry much less. As he grew older, the artificiality of Schiller's idealism repelled him, and he enjoyed telling Lassalle that in his attempt at tragedy he had been foolish to imitate Schiller rather than Shakespeare. Marx must have been so eager to beat Lassalle with any stick that came to hand that he forgot the disaster which has overtaken any would-be imitator of Shakespeare, and the obvious fact that any degree of fidelity to that model would have meant that the propaganda element in the play would have to go. He twice trots out Schiller's sentatious line about a childlike spirit seeing the truth when wise men fail; and he quotes from the Wallenstein trilogy the story of the sergeant-major who tries to copy Wallenstein, but reproduces accurately only the way in which he spits.

Marx cites the poetry of Uhland, Bürger, Rückert; the ponderous 'tragedies of fate' of Müllner; the fantastic tales of E.T.A. Hoffmann. Among his literary contemporaries he ridiculed Kinkel and his wife;

he ended by quarrelling with Herwegh; and he finally turned against his old collaborator Freiligrath. Far more important was his relationship with Heine. At school and as a student he had imitated Heine's poetry; during the Paris period they became friends, and when Marx left he would have liked to take Heine away in his luggage. Later they no longer saw eye to eye; Marx repeated scandal about Mathilde, and Heine's return to a belief in God disgusted him; yet he would still listen to no criticism of Heine's work.

He was familiar with that work and often quotes it; *Deutschland: eine Winterreise* in particular supplied him with many illustrations. More important is the influence of Heine's satirical and polemical prose on that of Marx; it is most instructive to compare the two. Even when Heine is at his bitterest, as in the unedifying pamphlet against Börne which Marx, characteristically, so much admired, he has a lightness of tone and playfulness of fancy which Marx, for all his warmth of feeling and sardonic humour, never equals.

Marx cared deeply about style, and at his best, as in the *Communist Manifesto*, he can appeal powerfully to the emotions as well as the intelligence of his reader. Undeniably he has wit, and even humour, though of a rather ponderous kind; but just as the gods denied him the gift of poetry, so they denied him the gift for prose writing of a Heine, a Swift or a Voltaire. The moment these names are mentioned, one remarks the heaviness of Marx's prose, the coarseness of its texture, the crude brightness of its colours, its typically German lack of the French virtues. As a writer and as a man, Heine with all his faults had charm; Marx despite all his great qualities lacked charm completely.

The picture of Marx as reader which emerges from the study of Professor Prawer's book fits well with the impression derived from other sources. The greatest writers are indeed preferred above the rest; but they supply material, for the most part, for the expression of irony or indignation. Certain significant blind spots are found; the greatest French poetry, almost all lyric verse that is not German, the subtler novelists of Marx's own time. The study brings out many of his great qualities; it also brings out his alarming limitations.

Reading the book, one remembers how strongly Marx insists on the objectivity of his own approach to history. Yet his account of some of the effects of capitalism in his time, based upon the data supplied by Engels, reveals a fierce moral indignation. So, in a different way, do his countless attacks on individual persons, many of them so insignificant that one wonders why Marx should have troubled to notice their existence.

It is not easy to avoid the impression that Marx from the beginning had a chip on his shoulder. How is this to be explained? He had a happy childhood; his family was well off; his parents loved him; he had an excellent education; he was encouraged by the generous friendship of Westphalen and the love of his delightful daughter. He had a perfect wife, and children to whom he was devoted; in the early years of exile he had to endure bitter poverty, but that came too late to affect his psychological development.

An obvious explanation is at hand. Marx did not suffer from disabilities imposed upon the Jews, since his father's acceptance of Christianity had exempted him. But in the Rhineland of his time a certain social stigma undoubtedly attached to Jewish origins. He seems to have felt this keenly. In all his voluminous writings Professor Prawer has unearthed only two references to his Jewish birth, both made in private letters and to injure others. In the early essay in which he advocated the assimilation of Jews into the general population, Marx identified the Jew with 'gross and unrelieved commercialism'; in Professor Prawer's words, he chose 'to overlook the Jewish tradition of spirituality, intellectual adventurousness, and prophetic fervour whose heir he himself unwillingly was'. One of his *bêtes noires* was Moses Mendelssohn, partly, it would seem, because he was a Jew. His remarks about Lassalle sometimes recall the tone of Goebbels. An innocent blue-stocking, Ludmilla Assing, who bored him during a visit to Germany, he called 'the ugliest creature I ever saw in my life, a nastily Jewish physiognomy'. Marx's attitude to his own ancestry was surely a potent factor in the formation of his character.

Judaism, ignored and rejected by his conscious mind, comes out strongly in his philosophy. Toynbee pointed out that we find here the sacred book, the inspired prophet, the chosen people being guided to the promised land. Impatient as Marx often became with the representatives of the proletariat whom he had to deal with, the references to it in his writings are deeply permeated with the wholly German sentimentality that was so deeply rooted in his nature. During his lifetime Burckhardt was warning his readers that during the twentieth century power would pass into the hands of the masses, and was expressing doubts about their suitability to exercise that power; Marx had no such worries. In his works the utopian approach that insists on the most radical alteration of existing society is never questioned; the possibility that when the proletariat is in sole command new class divisions might appear within it is never raised. As for the notion that the condition of the workers might be best improved by piecemeal social engineering, that could never have been entertained by one who through Hegel had absorbed so much of Plato.

12

Burckhardt

Dr Janssen has now done for the *Griechische Kulturgeschichte* what he has already (in No. 5 of the same series) done for the *Kultur der Renaissance*. After a short chapter on the book's fortunes since its posthumous publication in 1898, he offers a careful analysis of Burckhardt's views on a series of well-chosen topics, which occupies 75 pages; in the footnotes, which occupy 154 pages, he supplies references to the relevant sections of the *GKG* itself, as well as to Burckhardt's other works, to his letters and to Kaegi's biography, and also to books used by him and to discussions of his views by other scholars. The book is prefaced by a very full table of contents and rounded off by a useful bibliography and indexes. The author disavows any claim to be an ancient historian or to have offered a complete study; but the keen intelligence of his analysis and the discriminating thoroughness of his documentation make his book a precious instrument of study, which will be gratefully received by all who regard the *GKG* as a notable part of the great historian's achievement.

That view has by no means been universally accepted. Soon after the book appeared, Wilamowitz pronounced that it was 'non-existent for learning'; Burckhardt, he complained, was ignorant of the gains made by the researches of the second half of the nineteenth century. Beloch was politer, but deplored the neglect of economic matters; Eduard Meyer compared the work to a book on mathematics by an author ignorant of the first principles of the subject. These learned men did not understand that Burckhardt's purpose differed from their own. He was concerned to grasp the essential features of Greek culture and its history and to indicate their significance, as he had done in the case of the Italian Renaissance; as Kurt von Fritz puts it, he was 'nie ein ganz reiner Geschichtsschreiber im Sinne des Geschichteerzählers, sondern überall in starkem Masse analytischer

* A review of *Jacob Burckhardt und die Griechen* (Jacob Burckhardt – Studien, zweiter Teil) by E.M. Janssen in *Speculum Historiale* 10 (1979), which appeared in *History* 65, no. 213, (1980), 92f.

Betrachter des geschichtlichen Geschehens'. Now that Burckhardt is coming to be generally recognised as the greatest historical thinker of the nineteenth century, and the only one to foresee the nature of the twentieth, this is beginning to be understood even by classical scholars.

Burckhardt fully grasps the central importance of Greek religion and sympathises with the modest view of the human race and its prospects which it took. He appreciates the power and the significance of Greek myth; he remarks that something like Greek philosophy might have been achieved by other peoples, but that the Greek myth is unique. He does not overrate the importance of Orphism or Pythagoreanism; but he feels that the Greek gods did little to promote morality, perhaps underestimating the importance of the justice of Zeus. He sees a tragic element in the transition from mythical to rational thinking, and also in that from the early community to the polis in its full development; the ambivalence of his feelings about the polis is shown by his prefixing to the chapter in which he deals with it Dante's words 'per me si va nella città dolente'. He is far from idealising the Athenian democracy; here his experience of a small civic community saved him from the false analogies which learned Germans were so quick to draw. Yet he is so far from sympathising with Plato's reaction against fifth-century Athens that in many ways his attitude to Plato anticipates that of Popper. Like a good pupil of Droysen, he appreciates the achievements of the Hellenistic age, while not blind to its deficiencies. He admires Diogenes and Epicurus, but has relatively little use for the Stoics or the Neoplatonists. His book is full of excellent observations on individual matters. We all know that he strongly stressed the importance of competition in Greek life; he also remarked on the Greek love of fiction and indifference to exactitude. Although not concerned to make use of the results of the most up-to-date research, he seldom misleads on questions of fact, though Dr Janssen points out that he takes too gloomy a view of fourth-century democracy, and he accepts a picture of Euripides, largely due to Wilamowitz, that now seems obsolete. On the whole one must agree with Alfred von Martin that his book is still the most readable and the most highly-concentrated presentation of Greek cultural history.

13

Max Müller

Few eminent Victorians are so forgotten as Max Müller; and few once famous scholars have so lost their fame. Even in Oxford, where he spent fifty-two years and became a celebrated character, we seldom mention him except as the eagerest entertainer of foreign royalty, the man who spoke of Wilhelm II as 'the nicest emperor I know' and whose wife, after they had given luncheon to the Sultan of Turkey, received in the post the Imperial Order of Chastity, Third Class. Yet in his day he was a figure of national and indeed of international importance. Relying on his achievements as a Sanskrit scholar, but aided by his rare gift of presentation and by a personal charm not always found in learned men, he won a great reputation as a comparative linguist and as an investigator of the early history of religion. During the nineteenth century the knowledge of the connection between Sanskrit and the classical and modern European languages profoundly influenced thought and even politics, and in the age of Darwin the origins of religion were a burning topic. This part of Müller's reputation has now vanished. What makes him important is the effect both in India and in England of his championship of Hindu literature and civilisation. He deserves the honour of having his life written by the most distinguished living Indian writing in English.

With the publication in 1951 of *The Autobiography of an Unknown Indian* Nirad C. Chaudhuri became known as a writer of striking originality, able to convey the feel of places and personalities and to reflect upon happenings and ideas with a cool detachment that contrasts strikingly with the warmth of his intellectual enthusiasm. In *A Passage to England* (1959) he gave a delightful description of his first visit to that country, paid at the age of fifty-seven; and in *The Continent of Circe* he offered by far the best general account of modern India, infuriating most Indians and many Englishmen by his total

* A review of *Scholar Extraordinary: The Life of Professor the Rt. Hon. Friedrich Max Müller*, by Nirad C. Chaudhuri. (An abridged version of this review appeared in the *New York Review of Books*, 20 March 1975).

independence of received opinions.[1] Since Tagore, to whom he has lately devoted a brilliant essay, no Indian writer has gained in the same way the ear of the English-speaking world. He has now made Müller the subject of a biography which is both delightful to read and enormously instructive. The book fully brings out what I have argued above to be Müller's principal claim to notice; but Mr Chaudhuri also tells us much about nineteenth-century England, which he sees from a distinctive point of view. I shall argue that he is a little too kind to the Victorians in general and to his hero in particular; but I have enjoyed and learned from every page of his admirable book.

Max Müller was a child of the Romantic Movement. He was the son of the poet and scholar Wilhelm Müller, who wrote *Die schöne Müllerin* and the verses set to music by Schubert in *Die Winterreise*. Wilhelm Müller had a comfortable position as librarian to the ruler of the small German principality of Anhalt-Dessau; but he died at thirty-three, leaving his widow and four-year-old son with very little money. But they lived happily in the small capital town, whose agreeable atmosphere Mr Chaudhuri most attractively describes. There was much good music in the place, and Müller got an early training that later made him the best amateur pianist of Victorian Oxford. He had an excellent education at a school and later at the university in Leipzig. In that city he consorted with Mendelssohn and Schumann, had Fontane as a fellow-student, and fought a duel with someone who had spoken disrespectfully about his Professor of Greek. That Professor happened to be Gottfried Hermann, one of the greatest Hellenists. Müller studied a variety of subjects, began Sanskrit under Brockhaus, and took his doctorate at twenty.

Poor as they were, the Müllers had some useful connections, and Max managed to continue his education in Berlin and Paris. Through a cousin morganatically married to a member of the ruling house of Anhalt-Dessau he became friends with the mysterious Baron Hagedorn, whose mother had come to a forester's cottage to give birth to him and then disappeared for ever, leaving her son to enjoy a large income emanating from an unknown source. In Berlin Müller attended the lectures of the great comparative linguist Franz Bopp and the eminent philosopher Friedrich Schelling. Bopp turned out to be a poor teacher, but Schelling lectured admirably and interested himself in Müller. It was a pity that the relations were not reversed. Müller needed a sound grounding in the grammars of other languages besides Sanskrit; he did not need to be encouraged in the metaphysical flights of fancy prompted by Schelling's belief that the

[1] He has now published an important study of *Hinduism* (1979).

philosophy of the Vedanta was like his own. In Paris he got valuable instruction in Sanskrit from Eugène Burnouf, and now formed the ambitious plan of editing the formidably long and difficult *Rig-Veda*. The last to try, Bopp's pupil F.A. Rosen, had succumbed when only an eighth of the way through.

Important manuscripts of the *Rig-Veda* were in the East India Company's library in London, and Müller made his way there and got permission to make use of them. He was most effectively befriended by the genial polymath Baron von Bunsen, then Prussian Minister in England, who gave both material support and many useful introductions. With Bunsen's powerful aid he persuaded the Directors of the East India Company to join the governments of France and Prussia in sponsoring his vast undertaking. Visiting Oxford to collate a manuscript in the Bodleian Library, Müller was enchanted by the place; and since it had been decided that his work was to be printed there, he moved to lodgings there in May of 1848. As it turned out, Oxford was his home for his fifty-two remaining years of life.

The somnolent beauty with whom Müller fell in love was slowly awakening from the clerical slumbers of the preceding century. The institution of serious examinations for a degree had failed to promote an interest in research. But it had encouraged intellectual activity of a kind, and it was presently followed by the rise of genuine interest in modern scholarship, which the Noetics diffused from a single college, Oriel. Before Müller's arrival the clerical and conservative reaction had arisen in the same college; Newman and his followers had begun the movement which in Mark Pattison's words 'desolated Oxford life and suspended, for an indefinite period, all science, humane letters, and the first strivings of intellectual freedom which had moved in the bosom of Oriel.'

Müller was captivated by the beauty of the place, and was fully sensible to the charm and intelligence of many of its inmates. Yet he sighed for the learned professors of his own country; he was distressed, as some more recent German visitors have been, by the lack of respect shown by the young towards their elders; and he was puzzled to hear religious discussion centring not upon the great questions touching the nature of revelation, the divinity of Christ and the early history of the Church which were so eagerly pursued in Europe, but upon the validity of Anglican orders or the niceties of Anglican ritual. He wrote home that the place was a high-school rather than a university, and he was right. The abler undergraduates learned a few texts well, and some excelled at the translation of English into Greek and Latin; but of modern European classical and historical scholarship they were given no notion. Mr Chaudhuri finds it strange, in view of Jowett's greater success in undergraduate exercises, that Pattison should be called a better scholar than Jowett. Jowett defined a scholar as a man who read Thucydides with his feet on the mantelpiece; by that test he was a scholar, scarcely by any other.

The Oxford of that time was not an easy society for any outsider, especially if he were a foreigner, to penetrate, and Müller's ability and energy by themselves scarcely explain the success which he enjoyed there. Even the musical gifts which won him so many invitations cannot account for it; Müller later said that when he first came to Oxford music was so looked down on that 'it would have been an insult to invite a Don to play'. Müller owed much to the boyish charm and enthusiasm which surprised people when conjoined with so much learning, and to what the poetaster Sir Henry Newbolt later called his 'power, which the English as a nation lack, of entering with ease and sincerity into relations, however sudden and unexpected, with strangers or foreigners'. People who might have been opposed to Müller on one count welcomed him on another; Gaisford, the Dean of Christ Church, and Pusey, the leader of clerical reaction, were both learned scholars, and despite their conservatism welcomed Müller for his erudition; people like Jowett might be afraid of serious scholarship, but as liberals felt that they must favour progress, which they thought Müller represented. Most of his supporters were liberals, for most conservatives were against foreigners, as Müller was to learn; it was fortunate for him that in 1850 a Liberal Government appointed the University Commission whose proposals for reform, adopted four years later, were to revolutionise the place.

Müller was made a member of Christ Church, which gave him social status but no standing in the university. But the Taylorian Institution had lately been founded and provided with a professor to teach modern languages; this professor obligingly went mad, and Müller was the nearest person available qualified to act as substitute. After a few years, in 1854, Müller succeeded to this chair; and after the reforms of the Commission the Fellows of All Souls, anxious to rescue their college from its reputation of being a sleepy drinking-club most of whose members owed their places to their kinship with the fifteenth-century founder, chose him to be one of their number. Two years later, in 1858, the Boden Chair of Sanskrit became vacant. Müller was the best qualified candidate; but Colonel Boden had founded the chair so that its occupants might train missionaries to convert the natives of India to Anglicanism, and a Tory rival claimed, with truth, that he was fitter for this purpose. The professor had to be elected by the full body of 3,786 senior members, many of whom were clergymen; Müller was not elected, and was sorely disappointed. But his friends were not powerless, and in 1868 his chair at the Taylorian was converted into a new University Chair of Comparative Philology.

In 1853, a year before his appointment to the Taylorian Chair, Müller met a beautiful English girl of good family, Georgina Adelaide Grenfell, and in the Romantic manner experienced the *coup de foudre*. Although the Grenfell family liked Müller personally very much, the girl's father opposed the match for the solid eighteenth-century reason that his means were insufficient. When Müller put out a feeler through his friend the historian J.A. Froude, who was married to an aunt of the young lady, he elicited from an unmarried aunt who kept house for Georgina's father – the aunt was also called Georgina, but was known in the family (as Mr Chaudhuri does not mention) as 'Gommy' – a letter that might have been written by Jane Austen's Mrs Norris with the aid of Forster's Reverend Mr Beebe. She sang Müller's praises, but pointed out that 'without an adequate provision for the *future* as well as the present' the idea could not be entertained. But Müller was not forbidden to see Georgina, and she became so much attached to him that in 1859, the year after he became a Fellow of All Souls, she was able to overcome her family's opposition by using the last resort of the Victorian girl in such circumstances, the threat of *going into a decline*. The marriage turned out blissfully successful; Müller's romantic passion for his wife lasted all his life, and there is no evidence that either of them afterwards thought of any other person. Müller was a devoted father to his family of three daughters and a son; the early deaths of the two elder daughters saddened his declining years.

Mr Chaudhuri has already contrasted the attitude of his own countrymen towards marriage and the family most unfavourably with European notions, and he eloquently praises the Victorian conception of passionate love between man and wife. It certainly works well for the right people; but the same may be said for other kinds of union, and this kind requires unusual qualities in both partners. Not everyone will relish its religious element; Housman called the poetry of Coventry Patmore, whose *Angel in the House* established him as the laureate of this theory of marriage, 'a nasty mixture of piety and concupiscence'. Mr Chaudhuri's partiality for the Victorians, in reaction against their denigration by writers such as Lytton Strachey, manifests itself in what seems to one who has himself had Victorian aunts a surprising tenderness towards the sinister Gommy, even though he knows what one would in any case have guessed, that she herself had suffered severely from a matrimonial disappointment. It happens that some years before she obstructed the marriage of her niece with Müller Gommy had obstructed the marriage of her younger sister Fanny with the poet, novelist and Christian Socialist clergyman Charles Kingsley, lately the subject of an excellent new biography by Susan Chitty called *The Beast and the God*. The relation hardest to win over, Lady Chitty writes, was this particular aunt, she being 'domineering, hysterical and too stupid to be convinced by argument'. Despite Mr Chaudhuri's indulgent treatment, I had recognised this horror, even from the material he provides, for what she was before coming upon Lady Chitty's book.

Something about Müller's notions above love may be gathered from his novel *Deutsche Liebe*, first published in 1857, translated into English and then retranslated by Mrs Müller herself. It describes a love affair between a crippled princess and a commoner in a small German principality; a letter quoted by Mr Chaudhuri indicates that it was to some extent autobiographical. In his words the book 'seems to have appealed to a deep and universal human need'; by 1901 it had gone into its fourteenth edition, and its author, as my friend Erich Segal will be glad to know, 'was particularly pleased that it had succeeded in winning friends even among the hard-headed readers of the United States'. Froude in a review compared his friend's production with Goethe's *Wilhelm Meister*, which Müller's mother had when he was a boy judged unsuitable for his reading, and remarked with satisfaction that the comparison showed 'how much half a century had done to elevate and purify the tone of society'. Exactly fifty years after *Deutsche Liebe*, an equally successful novel appeared with rather similar subject-matter, Elinor Glyn's *Three Weeks*. If Froude could have compared that with Müller's book, I doubt whether he would have thought the intervening half-century had much elevated or purified the social tone; but I find the absurdities of the Edwardian best-seller many times more agreeable and many times more pardonable than those of its mawkish mid-Victorian predecessor.

Once established as a proper Oxford professor, Müller went from strength to strength. In 1873 he completed his tremendous task of editing the *Rig-Veda*, with the fourteenth-century commentary of Sayanacharya, in six large volumes. Offshoots of this work were a history of Sanskrit literature, a Sanskrit grammar, other editions of Sanskrit texts and many minor writings. In the meantime he had boldly plunged into the fields of comparative linguistics and comparative religion and mythology; and to the end of his life he poured forth a stream of writings on these topics, together with such parerga as an edition of Schiller's letters, a translation of Kant's *Critique of Pure Reason*, a defence of Germany published during the

Franco-Prussian War and a defence of England published during the Boer War. During the last part of his life his main function was that of general editor of the valuable series of *Sacred Books of the East*, in forty-nine volumes.

Müller collected innumerable honours, in which he took an innocent delight. In 1886 he received the offer of a knighthood. This was before Lloyd George had revived the pre-Victorian custom of the sale of such distinctions, and long before modern politicians had begun to seek the favour of the people by bestowing them on games-players or the writers of detective stories; but Müller politely explained that foreign governments had already accorded him higher honours than this, and the proposal lapsed. Ten years later Queen Victoria got round the difficulty by making him the only non-political member of her Privy Council. Müller's family dropped the *umlaut* and oddly attached the word Max by means of a hyphen to its surname, provoking the Regius Professor of Modern History to remark that his own daughter did not call herself 'Miss Ned-Freeman'.

On the famous day on which Mommsen, visiting Oxford to receive an honorary degree, began by rapping on the door of the Bodleian Library at six in the morning, he noticed Müller among the crowd in the Sheldonian Theatre and asked in audible tones, 'Do you breed no humbugs in your own country, that you must import them from mine?' Mommsen was a severe judge, but as Mr Chaudhuri, whose youthful ambition was to be like him, will agree, he was entitled to an opinion, and he was not unjust. Mr Chaudhuri points out that his book is not, except incidentally, a discussion or evaluation of Müller's work as a scholar, and it would not be reasonable to reproach him with failing to tell us why Mommsen held this view; yet an explanation of it would be welcome. We cannot help wondering why Müller's views about language, religion and mythology, at one time listened to with great respect, went altogether out of fashion during his own lifetime and have never since returned to favour.

Mr Chaudhuri was told by his father early in life that Müller had established the connection between Sanskrit and the European languages. That is quite untrue; the discovery was made long before Müller by much greater men; and though Müller did much to popularise the results of comparative philology, he was by no means proficient in the subject. Sanskrit was the only language of which he could claim expert knowledge; despite his duel fought on behalf of Gottfried Hermann, his Greek and Latin were hardly sufficient for his purposes. His view of the origin of language, like his view of the origin of religion, was manifestly conditioned by the simple Lutheran faith which he had imbibed in Dessau, and by the Kantianism that supplied his basic philosophy. The brilliant Italian Marxist Sebastiano Timpanaro has lately reproached Noam Chomsky for bringing in Kant by the back door. What would he say of Müller's argument that there was a mystic harmony between sound and sense, to be perceived by means of a special human instinct? Each substance had its peculiar resonance, and each impression from without received its correct impression from within. Müller came to modify this view considerably; but he never ceased to insist that language was inseparable from, though not identical with, thought.

With regard to the origins of religion, Müller believed that men had always had an intuition of the divine, derived not from religious instinct but from sensory impressions. Their observation of the sky and planets, above all the sun, suggested the notion of the infinite, which he described by metaphors and symbols drawn from such observation. Later the metaphors ceased to be thought of as metaphors, so that the heavenly bodies themselves came to be personified and deified into a kind of religion Müller described as 'a disease of language'. Müller explained all myths in terms of this theory, his incapacity as a comparative linguist greatly facilitating the often absurd etymologies by which he did so. Littledale's famous demonstration that Max Müller himself was nothing but a sun myth was to the point; Andrew Lang is rightly blamed by modern critics for his dislike of every new writer of genius who appeared while he was a reviewer, but he deserves much credit for his demolition of Müller's sun myth fantasies. Few scholars now believe that linguistics can furnish comparative mythology with any data of real value. Mr Chaudhuri speaks disapprovingly of academic controversies, and indeed many of them generate more heat than light. But they sometimes serve to establish truth, or at least to combat error. T.D. Seymour, President of Yale, wrote that the ruling passion of Müller's chief adversary, the Yale linguist William Dwight Whitney, was his love of truth; and there is more to be said for some of Müller's critics than one might gather from these pages.

Müller's reputation as a scholar, as distinct from his reputation as a propagandist, must rest chiefly upon his editing of the *Rig-Veda* and his history of Sanskrit literature. Here I can offer no independent judgment; but though he was not the leading Vedic scholar even among his contemporaries, his achievement is said to be substantial. What is undoubtedly of great significance is the effect upon the Hindus of Müller's editing of the *Rig-Veda*, which they invested and still invest with talismanic properties. A great congress of Brahmins once met at Poona and discussed Müller's edition. They could not handle the book, for they believed the ink used to print it to contain cow's blood; but they had it read to them, and pronounced the editing to be the work of a great pundit. European Sanskrit scholarship, as Mr Chaudhuri has already pointed out in his autobiography, did much to restore the bruised self-respect of nineteenth-century Hindus. The discovery of a racial affinity between themselves and their conquerors soothed their pride; and the stress now laid upon the great achievements of their ancestors fostered the almost chauvinistic satisfaction in being Aryans which was deeply embedded in their minds long before the Muslim scholar Alberuni observed it during the eleventh century. In India Müller had an enormous reputation; many distinguished Indians came to visit him, and he was much respected even by conservative Hindus who had little use for other Europeans.

In fact Müller seems to have had little sympathy with the concrete reality of post-Vedic Hinduism, except for the philosophy of Vedanta in its religious aspect. His admiration was reserved for what he thought the higher and purer monotheistic religion of the Vedas; he was too Lutheran to feel the fascination of the later polytheistic Hinduism. At first he thought that Hindus ought to renounce their own religion and turn to Christianity. The Hindus whom he regarded with most sympathy were the monotheistic imitators of Christianity of the Brahmo Samaj, and near the end of his life he tried to persuade one branch of that organisation to declare itself as Christian, though since he did not wish them to join any particular Christian sect he was attacked by High Church Anglicans.

Strangely, Müller never visited India. Mr Chaudhuri says that when he was young his mother thought England was far enough, and that later the pressure of work and family life prevented him from making the voyage while he was still young enough; but I wonder whether his case does not resemble that of his colleague the eminent Greek scholar Ingram Bywater, who is said never to have gone to Greece because the reality might interfere with his imaginative picture of the country in ancient times. Perhaps Müller was wise not to go to India; it is even truer of India than of other countries that the experience of having seen it is apt to make a difference in what people feel about it.

But despite this limited sympathy with Hindu religion, Müller was a loyal and effective champion of Indian civilisation in England. In 1882 he delivered at Cambridge and published a course of lectures on the theme 'India: What can she teach us?'. The mere title must have come as a shock to most Englishmen then resident in India who came to hear it; and not only to those resident in India. In 1835 Macaulay had contemptuously brushed aside the notion that the native literature and civilisation might be a worthy object of study; the same cocksure confidence in western superiority permeates the *History of British India* published in 1817 by the dogmatic utilitarian James Mill. The Mutiny of 1857-58 and its aftermath had done little to diminish English contempt for India and Indians. Yet in this book Müller singled out India as the country most richly endowed with wealth, power and beauty, as the place where the human mind had most deeply pondered on the great problems of life, and as the producer of a literature 'most able to make our inner life more perfect, more comprehensive, more universal, in fact more truly human, a life, not for this life only, but transfigured, eternal life'. It is satisfying to know that in that place and at that time someone was found to voice this attitude.

Müller's defence of India and Indian civilisation was not restricted to his writings. As early as the fifties he put forward a scheme for establishing at Oxford a kind of graduate school to educate young Englishmen so as to enable them to take part in a kind of cultural mission to India. Had this suggestion been adopted, the effect might have been considerable; Mr Chaudhuri himself in his autobiography has shown that the cultural situation in India at that time offered great opportunities for such an experiment. Müller might also have been able to provide more suitable training at Oxford for Indian students. As it was, the Indians who went there came mostly from the wealthiest families, and were by no means always the best qualified to take advantage of what the place could offer.

Max Müller's real importance lies in the effect exercised both in India and in England by his assertion of the claims of Hindu civilisation. But English people must remember with regret as well as gratitude that Müller offered them a chance of understanding the Hindus and coming to terms with them which their ancestors failed to grasp. However exaggerated Müller's contemporary reputation as a scholar may now appear and whatever elements of vanity and absurdity his story may expose, these achievements lend his career a significance which Mr Chaudhuri's deeply intelligent and sympathetic study most effectively reveals.

14

Nietzsche

The late Eduard Fraenkel (1888-1970) once remarked to me that the
most powerful factor in the difference of outlook between Wilamowitz
and his own generation was the influence of Nietzsche. I remembered
his remark when, looking back at the end of a study of early Greek
religion and thought[1] undertaken in terms of the concept of *dikē*, that
term which can mean 'justice' but can also mean 'the order of the
universe which the gods maintain,' I found the turning-point in the
modern understanding of early Greek thought to be the publication
just a hundred years ago of Nietzsche's *The Birth of Tragedy*.

In Germany, the importance of Nietzsche's influence upon classical
studies has been recognised a good deal more clearly than it has been
in English-speaking countries. Notably, Karl Reinhardt, who had
perhaps the finest feeling for poetry and the most sensitive
understanding of the Greek intellectual world among Wilamowitz'
pupils, grew up under this influence;[2] Nietzsche's friend Paul Deussen
was a habitué of his father's house. Many German and Italian
scholars have been more or less aware of it. In English-speaking
countries scholars have been less willing to recognise it, at least until
lately.

This is largely due to the unfortunate prejudice which for most of
this century has prevented most American and English people from
recognising the immense importance of this writer; a comparable case
is that of Wagner. That prejudice is due largely to the evil work of
Nietzsche's sister, a Nazi before the Nazis, who took over all his
papers and did her best to credit him with her own detestable
opinions; it was also fostered by the excessively strong language in
which Nietzsche's fatal vanity and his natural resentment at the

---

* This chapter first appeared in *The Times Literary Supplement*, 21 February 1975; it
was later included in *Studies in Nietzsche and the Classical Tradition* (1976), ed. J.C.
O'Flaherty, T.F. Sellner and R.M. Helm.

[1] *The Justice of Zeus* (1971).

[2] See p. 238f.

neglect he suffered led him to express himself.

In our time there is no excuse for such a misconception of Nietzsche; Karl Schlechta's edition of 1954-6 began the necessary task of a proper publication of the vast mass of material in the Nietzsche-Archive at Weimar, and now the splendid complete edition of Colli and Montinari[3] has come half way to a satisfactory completion of the work. In America Walter Kaufmann's pioneer study has made it easier for the reader to do justice to Nietzsche;[4] from different points of view, R.J. Hollingdale and Arthur Danto[5] have supplemented his work. There is ground for hope that even in English-speaking countries the general reader may come to realise how impossible it is to understand the origins of existentialism, and other movements now prominent, without taking account of this formerly proscribed writer; how great a part of the advance in understanding the workings of the human mind popularly ascribed *en bloc* to Freud properly belongs to Nietzsche; and how Nietzsche's reservations about language point forward to the linguistic philosophy of Wittgenstein.

It is generally known that Nietzsche in his mature philosophy took the motive force of all human activities to be the will to power and saw the only hope of improvement in the future in the procreation of more specimens of a superior type of human being, the *Übermensch*. On the surface that sounds akin to Nazi doctrines, and Elisabeth Nietzsche told Hitler that he was what her brother meant by an *Übermensch*. She lied. First, Nietzsche made it abundantly clear that he regarded racial purity as a delusion, and thought the highest human types resulted from a racial mixture; we can now know that he often spoke with special admiration of the Jews. Secondly, when Nietzsche spoke of power, he meant much more than the strength that can achieve physical or political domination. In its highest manifestations, he thought, the will to power produced great saints or great artists; his favourite example of the *Übermensch* was not Napoleon, but Goethe. The educated reader is nowadays aware that Freud's view that the erotic instinct is the mainspring of human behaviour made it fatally simple for people to make fun of Freud by taking as literal the meta-language which he had to use in order to expound his theory. Thus when Freud says that an infant is in love with his mother he is using not ordinary language but a meta-language. In the language of

[3] *Werke: Kritsche Gesamtausgabe*, ed. Colli and Montinari (Berlin, 1967 –), hereafter *WKG*.

[4] *Nietzsche: Philosopher, Psychologist, Antichrist* (1960; 1974[4]).

[5] *Nietzsche: The Man and his Philosophy* (1965); *Nietzsche as Philosopher* (1965).

ordinary life his statement is absurd, so that people who neglect the distinction can make fun of him. But nowadays educated readers will not do this in the case of Freud; and there is no reason why they should do it in the case of Nietzsche.

Nietzsche is commonly regarded, even by those who know how much people like his sister have misrepresented his real views, as a dangerous subverter of established ethics. He himself is partly to blame, for he often uses language that gives colour to this notion; it recalls to Dodds,[6] for instance, the arguments of the immoralist Callicles in Plato's *Gorgias*. Yet as Kaufmann has pointed out, Nietzsche is not an immoralist, except in the sense that he criticises modern notions about morals. From the moment when, as a schoolboy, he came in contact with the views of Darwin, Nietzsche rejected the belief in God. He thus denied the existence of a divine sanction for morality; and being strongly opposed to a distinction between spirit and matter, he rejects abstract notions of the good like that of Plato. He is concerned to base a relativist ethics upon a realistic psychology. But that does not make him an immoralist. His superman is no more overbearing than Aristotle's megalopsych. The passions, he holds, should be subordinated to the will to power; but they must not be weakened or repressed, but sublimated by the controlling action of the will. Courage is the supreme virtue, and pity is looked on with suspicion; but generosity is commended, and the power to be pursued is not power in the sense of arbitrary dominion over others. Instinctual reactions are favoured, but instinct must be controlled by reason.

Unlike Kant and Hegel, but like most great philosophers, this man of genius was not a professional philosopher. But he was for ten years a professor in an important university; and he was by training and profession a classical philologist, and from an early age showed a very marked aptitude for that subject, one which in Germany in his time and for long before and long after was of central importance to the whole culture of the nation. In the formation of his philosophy he was influenced by many modern thinkers, including, for example, Spinoza and Hume, Kant and Hegel, Darwin and Lamarck, Schopenhauer and Wagner. But his impetus towards philosophy derived initially from his study of the ancient world, and not only of its philosophy but still more of the religious and intellectual climate in which those philosophies developed.

Like many original thinkers, Nietzsche found himself at odds with the members of his own profession. His first book was savagely

[6] E.R. Dodds, *Plato, Gorgias* (Oxford 1959), 387f.

attacked by some of them and condemned in conversation by others;[7] and after ten years he resigned his chair to concentrate upon philosophy. These facts, and also the nature of their own training, have caused some of his interpreters to write as if Nietzsche had only drifted into classical philology by mistake, and to ignore the part played by the influence of Greek antiquity in the formation of his opinions. That, I think, is a mistake.

I am no philosopher, but a classical scholar, and much of what I have to say is concerned with *The Birth of Tragedy*; but I think it unfortunate that so many people begin the study of Nietzsche by reading this, or by reading *Thus Spoke Zarathustra*. The overheated tone of the former work and the biblical and prophetic manner of the latter are not calculated to reassure the sceptically or empirically minded reader. But Nietzsche is in many ways a sceptic and an empiricist. He detested Hegel, he finally rejected Wagner, and he purified himself from the influence of the latter's music by listening repeatedly to *Carmen*. Correspondingly, he often writes in very different style, sharp, elegant and crisp. 'Only a genius,' he said, 'can write clearly in German.' Nietzsche certainly survives the test. What makes his philosophy difficult to understand is his habit of stringing together separate aphorisms or disconnected paragraphs; that is why it is hard to get a general view of his philosophy till you have read all of him. Still, it is a delight to read him; he is one of the greatest writers of German prose, and might be considered a greater writer than any philosopher since Plato.

To understand Nietzsche's criticisms of the classical philology of his time, and also the importance of the subject in his own formation, one must take account of the history of classical studies in Germany, and indeed in Europe. In modern times there have been two revivals of interest in the ancient world. The first arose in Italy during the late middle ages and reached its climax there during the fifteenth and in France during the sixteenth century; its impetus was finally exhausted by the wars and supersititons of the early seventeenth century. The second originated late in that same century, reached a high point in Germany late in the next, and maintained great vigour until 1914; since then, its impetus has been declining under the pressure of the wars and superstitions of our own time. Despite the progress in Greek studies made by individuals like Politian and the great French scholars of the sixteenth century, the first renaissance was largely concerned with Greek civilisation in its Latin dress. The second concentrated far more upon Greek; and with its beginning, Greek

[7] See below, p. 172.

literature for the first time re-entered the bloodstream of European civilisation in an undiluted form.

Before the second renaissance, classical philology had seldom been anything but a secondary pursuit. Men used it to perfect some other skill; they were first divines, lawyers or doctors, and only in second place classical scholars. Nietzsche rightly noted[8] that a new era dawned on 8 April 1777, when Friedrich August Wolf, entering the university of Göttingen, insisted on being set down as 'studiosus philologiae'.

Yet at its beginning the second renaissance was, like the first, a movement of men eager to make use of the ancient world to illuminate the modern. German classicism had its links with the universities; yet it was not an academic but a literary movement. Winckelmann was in a sense a great scholar, but he was less concerned with art history than with art itself; Lessing and Goethe made serious and sustained efforts to become familiar with the ancient world, but did so not for the sake of scholarship but for that of literature and art. During the early stage of this second renaissance, even professional scholars had something of this attitude. Gottfried Hermann was a close student of Kant, and interpreted Aristotle's *Poetics* in the light of Kantian aesthetics; he and Wolf[9] were both in touch with Goethe, and helped him in his Greek studies. Karl Otfried Müller's history of Greek literature is a learned book which the general reader as well as the scholar can enjoy and admire. The link between the two worlds is seen most clearly in the person of Wilhelm von Humboldt, eminent both as scholar and as statesman and prominent among the founders of that University of Berlin which was to provide Europe with the pattern of a modern education.

But philology could not remain unaffected by the vast development of historical studies that marked the nineteenth century. In the early decades the older type of literary scholarship, personified by Hermann, came into conflict with the newer type, making use of the findings of archaeology, epigraphy, and the new science of comparative linguistics, personified by Karl Otfried Müller, August Boeck, and Friedrich Gottlieb Welcker. On the whole the victory rested with the latter; what was now called the science of the ancient world, *Altertumswissenschaft*, was dominated by the historical outlook. Not all the scholars of this period lost touch with literature. We can

[8] *WKG*, IV-1, 90, an epoch-making event, despite the precedents mentioned by E.J. Kenney, *The Classical Text* (1974), 98[1].

[9] See the references to the two men in the index of Ernst Grumach's *Goethe und die Antike; Eine Sammlung* (Potsdam 1949).

remark, for instance, the link between romanticism and the new
growth of a historical sense; the new historical writing, rich in cultural
and social detail, owed a debt to the romantic novels of Scott, as
Ranke, for example, was well aware.[10] But it was now that scholarship
became separated from literature, and indeed from other departments
of life. Seduced by the example of the natural sciences, whose results
seemed so easily to be expressed in concrete terms, scholars showed
an increasing appetite for facts collected for their own sake and an
increasing pride in 'production'; specialisation was carried to an
extreme degree, and the new historicism came to despise, as
sentimental and superficial, the classicism of the age of Goethe. Of
course by no means all scholars of the new type were dull or dry; but
in the new climate dullness and dryness throve. By 1869, when
Nietzsche began his professorial career, the second renaissance was
showing distinct signs of a decline.

Born in 1844, Nietzsche was educated at Schulpforta, by far the
most famous classical school of Germany, which had educated Ranke
and – four years after Nietzsche – Wilamowitz, as well as countless
classical philologists of note. In this strict establishment, in the face of
the keenest competition, Nietzsche won high honours; and he
maintained his progress after entering the University of Bonn in 1864.
At the end of his first year, the famous quarrel between Otto Jahn and
Ritschl[11] ended in the depature of the latter to Leipzig, and Nietzsche
was among those who followed him. Nietzsche might have been
expected to side with Jahn, whose strong aesthetic sense came out in
his famous life of Mozart and in his pioneer studies in Greek art,
rather than with Ritschl, whose claim to fame lies in his immense
services to the study of early Latin, particularly Plautus. But in fact
Nietzsche attached himself to Ritschl, for whom, as he noted,
philology meant the attempt to understand an entire civilisation.
Ritschl was so much impressed by Nietzsche's work that in 1869 he
secured his appointment, at the age of 24, as Professor
Extraordinarius at Basel; he became full professor a year afterwards.

Karl Reinhardt, who cannot be accused of prejudice against

---

[10] See H.R. Trevor-Roper, *The Romantic Movement and the Study of History: John Coffin Memorial Lecture delivered before the University of London on 17 February 1969* (London 1969), 13ff.

[11] For an excellent brief account of the quarrel, see Alfred Körte, *Die Antike* 11 (1935), 212f. Nietzsche's letter to Rohde of 8 October 1868 shows that the attack on Jahn in *Die Geburt der Tragödie* that so angered Wilamowitz (cf. *Erinnerungen*, 1843-1914, 129) had been provoked by Jahn's unfavourable criticism of Wagner. Körte, p. 216f., shows how strongly Wilamowitz sided with Jahn in the quarrel with Ritschl's supporters.

Nietzsche, has written that 'the history of philology has no place for Nietzsche; his lack of positive achievement is too great.'[12] It is true that his contribution to detailed scholarship is comparatively small; but when we remember that he gave up his chair at thirty-five, he must be acknowledged to have made himself a place in the history of the subject, even if we think only in terms of concrete achievement. His early work on Theognis (1864)[13] is interesting chiefly on account of the resemblance of this poet's uncompromisingly aristocratic outlook with Nietzsche's own. His doctoral thesis[14] advanced the investigation of the problem of the sources of the second-rate compiler Diogenes Laertius, on whom part of our knowledge of the history of Greek philosophy unfortunately depends. More interesting, from the point of view of Nietzsche's own development, is his work on Democritus;[15] but we should hardly read it now if it were by another author. On the other hand, the three articles on Greek rhythmic[16] contain a statement of the case against believing in a stress accent in Greece that is referred to with approval in Paul Maas' standard manual on Greek metre.[17] A distinct contribution to learning is made by Nietzsche's work on the fictitious contest between Homer and Hesiod preserved in an ancient life of Homer;[18] his guess that the work depended on the *Mouseion* of the late fifth-century sophist Alcidamas, ridiculed by Wilamowitz in 1916, was confirmed when J.G. Winter published a Michigan papyrus in 1925.[19] It is more interesting to note that in this study we see the origins of Nietzsche's important observation of the significance in Greek life of contests and competitions. This is emphasised in the history of Greek culture of

[12] In a lecture on 'Die klassische Philologie und das Klassische,' given in 1941; see *Vermächtnis der Antike: Gesammelte Essays zur Philosophie und Geschichtsschreibung*, ed. Carl Becker, 2nd ed. (Göttingen 1966), 345.

[13] *Gesammelte Werke: Musarionausgabe*, ed. Oehler, Oehler and Wurzbach (Munich 1920-29), hereafter *MusA*, I, 209f.

[14] *MusA*, II, 33f.; cf. 1, 299f.

[15] *MusA*, II, 85f. [16] *MusA*, II, 279f.

[17] Paul Maas, *Greek Metre*, trans. Hugh Lloyd-Jones (1962), sec.4, p. 4.

[18] *MusA*. II. 369f. See E. Vogt, *Rh. Mus* 102 (1959), 193f., *Antike und Abendland* 11 (1965), 103f.

[19] *Transactions of the American Philological Association*, 56 (1925), 121f.; M.L. West, *Classical Quarterly*, 17 (1967), 433f. believes that the papyrus comes from a manuscript of Alcidamas; G.S. Kirk, ibid., 44 (1950), 149f., E.R. Dodds, ibid., 46 (1952), 187f., and G.L. Koniaris, *Harvard Studies in Classical Philology*, 75 (1971), 107f., think lines 15-23 come from Alcidamas; R. Renehan, ibid., 85f., thinks that 'we must either accept the entire papyrus as a fragment of Alcidamas or pronounce it an obscure piece of Greek of unknown authorship' (ibid., 104). M.L. West, *Class. Quart.* 17 (1967), 433, argues convincingly that the papyrus is a text of Alcidamas. Cf. A. Momigliano, *The Development of Greek Biography* (1971) 26f.

Jacob Burckhardt,[20] a senior colleague of Nietzsche in the University of Basel; and though Burckhardt always kept his distance from Nietzsche, and later came to mistrust him, it seems certain that this feature of his work was due to Nietzsche's influence. The lecture notes published in the Musarion edition of Nietzsche's works in 1920[21] are highly interesting to students of the origins of his philosophy, or of the general contribution to the understanding of Greek thought which I shall come to presently; but they contain little positive establishment of concrete facts. In that respect, Nietzsche has rather more to his credit than Reinhardt's judgment would imply; Reinhardt, who himself was denied by some colleagues the title of philologist, may have been afraid to claim too much for him. But Nietzsche's own achievement in professional scholarship is trivial in comparison with his general contribution to the understanding of Greek life and thought.

The main elements of this are present in *The Birth of Tragedy*, published in 1872. This work was greeted with derision by most of his professional colleagues. Soon after publication it was bitterly attacked in a pamphlet entitled *Philology of the Future*, with allusion to Wagner's 'Music of the Future,' by a doctor of philology four years Nietzsche's junior and like him an alumnus of Schulpforta. This was Ulrich von Wilamowitz-Möllendorff, destined to become the most celebrated Greek scholar of his time. Nietzsche was defended in an open letter to a Swiss newspaper by no less a person than Richard Wagner, and in a pamphlet no less bitter than that of Wilamowitz and bearing the unfortunately chosen title of *Afterphilologie* by his friend and contemporary Erwin Rohde, destined in the 1890s to bring out a study of Greek beliefs about the soul that is one of the landmarks in modern classical scholarship; then Wilamowitz returned to battle in a second pamphlet. The firm of Olms has lately reprinted all this literature inside one cover.[22] It makes distressing reading; the over-excited tone and utter lack of humour of all parties to the dispute – it is significant that the most moderate of them was Richard Wagner – is the kind of thing that makes foreigners despair of the whole German nation. The condemnation of his book by older, more established scholars may have distressed Nietzsche more. Usener, the great authority on Greek religion, pronounced its author 'dead from the point of view of scholarship'; and Nietzsche's own teacher, Ritschl,

---

[20] See especially *Griechische Kulturgeschichte* iv, 84f., rpt. in *Gesammelte Werke* viii (1962), 84f.

[21] *MusA*, II, 337f.

[22] *Der Streit um Nietzsches 'Geburt der Tragödie,'* ed. K. Gründer (Hildesheim 1969).

was more polite but hardly less severe.[23] On the other hand, Rohde in a letter of 12 January 1873 claims that Jacob Bernays recognised in the book ideas that had long been in his mind.[24] This, if true, is highly significant, for Bernays had a more penetrating intelligence than either Usener or Ritschl.[25]

Considered as a work of scholarship, *The Birth of Tragedy* has many failings. As Wilamowitz saw, it contains some annoying mistakes in scholarship; and the author even leaves out several facts which might have been used to support his thesis.[26] That thesis, that tragedy originated through a synthesis of Apollonian and Dionysian elements, is as a statement of fact to say the least unprovable; and the defectiveness of the arguments confidently asserted to prove it is rendered doubly infuriating by the over-confident and hectic tone in which it is written. Nietzsche failed entirely to control the two intellectual passions which at that period of his life had taken possession of him, the passion for Schopenhauer and the passion for Wagner. The latter passion was not simply for Wagner's music, but for his critical writings, so that Nietzsche took over from his hero the notion that Wagnerian opera was in a real sense a revival of Greek tragedy. In consequence, the importance assigned to music in the emergence of tragedy is quite out of proportion. Wilamowitz rightly pointed out that the very different music of ancient Greece was always kept in strict subordination to the words. Later Nietzsche came to regret that he had ever added to the original fifteen sections of the book the ten sections about Wagner with which it concludes.

Niezsche's Apollo and Dionysus bear an obvious resemblance to the notions of idea and will in the philosophy of Schopenhauer. Later, when Nietzsche had abandoned his Schopenhauerian dualism in favour of a monistic position, he would have operated with Dionysus only. The manner in which the two elements became interfused, and the whole functioning of the Dionysian, are described in over-heated

[23] See Charles Andler, *Nietzsche: Sa vie et sa pensée* (Paris 1920-31) ii, 59.

[24] See ibid.; cf. *Nietzsches Briefwechsel mit Erwin Rohde*, ed. Elisabeth Förster-Nietzsche and Fritz Schöll (Leipzig 1923), 273 = *WKG* II-4, 168 (no.400).

[25] On Bernays, see A. Momigliano, 'Jacob Bernays,' *Mededelingen der Koninklijke Nederlandse Akademie van Wetenschappen*, afd. Letterkunde, Nieuwe Reeks, Deel 32, No. 5 (1969), 17 = *Quinto Contributo* i (1975), 127f.

[26] It is astonishing that Nietzsche does not mention Aeschylus' trilogy about Lycurgus, in which the devotees of Dionysus seem to have clashed with those of Apollo, led by Orpheus; see Karl Deichgräber, *Göttingische Gelehrte Nachrichten*, 8 (1938-39), 231f. for critical discussion; the fragments are on pp. 25f. of Hans Joachim Mette, *Die Fragmente der Tragödien des Aischylos* (Berlin 1959). See in particular fragment 83 (the texts with evidence for the clash between the two cults) and fragment 71, the wonderful fragment describing Dionysiac revelry preserved by Strabo X, 3, 16.

tones not calculated to appeal to the judicious reader; and the assertion that tragedy was killed by an alliance between Euripides and Socrates, grounded as it is on a belief in a community of opinion between these two persons, which is wholly unacceptable, leaves the book wide open to attack. Its author himself later became dissatisfied with it; in 1886 he wrote that he should have done what he had to do 'as an imaginative writer.'[27] Yet with all its appalling blemishes it is a work of genius, and began a new era in the understanding of Greek thought.

Through Nietzsche's writings runs a vein of criticism of the view of the Greek world taken by the old classicism, much as he preferred its attitude to antiquity to that of the new historicism. Behind the calm and dignity praised by Winckelmann, Nietzsche saw the struggle that had been needed to achieve the balance; he saw that the Greeks had not repressed, but had used for their own purposes, terrible and irrational forces. Nietzsche, and not Freud, was to invent the concept of sublimation, so important in his mature philosophy. Nietzsche saw the ancient gods as standing for the fearful realities of a universe in which mankind had no special privileges. For him what gave the tragic hero the chance to display his heroism was the certainty of annihilation; and tragedy gave its audiences comfort not by purging their emotions but by bringing them face to face with the most awful truths of human existence and by showing how those truths are what makes heroism true and life worth living. In comparison with such an insight, resting on a deeper vision of the real nature of ancient religion and the great gulf that separates it from religions of other kinds, the faults of Nietzsche's book, glaring as they are, sink into insignificance.

Reinhardt[28] says that Nietzsche did not discover the Dionysian element in Greek thought, for archaeologists, whose work he had neglected, knew about it before. He might have added that the investigation of the whole problem of the irrational did not begin with Nietzsche. Its origins may be seen in the now forgotten but perhaps still instructive controversy stirred up by the symbolistic theories of the Heidelberg professor Creuzer; his book on Dionysus appeared in 1809 and his *Symbolik und Mythologie der alten Völker, besonders der Griechen* in 1810-12. Reinhardt might have inquired whether in Basel Nietzsche had become acquainted with Bachofen, whose work might well have influenced him. According to Reinhardt, Rohde would have written his great book *Psyche* without the influence of his early friend. Perhaps that is true; perhaps the spirit of the time made it inevitable

---

[27] In his introduction to the reprint of that year.
[28] See n.12 above.

that the anthropologically minded scholars of the Cambridge school should approach Greek antiquity in the light of Durkheim's teaching; and that the course of classical studies should be transformed by the great movement that culminates, or seems to us to culminate, in *The Greeks and the Irrational* of E.R. Dodds.[29] But the man who first set this in motion was Nietzsche; and by that alone he acquired an importance in the history of philology far greater than that which his positive discoveries of fact could have won him. More significantly still, Nietzsche's writings show an unprecedented insight into the nature of divinity as the Greeks conceived it. The scholars of modern times who have best apprehended this are Reinhardt himself and Walter F. Otto.

Anyone who shares the view of Nietzsche's importance in the history of scholarship which I have put forward must accord some interest to the criticisms of scholarship and scholars which are scattered through his writings, particularly those of the early period. We see these criticisms beginning to take shape in the notes for a course entitled 'Introduction to Philology', which Nietzsche delivered in the summer of 1871. This remarkable document may be read in the Musarion edition;[30] the criticisms of contemporary practice which it implies arise naturally out of the subject-matter, and lack the almost waspish sting they carry in Nietzsche's later writings. Above all, Nietzsche insists that the philologist must love his subject; in listing the three requirements of philology: a bent for teaching, 'delight in antiquity' ('Freude am Altertume'), and pure desire for knowledge, he clearly gives special consideration to the second. Modern classical education, he ruefully remarks, is designed to produce *scholars*; how different that is from the purpose of the Greeks themselves! There is something comic, he says, about the relation of scholars to the great poets.[31] The most important thing, and the hardest, is to enter into the life of antiquity and to feel the difference. He warns against overspecialisation, and insists that the acquisition of knowledge is a means and not an end; in defiance of the spirit of his time, he pleads for concentration on the real classics, which have a permanent value. In a magnificent passage he insists upon the essential simplicity of the Greeks; they are 'naiv', he says, and this word connotes both simplicity and depth.

In the essay on the future of German cultural institutions of 1872,[32]

---

[29] E.R. Dodds, *The Greeks and the Irrational* (Berkeley 1951).

[30] *MusA*, II, 337f.

[31] Nietzsche would have enjoyed the poem of Yeats that begins, 'Bald heads, forgetful of their sins.'

[32] *WKG*, III-2, 133f.

Nietzsche attacks philologists as being unable to teach their pupils art and culture. In the essay of 1874 on the uses and disadvantages of history, very similar arguments are directed against historians. The four *Untimely Meditations*, published between 1873 and 1876, were originally to have numbered eight. The fifth was to have been entitled 'We Philologists'; a number of the notes collected for it have appeared in the Colli-Montinari edition.[33]

From this early date in his career, Nietzsche, more than any German writer of his time, condemned the vulgarisation and brutalisation of many elements of German life and culture which acquired such frightening momentum from the foundation of the Empire in 1871. He was now beginning to emancipate himself from Wagner's influence; and the more he did so, the more scathingly he attacked the crude and stupid nationalism which saw in the triumph over France convincing evidence of the superiority of German culture. He saw that this affected science and scholarship, just as much as it affected trade, commerce, and technology. Dominated by the prevailing materialism, scholars had become fatally ambitious to emulate the positive and concrete achievements of natural science. The passionate devotion to antiquity that still marked German scholarship had become mechanised; and most members of the vast learned profession that had been created were devoted to the accumulation of facts for their own sake. So far as it concerns German classical scholarship, Nietzsche's criticism finds a striking parallel in Housman's inaugural lecture given at Cambridge in 1911.[34] Yet what Nietzsche says about his own profession is only a part of his criticism of German culture in general.

The preference accorded to classical studies, he says in 'We Philologists,' is due to ignorance of the rest of antiquity; to false idealisation of the humanity of the Greeks, who were really less humane than Indians or Chinese; to the arrogance of schoolmasters; to the tradition of admiration of the Greeks inherited from Rome; to prejudice for, or against, Christianity; to the belief that where men have so long dug there must be gold; to aptitude and knowledge

---

[33] *WKG*, IV-1, 87f. The merit of having translated a selection from these notes and of having drawn attention to their importance belongs to William Arrowsmith, 'Nietzsche on Classics and Classicists,' *Arion*, 2 no. 1 (Spring, 1963), 5-18 and 2, no. 2 (Summer, 1963), 5-27. His brief introductions to them are admirably vigorous, but devote too much of their limited space to the negative side of Nietzsche's attitude. Nietzsche's views on this topic have to be considered in their historical context and in some detail; otherwise there is danger of their being invoked to give a charter to people who wish to write about the classics, but who lack the ability or the industry to equip themselves to do so competently.

[34] Published under the alien title 'The Confines of Criticism' (Cambridge 1969).

derived from philological studies. In sum, it derives from ignorance, false prejudice, wrong inferences, and professional interest; he speaks also of escapism, 'Flucht aus der Wirklichkeit.' The grounds for this preference have one by one been removed, and one day people will notice this. Many philologists, he thought, had drifted into the profession without being really suited to it. Such people were unfit to teach others, because they had no real conception of the object of their study; if they could grasp the real nature of antiquity, they would turn from it in horror. He accused scholars of lack of respect for antiquity, excess of respect for one another, having ideas above their station, sentimentality, and loose rhetoric. Classical culture, he said, was for the few; there ought to be special police to stop people from being bad scholars, as there ought to be a special police to stop people from playing Beethoven badly. He thought people would get more out of the subject if they began the study late in life. He quotes with approval Wolf's remark that people who are not scholars may understand the ancients better, if they have a real affinity with them, than people who are. The most notable products of our study of the ancient world, he said, are not scholars, but Goethe, Wagner and Schopenhauer; later in his life, he might have said Goethe, Leopardi and himself.

What comment can be made on these criticisms? It is easy to see that Nietzsche became dissatisfied with philology partly because it gave no scope for his philosophic and prophetic mission. *The Birth of Tragedy* turned out to be not a work of scholarship, but an imaginative construction; and Nietzsche was right when he finally took the advice of Wilamowitz and gave up his profession. But to say that hardly disposes of Nietzsche's criticisms. It must be recognised that many other persons, by no means prejudiced against the subject, have held that, at the time when Nietzsche began his professorial career, philology was passing through a difficult period, when one wave of inspiration had become exhausted and the next had not yet gathered strength.

In the event, philology made a remarkable recovery, thanks to the great generation of Nietzsche's contemporaries. With the example of Mommsen to guide them, and by an immense *tour de force* of comprehensive learning, men like Eduard Meyer, Hermann Diels, Eduard Schwartz, Friedrich Leo, and above all Wilamowitz broke down the barriers between specialised compartments of the subject. Wilamowitz in a lecture at Oxford[35] once said that as Odysseus in the underworld had to give the ghosts blood before they could speak to

[35] Ulrich von Wilamowitz-Möllendorff, *Greek Historical Writing, and Apollo: Two Lectures Delivered before the University of Oxford, June 3 and 4, 1908*, trans. Gilbert Murray (Oxford 1908), 25.

him, so the philologist had to give the spirits blood – his own – before they would reveal their secrets. By the astonishing vitality of his teaching and writing, and with the aid of his colleagues, Wilamowitz was able for a time to put off the crisis of philology. But throughout his lifetime the dangers indicated by Nietzsche were drawing nearer.

During the 1920s Werner Jaeger tried to institutionalise the now evident reaction against historicism by proclaiming the need for a 'third humanism' in the wake of the two revivals of interest in ancient culture of the past. Philology was not to renounce the burden of comprehensive learning imposed on it by the nineteenth century; how could it, without degenerating into mere *belles lettres*? But it was to publish its official divorce from history; and while it went about its business, it was to keep reminding itself that it was all the time reflecting on its purpose. So Jaeger rewrote the intellectual history of the Greeks from the stand-point of culture conceived as education, and produced one of the most respected, and one of the dullest, learned books of our century.

Bruno Snell in a famous review of Jaeger[36] truly said that the business of philology is not to proclaim new humanisms, but to investigate and present antiquity with honesty and truth. The self-conscious attitude recommended by Jaeger has fortunately not caught on. But to do in our time what Snell demands is not easy. Unless the noble conception of the unified study of the ancient world as a whole is to be abandoned, a large labour force is needed; and in the nature of things most of these labourers must be mere technicians. Can we do without them?

Nietzsche was prepared to sacrifice the concept of antiquity as a whole, and to concentrate attention on the really creative period of Greek thought. Wilamowitz asked, 'What can we do for philology?'; Nietzsche preferred to ask, 'What can philology do for us?' To the classicists, with whom Nietzsche's standpoint has so much in common, the ancients had supplied a pattern, an ideal standard of excellence; for the historicists with their relativistic outlook no such thing could exist. Even those who do not accept the notion of an ideal pattern may feel that we must get from antiquity what we can; and in modern conditions, which have notably reduced our labour force, that is what we are being forced to do. Even in modern conditions, and in our new awareness of the dangers of historicism, we cannot renounce the idea of *Altertumswissenschaft* as a unity; if only as an ideal notion, it must still be kept in mind. But scholarship involves a subject as well as

---

[36] *Göttingische Gelehrte Anzeigen*, 197 (1935), 329f., reprinted in *Gesammelte Schriften* (Göttingen 1966), 32f.

an object; and if our studies are to enhance the value of life, we must ask the questions which will yield the most interesting results. Often the people who ask those questions are those who, like Nietzsche, are not restricted by narrowly professional limits. Such people have to guard against reading back into the ancient world the things they want to find in it. All generations have to some extent done that, as, when we look into the past of scholarship, hindsight easily reveals. At least we can be quick to suppress movements which are still looking for what our predecessors wanted to discover, and instead look for those things in the past – real things to the best of our ability – which our own position in history makes it possible and desirable for us to find. That can be done, if it can be done at all, by him who is willing to enter in imagination completely into the life of the past, while carrying back with him as little as possible of the mental furniture of the present. In the past, we can find working models of culture and civilisation that may be of value to us when we make our own experiments. The main value of historical scholarship is that it can furnish such models to those who can make profitable use of them. Nietzsche himself was such a one. Ernst Howald[37] rightly says that Nietzsche owed nothing to philology, but much to antiquity; and in a few pages of *The Twilight of the Idols*, written in 1888, the last year of his activity,[38] Nietzsche speaks of his debt to the ancients in a tone of open-minded detachment. He acknowledges a debt to Sallust, who he says awoke his feeling for style and for the epigram as a stylistic medium, and to Horace; the sketch for this chapter in the notebooks adds Petronius.[39] To the Greeks, he says, he owes no such definite impressions; he repeats what he has written earlier, that the Greeks are more remote from us than the scholars of his day believed. We may well wonder whether he was altogether true to his earlier self at this point; but one can understand his wish to avoid the all too easy self-identification with the Greeks of so many of his contemporaries. His scepticism about Plato extends to style as well as matter; Plato, like a true decadent, wrote in too many different styles, a judgment in which he fortifies himself by quoting 'the most refined judges of taste of antiquity' – an odd way of referring to Dionysius of Halicarnassus. His relief from Plato has always been Thucydides; Thucydides, and

---

[37] Ernst Howald, *Nietzsche und die klassische Philologie* (Gotha 1920), 1. Brief as it is, Howald's lecture is necessary reading for anyone seriously interested in the subject; it well deserves to be reprinted. See also the literature quoted by Marcello Gigante in the course of his excellent remarks about Nietzsche in *La parola del passato*, 156 (1974), 15ff.

[38] *WKG*, VI-3, 148f.

[39] *WKG*, VIII-3, 436.

also Machiavelli's *Prince*, have always been close to him because of
their unconditioned will to take nothing for granted and to see reason
in reality. Thucydides, who for Nietzsche incarnates all those Sophists
whom he much preferred to Socrates and Plato, is the great
summation, the last revelation of that strong, strict, hard factuality
which lay in the instinct of the early Greeks. Plato, he says, is a
coward in the face of reality.[40]

Next, with the German classicists in mind, Nietzsche rejects all
attempts to see in the Greeks beautiful souls, golden means or other
types of perfection. Their strongest impulse was the will to power, and
all their institutions arose from safety regulations, to protect
themselves from the potentially explosive matter lying all around
them. The inner tension in a Greek state burst out in ruthless external
enmities; strength was a necessity, and so was realism.

He himself, Nietzsche claims with pride, has been the first to see the
significance of Dionysus; Burckhardt saw at once the importance of
his discovery. He pours contempt on the matter-of-fact, rationalistic
explanation of Dionysiac mysteries given by Creuzer's learned
antagonist, Christian August Lobeck. Goethe would not have
understood the mysteries; therefore Goethe did not understand the
Greeks. They signified eternal life, the eternal return of life, a
triumphant Yes to life beyond death and change; true life as the
continuance through generation, through the mysteries of sexuality.
The key to the concept of tragic feeling, misunderstood by Aristotle,
was given him, he claims, by the psychology of orgiasm. Tragedy –
and here he is correcting his own early treatment – is far removed
from the pessimism of a Schopenhauer; it is above all an affirmation of
life. Its purpose is not to free us from terror and pity nor to purge us by
allowing us to discharge these feelings, but by means of them to allow
us to participate in the eternal delight of being, that delight which
incorporates also the delight of annihilation.

It is not hard to see that in the formation of philosophy designed to
meet the needs of his own time Nietzsche made use of the work of
many modern thinkers. The influence upon him of classical antiquity
receives less attention in most current manuals; even the exhaustive
study of Charles Andler,[41] who painstakingly lists every conceivable
influence upon Nietzsche's thought, hardly does it full justice. It
would, I think, have been better apprehended if it had been easily
resolvable into the influences of individual philosophers. Thus the
love-hate relationship with Socrates which Nietzsche often mentions

[40] It must have been in unconscious memory of this remark that I wrote: 'The first
important failure of nerve was that of Plato' (*The Justice of Zeus*, 136).
[41] See n.23 above.

has received much attention; yet this is not positive but negative. The truth is that in building his philosophy Nietzsche used not so much the doctrines of any individual ancient thinkers, not even that of Heraclitus, whose thought seems to provide several striking parallels, as the religious and ethical attitude held generally in Greece down to the fifth century, and expressed, with variations, by many Greek poets, historians and thinkers. The influence of Greek ethics upon Nietzsche's ethics is, or should be, obvious. Equally undoubted, in my view, is the influence of the early Greek world outlook upon his philosophy. The Greek universe was god-controlled, but not anthropocentric; the gods granted men occasional favours, but ruthlessly held them down in their position of inferiority; it was in the face of this that heroes showed their heroism. Nietzsche's theory of tragedy contains the essence of his whole metaphysic; so that the Greek influence on this can hardly be disputed. An important difference is that the Greeks, unlike Nietzsche, believed that gods controlled the universe. But, as modern experience has shown, a metaphysic like that of Nietzsche is not necessarily atheistic.[42]

[42] Dr Peter Walker, Bishop of Ely, draws my attention to the influence of Nietzsche upon Dietrich Bonhoeffer, who even finds in Nietzsche's *Übermensch* 'many of the traits of the Christian made free, as Paul and Luther described him.' André Dumas, *Dietrich Bonhoeffer, Theologian of Reality*, trans. Robert McAfee Brown, (New York 1971), 285.

15

A.E. Housman 1

When A.E. Housman in his will expressed the wish that none of his contributions to periodicals should be reprinted, he was showing an attitude to his own writings that is not uncommon among learned men. A scholar often prefers that his writings, particularly his early writings, should not be reprinted, at least without his being given an opportunity to correct them. But potential readers of such collections on the whole prefer them to appear uncorrected, unless the corrections are clearly marked as such. The editors of *The Classical Papers of A.E. Housman* have rightly confined themselves to the correction of misprints, and they have added references to the editions of works cited which are now in general use.

One must sympathise with Housman in that his request has been disregarded, and one may wish that this had not happened in the lifetime of his literary executor; but one can hardly blame the publishers. The demand for the book undoubtedly exists; if an author's wishes had always to be respected, the *Aeneid* itself would have been lost and, as the editors remind us, Housman himself prefaced to his London inaugural lecture the words of Horace, 'nescit vox missa reverti'. The three volumes are handsomely produced, and have been edited by two well-qualified scholars, who have added a list of contents and valuable indexes of passages and of subjects discussed. The publication has atoned to scholars, if not to Housman's ghost, for the undeniably useful but in some respects unsatisfactory selection of Housman's prose which came from the same publishers twelve years ago.

The best account of Housman's career in scholarship is given by A.S.F. Gow in the memoir which he published in the year of Housman's death; a brilliant short appreciation may be found in a talk broadcast by the least unlike Housman of modern Latinists, D.R. Shackleton Bailey (published in *The Listener* on 26 March 1959). Now

* A review of *The Classical Papers of A.E. Housman* edited by J. Diggle and F.R.D. Goodyear in *The Times Literary Supplement*, 9 February 1973.

we can read the articles and notes in their order of publication and so follow the author's development.

Housman did not attain immediately to his full power. From the start he writes clearly, elegantly and wittily; from the start his knowledge is impressive and his ingenuity remarkable. But though they contain some brilliant suggestions, the pieces in the first volume, first published between 1882 and 1897, seldom show the quality singled out by Professor Shackleton Bailey as most singular in Housman: 'the unremitting, passionate zeal to see each one of the innumerable problems in his text not as others had presented it or as he might have preferred it to appear but exactly as it was'.

The earliest article specially praised by Gow is a series on Ovid's *Heroides* published in 1897, when Housman was thirty-eight. Before that time Housman published a number of articles on Greek authors, particularly the tragedians; all this work is learned and clever, but very little of it is right. The rhetorical manner which makes it look as if only one approach to a problem – the author's – is worthy of a rational man, is not well suited to the treatment of Aeschylus and Sophocles, whose corrupt texts are made still more difficult by the lack of material for comparison.

After the late 1890s, Housman wrote little about Greek, except when tempted by a new papyrus, though he contributed effectively to the emendation of the new fragments of Bacchylides, Menander, Callimachus and, most particularly, of Pindar. When asked why he had ceased to write on Greek, he said it was because he had come to despair of attaining excellence in both languages. In Greek the law of diminishing returns has set in, and problems are not easily solved with finality. But Housman's younger contemporary, John Jackson, produced a remarkable series of emendations of the tragedians; and, if Housman had chosen to go on with Greek, he would doubtless have improved greatly on his early attempts. All the same, he was wise to prefer Latin, which offered a field better suited to the peculiar nature of his gifts.

The second and third volumes contain an extraordinarily large quantity of detailed work of the highest quality. Few people now living are qualified to praise it, but one may record the impression that hardly any scholar has left a collection of textual notes of similar size whose average quality, over a long period, may be compared to what we find here. The early pieces were learned and ingenious. In the later ones the erudition is enormous, covering every topic which might illuminate the matter in hand, and extending over the difficult and rarely mastered fields of ancient astronomy and astrology. The ingenuity is as great as earlier, or greater; but now it comes to be controlled by a sure and steady judgment not often developed by the specially ingenious.

The second volume contains notable articles on Lucilius, on Statius' *Silvae*, on Martial and on Persius; the third has superb pieces about Ovid (particularly the *Ibis*), Martial again, and Statius' *Thebaid*, besides the famous papers on 'The Application of Thought to Textual Criticism' and on 'Prosody and Method'. Yet articles and notes, because they deal not with a complete text but with a selected problem, give less opportunity to appreciate the quality singled out by Professor Shackleton Bailey than do the commentaries. No one can form a proper notion of the greatness of Housman without working through the *Manilius*, and then comparing with the text of the commentary the text printed in the *editio minor* of 1932. Here even brilliant suggestions are relegated to the foot of the page or dropped altogether if they do not satisfy the editors's standards with regard to probability.

Why did Housman, whose verse belongs so entirely to the nineteenth century, choose in his scholarship to continue an eighteenth-century tradition and concentrate almost exclusively on textual criticism? In nineteenth-century Germany the tradition in question, represented there until his death in 1848 by Gottfried Hermann, a very much greater scholar than his English contemporary Porson, was replaced by the new concept of *Altertumswissenschaft*, the study of the ancient world as a whole. Textual studies took their place together with history, archaeology, and the new discipline of comparative philology and with other ancillary disciplines; and the study of ancient literature no longer stopped at the constitution of the text. Wilamowitz, born in the year of Hermann's death and so eleven years older than Housman, wrote commentaries on works of literature in which every branch of the study of antiquity was used to illuminate the text in hand. He made important contributions to textual criticism, but he did not shrink from attempting literary interpretation and nothing that he wrote is dull. Leo, three years younger than Wilamowitz, brought out the first volume of a history of Latin literature not only learned but admirably written and exceedingly intelligent, in which the central problems, including purely literary ones, are discussed in a way that even now, more than fifty years after the author's death, commands the attention of any person seriously interested in the subject. Housman was intimately acquainted with the new German scholarship of the nineteenth century; he more than once expressed admiration for Wilamowitz. Why did he stay outside the movement that revolutionised his subject?

That he did so is greatly to be regretted, for English scholars after 1830 failed entirely to profit from the momentous developments in Germany. The triumph of the new scholarship in that country coincided with the moment when the ancient universities of England became absorbed in teaching to the virtual exclusion of research. The opinion of enlightened persons like the great German educational reformer, Wilhelm von Humboldt, that the two activities were necessary to each other was not comprehended in the world of Jowett. Mark Pattison wrote that in the Oxford of his day young MAs of talent abounded, but that each was rapidly set to turning some wheel in the vast machinery of cram. British scholars did indeed attempt the general interpretation of the ancient world, but with few exceptions – most of them, like Grote, outside the universities – they did so in a way that did not increase understanding. In the inaugural lecture which Housman gave at Cambridge in 1911 he ridiculed their efforts. They took it for granted, he observed, that the taste of the ancients was identical with their own Victorian romantic taste; they believed, in his words, that 'the secret of the classical spirit is open to anyone who has a fervent admiration for the second-best parts of Tennyson'. Many of their German contemporaries suffered, as Nietzsche pointed out, from a similar delusion; but most of these were at least active in adding to our factual knowledge of antiquity.

Gilbert Murray, himself a minor poet in the late Victorian manner, assumed that the poetical intentions of such a writer as Euripides were not very different from his own. Housman also was a romantic poet; but he never for a moment suffered from such delusions. He saw that the so-called literary criticism of classical authors in terms of romantic canons was altogether worthless. But why, instead of trying to overthrow it by introducing a kind of criticism that took account of the poetical intention of the authors criticised, did he take refuge in asserting that literary criticism was no exercise for a scholar?

Housman throughout his life upheld the narrow restriction of the term 'poetry' to verse productive, in his experience, of particular emotional effects. That definition excluded most of the poets on whom he worked, poets like Ovid, Lucan, Juvenal and Manilius, whose stock-in-trade was wit, elegance, all kinds of rhetoric. Housman's textual criticism of these poets shows that he was supremely capable of appreciating these qualities, which he justly complains were better perceived by the critics of the seventeenth and eighteenth centuries than by their supposedly more learned successors of his own age. Since by Housman's romantic definition of poetry these poets were not 'true poets', one can see why he should not have thought it his duty to explain their literary technique. But it would not be hard to show that these same qualities also formed part of the attributes of poets whom Housman would have agreed to be worthy of the name. Yet Housman equates literary criticism, except as practised by a few rare spirits like Lessing and Arnold, with the wearying repetition of sentimental adulation.

Scholarship, he tells us in his Cambridge inaugural, not to mention the London lecture of 1892 which he later called 'rhetorical and not wholly sincere', is a department not of literature but of science. Yet later in the same lecture, when he is warning against the tendency to practise scholarship mechanically – which he rightly saw as one of the greatest dangers that may threaten scholars – he says that 'the criticism and interpretation of the classical texts is not an exact science'. 'Its subject-matter,' he continues, 'is a series of phenomena which are the result of the play of the human mind ... To deal with the mutable and evasive you want no cut and dried method.' Exactly; even textual criticism requires not merely exact knowledge of language and technique, but a measure of tact and intuition – a measure, in fact, of literary understanding. Housman cannot have it both ways; the hard and fast barrier which his romantic dogmatism seeks to erect between textual criticism and literary analysis cannot be maintained between two territories which shade so imperceptibly into one another.

Housman, like Nietzsche, deserves our admiration for having ridiculed the false assumption that Victorian taste was like that of the Greeks and Romans; and he was right to remind scholars that the possession of a powerful technical equipment does not by itself convey a gift for literary discrimination. But does that exempt professional teachers of the classics, whose duty is to explain a difficult literature, from any duty but that of constituting the text? Their task requires not only factual and linguistic knowledge, but sympathetic understanding of beliefs and attitudes unfamiliar to the modern man; and if they are to perform it adequately they must have the courage to try to achieve both. Their task is not easy. Many people who have taste and understanding are hampered by inadequate knowledge of the facts; many learned people suffer from an insufficiency of taste and understanding. But a knowledge of the difficulties of the enterprise ought not to discourage a true scholar from attempting both halves of what his choice of a career requires.

People often say that Housman's romantic poetry was a kind of protest against the austerity of his life of scholarship. From a different point of view, Housman's life of scholarship can be seen as a kind of protest against the tyranny of 'sub-Tennysonian taste' which he from his earliest years found all around him. Talking about scholars and their personal literary tastes, he wrote in his Cambridge inaugural:

> Our first task is to get rid of them, and to acquire, if we can, by humility
> and self-repression, the tastes of the classic; not to come stamping into the
> library of Apollo Palatine without so much as wiping our shoes on the
> doormat, and cover the floor with the print of feet which have waded
> through the miry clay of the nineteenth century into the horrible pit of the
> twentieth.

Housman read widely in several literatures and keenly appreciated
the quality of many different kinds of verse, even though his romantic
dogmatism, tenacious as a Calvinist's belief in hell-fire, always
prevented him from according any but a little of it the title of true
poetry. As the reader of these three amazing volumes admires the
writer's powerful intellect and revels in his wit, he cannot help asking
himself what would have happened had Housman by some lucky
accident ever thrown off the chains of the rigid romantic prejudice
which restricted his attitude to literature. If he had been able to
employ his strong and supple intelligence in unison with his
imaginative powers, might he not have become a major instead of a
minor poet? Might he not, instead of dogmatically upholding the
critical attitudes of Arnold, have come some way towards those later
voiced by Eliot? If Housman had rightly appreciated Leopardi, an
author not to be understood if he is considered simply as a romantic,
or if he had come upon Nietzsche at an early age, the thing might have
happened. Could he not, as he does in one of his most startling poems,
have shot the devil? But perhaps events in his own private life so
checked his emotional development as to rule out such possibilities.

Nowadays Housman is from time to time abused by people who
wish to insist upon the importance of the literary study of the classics.
When such people find it necessary to abuse Housman we usually find
that they are ignorant or slipshod scholars. Housman is an object of
cult among a few young lions, who with a jacobite-like gallantry
which one cannot help admiring a little – unless, perhaps, one
happens to be a pupil of one of them – claim that a scholar's chief or
only duty is to purify his authors' texts. Some of his tirades against
other scholars share with the witticisms of F.E. Smith the annoying
quality, not their author's fault, of being specially appreciated by
people not usually sensitive to forms of humour less promptly to be
apprehended. We should guard against allowing any of these things to
prevent us from appreciating and admiring Housman.

16

A.E. Housman 2

There is, as Richard Graves points out, no general biography of Housman. The books about him by Laurence Housman, Grant Richards and Percy Withers are valuable, because these men knew Housman and could describe him: but they are not biographies. George Watson's *A.E. Housman: A Divided Life* is more like one, but it is not quite one; of Norman Marlow and Maude Hawkins I say nothing. The most satisfying book about Housman is A.S.F. Gow's *Housman: A Sketch*, but as Mr Graves says, its aims are limited, since it is mainly concerned with Housman's scholarship.

Mr Graves's book takes us through Housman's life, stage by stage. It gives full, rather too full, details about the Housman family; it gives much information about the Patent Office, University College and Cambridge periods, using printed sources and adding some material from unprinted papers and from personal communications. A few interesting facts and good stories appear here for the first time. Mr Graves treats Housman with sympathy, is enthusiastic about his poetry, and tries hard to do justice to his scholarship. The disappearance of the taboo on writing frankly about homosexuality makes things easier for him. He has worked hard and seems accurate, though there is an unfortunate mix-up on page 89, where I do not think he means to say that Housman was in love with Professor A.W. Pollard. His prose is clear, though not very distinguished, and he has excellent intentions: so that one is sorry to have to say that his book is only mildly interesting.

The truth is that although it is good to have a general biography of Housman, it was not a particularly urgent need. The main facts have long been known: the early loss of his mother and his faith, the failure in Greats, the relationships with Moses and Adalbert Jackson. One could write a more interesting book by cutting biographical data to a minimum and concentrating on Housman's work. One might then

* A review of *A.E. Housman* by Richard Graves in the *London Review of Books*, October 1979.

place his poetry in its historical context and assess it critically, taking account of the literary attitudes expressed in the London Introductory and Leslie Stephen Lectures. The author of such a study would find it helpful to have some understanding of the scholarly work which was the main business of Housman's life, since the relation of this activity to his poetry is of great interest.

Mr Graves quotes copiously from the poems, and speaks of them with enthusiasm, though not always with approval. But since he wishes to introduce a new generation to the beauties of Housman's poetry, enthusiasm is not quite enough: we need critical evaluation, and we do not find it here. Mr Graves is a biographer, not a critic, and may plead that in the case of a romantic poet like Housman it is legitimate to make biographical inferences from his poems: but one becomes infuriated by his unvarying assumption that every poem may be related to some incident in the poet's life. For example, 'The rainy Pleiads wester' is described as 'a love poem about Moses Jackson'. A group of poems about war, says Mr Graves, 'taken together, show the complexity of Housman's attitude. On the one hand, he writes admiringly of bravery; on the other, he cannot but feel the tragedy when brave men die, and that they have missed their real purpose in life.' That gives an idea of how much complexity Mr Graves is able to perceive. His nadir is reached on page 240, where an awful stanza that contains the line 'Be good to the lad that loves you true' is quoted with admiration, forming the peroration to a chapter.

Mr Graves's treatment of the question of influences is correspondingly superficial. He quotes Housman as saying that he was conscious of three models, the Border Ballads, Heine, and Shakespeare's songs, and he names other influences: the Bible and Arnold are the two most important of those he names, and Hymns Ancient and Modern and Hardy the two most important of those he omits. But he is interested principally in echoes, and cannot show how each of these influences affected Housman. The strongest influence, not only because the echoes are so frequent – G.B.A. Fletcher's long list in Richards's book could be expanded – is surely Heine: compared to his, the influence of Shakespeare and the Ballads is remote. But instead of critical discussion of such questions, Mr Graves offers only lengthy and repetitive descriptions, without explanation, of Housman's rhetorical attitude of cosmic despair. It does not occur to him to set it against the cosmic despair of a poet such as Leopardi – a process that might be revealing.

Mr Graves's section about Housman's reading is interesting, though heavily indebted to Grant Richards. Housman read Proust and James; he enjoyed Colette; he much admired the work of Edith

Wharton. Mr Graves finds it surprising that he neglected the opportunity to cultivate the society of E.M. Forster: my guess would be that he did not think much more highly of Forster's work that he did of Galsworthy's. The only Lawrence he is recorded to have read is *Lady Chatterley*, from which, like the unlearned readers who had heard that his *Manilius* contained a scurrilous preface, he doubtless hoped to extract a low enjoyment. Mr Graves is artlessly surprised at his having read Heine in the original, not realising that any serious classical scholar has to read a great deal of German: but Housman seems to have read very little German literature for pleasure. One wonders if he ever tried Nietzsche, who might have interested him greatly. He had an affinity with Kipling. One of the most interesting things Mr Graves tells is that in the text of 'Heriot's Ford' in his copy of Kipling's poems, Housman crossed out the last six verses and changed 'your might' to 'the night' in v.I 1.4 and 'judgment follows' to 'darkness gathers' in v.2, 1.4.

Mr Graves records with satisfaction the triumphant reception given to the lecture on *The Name and Nature of Poetry* in 1933, in which Housman declared that 'the peculiar function of poetry was not to transmit thought but to transfuse emotion,' and asserted 'that poetry had nothing to do with intellect.' Only Leavis, we are told, disapproved, and that because he construed the lecture as a personal attack upon himself.

Mr Graves makes a valiant effort to do justice to Housman's scholarship, but altogether lacks equipment for the task. He is aware that Housman concentrated on textual criticism, but he has little notion of the distinctive qualities of his work in that domain. 'Sensitivity,' he writes, 'combined with his knowledge of what it was to be a poet and to write poetry, particularly fitted Housman for the task of emending the Latin poets.' That is in a sense true, but Mr Graves's way of expressing himself shows that he is not aware that the Latin poets whom Housman emended wrote a very different kind of poetry from his own, or that sensitivity would have been of little use without extensive and exact knowledge. When he wants to tell us what a good scholar Housman was he quotes the late John Carter's comment on the testimonials supplied by various scholars when Housman was candidate for the Chair of Latin at University College, London. 'Perhaps only those conversant with the trades-union of Academe,' wrote Carter, 'can appreciate to the full the exceptional character of such a volley of endorsements.' Mr Graves might have made better use of Gow; and although he quotes the excellent talk on Housman broadcast by D.R. Shackleton Bailey on the 100th anniversary of his birth and published in *The Listener* for 7 May 1959, he quotes it only at second hand and cannot, I think, have read it.

Mr Graves applies a mild variety of the psychological technique favoured by so many biographers. 'Alfred,' he writes, 'had been brought up by a weak father and a powerful mother, and it is reasonable to suppose that his unusually strong relationship with his mother had led to an early development of the more feminine aspects of his psychological make-up – a development which may indeed be largely responsible for the sensitivity of his poetry and the imaginative insight of his textual scholarship.' Wondering why Housman chose to call his Mr Hearsay Terence, Mr Graves ventures, unusually, upon a daring speculation. 'The Greek poet Terence,' he writes (Terence was an African who wrote Latin, but no matter), 'was brought to Rome as a slave, and lived there in exile; no doubt Housman, thinking of his own exile in London from the world of his childhood, saw some similarity in their situations.'

Mr Graves is surely right to point out that the failure in Greats, due, it would seem, to youthful arrogance and over-confidence, must have sharpened the extreme ambition which drove Housman to apply himself to scholarship with such an exceptional degree of thoroughness. Later, he thinks, Housman realised that he was homosexual, and this, together with the consequent realisation that Moses Jackson was not, combined with the failure in Greats to drive him in upon himself. It is to Mr Graves's credit that he does not exaggerate the bitter element in Housman's character. He shows that in the company of people whom he knew and trusted Housman could be a delightful and entertaining companion. Although his pupils of both sexes were often repelled by his reserve, his colleagues both at University College and at Cambridge found him a congenial member of their society, and with some of them, like Arthur Platt and Andrew Gow, he was on easy terms.

It is interesting to learn that on the trips abroad which he began to make after his appointment to the London Chair Housman was able to find satisfaction for his sexual needs in a manner he would not have ventured to attempt in England. At home, he was a model of propriety, sternly rebuking Grant Richards for returning through the English post a Tauchnitz volume he had lent him. 'Even in the Cambridge of Forster, Brooke and Keynes,' writes Mr Graves, Housman 'felt imprisoned': but he accumulated a large collection of curiosa, as has been known since part of his library was sold in Oxford. Mr Graves reveals that a document in Housman's writing found among his papers contains 'what seem to be references to a number of male prostitutes, including sailors and ballet-dancers, together with a mark which indicated the value of their

services, and a marginal note in which Alfred refers with some
satisfaction to the large number of these homosexual encounters
which he had enjoyed in the space of little over a fortnight'. We must
note the 'seem to be', and be cautious. I remember hearing, though I
cannot vouch for the story's authenticity, of a notebook, containing
numbers, found among Housman's papers. An American scholar
worked on it for many years, decoding a number of poems thought to
resemble Housman's, only to be made aware that the numbers were
actually those of the dogs which, during his afternoon walks, the
Professor had contrived to kick. In early years, Housman often went to
Venice, but the gondolier Andrea seems in the end to have proved
wearisome; the fine poem about the fall of the Campanile seems to
have indicated a recognition, if I may employ Mr Graves' method,
that Andrea could not console the poet for the loss of Moses Jackson.
After that, Housman went usually to Paris. Sometimes he was
accompanied by mysterious companions; once when he was in France
and Richards proposed one of their gastronomic expeditions,
Housman replied that he was travelling with a companion whom
Richards would not get on with. Housman sent a copy of *The
Shropshire Lad* to Wilde, who was delighted with the present; Mr
Graves is not the first to detect Housman's influence in *The Ballad of
Reading Gaol*.

Housman came at the end of the Romantic movement, when it was
already moribund. His verse was simple and easy to understand, and
was therefore extravagantly praised by many people whose taste in
poetry was conventional and who were incapable of appreciating
more distinguished work by writers who had turned their backs on
Romanticism. In his London Introductory Lecture of 1892, and again
in his Leslie Stephen Lecture of 1933, Housman expressed in its most
extreme form the romantic dogma that real art is concerned simply to
excite emotion, and has nothing whatsoever to do with intellect. Even
in 1933, the more critical section of the public was aware that this
theory had come under heavy fire and had had its credit seriously
undermined. It is not surprising that Housman's critical
pronouncements, and his poetry also, were strongly attacked by
several formidable antagonists.

Nothing could better illustrate the weakness of Housman's critical
position than the strange difference between his poetry and his
scholarship. Housman's skill in the editing of texts was principally
exercised on writers powerfully influenced by rhetoric. Like the
English poets of the school of Pope, whom Housman regarded as
being no true poets, they had as their stock-in-trade wit, polish,
elegance. Some set much store by the content as well as the manner of

their work: Lucretius, whom Housman particularly admired, happened to be of all things a didactic poet. The cliché that Housman took refuge in his poetry from the austere world of scholarship is false as well as stale, for the exact opposite is the truth. When Housman was exercising his profession, he could indulge the love of wit, rhetoric and persuasive exposition which his learned work displays: all these things were proscribed by the stern laws of extreme romanticism, as rigid as the decrees of his own fate-bound stoic universe, which he bowed down to. Housman often denied that Manilius, to whom he devoted the main effort of his working life, was more than a mediocre poet. In fact, by the canons of his own kind of art, he is a poet of considerable merit: I wish someone would reprint an article in the *Spectator* in which the late Darsie Gillie demonstrated this effectively. Housman also did brilliant work on Ovid and Lucan, of whose high quality he must, even if subconsciously, have been keenly aware.

Housman claimed that the rarest of gifts was that of literary criticism: once in a while there arose a Lessing or an Arnold, but ordinary men had better not attempt anything so difficult. Mr Graves repeats the well-known story of how Housman, lecturing in Cambridge, carefully dealt with the textual problems of the seventh ode of Horace's fourth Book, and then said: 'I should like to spend the last few minutes considering this ode simply as poetry.' His way of doing that was to read the Latin, and then his own beautiful romantic translation, and after that to blurt out in embarrassed fashion, 'I regard that as the most beautiful poem in ancient literature,' and to leave the room. He did not think it necessary to explain why he felt this about the poem, and seemed distressed at having touched publicly on an emotional matter.

It is true that in Housman's time much of what passed for literary criticism was sentimental adulation. Classical scholars were among the worst offenders in this respect. People with romantic taste took it for granted that the ancients also had it: Gilbert Murray, seven years Housman's junior and gifted with an unusual flair for Greek, won immense applause for rendering Greek tragedy into Swinburnian verse. Dominated though he was by the tyranny of Romanticism, Housman was too intelligent to share this delusion. In the Cambridge Inaugural Lecture which was delivered in 1911 but not published until 1969, he ridiculed the prevalent opinion that 'the secret of the classical spirit is open to anyone who has a fervent admiration for the second-best parts of Tennyson'. His reaction to that kind of literary criticism was to avoid literary criticism altogether: it seems not to have occurred to him that it might be possible to write literary criticism in a different way.

Mr Graves alludes to an essay written many years ago in which John Wain says of Housman: 'His stock of ideas was tiny; his human responsiveness, after early life, almost nil; his general intelligence poor.' Anyone who reads Mr Graves's book will be inclined to doubt all these propositions, particularly the last; anyone acquainted with Housman's learned work and able to understand it will dismiss them with derision, as I have no doubt Mr Wain himself would now do. Housman was a man of the greatest intellectual ability, so that there is something tragic about his failure to attempt the great deed of breaking through the ring of fire with which Romanticism had encircled the sleeping Brünnhilde of the critical intelligence applied to literature. Had his emotional life not been stunted by early misfortune, he might have been capable of the attempt. Perhaps a latent consciousness of this conspired with other frustrations to make him seek relief in writing what Auden called 'savage footnotes on unjust editions'. Even the greatest admirer of his scholarship must admit that there is something unbalanced about much of his polemic: as a distinguished Cambridge scholar told Mr Graves, his influence on Latin studies has not been entirely beneficial.

Housman's poetry was greatly overrated by the latest survivors of the Romantic tradition, though never by himself. The late Cyril Connolly, during an exchange in the *New Statesman* soon after Housman's death, now conveniently reprinted in Christopher Ricks's Housman volume in the series '20th-Century Views', drew attention to many weaknesses: but if one can accept them on their own terms, a fair number of his poems surely stand up. Eliot, whose surprisingly sympathetic review of *The Name and Nature of Poetry* gave Housman pleasure, certainly held this view. On the only occasion on which I met Eliot, I told him that Grant Richards had recorded Housman's admiration for his own work. Eliot seemed surprised and greatly pleased; he told me that Housman had attended all his Clark Lectures, but with a face so impassive that he had no idea whether or not Housman had approved. Then he mentioned some of his favourite poems of Housman. He spoke of 'Her strong enchantments failing', and remarked that the penultimate line of the stanza of 'Fancy's Knell' made against the notion that Housman had not a subtle ear. If Housman had been able to effect a junction between his poetic and his critical self, if like the mutinous Ned in one of his finest poems – how characteristic that when he submitted *Last Poems* to J.W. Mackail for criticism, 'Hell Gate' should have been the one he had most doubts about! – he had found the courage to shoot the devil, might he have become a major poet, instead of a minor poet who was also a great scholar?

17

Gilbert Murray

About a hundred years ago – he did not know whether it was in 1879 or 1880 – an argumentative red-haired Australian boy entered Merchant Taylors' School, then in its old buildings in Charterhouse Square. He was to become a universally respected figure, not only the main propagandist for Greek studies for more than half a century but a leading Liberal and a powerful advocate of the League of Nations. Half in and half out of the academic world, he was the friend of many celebrated persons; of Bernard Shaw and Bertrand Russell, of William Archer and Sybil Thorndike, of Asquith and H.A.L. Fisher. His translations of Greek drama were staged successfully over a long period; during his lifetime they sold nearly 400,000 copies. He received the Order of Merit and the German order *Pour le Mérite*; he came near to being appointed British Ambassador in Washington; a lifelong atheist, he was buried in Westminster Abbey.

It would be idle to pretend that his fame had suffered no diminution since his death. Gladstonian Liberalism is a thing of the past, and its values are commonly derided, even by those who are in a sense its spiritual descendants. Even during his lifetime the famous translations were devastatingly attacked, and they are now seldom read. His academic work, like that of most scholars after a generation or so, is in large measure superseded, and I know gifted young scholars to whom it means little, even though it helped to make

*Given as Jane Ellen Harrison Memorial Lecture at Newnham College, Cambridge, on 8 February 1980; a version has also been given at Merchant Taylors' School, and to the Academy of Israel in Jerusalem. In general, see: *Essays in Honour of Gilbert Murray*, ed. J.A.K. Thomson and A.J. Toynbee (1936); Gilbert Murray, *An Unfinished Autobiography, with contributions by his friends* (foreword by A.J. Toynbee, introduction by E.R. Dodds, reprinted from *Gnomon* 29 (1957), 476f., and contributions by Jean Smith, Isobel Henderson, Sybil Thorndike and Lewis Casson, Salvador de Madariaga, Bertrand Russell, Arnold Toynbee) (1960); J.A.K. Thomson, *PBA* 43 (1957), 245f.; C.M. Bowra, *Memories, 1898-1939*, (1966) 214f.; Bertrand Russell, *Autobiography* (1971); J.G. Stewart, *Jane Harrison* (1959); K. Reinhardt, *Vermächtnis der Antik*, 2nd ed. (1966), 373f.; Isobel Henderson in *JHS* 77 (1957), xvf. and in *DNB*, s.v.

possible the work of younger writers who mean much to them. Yet I shall argue that he was a figure of uncommon interest, whose place in the political and cultural history of his time remains important. Whether that is true or not, he was an unusual and remarkable human being; and since at the end of his long life I was the last person who got to know him well, I can describe the impression that he made on me.

Gilbert Murray was born in Sydney on 2 January 1866. The ancestors of his father, Sir Terence Murray, had come to Ireland from Scotland in the seventeenth century and had become thoroughly hibernicised. They had taken part in every Irish rising against England; one had lost his father and six brothers fighting for James II against William III in the Battle of the Boyne. The Murrays remained Irish in their attitudes; radical in politics, sceptical in religion, with occasional bouts of Roman Catholicism, critical of England. Sir Terence had been a rich man, owning three fine cattle-stations; but droughts and floods destroyed his wealth, so that he ended by having to sell his splendid library. In a tough school in the bush, the young Gilbert learned to hold his own; his fierce hatred of cruelty led him into many fights. He was not an antagonist to be despised, for he was far from unathletic. He was a good enough cricketer to make 40 in the Freshmen's Match at Oxford, and when a visiting team of Australian aborigines staged a boomerang demonstration, Murray proved himself as good as any of them. He had an extraordinary sense of balance that helped him to cross Swiss glaciers on foot, and at seventy he could still walk up a ladder without using his hands. At his Sydney school he started Greek, which fascinated him from the first; the first word of it he learned was Μοῦσα.

After his father's death, his mother – born Agnes Edwards, of Welsh descent – brought him to England in January 1877; he nearly went to Malvern, but Merchant Taylors' turned out to cost less. It supplied a good classical education; Hebrew was among the subjects studied, though it was not well taught. Murray felt respect for the headmaster, Dr Baker, and for Mr Bampfylde, who taught the sixth form; but the master who taught him most was Francis Storr, who though head of the modern side was a good classical scholar in the severe Cambridge manner. 'He knew how to make us think and enjoy literature,' Murray wrote in the unfinished autobiography published after his death (p. 81), 'opening up to us the vision of another world.' Murray must have worked hard at Greek and Latin, and excelled in translation of English verse and prose into both languages, 'the one form of art', as he wrote, 'which the traditional education of the day supplied'. But he also read widely in modern literature. Mill, Spencer and Comte influenced his opinions; Shelley and Swinburne were his favourite poets, both for their style and for their matter. In 1884 he won a Merchant Taylors' Scholarship to St John's College, Oxford.

The Oxford education of that day laid a grossly exaggerated emphasis on translation from English into Greek and Latin, and proficiency in that exercise was then popularly equated with classical scholarship, as it still is by old gentlemen who write to the newspapers from clubs saying that Raymond Asquith or Ronald Knox was the finest classical scholar of his time. Most of the Oxford tutors for Moderations, the first part of the School of Literae Humaniores, thought it their main duty to coach their pupils in this accomplishment. The absurdity of this was evident, to nobody more so than to Murray, who later did much to redress the balance; but the value of the exercise to someone well qualified to profit from it is considerable, and the disrepute into which it has now fallen is to be regretted. First, it forces the student to look closely at a piece of English and consider what it really means; I remember being asked to translate an apparently brilliant account of the contradictory character of Gladstone by Lytton Strachey and being forced to the conclusion that it meant hardly anything at all, being simply a collection of cheaply paradoxical antitheses. Secondly, the shape and syntax of ancient and modern languages are so different that the student is forced to recast the content of the text for translation in his mind and to refashion it completely. Finally, he acquires a grasp of ancient grammar, syntax and metre that is not easily acquired by other methods.

A great many of the translations into Greek and Latin published by Victorian scholars are mere centos of tags taken direct from ancient writers; few will stand up to examination by professional scholars well acquainted with the models. Murray's compositions form a remarkable exception; I do not think any others, except the Greek prose versions of J.D. Denniston,[1] are their equals. For the benefit of people who know Greek, let me give a few examples. 'The world is too much with us,' writes Wordsworth; Murray renders that by Πρήγμασιν ἦ λίην προσκείμεθα. Tennyson writes:

Come down, O maid, from yonder mountain height:
What pleasure lives in height (the shepherd sang)
In height and cold, the splendour of the hills?

[1] See Sir Maurice Bowra's obituary notice of Denniston (*Proc. Brit. Acad.* xxxv, (1949), 219f.)

Murray renders that as follows:

Ἔρχεό μοι τρίλλιστε κατ' ὤρεος, ἔρχεο, κώρα·
ποῖον ἄρ' ὔψεος ἆδος ;—ὁ βωκόλος ὧδε μέλισδεν·—
ὔψεος ἢ πάχνας, ταί τ' ὤρεσι κόσμος ἕπονται ;

William James in a passage about the eternal fascination which war exercises upon human beings wrote: 'The horror makes the thrill; and when the question is of getting the extremest and supremest out of human nature, talk of expense sounds ignominious.' Murray's version runs: δι' αὐτὸ γὰρ τὸ δεινὸν καὶ τὸ λαμπρὸν γίγνεται, αἰσχρον δέ πως ἐν οἷς τῆς ἀρετῆς τὰ μέγιστα καὶ κάλλιστά ἐνεργεῖ, ἐν τοιούτοις περὶ δαπάνης ἀργυρίου λέγειν.[2] Later, when Murray taught translation at Oxford, the exercise became in his hands an educational weapon of the highest power. Not surprisingly he was supremely successful in the university scholarships and in the schools; he won the Ireland and Hertford Scholarships in his first year, added three other prizes and obtained First Classes in both Mods and Greats. At the earliest possible moment, in 1888, he was elected to a Fellowship at New College.

The Oxford of the time included a few scholars of international eminence, like Ingram Bywater, the Aristotelian expert, and D.B. Monro, the authority on Homer; but we hear nothing of Murray's personal contact with them, and perhaps he found them dry. He had a good tutor in the kind-hearted and eccentric radical T.C. Snow; he was kindly treated by the learned but silly Professor of Latin, Robinson Ellis; and he warmed to Arthur Sidgwick, a gifted if not learned scholar, an enthusiast for Greek and a convinced Liberal. At a boating party given by the Sidgwicks he met the formidable Mrs Howard, later Rosalind Countess of Carlisle. 'I hear you are a teetotaller, Mr Murray,' said she. 'Yes,' he replied, 'do you disapprove?' Perhaps Murray hoped the alarming lady did disapprove, but if so he was disappointed, for she was President of the Temperance Union. Being by birth a Stanley of Alderley, she came of a family whose men had been drunkards and its women temperance addicts since the eighteenth century. At Castle Howard she had all the priceless port poured into the moat. The villagers were drunk for months afterwards. Not surprisingly, her husband and son both showed a propensity for drink. 'Don't touch that stuff,' she called out across the table when she saw the Earl helping himself to trifle at a tenants' lunch, 'it might bring on the old craving.' Many more stories

---

[2] The first two versions are in *Nova Anthologia Oxoniensis*, ed. R. Ellis and A.D. Godley, 1899, p. 3 and p. 92; the third is on pp. 118-19 of the *Unfinished Autobiography*.

of her will be found in the memoir of her by her daughter Lady Henley.[3] In consequence of this meeting Murray was invited to Castle Howard, where he met the Countess's ardent and beautiful daughter, Lady Mary Howard. At that time, Lady Mary must have been a fascinating creature; the distressing likeness to her mother which was later to overtake her will not have been apparent. She spoke French and Italian; she was a passionate supporter of all liberal causes; and she and Murray fell immediately in love.

In 1889, at the astonishingly early age of twenty-three, Murray was appointed to succeed the famous scholar Sir Richard Jebb in the Chair of Greek at Glasgow; the salary together with Lady Mary's private means enabled them to marry. 'He is devoted to the study of literature,' wrote Henry Nettleship, Corpus Professor of Latin, in a testimonial supporting Murray's candidature,[4] 'but if I am not mistaken this devotion is the expression not merely of his taste and pleasure in reading but of his whole moral nature. Classical education in his hands will not be a mere engine of literary culture, but a general training of the character and affections.' This expectation was fully justified by Murray's tenure of the Chair. He proved an inspiring lecturer and teacher, who attracted large audiences, had a powerful effect on them and devoted himself to his pupils with striking results. 'I combined – or tried to combine,' he wrote later, 'an enthusiasm for poetry and Greek scholarship with an almost equal enthusiasm for radical politics and social reform.' He threw himself into the unpopular cause of opposition to the South African War, and was regarded by conservative persons as a dangerous radical.

At the same time Murray was actively laying the foundations of a distinguished career in scholarship, and also planning a second career as a man of letters. In 1894 he wrote to Ulrich von Wilamowitz-Moellendorff, the most eminent Hellenist of his time, to consult him about a plan for a new series of Greek texts and a lexicon to Murray's favourite author, Euripides; he wrote in excellent Greek, and the great man responded warmly and in detail.[5] Wilamowitz was at that time forty-six years old. He was a man of phenomenal energy, and of the greatest learning in almost every department of Greek studies; but he was also intensely alive and wholly free from pedantry. Coming from a background utterly remote from the academic world, that of an East Prussian Junker, he never wholly belonged to it, and from the start he showed no patience with the dry and pedantic phase through which German scholarship was passing when he started his career.

[3] Dorothy Henley, *Rosalind, Countess of Carlisle* (1958).

[4] Cited by A.J. Toynbee in *An Unfinished Autobiography*, 212.

[5] See Gilbert Murray, 'Memories of Wilamowitz', in *Antike und Abendland* 4 (1954), 9f.

Wilamowitz was eager to make Greece intelligible not only to scholars but to the general reader, and brought out a series of verse translations of Greek tragedies which for some time enjoyed a great success. His poetic manner owes something to Schiller, but recalls rather the verse of Wagner; the versions are not now highly regarded, but they have clarity and vigour, and for some time held the stage. From the start of his career Wilamowitz did important work upon Euripides, a writer not highly estimated by the German classicists of the early part of the nineteenth century; in the year in which Murray went to Glasgow, he had made Euripides' *Heracles* the subject of the first modern commentary on a Greek text, using all the methods and results of modern scholarship to explain the play and doing so with incomparable clarity and liveliness. Years afterwards, in a lecture given at Oxford,[6] Wilamowitz was to say that to make the ancients speak to us we must feed them, like Odysseus in the underworld, upon blood, and that it is our own blood that we must give them. A scholar who does this runs the risk of fathering upon the ancients beliefs and attitudes rooted wholly in the modern world, and even Wilamowitz was no exception. In 1891, a year after the première of Ibsen's *Hedda Gabler*, he wrote this of Phaedra in his commentary upon Euripides' Hippolytus. 'No vulgar woman – she is altogether the high society lady, knows and does her duty; she has a husband and children, relations and a social position, and knows how to render all these the regard she owes them. But she has no inner relationship to husband or children; let alone to any other object. Her life lacks the blessing of work, and she is too intelligent to be content with idleness and empty social activity ... So she is ripe for passion. Suddenly she encounters in her stepson a being who astonishes her just because she cannot understand him ...'.[7] It is easy now to see that this description is far more relevant to Ibsenian heroines like Nora, Rebecca West or Hedda Gabler than to Phaedra; Euripides took no interest in Phaedra's disposition or her social situation, only in her passion. Murray was eager to follow Wilamowitz in combining real learning with an active understanding of the ancient world that would help him to interpret it to his contemporaries; but in doing so he ran the risk of importing into his picture of antiquity more of modernity than the facts justified.

In 1897 Murray brought out a book called *Ancient Greek Literature*. 'To read and reread,' it begins, 'the scanty remains now left to us of

---

[6] See the quotation prefaced to this book.

[7] See Karl Reinhardt, *Tradition und Geist* (1960), citing Wilamowitz, *Euripides: Hippolytos* (1891), 48; cf. below, p. 241. W.M. Calder III, *GRBS* 20 (1979) 219 protests against this notion; he thinks that when Wilamowitz wrote about Phaedra, he had in mind one of his aunts.

the literature of Ancient Greece is a pleasant and not a laborious task'; against these words Henry Jackson, later Professor of Greek at Cambridge, scrawled in the margin 'Insolent puppy!'. But though the book is not learned it is fresh, stimulating and inspiring. During the Glasgow period Murray was already at work on what was to prove his main work of technical scholarship, the Oxford text of Euripides whose three volumes were to appear in 1901, 1904 and 1910. He lacked the sound training which study in Germany would have given him, and in some ways never quite made up that deficiency; but his wide knowledge and his strong feeling for Greek stood him in good stead. In many places he is right where Wilamowitz and other eminent critics have been wrong, and his edition is only now in process of becoming superseded. He was a subtle and ingenious textual critic; indeed, his main fault lies in an excess of these qualities, fostered by the disastrous influence of the clever but sophistic Cambridge scholar, A.W. Verrall.

In 1895 Murray made friends with the dramatist and pioneer translator of Ibsen, William Archer, who was his advisor about things connected with the theatre. A prose play attacking imperialism, *Carlyon Sahib*, was produced by Mrs Patrick Campbell in 1899, but proved a flop; a drama called *Andromache* was put on in 1901, with Janet Achurch in the title role, but was hardly more successful. But in 1902 Murray brought out a book on Euripides which contained versions of the *Bacchae* and *Hippolytus*; and two years later the famous management of Granville-Barker and Vedrenne at the Court Theatre opened with Murray's *Hippolytus*. It proved a success, and Granville-Barker went on to stage his *Trojan Women* and *Medea*. He and Vedrenne left the Court in 1907, but Murray's versions continued to be successful, notably when Max Reinhardt staged his *Oedipus Tyrannus* at Convent Garden Opera House in 1922.

In the end Murray's health proved unequal to the strains which he imposed on it at Glasgow, and in 1899 he was compelled to resign his Chair and move to Churt, in Surrey, where he and his wife and family – the Murrays had five children – spent three restful years. In 1905 he was sufficiently recovered to return to Oxford as a Fellow of New College, where though he was not a tutor he did some teaching. In 1907 he published *The Rise of the Greek Epic*, a work based on lectures given during his first visit to Harvard. Murray's purpose was to mediate between unitarian and analyst theories of the composition of the Homeric poems by postulating an original work gradually

[8] Interesting letters from Murray are quoted in J.G. Stewart's *Jane Harrison* (see note on p. 195).

augmented by later accretions, a theory which he supported by the
analogy of other 'ancient traditional books', particularly those of the
Old Testament. The book belongs to a past phase of Homeric
scholarship; but it is beautifully written, it contains many interesting
remarks, and its first chaper contains an exposition of Murray's view
of Hellenism as an instrument for the betterment of man's condition
that retains its interest, even for those who have no sympathy with his
conception.

In 1908 the Regius Chair of Greek was vacated by the resignation of
Ingram Bywater, and the appointment rested with the Prime
Minister, Asquith. Murray was not the only possibility, for as he
himself acknowledged John Burnet, the eminent authority on Greek
philosophy, was a strong candidate; but Asquith was eager to choose
the person most likely to interest and enthuse his audiences, and this
rather than Murray's Liberalism was the decisive factor in his choice.
I have heard people who were undergraduates at the time describe the
immense difference which this appointment to the Chair made to the
whole character of classical teaching in the place. His success as a
lecturer was legendary, aided by his mellifluous voice and strong
dramatic sense. In 1910 he voted for the abolition of compulsory
Greek; he thought that Greek was capable of looking after itself
without compulsion, and so far it has done. In 1912 he brought out the
first edition of what is in many ways his most important book; it was
originally called *Four Stages of Greek Religion*, the fifth stage being added
in the second edition of 1925.

The classical colleagues who had most influence on Murray lived
not in Oxford but in Cambridge. I have already mentioned what
Housman called 'the baleful influence' of A.W. Verrall. Jane Harrison
started as an archaeologist, and had a wide knowledge of Greek art.
Later she read Durkheim and other anthropologists, and became a
pioneer of the anthropological approach to early Greek religion.
Unlike her fellow-pioneers in Cambridge, Sir James Frazer and A.B.
Cook, she did not know Greek well; her judgment was erratic, and like
other pioneers she made many errors. But she did much to expedite
the adoption of new methods that finally led to valuable results, and
her charm and enthusiasm had a remarkable effect upon her friends
and pupils. Murray was also a pioneer of the new approach, and in
this capacity did important services to learning; yet his study of
anthropology led him into grave mistakes. What interested him about
what he termed 'the dark and fascinating department of the human
mind which we may call religious origins' was its appeal to the
imagination. Thus he came to fasten on the notion that early Greek
religion centred upon the Year-Daemon, the vegetation spirit who is

annually born, killed, buried with the crop and resurrected; and this led him to espouse a theory of the origins of tragedy which in his own time was effectively refuted and for which few scholars now say a good word.

Jane Harrison in her enthusiasm for the new discoveries treated the Olympian religion of Greece with scant respect; Murray too was critical of the attribution of human passions to the gods, and could not refrain from transferring to the Olympian religion some of the aversion which he felt for orthodox Christianity. Yet he felt it his duty to defend that religion against Miss Harrison, seeing that it stood for cosmic order and rationality. One application of that belief was his suggestion that we find in the Homeric poems a definite tendency to ignore certain topics which were thought unsuitable to the epic style, a suggestion which has been taken up by others since. Yet Murray failed to perceive the merits of the Olympian religion as they were perceived by his German contemporary Walter F. Otto; he failed to appreciate its insistence that the gods governed the universe for themselves and not for men, its reminder that the human condition imposed limitations that no action on the part of men could overcome, its teaching that human life was for the most part miserable but might by the favour of the gods and the supreme efforts of men themselves contain moments of felicity. Murray was most at home with the religious philosophies evolved during the fourth century, which supplied the fifth stage placed in the middle of his original *Four Stages of Greek Religion* in 1925, again figured in the small but interesting book called *Stoic, Christian and Humanist*, which he brought out in 1940. He wrote with deep sympathy of Epicureanism and even of Cynicism; but his obvious affinity was with Stoicism, perhaps because of a residue of a kind of Scotch Calvinism. 'The Stoic school,' he wrote, ' ... has on the whole weathered the storms of life with great success. It largely dominated later antiquity by its imaginative and emotional power. It gave form to the aspirations of early Christianity. It lasts now as the nearest approach to an acceptable system of conduct for those who do not accept revelation, but still keep some faith in the "Purpose of Things".' One can easily see the Stoic residue in the neoplatonic paganism of late antiquity, of which Murray gives such a sympathetic sketch in the last of his *Five Stages*, built around the treatise of the fifth-century writer Sallustius 'On the Gods and the World'. *Five Stages* is a fine book; Murray shows remarkable familiarity with the great body of detailed work done upon the subject and fully acknowledges his debt to it, but his interpretation of the results which it attained is quite his own, and is expressed with clarity and elegance.

In 1913 Murray published in the popular and influential Home University Library, of which with his friend H.A.L. Fisher he was long a general editor, a small but important book called *Euripides and his Age*. This book summed up the general view of Euripides on which his translations rested, and its conclusions will best be dealt with when I come to speak of his translations.

The First World War marked a turning-point in Murray's life and thought. He had opposed the South African War with all his power; but this time he had no doubt of the justice of the British cause, which he most effectively served by pamphleteering, lecturing abroad and undertaking other governmental work. At this time he began his practical efforts to help the victims of war and persecution, which grew steadily and reached their climax during the period of Hitler's rule. After the war, Murray threw himself into work in support of the League of Nations, acting from 1922 to 1938 as Chairman of the League of Nations Union and presiding for eight years over the League's Committee for Intellectual Cooperation, a distinguished body that was a precursor of Unesco. Unlike many other enthusiastic supporters of the League, Murray was never an unconditional pacifist – he opposed appeasement of Hitler in the thirties – and he was never unduly optimistic about the League's prospects of success; he was too much a Hellenist to be over-sanguine about the capacity of human beings. But he saw in the League the only serious attempt to prevent a recurrence of world war, and believed that as such it deserved all possible support. Nor was the League the only cause he fought for; at a time when such support was badly needed he gave ungrudging support to women's rights and women's education. The time given up to this work represented a very great sacrifice; but Murray had far too strong a sense of civic duty to be able to concentrate, in such an age as that in which he lived, on nothing but his scholarship. To him the work to spread the knowledge of Hellenism and the work to preserve peace were one and the same thing.

After the war Sybil Thorndike acted in a series of performances of Murray's *Trojan Women*, *Medea* and *Hippolytus*, and these works continued to be staged at home and abroad, though with diminishing success, into the thirties. Even after the second war there were occasional revivals, and Murray's accomplished rendering of the newly-discovered play of Menander whose title he translated as *The Rape of the Locks* was put on with some success by amateur companies.

But in 1920 the translations were fiercely attacked by a thirty-two-year-old poet and critic whom the public thought of, if it thought of him at all, as a disreputably modern writer. 'Greek tragedy,' T.S.

Eliot wrote,[9] 'will never have the slightest vitalising effect upon English poetry if it can only appear masquerading as a vulgar debasement of the eminently personal idiom of Swinburne.' Euripides writes, Eliot complains, 'Women of Corinth, I have come out of the house'; Murray writes:

> Women of Corinth, I am come to show
> My face ...

'Show my face, therefore,' Eliot says, 'is Mr Murray's gift.' Later, Medea says 'This thing has fallen on me and has ruined my life; I have let go my delight in life and long for death.' Murray says:

> This thing undreamed of sudden from on high
> Hath sapped my soul: I dazzle where I stand,
> The cup of life all shattered in my hand.

'So here are two striking phrases which we owe to Mr Murray,' Eliot writes; 'it is he who has sapped our soul and shattered the cup of all life for Euripides.' Murray, Eliot continues, 'has simply interposed between Euripides and ourselves a barrier more impenetrable than the Greek language'; as a poet, Eliot declares, Murray 'is merely a very insignificant follower of the pre-Raphaelite movement'.

In the examples chosen by Eliot, the spareness and tautness of the Greek original has been replaced by faded and tawdry ornament of a kind typical of verse; the style derives ultimately from Swinburne, as its rhyming metres and alliteration and countless tricks of style reveal. In Swinburne romanticism is already decaying, but this verse belongs to the category of faded sub-Swinburnian verse of the nineties, typified by the now deservedly forgotten dramatist Stephen Phillips. The verse of Greek tragedy is by no means all spare and taut; much of it is highly elaborate and ornate; but the ornament is of a very different kind from that found in the verse of Swinburne, who despite Murray's reluctance to admit it – he always maintained that he was far more influenced by the verse of his mother's first cousin W.S. Gilbert, to whom he owed his name – was surely Murray's principal model. Part of Murray's ornament consisted in the fatal use of rhyme, employed by him in the hope of lending to his verse a solemnity comparable with that of the original; the rhyme leads to the interpolation of alien matter and to much distortion of the sense, and frequently results in a displeasing jingle. Let me offer an example from his translation of a passage from the second stasimon of the *Agamemnon* of Aeschylus (736ff.). Murray offers:

[9] In 'Euripides and Professor Murray', now in *Selected Essays*, 59f.

And how shall I call the thing that came
At the first hour to Ilion city?
Call it a dream of peace untold,
A secret joy in a mist of gold,
A woman's eye that was soft, like flame,
A flower which ate a man's heart with pity.
But she swerved aside, and wrought to her kiss a bitter ending,
And a wrath was on her harbouring, a wrath upon her friending,
When to Priam and his sons she fled quickly o'er the deep
With the god to whom she sinned for her watcher on the wind,
A death-bride, for whom brides long shall weep.

Louis MacNeice in his version of 1936 offers a rendering which, whatever one may think of it as poetry, is a great deal closer to the actual Greek; that is made easier for him by his use of blank verse instead of rhyme.

So I would say there came
To the city of Troy
A notion of windless calm

Delicate adornment of riches
Soft shooting of the eyes and flower
Of desire that stings the fancy,
But swerving aside she achieved

A bitter end to her marriage,
Ill guest and ill companion,
Hurled upon Priam's sons, convoyed
By Zeus, patron of host and guest,
Dark angel dowered with tears.

Taste in poetry shifts from generation to generation; pre-Raphaelitism is again in fashion; and some of my readers may well prefer Murray's version to that of MacNeice. That would give me pleasure, since I was personally devoted to Murray; but I cannot pretend for a moment that I prefer his rendering as poetry, and I have no doubt whatever that MacNeice's version is far closer to the words of Aeschylus. The truth is that, as I shall argue presently, Murray's pervading romanticism led him to distort the content in a way even more damaging to the truthfulness of his rendering than the distortion of the form resulting from the nature of his style. Yet at his best, seen most often in his renderings of certain choruses of Aristophanes, Murray was a highly skilful writer of Swinburnian verse, from whose work, once we have decided to regard it as a period piece and have ceased to expect it to render anything like the full impact of a Greek tragedy, we can legitimately get pleasure of a certain order. Consider, for example, this rendering of the opening stanza of the second stasimon of Euripides' *Trojan Women*:

In Salamis, filled with the foaming
    Of billows and murmur of bees,
Old Telamon stayed from his roaming
    Long ago, on a throne of the seas;
Looking out on the hills olive-laden,
    Enchanted, where first from the earth
The grey-gleaming fruit of the Maiden,
    Athena had birth;
A soft grey crown for a city
    Beloved, a city of light:
Yet he rested not there, nor had pity,
    But went forth in his might,
Where Heracles wandered, the lonely
    Bow-bearer, and lent him his hands
For the wrecking of one land only,
    Of Ilion, Ilion only,
Most hated of lands!

That is not much closer to its original than the translation of Aeschylus just quoted: but though its tone and impact are distinctly different from those of Euripides, it is not without poetic merit.

But as I said earlier, Murray's distortion of the style of Greek tragedy went together with a distortion of the meaning. His master, the great Wilamowitz, had given the world an Ibsenian Euripides; Murray's Euripides was Shavian. From about 1899 he had been a close friend of Shaw; and *Major Barbara*, produced in 1905, contains easily recognisable and highly entertaining portraits of Murray himself (Professor Adolphus Cusins), his wife (Barbara) and his formidable mother-in-law (Lady Britomart). The play ends with the idealistic Greek scholar taking over the armaments business founded by Andrew Undershaft; Shaw understood the underlying determination of Murray's character, and knew that he would not flinch from positive action in order to achieve his idealistic aims. In the film based on that play, you may see Murray being acted by Mr Rex Harrison, a fine actor but one who does not correspond very closely with my impression of him.

Observing that Euripides in his dramas often makes play with the philosophical and cosmological speculations of the contemporary sophists, Murray concluded that he must have been concerned to propagate belief in these ideas. From the many debates in which one character puts forward his point of view with all the resources of contemporary rhetoric and another then states the opposite one, Murray deduced that Euripides was arguing the case for new and revolutionary moral attitudes. In both these assumptions, he was guided by the apparent analogy with Ibsen. Some of Euripides' plays contained passionate pleas for women; Murray therefore assumed the poet to have been a committed feminist, taking no account of the context of these pleas within the play in question. One chorus of the *Medea* in his version was chanted by a horde of suffragettes. In Euripides' play *Ion* Creusa, Queen of Athens, at one moment believes Apollo to have allowed her son by him to perish, and in a superb monody in lyric anapaests delivers a passionate diatribe against the god. Murray seizes upon this as a denunciation of mythological deities who feel human passions and treat mortal women as their playthings; but Creusa happens to be mistaken, as she learns not long afterwards, and since her son is restored to her and becomes her only heir, at the end of the play she has good reason to be grateful to Apollo. The *Trojan Women* powerfully depicts the horrors of war, and Murray assumes that Euripides meant it as a protest against atrocities committed by his own side in the war against Sparta and her allies that Athens was fighting at the time. This view still has some advocates; but those who are aware of the difference between a tragedy and a *drame engagé* see the play not as a protest against the behaviour of any actual persons, but as a portrayal of what the poet regards as a permanent feature of the human situation. This view of Euripides as a crusader for contemporary causes is eloquently expressed in Murray's book *Euripides and his Age*, published in 1913; the work is delightfully written, and (if you will forgive a personal reminiscence) did more than any other to make me want to be a scholar when I read it at the age of fourteen. But I now believe it to be almost totally misguided.

In the early part of his career Murray did not much care for Old Comedy; it was full of obscenity, and he was a trifle straitlaced; it was robust, and Murray's taste had been formed during the eighties and nineties, when that quality was not in fashion. But Aristophanes constantly attacks the politicians who kept the war going, and his heroes triumph by restoring peace, so that they can indulge the most pervasive human fantasies. It was therefore possible to represent Aristophanes as an enlightened pacifist writing in a popular form in the hope of curing the bellicosity of his audience, and in this good cause making certain concessions to the groundlings' taste. Murray drew confirmation for this view from the beauty and delicacy of many of Aristophanes' lyrics, and these inspired him to some of his most successful versions. But for understanding of the full-bodied humour of Aristophanes and his sympathetic and satiric view of the human condition you must not look to Murray. His limitations as a critic of both tragedy and comedy are clearly revealed by his inability to appreciate Shakespeare, in whom an explicit moral message is not easily to be apprehended.

The strong measure of suppressed Calvinism that lay behind Murray's lifelong agnosticism may plainly be perceived in his treatment of Aeschylus. 'The Olympian religion,' he wrote, 'brought to man the Good News that, as Plutarch expresses it, "the world is not ruled by fabulous Typhons and Giants" – nor, we may add, by blind mechanical laws – "but by One who is a wise father to all".' 'The Aeschylean doctrine,' he added, 'is in essence an early and less elaborate stage of the theological system which we associate with St Paul: the suppression of the Law by a personal relation to the divine person, and a consequent disregard for the crude coarse test of a man's "works" or "deeds" in comparison with the one unfailing test of the spirit, its "faith" or "faithfulness" towards God.' But the stern assertion of the chorus of the Agamemnon that Zeus has given mortals a grace that comes by violence in that he has ordained that their crimes against each other must eventually be punished is a long way from Christian notions of sin and repentance. Orestes is acquitted not because of his faith, but because the reasons for his condemnation and the reasons for his acquittal cancel each other out, and the gods decide to give him the benefit of the doubt. Aeschylus and St Paul are worlds apart.

After the war Murray devoted much of his time to work designed to preserve peace; one Vice-Chancellor of Oxford even asked him if he should not resign his Chair. But if he had wished to do so his colleagues, not to mention his audiences, would have done everything they could to stop him. In 1925 he brought out the augmented second edition of his *Five Stages of Greek Religion*. Two years later appeared his Charles Eliot Norton Lectures given at Harvard on *The Classical Tradition in Poetry*. This is not among his best books; in particular, the perverse ingenuity of the equation of Hamlet and Orestes with the Corn Spirit has provoked adverse criticism. The *Aristophanes* of 1933 and the *Aeschylus* of 1940 are beautifully written, but are not among his best works; and the first Oxford text of Aeschylus, which appeared in 1937, has little that is new and good to set against its marked perversity and eccentricity.

Murray's achievement as a scholar is by any standards considerable. His text of Euripides is only now being superseded; and

anyone who doubts his capacity for pure scholarship ought to read
through his often brilliant contributions to the early publications of
Oxyrhynchus Papyri by his Oxford colleagues Grenfell and Hunt. *The
Rise of the Greek Epic*, and, still more, the *Five Stages* are works whose
value cannot be ignored. Yet when one considers Murray's
extraordinary flair for Greek, one cannot help feeling sad that he did
not achieve more in scholarship. This happened partly because he felt
it his duty to devote much time to public work; but it happened also
because his minor but real gift for poetry got in the way of his
approach to Greek realities. He had a weakness for what he called
originality, and sometimes he seemed to care more for originality than
for truth; he was fascinated by the irresponsible conjectures of Verrall
and the ingenious fantasies of the learned Arabist D.S. Margoliouth.[11]
Housman, who was seven years his senior, liked him but disapproved
of his activities. Reviewing a lecture by Murray's learned predecessor
in the Oxford Chair, Ingram Bywater, Housman called it 'the
businesslike production of a good scholar who did not aspire to be an
indifferent man of letters'; 'readers who wish to hear about the Greek
spirit,' he added, 'may leave it alone.'[11]

Housman clearly understood that the spirit of classical poetry and
that of the romantic poetry of his own age were totally different; in his
Cambridge inaugural lecture, he spoke disdainfully of 'the prevalent
opinion that the secret of the classical spirit is open to anyone who has
a fervent admiration for the second-best parts of Tennyson'. Housman
kept his romantic poetry quite distinct from his classical scholarship.
People think his poetry was a refuge from the austere world of his
scholarship. On the contrary, his work opened to him a world in
which he was able to enjoy witty, elegant writers like Ovid and
Manilius, free from the tyranny of romantic taste and romantic
pessimism which oppressed his poetry. Had he been able to use his
vein of poetry to make his scholarship less dry, or his appreciation of
classical poetry to make his romantic poetry less limited in scope, he
might have published even more. Murray failed to perceive the
incongruity between his poetry and his scholarship. This caused his
translations to be false to the character of the originals they purport to
render; but it enabled him to breathe life into his teaching and his
written scholarship. Housman's own contribution to technical
scholarship was immeasurably greater; he too was a minor poet, and
a better one than Murray. Whatever Murray's failings, his influence
upon others was powerful; and among the countless pupils and

[10] See Murray's obituary notice of Margoliouth in *PBA* 26 (1940).
[11] See *The Classical Papers of A.E. Housman* (1972), iii, 1004; cf. above, pp. 182f.

readers whom he influenced were eminent professional scholars like A.D. Nock and E.R. Dodds. Not everyone will feel that he did less for scholarship and education than his eminent contemporary.

In the end Murray's tenure of the Chair was specially prolonged for five years, and he retired in 1936. He lived on at Yatscombe, the pleasant house on Boar's Hill where he had moved from the Woodstock Road in 1919, retaining his faculties to an astonishing degree, until his death aged ninety-one on 20 May 1957. He received all kinds of honours, including the Order of Merit, conferred on Churchill's recommendation on his seventy-fifth birthday in 1941, the German order *Pour le Mérite*, and in the end burial in Westminster Abbey.

The Murrays' household was unusual. At their table Cabinet Ministers, famous authors, eminent scholars and raw undergraduates might sit together eating nut cutlets and sipping orangeade. Most visitors were to some extent cowed by the dominant personality of the hostess. At the time of her marriage in 1889, Lady Mary Murray must have been very like one of Shelley's heroines. In old age she retained her generous enthusiasms, and she was basically kind-hearted; but she inherited a large measure of her mother's bossiness, censoriousness and complete lack of sense of humour. Maurice Bowra described how she ordered one of the refugees to whom she was so kind to repeat a story he had told, then suddenly noticed that it was boring and cut him short with 'Never mind! That will do for the present. Get on with your pudding!' The first time I had lunch with them they had given up their vegetarianism; one of them had had to have a blood transfusion, and they felt that after that it would be hypocritical to refuse meat. There was chicken for lunch, and their son Stephen carved; when he very naturally served his mother first, she fixed him with her eye and said, 'I always used to help a guest first, however young.' In a domestic atmosphere strongly coloured by the powerful personality of his wife, Murray held his own with charm, wit and unfailing good humour. Once Lady Mary rapped the table with a spoon, and announced that everyone at the luncheon-table was to tell the worst thing he or she had ever done. She herself began, and explained that as a small girl at Castle Howard she had once stolen green plums, a thing she never could resist – from the church where they had been offered at a harvest festival. 'But I like to think it was all right,' she said, 'because next Sunday I put a shilling, all the money I had, in the collection-box.' 'My dear,' said her husband from the other end of the table, 'the last time you told that story it was sixpence.'

Murray was an extremely entertaining talker; and like Addison he was this without the aid of alcohol or obscenity. A man at a party once took him for a waiter and said, 'Call me a cab.' 'You're a growler,' said Murray. 'You can't talk to me like that, my man.' 'Well, at any rate you're not a hansom.' One day I was with him just after having gone to Cambridge to read a paper about the textual criticism of an Aeschylean chorus. My audience had included the late A.Y. Campbell, once Professor of Greek at Liverpool, a most agreeable person but a notoriously wild emender. During the discussion after my paper, A.Y. was on his best behaviour, but suddenly he suggested dealing with a problem by transposing a whole stanza of the chorus. I pointed out that this would disturb the pattern of metrical responsion between the strophe and the following antistrophe. A.Y. retracted his suggestion; but during dinner that night he telephoned me with a new emendation of the passage, and when I got home next day I found waiting for me a letter from him putting forward a third. When I told Murray this, he was reminded of a weekend party at which the chief lion had been the celebrated Mme. Blavatsky. On the first day she asked one of the company to go into the village and buy a quantity of gauze; and during the first séance, this gauze became entangled with one of the audience. Mme. Blavatsky at once gave an explanation that was totally convincing, or at least would have been had she not given at breakfast next day another explanation that was equally convincing but different, and had not each of the guests on his return home found a letter from her giving a third explanation, in itself equally persuasive.

I hope it will not seem tiresomely egoistical if I say a word about my own relations with Gilbert Murray. At school I read his writings with passionate enthusiasm; no other modern books did as much to make me want to be a scholar. Then I reacted against them, with the excessiveness of youth. I am a Conservative, with very little belief in the intrinsic goodness of human nature; I came to think that Murray brought too much of the modern world into his interpretation of antiquity; and like many young scholars I went through a tiresomely protracted phase of aggressive dryness. After I won the Ireland in December 1947, I was asked up to Yatscombe for lunch, and met Murray for the first time. Lady Mary was extremely nice to me, even though she discovered the awful truth about my politics. In spite of the obvious incompatibility between us, I found the experience exciting; but there were a good many people there, and I did not have any specially memorable contact with Murray himself. The next year I was appointed to a post at Cambridge and saw nothing of him, except for occasional encounters on trains going to London, for about seven years. Then after my return to Oxford my old tutor R.H.

Dundas took me up to tea at Yatscombe. This time Murray must have mentioned me to his friend Paul Maas,[12] the famous German scholar who had come to Oxford as a refugee and was working for the Clarendon Press. Murray had become aware of the deficiencies of his text of Aeschylus of 1937, and had carefully revised it with the aid of Maas before publishing the second edition in 1955. In 1957 the Press had just told him that the book was almost sold out, and that he could if he wished make further changes; I already knew Maas well, and often went to see him; and now I was invited to join the two in the revision of the Oxford Aeschylus. For about four months Maas and I travelled up to Boar's Hill about four times a week, and the three of us went through the whole of Aeschylus together. It was a delightful experience. Maas was a scholar as different from Murray as anyone could imagine; both extremely learned and extremely exact, he aimed at giving to his scholarly work the conciseness and preciseness of a mathematical demonstration. In Germany he had been a rich man; deprived of everything by the Hitlerian persecution, he accepted his ill fortune in the spirit of a man who knew that human beings can count on nothing, and was content to live on a minimal stipend provided he could do his work. He had been a friend of Murray for nearly half a century. In 1909 Maas, in Switzerland for winter sports, had noticed a well-brought-up English girl accompanied by a Nanny carrying her Liddell and Scott, and had introduced himself as a Professor of Greek. 'My father too is a Professor of Greek,' replied the girl, 'and when you come to Oxford you must come and stay with us.' The girl was Murray's daughter Rosalind, and very soon after Maas did come and stay with the Murrays in the Woodstock Road. He asked Murray what principles he had adopted in his arrangement of Euripides' choruses, as Murray records in the third volume of his edition, and Murray was unable to satisfy him. No two men were more different and no two men were better friends. Most people treated Murray with great deference; Maas if he disagreed said so straight out, and Murray was delighted. To hear these two famous men talk together, and to go through Aeschylus with them, was an exhilarating experience. By this time Murray had almost entirely given up his public life; but he still knew very large parts of Greek poetry by heart, and to hear him recite it in his melodious voice was an exciting experience. He was still an incomparable talker, and his memory for the early part of his life was unimpaired. Once he did make a speech at a United Nations function, and he still wrote the occasional letter to *The Times*. Unlike other elderly Liberals I knew at that time, whose inability to see how times

[12] See pp. 215ff.

had changed made them gullible victims of collectivist cant, Murray perfectly understood the altered situation, and regretted the decline of European influence upon the world. The disadvantages often held to excuse any behaviour on the part of those belonging to the so-called working class and the so-called Third World did not in his view palliate the barbarism often shown by both, and he was ready to call it by its proper name. In taking up this attitude he was entirely true to the liberal principles – aristocratic liberal principles, as Arnold Toynbee said – for which he had fought all his life, and he maintained it with his usual courage.

Murray's life, which had begun with singular felicity, was clouded by much sadness. He survived three of his children; his son Denis, his beautiful and tragic daughter Agnes, his gifted but erratic son Basil, said to have been the model for Evelyn Waugh's memorable character Basil Seale. Though he was an eminent public figure and a distinguished scholar, he was never exempt from criticism. He lived between the academic world and the great world, and was never quite at home in either. At all times it was possible for second-rate scholars to despise him as 'unsound'; like most scholars who give their own lifeblood to the ghosts, he seemed to many to have taken too much of the modern world into his picture of antiquity. Taste in poetry changed, so that the famous translations became the object of attack. The liberal values for which he had fought all his life were challenged everywhere. The influence of Europe and European culture declined; individualism was everywhere challenged by collectivism; the ignorant, invested with power at the demand of liberals in the name of justice, used it to oppress civilised people and discourage civilised behaviour. But Murray never became embittered, and never wavered in his loyalty to what he believed in.

18

Paul Maas

Paul Maas, who died at Oxford on 15 July 1964, aged 83, had been for more than sixty years one of the foremost figures in classical and Byzantine scholarship.

Born at Frankfurt-on-Main on 18 November 1880, he was at school there and at Freiburg (Baden) and attended the Universities of Berlin and Munich. As a student at Berlin he gave early proof of exceptional ability, and Wilamowitz, far from being offended by Maas's courage in sometimes opposing his own views in the discussions of the seminar, was quick to mark him out as a student of exceptional promise. Later Maas moved to Munich, and in Krumbacher's seminar laid the foundations of his great knowledge of Byzantine literature. The long series of his publications in this field begins as early as 1901; and at the same time he eagerly pursued the study of the classics. The famous article in which he extended Porson's Law to Bacchylidean dactylo-epitrite was published only in 1904 (*Philologus* 63, 297f), but it had been written as early as 1899, when its author was still a student at Berlin. His doctoral dissertation (*Arch. für Lat. Lex.* 12 (1902), 479f.) was a valuable study of the Latin poetic plural: and in 1906 he published a notable review of Mommsen's edition of the *Codex Theodosianus* (641f.) in which he used the results of recent investigation of the clausulae to make a number of improvements in the text. On appointment as Privatdozent in Berlin in 1910 he was expected to take charge of instruction in Byzantine literature; but he insisted on his right to lecture on classical subjects also, and with the support of Wilamowitz managed to uphold his claim.

Maas spent much of the First World War in Istanbul as a member of the medical unit attached to the German Military Mission, and was eventually repatriated to Germany by way of Odessa; returning to Berlin, he became Professor Extraordinarius in 1920. He now became a close associate of Wilamowitz, who celebrated in Greek verse a

---

* This chapter first appeared in *Gnomon* 36 (1965). Maas's *Kleine Schriften*, edited by Wolfgang Buchwald, appeared in 1973, and were reviewed by me in the *Classical Review* xxv (1975) 137-40.

conjecture of his in Lycophron (*Elegeia* (1938), XIV);[1] the great man much regretted Maas's departure to Koenigsberg as Professor Ordinarius in 1930, and chose him to be one of the editors of his *Kleine Schriften*. Expelled from his chair by National Socialist barbarism in 1934, he for many years refused to leave his country, but finally made his way to England not long before the outbreak of war in 1939.

Arriving in Oxford, Maas found employment as adviser to the Clarendon Press. From affluence he found himself reduced to poverty, but he bore all misfortunes without complaint, and from the first found himself at home in his new surroundings. He was able to enjoy the company not only of other learned exiles, but of English friends, notably Gilbert Murray, whom he had first visited in 1909; and younger English scholars soon began to seek his company. At first the Press employed his expert knowledge of textual criticism upon the English Book of Common Prayer; but before long he became an indispensable consultant upon all manner of classical subjects. As a young man he had served a strenuous apprenticeship in lexicography under Wilhelm Crönert, with whom he worked on the best of all Greek dictionaries as far as 'ἀνά, the revision of Passow's *Wörterbuch der griechischen Sprache* which was regrettably cut short by the outbreak of the First World War; and now he was the ideal editor for the Addenda to the revised edition of Liddell and Scott's *Greek Lexicon*. He made important contributions to most of the chief classical works published by the Press for nearly twenty-five years, not to mention those brought out by other publishers; the list is far too long to be given here, but mention should be made of the help he gave to Rudolf Pfeiffer's great edition of Callimachus. With the aid of C.A. Trypanis he completed the task, begun many years earlier, of making the first critical edition of the genuine works of Romanos; a second volume containing the dubious or spurious works is now in the press. He kept up all the while a constant stream of publications, most of them brief and concise, but all of them instructive. He maintained a vast correspondence with scholars all over the civilised world, and after the end of hostilities he played no small part in renewing the links between German scholars and their colleagues in other countries.

Maas published no large book except the *Romanos*; yet the contribution to learning contained in his numerous articles and notes is very great, and his influence upon the methods and principles of scholarship perhaps still greater. W. Theiler estimated (*Gnomon* 27 (1954), 140) that, if translated into an ordinary writer's style, the writings listed in the bibliography issued by the Clarendon Press in

---

[1] See F. Solmsen, *GRBS* 20 (1979) 89f.

1951 to celebrate Maas's seventieth birthday in the preceding year would cover ten thousand pages. His command of the techniques of textual criticism, grammar, metre and palaeography and his close acquaintance with the stylistic principles of Greek prose and poetry found expression in numerous articles, notes and reviews, all drafted with the same masterly concision and exactitude. Perhaps the most important of his writings are his summary accounts of textual criticism and of Greek metre, both first published in 1923 in Gercke and Norden's *Einleitung in die Altertumswissenschaft* and most recently issued at Oxford in English versions (Textual Criticism, 1958; Greek Metre, 1962). Maas had always been attracted by the study of mathematics, and his presentation of the principles of textual criticism has a mathematical elegance and exactitude. To some readers this may seem to obscure the undoubted truth that in many traditions 'horizontal transmission' is so common that no precise stemma can do justice to their complications; Giorgio Pasquali's famous book *Storia della Tradizione e Critica del Testo*, originating from a review in *Gnomon* (5 (1929), 417f.) more than twice as long as the book that was its subject, does justice to the frequently untidy and unmathematical nature of textual transmission. But Maas was not unaware of the truths made evident by Pasquali, as a glance at the passages referred to under the heading 'Contamination' in his index will reveal; 'no specific,' he wrote (49) 'has been discovered against contamination.' An achievement in the field of textual criticism to which he attached special importance was his demonstration that Byzantine scholars were capable of greater proficiency as editors and critics than used to be supposed; we think in particular of his investigation of the work of Eustathius on the text of Athenaeus (ByzZ 35 (1935), 229f; 36 (1936), 27f. = *Kl. Schr.* 505f.) though this remains controversial.

Maas held strongly that it was better to make a wrong conjecture than to ignore a difficulty; he strongly upheld the value of the 'diagnostic conjecture' and the usefulness of the crux; and he was the sworn enemy of the lazy acquiescence in the anomalous or the excessive caution which many scholars dignify with the name of judgment. After the publication in 1897 of the great papyrus of Bacchylides the enemies of criticism gleefully pounced on the freedoms of responsion which the manuscript appeared to offer in order to restore the similar freedoms which had long been removed by emendation from the text of Pindar. Maas by a critical examination of the text showed that in almost all instances the text was suspect for reasons independent of the responsion. His principles were exemplified in numerous conjectures and supplements whose average quality was very high indeed. At times his rigorous logic could carry him too far; but even the suggestions to which this applies had usually the value of drawing attention to a difficulty or of provoking curiosity as to why the author should have departed from his usual norm.

The eighteen pages of the original edition of Maas's handbook on Greek metre embodied the results of some ten years of intensive work, and the later editions added more. It is at once a most useful handbook, full of detailed observations of great value, and a theoretical treatise of the highest importance, which lays bare with pitiless clarity the weakness of the foundations on which all general theories of the development of Greek metre rest. Maas held that metrical study should go hand in hand with textual criticism, and had no use for any metrical theory that did not stand upon a firm basis of solid fact.

Persecution, poverty and (in his last days) ill health did nothing to diminish Maas's exceptional enthusiasm for scholarship. He was a man of wide interests, which included medicine, music and the literatures of France, Italy and England besides his own. In his Berlin days he was a keen agriculturist, and until well over seventy he used to swim every morning. But he had no time for small talk; the scholar who visited his lodgings would be asked what problem he came to discuss, and having explained it would find all the great scholar's resources put at his disposal. The scholar who wrote to him would get his answer, as a rule, on one of the famous postcards which have become a legend.

In 1959 the University of Oxford honoured Maas with the honorary degree of D. Litt.; in 1962 the King of Greece conferred on him the Royal Order of King George I; and next year the German Minister in London made a special journey to Oxford in order to invest him with the Knight's Cross of the Order of Merit.

In 1909 Maas married Karen Raeder, sister of the Danish scholar Hans Raeder (see *Gnomon* 33 (1960), 87); his wife died in 1960.

19

Tycho von Wilamowitz-Moellendorff

No project lay nearer to the heart of Eduard Fraenkel[1] during his last years than that of promoting a reprint of the famous book *Die dramatische Technik des Sophokles*, by Tycho von Wilamowitz-Moellendorff, which was first published as volume xxii of *Philologische Untersuchungen* in 1917. Tycho Wilamowitz, the son of Ulrich von Wilamowitz-Moellendorff and the grandson of Theodor Mommsen, was killed fighting against the Russians near Ivangorod on the night of 14/15 October 1914. After his death the manuscript was prepared for publication by his friend Ernst Kapp, who has explained in the foreword of the book the nature of his services.

Fraenkel's long efforts to arrange for a reprint of this important book seemed at one time to have been successful, and he began work on an introduction, which would have been of great interest to scholars. At his death he left a number of notes intended for this introduction, most of which had clearly been carefully written and would have been inserted in the text. After Fraenkel's death on 5 February 1970, I was asked by a publisher – not the original publisher – if I would write an introduction. I did so, but after about a year heard from this publisher that owing to legal difficulties he would be unable to proceed with the reprint. In July 1972 I became aware that a reprint by the original publisher, bearing the date 1969, was on the market.

Tycho's book, like the whole series of *Philologische Untersuchungen*, had been published by the firm of Weidmann. 'The progress of research,' wrote Wilamowitz (*Erinnerungen* (1928), 2nd ed., p. 196),

---

* This chapter was first published in the *Classical Quarterly* xxii (1972), 214f., where Fraenkel's notes appear in the original German.

[1] 'During the years of Fraenkel's maturity the tragedians he had studied most had been Aeschylus and Euripides; but during his last years a deeper need of "classicism" had caused him to prefer Sophocles, who in his tragic serenity was "more Greek". Both in articles and seminars he dealt increasingly often with Sophocles (in 1968 he had held classes on the *Philoctetes* both at Rome and at Oxford), and if he had lived longer he would certainly have continued to work on him.' Sebastiano Timpanaro, *Átene e Roma*, N.S. xv (1970), 97. (Rather than speak of 'classicism' or of 'tragic serenity', I would say Fraenkel was attracted by Sophocles' depiction of the hero who despite his suffering resists a hostile world.)

'owes a special debt to detailed studies which are too long to appear in learned journals and will be bought by only a few readers if they appear as books. A great firm of publishers (as to Germany's honour Weidmann has always been) may somewhat reduce the sacrifice by including such a book in a series.' This was not the only instance of what Wilamowitz called the 'noble readiness to make sacrifices' ... (ibid., p. 237) displayed by the firm of Weidmann under its then director, the enlightened Reimer, the friend of Mommsen and of Wilamowitz. All human institutions are subject to the law of change. Scholars will regret that Tycho von Wilamowitz's sister, Dorothea Freifrau Hiller von Gaertringen, who died on 24 March 1972 in her ninety-third year, did not see the book reprinted in the way she wished it to be.

In these circumstances it has proved impossible to use the introduction for the purpose for which it was composed. But Fraenkel's material should surely be given to the world; and as my introduction provides it with a framework, they may as well appear together. I apologise for my inability to provide an introduction such as Fraenkel would have written. At least I know from many conversations, as well as from Fraenkel's notes themselves, that though we differed over some of the problems discussed in Tycho's book, over the main features of his work we were in complete agreement. Nearly all the examples cited in the footnotes to what follows come from Fraenkel's notes, and all the parts of the introduction which Fraenkel had completed are reproduced verbatim.

'It may seem surprising,' Fraenkel's introduction would have begun, 'for the unfinished work of a young scholar to be reprinted after more than fifty years. But in fact it is necessary to make available once more a book now to be found only in the larger libraries. Naturally research has moved forward, and much of the book is now out of date, but we are still far from being able to do without it. The forward to the reprint attempts by means of some examples to show why this is so.' Few doctoral dissertations have had so great an influence, and both the study of recent literature and the experience of teaching and discussion in several countries have convinced me, as they did Fraenkel, that interest in *Tycho*'s book is particularly lively.

The book's influence took some time to make itself felt; as late as 1932 a reviewer of one of the first books markedly affected by Tycho's ideas[2] could say with truth that most later interpreters had preferred to approach tragedy from the standpoint of *Geistesgeschichte*. But now the situation is altogether different.

Tycho was the first to apply to the Greek dramatists a particular

[2] W. Schadewaldt, reviewing E. Howald, *Die griechische Tragödie*, at *Gnomon* viii (1932), 2 = *Hellas und Hesperien* i (1970), 238.

critical attitude that was highly characteristic of the time at which he wrote. Towards the end of the nineteenth century and for long afterwards, even as late as the nineteen-thirties, students of drama, both ancient and modern, were accustomed to look upon character portrayal as one of the main elements, if not the main element, in dramatic art; and by character portrayal they usually meant a minute psychological analysis. Most of Tycho's examples of this attitude are taken from the respectable Sophoclean commentaries of Ludwig Radermacher and of Ewald Bruhn. But they abound also in the notable English edition of Sir Richard Jebb, in the most learned Sophoclean commentary of the age of Wilamowitz – the *Elektra* of Georg Kaibel – and in the works of Tycho's own illustrious father.[3]

Tycho agreed with Aristotle that the characters are there for the sake of the plot, not the plot for the sake of the characters;[4] p. 216, 1.2: 'For Sophocles it is simply not true that exhaustive, psychologically exact and consistent character-drawing is the dramatist's main task, as people nowadays claim it is,'[5] and he points to countless instances

[3] 'Wilamowitz should still say, in the sketch called "Greek Tragedy and its Three Poets" published in 1923 [in vol. xiv of his series of translations of Greek tragedies]: "Here we miss the lovable Ismene, whom the poet treats as if she did not exist." This may do for us, or for many modern readers. But that it will not do for Sophocles and for those among his audience who were able to follow him is something we can learn, together with many other even more important things, from Tycho's book. Tycho writes (p. 41): "About Ismene as a human being Sophocles cares nothing whatsoever; she is merely a tool" (he says later "only a foil for Antigone") "which he uses when he needs it and discards when he does not". In general this was anticipated by Schneidewin (introduction to his *Antigone*, 1st. ed., 18, p. 26), who with his usual sensitivity wrote with only slight concessions to modern taste, "The minor characters in general serve merely to display the character of Antigone ... Ismene stands to her as Chrysothemis does to Electra, in order to emphasise Antigone's heroism by contrast with a female character who in herself is noble; the moment that has been accomplished, she departs, and we hear no more of her", Tycho (p. 42) says that "Ismene is not what we mean by a character" ': Fraenkel.

Karl Reinhardt, *Tradition und Geist* (1960), 236, gives a particularly amusing instance of this tendency in Wilamowitz. Yet only three years after writing as he did about Ismene, Wilamowitz wrote, 'I have long outgrown my mistaken interpretation of characters such as those of Heracles and Electra'. (*D.L.Z.* xlvii (1926), 854 = *Kl. Schr.* i. 466, in his review of Schadewaldt's *Monolog und Selbstgespräch*).

[4] *Poetics* 1450 20-22; on the text, see R. Kassel, *Rh. Mus.* cix (1966), 10.

[5] Cf. p. 78: 'The poet's purpose is not to depict some particular characters in a struggle determined by their own nature, but to bring out as powerfully as possible what one might call the effect made possible by the material given by the dramatic situation.' p. 145: 'Of course one must never forget that here also Sophocles did not write the whole play so that he could depict this one individual character (Deianeira), but was obliged by the requirements of the story he was telling to motivate the action performed by Deianeira, and since she stood at the centre of the action he gave her the character for this action'. p. 154: 'the requirement of thorough-going, unitary characterisation is quite foreign to Sophocles'.

where modern critics had put forward a psychological explanation of a problem posed by Sophocles' text which was in the light of reason totally untenable.[6] They took no account, he complained, of the conditions of performance or of the effect a given scene would have upon the audience, but tried to explain the actions of the play's characters as though they had been real people, often postulating hypothetical events off stage and assigning primary importance to things which were secondary for the poet;[7] their explanations started from the supposed intentions of the characters, instead of from the legitimately inferred intentions of the author.[8] Sophocles, he concluded, cared nothing for consistency of character; the behaviour

[6] p. 31: 'Of course it is easy to find some kind of psychological explanation of this, but that is not what we need to do ... p. 162: 'This explanation entirely ignores the fact that we need to explain the creation of a poet, not the behaviour of real people'. p. 171n.1: 'This explanation shows how completely people may forget the conditions of performance and the consideration of whether the audience will understand when they are only concerned to find some reason for the behaviour of the characters just as if they were dealing with reality'. p. 281: 'where instead of interpreting the indication given by the poet in an unprejudiced way people try to explain behaviour on the part of the characters that we find incomprehensible by expedients of their own invention'.

[7] p. 20: 'It is not his purpose to obtain a unitary prehistory for the action; rather he does not hesitate (and one cannot attribute this to a slip on his part) to allow the same person to give two directly conflicting indications in different situations about an event that happens off stage and outside the action'. Ibid.: 'So he cares more about the dramatic effect of the individual scenes than about the unity of the plot, and calculates that what the audience actually sees happening will have so powerful an effect that an incongruity affecting subordinate matters lying in the past will not be noticed'. ('The same is true of Aeschylus, as so early a writer as Wilhelm von Humboldt clearly grasped in strong contrast with the usual way of stating the problems': Fraenkel); p. 33: 'All this shows ... that the poet deliberately left all these processes in the dark and preferred not to worry about the exact connection between them'; p. 38: 'In this connection our interest is directed in a quite different direction, and we give no further thought to this subsidiary piece of information'; cf. p. 62 (on the *Ajax*).

[8] p. 131, n.2: 'To construct a psychological process in this way, without the support of any indication given by the poet constitutes a mistake from the very start, because it involves one in inventing the explanation one requires'; p. 193, n.1: 'This shows that only a reader who is analysing the whole plot in retrospect could arrive at such constructions'; p. 194: 'Such peculiar constructions only show how odd these scenes must seem to a critic who does not look on them first and foremost as a spectator and so can never forget what he knows about the real situation and how it will all end'; p. 144 (on the second report of Lichas in the *Trachiniae*): 'It was far from Sophocles' purpose to take it into account that one might reconstruct the story told by Lichas in the meadow off stage and before the beginning of the action'. ('In the case of Aeschylus' *Agamemnon*, writes Fraenkel, 'an interpreter who had learned so much from Tycho's book ought not to have let himself be tempted into trying to find out by psychological speculations why the king finally gives in to Clytemnestra's flattering entreaties and walks into the house where murder awaits him over the purple tapestry that is too precious to be trod by human feet'; see his *Agamemnon*, ii, 441-2).

of his people was always determined by the situation of the movement.[9] Not only consistency of character, but consistency of fact were in his view disregarded. A motive could be exploited for its effect at a particular moment, only to be totally forgotten later; an oracle could be said to have demanded one thing at one time and another thing, inconsistent with the first, a little afterwards.

Again and again Tycho asks what will be the effect of the scene he is discussing upon the audience; again and again he ruthlessly flings out the accumulated rubbish of over-subtle psychologising interpretation. He throws much light on Sophocles' dramatic methods. He was the first to appreciate the new effects made possible by experience in handling a third actor;[10] and with much acuteness he showed how in several instances the poet gained much by splitting up what might have been a unitary scene into two separate episodes.[11] His historical importance as the initiator of the whole genre of detailed studies of various aspects of dramatic technique which have done such valuable work since is very great. But the importance of his work is far from being only historical, for his rigorous analysis still offers the best starting-point for the consideration of many Sophoclean problems.[12]

[9] p. 70n: 'the traits shared by the two kings, Creon in the *Antigone* and Oedipus in the *OT*, are due to the similarity of their situations; what they show is that the characterisation always operates within restricted limits, that the poet always likes to use definite motives, such as the suspicion of bribery, and above all that the character's behaviour is always determined by the situation of the moment, so that similar actions recur in similar situations'; p. 222: 'how ... motives simply serve momentary purposes of the poet, and that what seems to us the natural requirement that he should connect them with the actual plot of the play counts for so little for him that the moment one inquires further into them one finds the ground vanishing beneath one's feet'; p. 39: 'Sophocles is always concerned most of all to present the momentary situation in such a way that whatever dramatic effect it can yield comes to the fullest expression, and this shows that he consciously counted on the spectator who was gripped by the actual scene never thinking more about what was happening off stage than the poet intended and on his failing to notice even incongruences and contradictions in what was actually happening on the stage and on his not feeling a lack of motivation, mainly because he was altogether absorbed in the impression made by what was being enacted before his eyes'.

[10] n.2; 'A historian of literature who is not a professional classical scholar has rightly pointed out that Tycho's book was the first to direct our attention to a substantial innovation in the construction of a play successfully introduced by Sophocles': John Jones, *On Aristotle and Greek Tragedy* (London 1962), 272 n. 2': Fraenkel. This important book has received less attention from classical scholars than it deserves; see my *Discipline and Imagination* (1981).

[11] See pp. 34, 62, 67, 143, 224.

[12] His book also contains some valuable contributions to the criticism of the text. Fraenkel singles out his treatment of *Ant.* 933f. (p. 49 n.1); of *Tr.* 362-3 (p. 109 n.1; Wunder and Blaydes anticipated Tycho here); of *Phil.* 671-3 (p. 284 n.1, in support of Jebb); of *Phil.* 850f. (p. 293 n.1). On *Tr.* 46-8 and 901-3, see below pp. 229, 230.

Part of Tycho's results are nowadays generally accepted. Most scholars would now agree that Sophocles showed his minor figures 'only in silhouette'; most would concur in countless places where he had rejected a psychological explanation of a speech or action; few would deny that the action, not the characters, is the central element of Sophoclean drama. But like most daring innovators he in some places pushed his thesis too far. If character-drawing is held to imply an interest in individuals as individuals and in psychological peculiarities for their own sake, then indeed it is unimportant in Sophocles. But character-drawing in a different, but perfectly legitimate sense, is of very great importance in this author; idiosyncrasies may count for nothing, but the main qualities of the character considered as a human being count for a great deal. An anecdote makes Sophocles claim that during the third period of his career he has achieved the style which is 'the most expressive of *ethos* and the best'.[13] The Greek concept of *ethos* requires that the characters shall be represented as being the kind of people capable of the actions assigned them by the story, and this requirement Sophocles certainly fulfilled. To take an obvious example, no reasonable person would dispute that the contrast between heroic figures, like Ajax, Heracles, Antigone, the two Oedipuses, Electra, and Philoctetes, and ordinary human beings is a leading theme in Sophocles' work. Jebb once encountered George Eliot and, knowing her to be a close student of Sophocles, asked her how he had influenced her and was told, 'In the delineation of the great primitive emotions'.[14] George Eliot put her finger on a central truth about Sophocles, which has been better understood since Tycho disabused people of the belief that Sophocles took great trouble about minor psychological complexities.

Some of Tycho's critics fail to bear in mind that he offers not a general treatment of Sophoclean drama, but a study of the poet's dramatic technique. The great difficulty of this enterprise, especially when it is undertaken at the beginning of a scholar's career, lies in the fact that dramatic technique is the servant of poetical purpose, which

---

[13] Plutarch, *De profectibus in virtute* 7, p. 79. See C.M. Bowra, *A.J.P.* lxi (1940), 385f. = *Problems in Greek Poetry* (1953) 108f. = *Sophokles*, ed. H. Diller (Wege der Forschung, Band XCV, 1967), 126f. (German version) and Giuliana Lanata, *Poetica Preplatonica*, Florence (1963), 146f.

[14] See Caroline Jebb, *Life and Letters of Sir Richard Claverhouse Jebb*, Cambridge (1907), 156; cf. Gordon Haight, *George Eliot* (1970), 173. For recent treatments of character in Sophocles, see H. Diller, *Wiener Studien* 69 (1956), 70f. = *Kl. Schr. zur antiken Literatur* (1971), 272f. and *Antike und Abendland* vi (1957), 157f. = *Sophokles*, ed. Diller (cited above), 190f. = *K. Schr.* 286f. B.M.W. Knox, *The Heroic Temper* (1964); R.P. Winnington-Ingram, *Sophocles: an Interpretation* (1980).

often requires not only taste but experience to understand.[15] Some men of taste have reproached Tycho with philistinism, and at least one arrogant philistine has claimed him as a predecessor. They are not wholly wrong, as a glance through the mentions of Tycho in the footnotes to Karl Reinhardt's *Sophokles*[16] will remind the reader. Repeatedly Tycho finds fault with the poet for departures from probability or consistency which simply go to prove what Tycho himself demonstrates, that Sophoclean technique is very different from nineteenth-century naturalism.[17] Modern readers, who are accustomed to more than one theatrical convention in which naturalism plays little or no part, find this unnecessary.

Reinhardt chose to treat of 'Sophoclean situations, or of ... the Sophoclean relation between man and god and between man and man, and how it develops, scene by scene, play by play and stage by stage.' (op. cit., p. 9). Starting from Tycho's results and using a similar method of close analysis, Reinhardt with his mature taste and judgment and his unusually fine feeling for poetry was able to show that the essential quality of the poet's art lies not in psychological refinements but in the depiction of the emotions which Sophoclean situations evoke from those involved in them.

Reinhardt's method is unlike that of those who approach tragedy from the standpoint of *Geistesgeschichte*, who usually proceed by extrapolating passages supposed to reveal the poet's thought. They have neglected Tycho's work, and their self-protecting instinct can easily be understood; for in the field of *Geistesgeschichte* also it had

[15] 'The framework which he had chosen did not allow Tycho to show how for Sophocles dramatic technique serves only as a means of shaping something far deeper, something that lies in the nature of his art and his humanity. But in order to advance towards an understanding of this one must first make oneself thoroughly familiar with the narrower approach indicated in this book': Fraenkel.

[16] 'It would be sad if our understanding of Sophocles had made no progress after Tycho's youthful work, and not least in consequence of the stimulating effect that work has had. The progress has been great, above all thanks to Karl Reinhardt's *Sophocles*. This is perhaps the finest book ever written on this poet. It is not an easy book; its intensity may sometimes alarm, I will not say a cold-blooded reader, but one who likes to think things over calmly, and so is glad to allow Tycho to take him down from a higher sphere to the permanent and solid earth': Fraenkel. Reinhardt's *Sophokles* first appeared in 1933; the latest edition is the third, of 1947. My introduction to the English translation appears below, Chapter 20.

[17] 'Since Tycho did not carry through his basic conception consistently, he was wrong to blame the poet repeatedly (especially in the *Trachiniae*, but also the *Electra* and in other plays) for hasty or careless composition of certain scenes or parts of scenes, often attributing this to dependence on motives taken from earlier plays of Sophocles or of plays of Euripides, but sometimes to "pretty hasty composition" Instead of taking offence at such imperfections, the reader should try to use Tycho's own deeper insights to correct them': Fraenkel.

revolutionary implications. First, the sharp reminder that above all things a Greek tragedy is a play, written to be acted in a theatre and designed to have a particular effect upon its audience, could not fail to distress those who are accustomed to treat it as though it were an ethical or metaphysical treatise. People who took it for granted that the main element of a tragedy was its religious or metaphysical content, and that the poets wrote to recommend beliefs and opinions, sometimes new and 'original', were bound to resist an approach which was a step on the way to the revolutionary view that, at least in the case of early tragedy, traditional beliefs supplied a background against which the action of the play took place. Further, a challenge to the assumption that an ancient dramatist's aims and methods were like those of a modern dramatist was likely to strengthen the challenge to the equally prevalent assumption that the religion, ethics, and general world outlook of the ancient Greeks were either very like those now fashionable or were of interest chiefly because they were such as to 'lead up to' them.

Tycho's treatment of the *Antigone* appeared in print during his lifetime (see Ernst Kapp's Forword, p. v). It is encumbered by a lengthy polemic against a now deservedly forgotten theory of A.B. Drachmann[18] and it suffers from an undue insistence on the improbability of Antigone escaping capture on the occasion of her first burial of Polyneices. But it is none the less an important contribution to the understanding of the play; and, perhaps because it appeared before the rest, it contains many important statements of Tycho's principles, several of which have already been cited in the footnotes of this article.

Minor improbabilities concerning Creon's proclamation (18f.), Antigone's claim to have buried Eteocles (19f.), and Haemon's movements (21f.) exist, but are not particularly significant; more important is Tycho's argument that Ismene has no importance except as a foil for Antigone (23f.).[19] More interesting still is his handling of the problem of the 'double burial' (26f.). He makes somewhat heavy weather of the question of how Antigone avoids detection on the first occasion (26-30); surely it is easy for the spectator to infer that she does so under cover of the darkness.[20] He thinks that her return to the body is left unmotivated simply because it is inexplicable (34); but is one guilty of psychologising unreasonably if one takes it for granted

---

[18] 'For a correct appreciation of what Tycho has done for the understanding of the *Antigone* one should take no notice of pretty well everything between p. 7 and p. 17 (before the second section)': Fraenkel.

[19] See n.3. above.

[20] See A.T. v. S. Bradshaw, *C.Q.* n.5. xii (1962) 201-4.

that she has heard of the desecration of the body and hastens to repair the damage? But Tycho made one important contribution to the solution of this problem; he saw why Sophocles found it necessary for Antigone to make two visits to the body. First, she has to triumph by cleverly eluding the guards and carrying out the burial, and Creon's reaction to the news had to be presented; then she has to be apprehended and brought before Creon. Only at that moment is the identity of the guilty person known; Antigone's appearance as a prisoner is a tremendous *coup de théâtre*. Tycho (33-4) correctly explained this.[21] His view that Sophocles cared nothing for consistency of character enabled him to deal summarily with the celebrated problem of the speech in which Antigone protests that she would have made such a sacrifice only for a brother (45f.); but few scholars now would be content with this.[22]

In the *Ajax*, Tycho showed that during the first stasimon Ajax and Tecmessa must be together in the tent (55f.). But though he may be right in thinking the *ekkyklēma* was used, one may doubt whether ll.579-85 are there, as he maintains, simply to fill in the interval needed for the machine to be employed; the dramatic value of the dialogue here is obvious.[23] Tycho's belief that Sophocles cared nothing for consistency of character allows him once more to take a short way with a celebrated problem, this time that of the 'deceptive speech' of Ajax at 646f.; in his view Ajax means to deceive his companions, although the audience is not deceived, and simply acts as though the deception were the truth, with no attempt at psychological verisimilitude on the poet's part. For an understanding of the poetic purpose of the speech and an explanation of the pathos of its relentless but gentle irony, one must turn to Reinhardt.[24] One of Tycho's best achievements is his explanation of why Sophocles makes Teucer defend his brother's honour in two successive *agones* against Menelaus and Agamemnon (65f.). Had there been only a single *agon*, settled in the end by the intervention of Odysseus, Teucer's unshaken resolution would not have received the emphasis the poet rightly wished to give it.[25]

Kranz in his review of Tycho's book[26] rightly observed that the

[21] See n.11 above.

[22] Reinhardt's (op. cit. 92-3) is the most notable discussion; more recent treatments (see H. Friis Johansen, *Lustrum* 1962-7, 198-9) do not add much.

[23] See W. Kranz, *Sokrates*, N.F. vi (1918), 333 = *Studien zur antiken Literatur und ihrem Nachwirken* (1967), 304.

[24] Op. cit. 31f.; again, later interpretations add little (Friis Johansen, loc. cit., 177f.).

[25] See n.11 above.

[26] Loc. cit. (n.23 above), 332 = 303.

treatment of the *Oedipus Tyrannus* is a good specimen of its author's methods. He shows convincingly that the justly famous plot, when closely scrutinised, reveals a number of small improbabilities and inconsistencies which a modern realistic writer would not allow himself. Creon's movements at the start are not quite consistently described (72-3). The Tiresias scene contains contradictions, but these do not justify the view of some modern writers that Tiresias is a 'sinister' figure, secretly hostile to Oedipus. The poet is not interested in Tiresias' character, and the contradictions are due simply to the requirements of the plot (73-89). Tycho truly says that the whole plot depends on the old Theban shepherd's incorrect statement that Laius was killed by more than one person. He must also be right in saying that the old man says this because it is essential to the poet's purpose; but is the old man's inaccuracy as motiveless as he supposed? Lines 758-64 make it clear that the old man chose deliberately to get himself out of the city, and it is not hard to imagine why he should have done so. Tycho observes that Iocaste's attempt to prove the uselessness of prophecy (707f.) is not really relevant, but is introduced in order to lead up to her use of the report of Polybus' death to comfort Oedipus (80-3); he shows also that in reality Oedipus would have known all as soon as he had learned that Polybus was not his real father, but that he was given to the Corinthian shepherd on Cithaeron by a slave of Laius; not that either inconsistency troubles the audience during a performance (83-5). His concluding remarks on characterisation in the play and the poet's lack of interest in the psychology of his persons are altogether to the point (85-8).

The chapter on the *Trachiniae* must be judged less satisfactory. Tycho is unduly severe about this play, which he regards as a hurried and careless piece of work; he devotes excessive space to the refutation of a once influential, but now deservedly forgotten treatment by Zielinski[27] and he is handicapped by his preoccupation with

---

[27] 'The book often becomes involved in polemic against mistaken interpretations which now seem to us purposeless, partly because of the effect of the book itself. This is true, for instance, of the justified but far too lengthy polemic against Zielinski in the chapter on the *Trachiniae*. In general this chapter is uneven and should be regarded as a preliminary sketch; it is one of the chapters which according to Ernst Kapp's testimony took only their preliminary shape in the dissertation of 1911. Anyone who had made himself familiar with Tycho's method will not doubt that he would have made far-reaching alterations if he had been granted time to think out and formulate the chapter once again. But even so this chapter contains only a few conclusions that have permanent value. A reader who is concerned to attain a deep understanding of the art of Sophocles should make the effort to make his way beyond the lower levels of polemical argument to the rich positive insights which rise above them with undiminished attentiveness': Fraenkel.

Dieterich's theory that the scene of Heracles' awakening shows the influence of the not dissimilar scene in Euripides' *Heracles*,[28] as well as by his own unverifiable guess that the character of Deianeira was derived by Sophocles from that of Penelope in his lost *Niptra*. His whole treatment of the obscure topic of the early treatment of the myth is not notably rewarding, though his conjecture that the false motive for Heracles' attack on Oechalia given by Lichas may represent a different version given in an earlier poem may quite easily be right.

Few would now agree with Tycho that the prologue 'is composed exactly in the manner of Euripides' (116),[29] nor that it displays 'lack of attention to motivation and an extraordinary disregard for verisimilitude' (117). In real life Hyllus would have told Deianeira where his father was long before, but Sophoclean technique obviously requires that he must do it when he does, nor will the audience be disturbed at his getting to Heracles and back so quickly. Tycho in his treatment of the difficulties raised by the different mentions of the oracle given at Dodona draws attention to some serious problems (119-33). But as early as 1921 Kranz showed that if the various references to this oracle are considered each in its own context, no really grave inconsistency is found, but it becomes clear that each time the poet lets the audience know just as much about the oracle at the present situation of the plot requires.[30] The obvious parallel is furnished by the oracle in the *Philoctetes*, which is far more freely handled.

The refutation of Zielinski's treatment of Deianeira's scene with Lichas (134-8) is followed by some good general remarks about the type of argument which Zielinski uses (138-42). Then comes an excellent explanation of Sophocles' reasons for arranging Deianeira's scenes with Lichas and the messenger as he did; the good news of the victory must come first and cause premature rejoicing, the bad news about Iole must follow after an interval, and the greatest possible dramatic effect must be obtained from both (142-5). Faced with Deianeira, whose character has charmed so many interpreters, not always to their advantage, Tycho concedes that there is hardly any other Sophoclean personage who comes so near to being a character

---

[28] See Johanna Heinz, *Hermes* lxxii (1937), 289f.

[29] See Heinz, loc. cit., 284f.

[30] Tycho had predecessors in Dobree, *Adversaria* iii, 36 and Wunder, *Sophoclis Tragoediae*, vol. ii, sect. iii (1841), 47f.; the theory has now been revived in a somewhat different form by M.D. Reeve, *Greek, Roman and Byzantine Studies* xi (1970), 283f. See Kranz, *Jahresberichte des Philologischen Vereins zu Berlin* xlvii (1921), 32f. = *Studien* (see n.23 above), 283f.

in the modern sense (145); but even here he finds inconsistencies. He rightly rejects the interpretation of her words at 494-7 as a kind of Freudian slip revealing an unconscious malice (145-9); but he makes somewhat heavy weather of the alleged discrepancy between 436f. and 531f. After all, Iole is the first among his mistresses whom Heracles has actually brought to live in the matrimonial home (note 536f.) (150-4). Surely he goes too far in arguing that Deianeira's use of the philtre is inconsistent with her words at 436f.; the poet conveys with great delicacy how a wife who has sincerely uttered these sentiments might still, not knowing the real nature of the philtre, be tempted to make use of it. Like many others, Tycho complains that the play falls into two halves (154-5); this complaint seems to issue from his assumption[31] that every play of Sophocles must have one central character about whose fortunes it revolves. For him Deianeira is the central figure of the first half, Heracles of the second, and this seems to him perplexing. But need either be the central figure? The play is about the events that led to the death of Heracles; it shows the fulfilment of the plan of Zeus. Tycho shows much acuteness in his handling of the problem of Hyllus' movements in the later scenes and of the authenticity of ll. 901-3; only lately has a convincing solution of the difficulties he exposed been put forward.[32]

The chapter on the *Electra* was left unfinished, though the first half had been revised (Ernst Kapp, p. vi); it is the least satisfactory of all. Here more than anywhere the reader is vexed by perpetual complaints of departures from naturalism which Tycho's own researches have shown to be typical of Sophocles' technique; and the long section on the play's chronological relation to Euripides' *Electra* (228-64), with the appendix on the *Helen* and *Iphigenia in Tauris* that follows, need not now be read.[33] The treatment of the *Electra* itself often leads to unacceptable conclusions; yet even here Tycho's arguments still deserve to be read carefully.

The lack of naturalism in the initial dialogue is hardly proof of

---

[31] See John Jones, op. cit. (n.10 above), ch.1.

[32] By R.P. Winnington-Ingram, *B.I.C.S.* xvi (1969), 44f.

[33] 'The long section on the relation of the *Electra* of Sophocles to that of Euripides (p. 228-68) starts from a dating of the Euripidean play that has now been refuted, wearies us by its polemic against obsolete theories, and, most significantly, contains only very little of Tycho's most characteristic and most valuable thinking. So to begin with, at least, the reader may omit this section without missing anything essential. As regards the chronological question, Tycho rightly claims that Sophocles' *Electra* is earlier, but this can be argued much more powerfully than it is by him': Fraenkel. See now the useful dissertation of Armin Vögler, *Vergleichende Studien zur sophokleischen und euripideischen Elektra*, Heidelberg (1967); see my review in *C.R.* xix (1969), 36f., for the account of Tycho's treatment in his historical summary.

carelessness (166-7); neither is the absence of a motive for the entry of the Chorus (169); on the other hand, the observation regarding the use of the *Choephori* at ll. 77-85 is excellent. It is in no way strange that the Chorus makes no reply to Electra's long speech after the parodos (171); a reply is not needed. Nor is it surprising, even after what has been said earlier, that after that speech the Coryphaeus should confirm the absence of Aegisthus and should inquire for news of Orestes. In terms of the technique of early tragedy, the repetition is not offensive, and it is important to the poet's purpose that both subjects should be recalled to the audience at this point. Equally in keeping with the poet's methods is the absence of motivation for the successive *agones* of Electra with Chrysothemis and Clytemnestra; however improbable it may seem that such scenes should take place at these particular moments, the plot obviously requires it. In his treatment of the first scene with Chrysothemis, Tycho insists that the threat to imprison Electra is a motive invented simply for the moment, and afterwards arbitrarily disregarded. Indeed it is disregarded later, but is there any further need for it to be mentioned? In the *agon* with Clytemnestra it is not required, and after that both Clytemnestra and, when he returns, Aegisthus have other things to think about.

It is hardly true that the first Chrysothemis scene is 'so lacking in results that a long quiet conversation can follow' (177-9); Electra's triumph in the *agon* is heightened by her success in forcing her sister to accompany the offering sent by Clytemnestra to the tomb with a prayer of Electra's own dictation, and its effect will later be accentuated by a triumph over a more formidable antagonist in Clytemnestra herself.[34] To say that the first stasimon (473f.) 'is expressed in a completely conventional manner, with ideas generally available in the myth, with no intention of any sort of special effect' (179) scarcely does justice to its significance; Dike and the Erinys have their significance in this play.[35] Sophoclean technique does not require that the debate between mother and daughter at 516f. must be specially motivated (179-82); Tycho rightly dismisses the psychological explanations offered by modern critics, but fails to recognise that no motivation is required. He rightly insists that the main feature of the *agon* is the triumph of Electra; but while he justly discounts its alleged psychological significance (185), one may doubt whether its bearing on the moral issue is so slight as he implies.

Tycho has some good observations about the prayer of Clytemnestra

[34] So Schadewaldt, *Monolog und Selbstgespräch* (1926), 58 n.2.
[35] See Winnington-Ingram, *Proc. Cambridge Phil. Soc.* clxxxiii (1954-5), 20f. (German version in *Sophokles*, ed. H. Diller [*Wege der Forschung*, Band XCV (1967), 400f.]). Lloyd-Jones, *The Justice of Zeus* (Berkeley 1969), 112-13.

at 634f. (186-7), and about the partial sincerity of her grief at the announcement of her son's death (187-8). But he can hardly be right in maintaining that an audience which has seen the Paidagogos talking with Orestes during the prologue is so carried away by his convincing fiction that it actually shares the delusion of his hearers on the stage. Yet it is true that the main function of the speech is to enable the audience to imagine its effect upon Electra, who believes it (188-93). Tycho rightly draws attention (193) to the effect of contrast secured by the return of Chrysothemis, but in his insistence that everything must be seen from Electra's point of view he misses the full impact of the scene's irony. Chrysothemis, he says (194), is made to appear childish; but the audience knows that she is right and Electra wrong. Is the scene really there, as Tycho thinks, simply because the motive of the offerings at the tomb had to be worked in?[36] His treatment of Electra's proposal that the sisters shall try together to kill Aegisthus is very like his treatment of the threat to imprison Electra; the suggestion is by no means so unreal as he supposes (195-202). While Electra is speaking, the audience will know that she means what she says; and Greek mythology offers several instances of actions such as she proposes. Naturally she makes no mention of her mother, for her aim is to persuade her sister; nor does Chrysothemis in her reply find it necessary to mention Clytemnestra. Considering what happens immediately afterwards, it is hardly surprising that we hear no more of this proposal.

The suggestion of the Coryphaeus that Electra as 'the nearest' shall introduce Orestes and his party is scarcely as surprising as Tycho finds it (202-4); the courts of the heroic age were not ceremonious in

---

[36] Fraenkel strongly agreed with Tycho here: 'In the *Electra* Electra tries to persuade her sister Chrysothemis to join her in murdering Aegisthus. Sophocles gives no indication as to how the two of them could carry out this plan. Ancient critics remarked the singularity of the poet's silence about such an important presupposition and tried to explain it psychologically; Electra, they said, stressed only the advantages that would accrue to the sisters from the deed they were planning but suppressed, knowing her sister's timid nature, any allusion to the danger that would attend the enterprise (see the scholion on 975 and the passage from the *Rhetoric* of Apsines quoted ad loc. in the edition of Jahn and Michaelis, *Rhetores Graeci*, ed. Spengel-Hammer i, p. 302, 2ff.) Tycho explains the real reason for such a surprising omission when he explains the function in the drama of Electra's altogether unrealisible plan. In this context he makes the effective observation that in Hofmannsthal's *Elektra* "Chrysothemis is told how the murder is to be carried out and how success can be attained even before Electra tries to persuade her, and the plan is graphically described in all its details." This is a typical example of the fundamental difference between what a modern reader or spectator thinks is necessary and what Sophocles wishes to represent on the stage and what would content him and his public.'

the manner of Versailles, and it would not have been unusual for the strangers to be conducted into the queen's presence by the only member of the royal family present at the moment of their arrival. Tycho conclusively refutes the view of Kaibel and others that Orestes really knows who Electra is at the moment when he orders the urn to be put into her hands (204-6); he seems to have convinced everybody. Less to the point are his complaints about the lack of verisimilitude in the actual *anagnōrisis* (206-10). A conventional pattern is being followed, and naturalism is not in place; yet the scene is written with passion, so that the conventional element does not detract from the emotional effect. Tycho finds that the following scene (1233-1383) serves simply to present Electra's feelings; yet the warnings against indiscretion given her by Orestes and by the Paidagogos may serve to remind the audience that these feelings are shown against the background provided by a world inhabited by others. Like so many scholars, Tycho finds that Clytemnestra's murder gets very little of the poet's attention (215-16).[37] Certainly its representation occupies very few lines of print; but in performance the impression made by this episode, and in particular by Electra's horrifying cries of encouragement to her brother, is far greater than Tycho's words imply; as usual, he is concerned to insist that the real climax of the whole action is the recognition scene. For him Clytemnestra's murder is only an introduction and a means to the killing of Aegisthus (218); yet Sophoclean practice suggests that a final dialogue scene may be little more than a pendant to a preceding lyric episode. He finds the concluding dialogue between Orestes and Aegisthus 'almost incomprehensible' (217); it does not occur to him that this conversation, during which Aegisthus is allowed to get in at least one not ineffective retort (1500), may help the audience to see the phase in the history of the house of Atreus which it has seen enacted from a standpoint somewhat different from Electra's own.[38] Tycho's concluding remarks about the play's construction (219-28) suffer from the defects indicated by the preceding criticisms. They contain some just objections to the psychologising interpretations current at the

[37] This opinion was evidently shared by Fraenkel, who in one of his notes has copied out the passage on p. 174 which contains the words 'The poet has put the received story of Orestes' matricide completely in the background so far as our interest is concerned and no one can think of a moral problem residing in this material'. For a different view, see H. Friis Johansen, *Classica et Mediaevalia* xxv (1964), 8f.; C.P. Segal, *T.A.P.A.* xcvii (1966), 473f.; H.-J. Newiger, *Arcadia* iv (1969), 138f. (an important article); Winnington-Ingram, *Sophocles: an Interpretation*, ch. 10.

[38] See Friis Johansen, loc. cit. 28-9. It is going too far to suggest that the justice of the revenge is doubted; but no attempt is made to minimise the horror of the matricide.

time when Tycho wrote; but Tycho's insistence that the play centres not upon Electra's character but upon the recognition scene is not well founded. Indeed Sophocles is not concerned with the idiosyncrasies of his heroine; but he is concerned with her heroic nature and its divergence from the human norm, and he has shown the drawbacks as well as the advantages attaching to such a character. In the sense of the word 'character' that corresponds with the Greek term ēthos, Sophocles is interested in Electra's character; and the final scenes contribute hardly less than the justly famous anagnōrisis to its depiction.

The chapter on the Philoctetes was written in 1913, and was more carefully revised by the author than any other part of the work; it is the best of all, and its excellence makes one keenly regret the absence of a chapter on the work nearest in date and method to the Philoctetes.[39]

Tycho rightly concludes that it is not certain whether an account of how Philoctetes was persuaded to leave Lemnos for Troy figures in early epic, and briefly describes its treatment by Aeschylus and Euripides (269-75). He rightly recognizes that though in reality Neoptolemus would certainly have learned what was expected of him before reaching Lemnos, Sophoclean technique requires that he must be instructed by Odysseus during the prologue (274-5). Odysseus, he observes, outlines no definite plan; and in the prologue the important question of whether the bow alone is needed or Philoctetes with the bow is left vague. That is true, although l. 112 seems to indicate that Neoptolemus assumes that Philoctetes as well as the bow must come to Troy (274-7). Tycho argues that during the parodos and the scene with Philoctetes that precedes the entry of the supposed merchant, Neoptolemus and the Chorus behave not as if they are skilfully playing a part, but as if the fiction they were enacting were the reality (278-81); the merchant scene, he thinks, makes no sense if one remembers that Neoptolemus means to betray Philoctetes (281-3). To modern taste it must seem strange that nothing indicates that Neoptolemus and the Chorus are skilfully playing a part. But Tycho exaggerates the improbabilities of the scenes in question; Neoptolemus' plan to get Philoctetes on board the ship, bow and all, and Odysseus' effort to hurry on the proceedings by sending the merchant make perfect sense in the context. It is true that Odysseus' stratagem works out unfortunately for himself in that it warns Philoctetes that Odysseus is on his track; but that is necessary for the working-out of the plot, and is not in itself improbable or inconsistent.

---

[39] Fraenkel says of the chapter on the Oedipus Coloneus supplied by Tycho's father that 'it forms no organic part of Tycho's book.'

Tycho is surely right to insist that the dialogue of Philoctetes and Neoptolemus at 628-75 is intended to stress the importance of the bow, and not to illuminate the psychology of Neoptolemus (283-5). He observes that the stasimon that begins at 676 has every appearance of being a sincere expression of the sympathy of the Chorus for Philoctetes. His contention that the Chorus is here only the instrument of the poet (295-9) cannot be refuted by saying that the Chorus has misunderstood the real situation, and assumes that now that Philoctetes and Neoptolemus have made friends, they will easily reach an agreement;[40] the Chorus says that Philoctetes will be taken home, but nothing about his going to Troy. A more plausible answer would be that the Chorus is playing the part of deceiver all too well.[41] Up till now, Tycho has insisted, attention has been concentrated on Philoctetes; during the scene that extends from 730 to 864 it is concentrated, he points out, on Neoptolemus, of whose ambiguous position the audience is now directly reminded. He shows how necessary it is to the poet's purpose that Neoptolemus shall not steal the bow, as he did in Aeschylus, but have it entrusted to him by its owner. While Philoctetes is sleeping, the Chorus urges Neoptolemus to make off with the bow. Tycho was the first to point out the singularity of Neoptolemus' answer; instead of protesting that it would be dishonourable, Neoptolemus declares that the bow will be no use without its owner. And yet in the opening scene of the play Odysseus has by no means made this clear; and later, when Odysseus proposed to abandon Philoctetes and sail off with the bow, he declares that Philoctetes himself is not needed, and Neoptolemus and the Chorus do not contradict him (289-95). Before Tycho, the acute problem presented by these facts had not been faced; since his time it has been hotly debated, but the authors of the two most notable recent contributions both accept his general conclusion that Sophocles allows himself great freedom in respect of the content of the prophecy of Helenus.[42]

When Neoptolemus finally decides to make a clean breast of it and tell Philoctetes the truth, that happens, Tycho argues, without warning; he strongly denies that the audience has been prepared for it by any delineation of Neoptolemus' psychology. This is surely true;

---

[40] Thus Gerhard Müller, in *Sophokles*, ed. H. Diller, pp. 213f.

[41] See Reinhardt's comments on the words of the Chorus at 391f. and 507f. (op. cit. in n.16).

[42] D.B. Robinson, *C.Q.* xix (1969), 45-51 (against A.E. Hinds, ibid., xvii [1967], 169f.), and O. Zwierlein, *G.G.A.*, 222 Jahrgang. Heft 3/4 (1970), 206f. (in a review of W. Steidle, *Studien zum antiken Drama*, Munich [1968]); cf. O. Taplin, *G.R.B.S.* xii (1971), 35 n.24.

but when he argues that Neoptolemus acts not out of pity, but because his intrigue is now bound to be discovered in the near future, he omits to mention the obvious signs of shame with which the revelation is accompanied (295-7). Sophocles, in Tycho's view, is unable or unwilling to represent a double situation[43] in which a character has to keep up a pretence; he makes Neoptolemus first act exactly as though the part he was playing were genuine and then suddenly reveal the truth to Philoctetes and betray his shame, without abandoning the mission entrusted to him by Odysseus (297-8). Tycho finds it surprising, and by the canons of naturalism it certainly is, that Neoptolemus makes no attempt to explain the whole situation to Philoctetes in the hope of persuading him to come voluntarily to Troy; neither does Philoctetes demand an explanation of Neoptolemus. But the poet could have replied that Philoctetes in his enraged state would neither have demanded nor listened to an explanation (298-300). Tycho shows most skilfully that it is the merchant's communication of the prophecy of Helenus and the expedition of Odysseus that render Philoctetes, being such as he has been presented as being in his first scene with Neoptolemus, so determined to avoid being taken to Troy (300-2).

Tycho clearly points out the contradiction between Odysseus' assumption that the bow only is needed, and not its owner, and Neoptolemus' words both earlier and later in the play, and deals decisively with the attempt of Radermacher to show that Odysseus is only bluffing. He shows how skilfully the exposition in the prologue is calculated to prepare for the vagueness about the prophecy necessary for the plot (302-6). If Odysseus were only bluffing, he points out (306-7), the lyric scene of Philoctetes with the Chorus (1081f.) would lose all meaning. Tycho, who is so severe with the *Trachiniae* and the *Electra*, fully acknowledges the excellence of the scene during which Neoptolemus returns the bow (1218f.); he acutely observes that if the volte-face had been led up to by psychological preparation, the poet could hardly have achieved such an effect of surprise (307-8). It may be doubted whether Tycho is right in finding it implausible, although dramatically effective, that before returning the bow Neoptolemus should make an unavailing attempt to

---

[43] Kranz writes in the review quoted above (n.23), p. 332 = 303: 'Even Wilamowitz is not quite free from the mistake of making out that the poet's capacity fell short or was impeded in some connection; for example, one should not say that "the representation of such a double, fragmented situation lay quite outside what was possible for Sophocles"; it does lie beyond what he aimed at, since "art can always do what it wants", and it is a question of showing why the artist has not wanted this or that.'

persuade Philoctetes to come to Troy (308-9). Tycho thinks it would have been quite possible for Sophocles to allow Philoctetes, after the discomfiture of Odysseus, to be persuaded by Neoptolemus to abandon his quarrel with the Atridae and go to Troy. Surely this would have been inconceivable for a Sophoclean hero, loving his friends and hating his enemies beyond the norm. He thinks Sophocles used the god from the machine to bring about the ending which the known myth required. In fact the poet's use of Heracles serves a deliberate poetic purpose; deeply distasteful as it is for Philoctetes to make his peace with the Atridae and Odysseus, the will of Zeus requires that he must do so, and only the command of Heracles can persuade him.[44]

[44] On the appearance of Heracles in the *Philoctetes*, see A. Spira, *Untersunchungen zum Deus ex machina bei Sophokles und Euripides*, Diss. Frankfurt a. M. (1960), pp. 12-32, and Karin Alt, *Hermes* lxxxix (1961), 167-72 = *Sophokles*, ed. H. Diller, 448-55.

Addendum. Here is an isolated observation of Fraenkel regarding p. 274 n.1: 'It is clear that Neoptolemus gives a thorough description of Philoctetes' cave because he is describing what the audience does not see; that he does so establishes that Neoptolemus can go inside and see, even though the inside of the cave is invisible to the audience.' Cf. A.M. Dale, *Wiener Studien* lxix (1956) 104-5 = *Collected Papers* (1969) 127-9 = *Sophokles*, ed. H. Diller, 249-50 (German version).

20

Karl Reinhardt

In our time classical scholars often tell each other that they should cease to concentrate too much on technical scholarship and do more for the literary interpretation of the classics. That is easier said than done; although Housman doubtless exaggerated when he claimed that the faculty of literary criticism was the rarest gift,[1] it is certainly not common, and it has been denied to many learned men. When a learned man does appear who is liberally endowed with that rare gift, he surely deserves to be read not only by those who can read him in his own language, but by others also.

Karl Reinhardt[2] occupied a unique place among the classical scholars of the particularly gifted generation to which he belonged. He was born on 14 February 1886, the son of highly cultivated parents; his father was head of the chief secondary school in Frankfurt, and later helped to found the famous school called Salem, whose former headmaster, the late Kurt Hahn, founded Gordonstoun. The Reinhardts were both keenly interested in the literature and art of their own time, as well as of the past; Paul Deussen, the early friend of Nietzsche, was among the interesting visitors who were often in their house. Karl Reinhardt might have become an imaginative writer, a

---

*This chapter first appeared as the introduction to the English translation of Reinhardt's *Sophocles* by Hazel and David Harvey, published by Basil Blackwell, Oxford, 1979.

[1] At the beginning of his Leslie Stephen Lecture on 'The Name and Nature of Poetry', reprinted in A.E. Housman, *Selected Prose*, ed. John Carter (1961), 168ff.

[2] Speeches about Reinhardt delivered at a memorial ceremony on 3 June 1958 by Helmut Viereck, Matthias Gelzer and Uvo Hölscher were printed in the pamphlet *Gedenkreden auf Karl Reinhardt* (Frankfurt 1958). The second chapter of Uvo Hölscher's pamphlet *Die Chance des Unbehagens* (1965), 31ff., contains an excellent account of Reinhardt. See also the obituary notice by Rudolf Pfeiffer in the *Jahrbuch der Bayerischen Akademie* (1959), 147ff. and the *Nachwort* appended by Carl Becker to the collection of Reinhardt's essays called *Tradition und Geist* (1960), 431ff. See n.13 below.

historian of art or a distinguished actor, and in his writing and his teaching he revealed the qualities that might have helped him to succeed at any one of these professions. He began his student career at Bonn and later moved to Munich; but in 1904 his father accepted an appointment in the Ministry of Education in Berlin, and Reinhardt moved to the university of the imperial capital. There he was fascinated by the inspiring teaching of Ulrich von Wilamowitz-Moellendorff, the last man to attempt to attain excellence in virtually every branch of Greek learning.[3] Reinhardt had already come to share Nietzsche's discontent with the dryness and materialism into which the dominance of historicism had led German scholarship, and his fastidious taste must have revolted from the start against the element of philistinism revealed by Wilamowitz' approach to literature. But he was captivated by the rare personal charm of Wilamowitz, was carried away by his daemonic energy and conceived a deep admiration for his profound learning. In his own person, Reinhardt contrived to combine the profound scholarship of a worthy pupil of Wilamowitz with the enlightened realism of a follower of Nietzsche and the refined feeling for poetry of a gifted contemporary of George and of Hofmannsthal.

In 1910 Reinhardt obtained his doctorate with a thesis on the allegorical interpretation of Homer current in antiquity,[4] and in 1914 habilitated with a study of the first three books of Strabo, in which that writer expounds the theoretical basis of his Geography. The choice of these useful but somewhat dry subjects is an index of his determination to acquire technical competence in his profession; yet though he never published the work on Strabo, it must have helped to lead him to Posidonius. After teaching for a while in Bonn and Marburg he became full Professor in Hamburg in 1919, but in 1923 he returned to occupy a chair at his birthplace, Frankfurt. In 1933, the year of Hitler's coming to power, Reinhardt offered his resignation. When pressed to remain, he decided with considerable misgivings that he should stay and try to keep the university alive through the period of crisis. In 1942, when the university of Frankfurt had almost ceased to function, he accepted a call to Leipzig; in 1946, when he and his wife were threatened with starvation, he returned to Frankfurt, where he remained even after his retirement until his death on 9

---

[3] Reinhardt's account of him will be found in the volume of his essays called *Vermächtnis der Antike*, 2nd ed. (1966), 361ff. I have attempted to give a brief account of Wilamowitz to English readers in the introduction to an English version of his *History of Classical Scholarship*, soon to be published by Duckworth.

[4] *De Graecorum theologia* (Diss. Frankfurt, 1910).

January 1958. He himself has sketched his early career, and also his experiences under the National Socialist regime, in two brief but highly interesting memoirs.[5]

In 1916 Reinhardt published a book about Parmenides[6] which, although many of its contentions are not now generally accepted, was a striking and original contribution to the understanding of pre-Socratic philosophy. He followed this with three successive studies of Posidonius[7] (135-51 BC), except Plotinus, the last great philosopher of the ancient world, who constructed an eclectic version of the Stoic philosophy more humane and tolerant than that of its earlier exponents and also did epoch-making work in history, geography and anthropology. The work of Posidonius has to be reconstructed from scattered testimonies and fragments, which were not adequately collected until 1972, fourteen years after Reinhardt's death.[8] His method of treatment is often open to question. In his first volume, in particular, he can hardly be said to offer sufficient evidence in support of his contentions, and his confidence that his grasp of the inner form of the philosopher's system has enabled him to re-establish it in detail has not been shared by all his critics. Not all the evidence which might be considered relevant has been taken into account, as the user of the learned encyclopaedia article on Posidonius,[9] to which Reinhardt felt it his duty to devote three of his precious last years, will thanks to him find it easier to see. Yet the three books not only represent a vast advance upon all previous efforts, but are written with a flair and sympathy rare in the historical study of philosophy.

The first half of Reinhardt's career had been devoted mainly to philosophy; the second was to be given mainly to poetry. The book on Sophocles appeared in 1933,[10] when its author was forty-seven years old. In 1949 he followed it with a short but most perceptive and imaginative book about Aeschylus,[11] whose spectacular stage effects Reinhardt held to be closely bound up with his theology. In 1961, three years after his death, his former pupil, Uvo Hölscher, brought

---

[5] 'Akademisches aus zwei Epochen', *Die Neue Rundschau* 66 (1955), 1ff. = *Vermächtnis der Antike*, 380ff.

[6] *Parmenides und die Geschichte der griechischen Philosophie* (1916; 2nd ed. 1959).

[7] *Poseidonios* (1921); *Kosmos und Sympathie* (1926); *Poseidonios über Ursprung und Entartung* (1928; in *Orient und Antike* vi, reprinted in *Vermächtnis der Antike*, 402ff.).

[8] See L. Edelstein and I.G. Kidd, *Posidonius* i, *The Fragments* (1972): the commentary is in preparation.

[9] 'Poseidonios von Apameia', in Pauly-Wissowa-Kroll, *Real-Enzyklopädie* xxii, 561ff. (also obtainable separately).

[10] 2nd ed. 1941; 3rd ed. 1947.

[11] *Aischylos als Regisseur und Theologe*.

out his study of the *Iliad*.[12] Its unitarian point of view is not shared by all, and its disregard for Parry's work on oral poetry has excited some disapproval in the Anglo-Saxon world; but it is written with its author's keen intelligence and fine feeling for poetry, and cannot safely be neglected.

Throughout his career Reinhardt produced important articles as well as books; these are collected in two volumes, published in 1960, one devoted to philosophy and history and the other to Greek and German poetry.[13] Reinhardt's studies of the adventures of the *Odyssey*, of Heraclitus, Herodotus, Thucydides, Euripides and Aristophanes, are of great importance; and his work on modern writers, especially Goethe, Hölderlin and Nietzsche, seems hardly less distinguished.

It is easy for the reader of these works to believe those who heard Reinhardt speak when they say that as teacher and lecturer he exercised a unique fascination. By speech and gesture he was able to convey, more adequately than by the written word, his awareness of the impossibility of returning cut-and-dried answers to many of the acutest problems and his sensitivity to the innumerable ambiguities of literature and of life itself. His method, as he says himself with reference to his *Sophocles*, was a comparative method; but it was far from the comparative method of those who are content to categorise a work in terms of its author's supposed psychology or supposed literary ancestry, or to enumerate the *topoi* under which each element of it is supposed to fall without explaining how these are modified by the nature and purpose of the writer or the requirements of the context.

During the later part of the nineteenth century and the early part of the twentieth century, Greek tragedy was too often interpreted as though its aims and methods were identical with those of modern drama. In particular it was assumed, as it was also in the case of Shakespeare and his contemporaries, that the portrayal of character was one of the main elements, if not the main element, in the tragic art. Most critical discussions of tragedy during this period abound with minute psychological analysis, most of it unprofitable. The great scholar Wilamowitz was no exception to the prevailing tendency, as many examples given by Reinhardt in his *Sophocles* help to show. Reinhardt in his essay on Euripides[14] quotes a particularly revealing instance from the great man's edition of the *Hippolytus* which Wilamowitz published in the year of the première of *Hedda Gabler*.

---

[12] *Die Ilias und ihr Dichter.*

[13] *Vermächtnis der Antike: Gesammelte Essays zur Philosophie und Geschichtsschreibung*, 2nd ed. (1966); *Tradition und Geist: Gesammelte Essays zur Dichtung* (1960).

[14] *Tradition und Geist*, 236; see above, n.7.

'She is no ordinary woman,' Wilamowitz writes of Phaedra, '... She is every bit the society lady, knows and performs her duties; she has a husband and children, relations and a social position, and is well able to accord to all these the consideration that she owes them. But she has no inner relationship to husband or children, let alone to anything else. Her life lacks the blessing of work, and she is too intelligent to find satisfaction in idleness and in empty society ... So she is ripe for passion. Suddenly she encounters in her stepson a being who fascinates her, simply because she cannot understand him ... She for her part dreams of a life free from the shackles of convention, a life of freedom and of feeling such as she has never known. To pick flowers with him beside the brook, to hunt and ride by his side; that would give content to her existence. That is what her feelings tell her. Her understanding does not fail to give her counsel. She knows that she must not and will not go astray ... It is not sin that she is afraid of; far from it, she knows that she cannot help being in love. What she is afraid of is disgrace. Acting her part was her whole life. She was the irreproachable wife, because it was proper to be so; because it would be proper, she wants to die; impossible that she, Phaedra, the daughter of Minos, the Queen of Athens, should create a scandal ...' This Ibsenite Euripides has little to do with the reality, like the Shavian Euripides of Gilbert Murray that was so popular in England.

The first sharp reaction against this kind of interpretation came with the posthumous publication in 1917 of the doctoral thesis of Tycho von Wilamowitz-Moellendorff, son of Wilamowitz and grandson of Mommsen, who had died fighting on the Russian front in October 1914. This was a study of the dramatic technique of Sophocles which is still of great value.[15] Tycho Wilamowitz agreed with Aristotle that the characters in a tragedy were there for the plot, not the plot for the characters. He denied that exact characterisation was the principal aim of the tragedians, and was able to point to countless cases where the holders of this view had tried to deal with a problem posed by Sophocles' text by means of a psychological explanation which was wholly untenable. Taking no account, he complained, of the conditions of performance or the likely effect upon an audience, such critics tried to explain the actions of the characters as though they were real people. So far, he argued, from aiming always at convincing characterisation, Sophocles did not even trouble to make his characters consistent. Just as a factual detail, like the content of an oracular pronouncement, could take one shape at one

[15] Tycho von Wilamowitz-Moellendorff, *Die dramatische Kunst des Sophokles* (1917; reprinted 1969); see Ch. 19.

moment and another later, according to the dramatist's convenience, so a character could behave now in one way and now in another wholly different fashion, if that suited his creator.

Tycho's work threw much light on the dramatic methods of the poet, and eliminated for good much unconvincing psychological speculation about the motives of his characters. Scholars were as slow to grasp the importance of his book as they always are when they are confronted with real originality; but from about the early thirties its effect became visible, and now many of his tenets have become generally accepted.

In some ways Tycho went too far. Many of the departures from probability or consistency, or at least from modern notions of those concepts, which he notes, simply go to prove the truth of what he himself argues, that Sophoclean technique is far removed from that of nineteenth-century naturalism. Further, there is a sense in which Sophocles is interested in character, or at least in what the Greeks call *ēthos*. He does not care about personal idiosyncrasies or psychological niceties; but he cares greatly about the main qualities of his chief characters as human beings, and about the emotions which in virtue of those qualities they reveal. The famous Sophoclean scholar Sir Richard Jebb once met George Eliot, who told him that she had carefully studied Sophocles, whom she read in the original, and had been influenced by his work. When Jebb asked how Sophocles had influenced her, George Eliot replied: 'In the delineation of the great primitive emotions.'[16] It is these, and not psychological complexities, that are the main objects of the poet's study; and the emotions felt by different persons tend not to be the same.

Reinhardt's book, which appeared as early as 1933, accepted and developed what was best in Tycho's work and provided an ideal corrective to what was wanting. Reinhardt chose to treat of 'Sophoclean situations, or ... of the Sophoclean relation between man and god and between man and man, and to show how they develop, scene by scene, play by play, stage by stage in the poet's career ...' Using Tycho's results and applying his own kind of close analysis, Reinhardt with his mature taste and his unusually fine feeling for poetry was able to throw light on the poet's methods of depicting those emotions which Sophoclean situations evoke from the persons who are involved in them.

An important part of Reinhardt's purpose was to throw light on the difficult problem of the chronology of the seven complete plays of

---

[16] See Caroline Jebb, *Life and Letters of Sir Richard Claverhouse Jebb* (1907), 156; cf. Gordon Haight, *George Eliot* (1970), 173.

Sophocles that have survived. In this aim he achieved considerable success; but it was only part of his purpose, it was not the most important part, and the success which he attained in it was not complete. Let us consider his theory of Sophoclean chronology before coming to the more general aspects of his treatment.

The only surviving plays whose date is directly attested by external evidence are the *Philoctetes* (409 BC) and the *Oedipus at Colonus*, produced in 401, three years after the author's death, at the age perhaps of eighty-nine. In view of the very limited amount of material on which statistics can be based, the evidence of style and metre must be used with great caution. It is true that, in the case of Euripides, Zielinski was able to establish that the indications of one particular criterion of date, the increase in the number of resolutions of long elements in the iambic trimeter, yielded inferences as to date that roughly corresponded with the chronological facts known to us from external sources. But we have nineteen complete plays of Euripides, eight of them dated by external evidence. Excessive confidence in our ability to date Sophoclean plays from the evidence yielded by their style and metre is, or ought to be, discouraged by our experience in the case of Aeschylus, of whom we have seven complete plays, five of them dated by external evidence. For the first half of this century it was almost universally believed that one of the remaining two, *The Suppliant Women*, must be a very early work, composed perhaps as early as 500 BC; in 1952 a hypothesis preserved on papyrus showed that the play was produced not before the sixties of the fifth century. Statistics seem to indicate that the *Prometheus Bound* shows in an accentuated form tendencies visible in the *Oresteia* (458 BC), and that has encouraged some scholars to conclude that it must have been written during the two years of life remaining to the poet after the production of that trilogy. Considering the limited amount of material available and the dangers of assuming a linear development in the stylistic tendencies in question, this inference seems to me exceedingly unsafe, even if we take it for granted that the *Prometheus Bound* is by Aeschylus. In guessing at the dates of the five plays of Sophocles not dated by external evidence, we have even more reason to be cautious.

Reinhardt recognised that the indications of style and metre could not safely be relied on here, and approached the problem by a wholly different method. He believed that a gradual artistic development could be detected by means of his own method of studying, scene by scene, Sophoclean situations. At the start, he argues, each character simply gives utterance to his own fixed point of view, never allowing it to be modified in the light of the positions adopted by the other persons present. Dialogue involving three persons does not occur before the *Oedipus Tyrannus*: in the latest plays, it is handled with increasing skill, and each actor is affected by the standpoint of the other persons present on the stage. Reinhardt believed that his close analysis of the plays, scene by scene, actually revealed the stages by which this development took place.

It must, I think, be admitted that he has somewhat overestimated the degree of exactitude in dating which this method can be expected to attain. So far as chronology is concerned, his greatest achievement has been to make it highly probable that the *Trachiniae* is one of the earlier extant plays and that the *Electra* is one of the later. Most scholars would agree with him in placing the *Ajax* early, but he has hardly made it certain that it is the earliest extant play, or that it is as early as the fifties; Paul Mazon thought the *Trachiniae* earlier, and it may be argued that it shows a less mature technique. Reinhardt's criteria certainly seem to indicate that the *Antigone* stands between these two supposedly early plays and the *Oedipus Tyrannus*. He does well to warn us that the anecdote that Sophocles was elected general in the expedition against Samos because people had admired his *Antigone* offers most inadequate grounds for thinking that that play must have been produced in 441; for all we know, the play might be earlier or later, even if we are right about its chronological relation to the other works. Again, the first *Oedipus* certainly seems to show a technical advance on the *Antigone*; no one has argued this more convincingly than Reinhardt. But we cannot be certain that the *Oedipus* was produced during the thirties; evidence for an earlier or a later date would hardly come as a surprise. Reinhardt seems to have shown that the *Electra* shows an affinity with the two late plays whose date is known. He thinks it somewhat earlier than the *Electra* of Euripides, which from the middle of the nineteenth century till 1955 was generally thought to be firmly placed in 413 BC. But in the latter year G. Zuntz[17] pointed out that the argument on which this date rested was really very feeble. The Dioscuri, about to leave the stage, say that they are off to the Sicilian Sea to protect mariners; and that was taken by many generations of scholars to show that the play must have been produced in 413, just as the great Athenian expedition against Sicily was about to sail. But the Sicilian Sea was notoriously dangerous for sailors, and washed the coast of that Peloponnese which had been the home of the Dioscuri; as an argument for dating the play the passage is as good as useless. Zuntz pointed out that the criteria which in general serve as a useful guide for dating the plays of

---

[17] G. Zuntz, *The Political Plays of Euripides*, (1955), 64ff.; cf. my review of A. Vögler, *Vergleichende Studien zur sophokleischen und euripideischen Elektra* (1967), in the *Classical Review*, xix (1969), 36ff.

Euripides would indicate for the *Electra* a date about 422. If this is approximately right, and if Reinhardt was correct in thinking the Sophoclean *Electra* to be earlier than the Euripidean, the *Electra* of Sophocles will have been produced during the twenties, perhaps about fifteen years before the *Philoctetes*. Despite the similarities between the two plays which Reinhardt pointed out, we know of no reason why this should not be so. None the less, his method seems likelier to yield results, in the absence of external evidence, than any calculation based upon the style and metre of a very limited quantity of material.

But though Reinhardt's contribution to the establishment of the plays' chronology is important, it is less important than his contribution to their understanding. He takes us through each play, or rather through the dialogue portions of each play, delineating the emotional impact of each scene and the means adopted to achieve it with great delicacy and sensitivity. Most classical scholars are more interested in facts than in emotions, and prefer what is tangible and concrete to its opposite; they therefore give most of their attention to the constitution of the text, the explanation of the verbal meaning, and the religious beliefs and attitudes supposed to be implicit in the plays. Reinhardt is concerned chiefly with the emotional effect of each succeeding episode, and unlike most scholars he was singularly well qualified to describe it. It must be remembered that he offers not a full-length study of the poet, but an examination of Sophoclean situations, and of the relation between man and god and between man and man so far as they are revealed in the speeches, the episodes and the movement of the drama. He seems to have thought it unnecessary to examine the lyric portions of the plays with anything like the care which he devoted to the dialogue scenes, and in this it seems to me that he was mistaken. The lyrics form an integral part of the plays, and the total effect cannot be grasped without taking account of them; in particular, the relation between man and god is illuminated by the lyrics. Gerhard Müller in an interesting article[18] has lately argued that the Sophoclean chorus has simply the status of an actor, and does not serve, as an Aeschylean chorus may, as the mouthpiece of the poet. Kranz in his great book *Stasimon*, 1933, wrote (p. 171) that the chorus is at once a character in a tragedy, an instrument that can be used to accompany, to divide up, and to deepen the significance of the drama, and an organ of the poet's individual self. If Müller is right in denying the chorus the third of these functions, is he also right in denying it the second? Reinhardt throws no light upon this problem.

[18] In *Sophokles* (Wege der Forschung xcv) ed. H. Diller, 1967, 212ff.

But his positive achievement is very great, and it cannot be summarised. What he has written must be read carefully and as a whole in order to be fully understood.

Reinhardt did much to set the stage for the debate over the part played by the gods in Sophoclean drama that has occupied so much space in the extensive literature devoted to Sophocles during the last thirty years. He sees the relation between man and god in Nietzschean terms. According to Nietzsche, it is through his defiance of the universe and the ruling powers that the hero meets his end, and in the moment of annihilation confirms for ever his heroic status. The man who practises 'safe thinking' – *sōphrosunē* – will remember the limitations imposed upon him by his mortality; the hero will ignore them, and so provoke the gods to destroy him and so attest his heroism.[19]

Nietzsche's conception of the hero enables Reinhardt to do justice to aspects of Sophocles that had been most inadequately explained by the attempts of nineteenth-century scholars to discover the workings of divine justice in his plays. We are in certain cases given information that might enable us to account in Aeschylean terms for the actions of the gods. Yet in other cases we are given no such information; and even when we are given it, it makes little difference to the drama. In the *Ajax*, we are told which god punishes Ajax and why; yet how unimportant this is in the total sum of the impressions we are left with! In the *Trachiniae*, the mentions of Zeus in relation to Heracles in the early part of the play may cause the spectator familiar with the genre to wonder what Zeus may now intend, and when Lichas describes Heracles' dealings with the family of Eurytus, such a spectator may guess that Heracles may expect trouble; at the end of the play, the chorus pronounces that all that has happened is Zeus. Yet the fulfilment of Zeus' justice is never insisted on, only barely hinted at, richly though Aeschylus might have developed such a theme. In the *Antigone* Tiresias makes it plain how Creon has angered the gods, because the plot happens to demand it. Yet the gods do not intervene to save Antigone, who has vindicated their rights at the cost of her own life. There is indeed sufficient mention of the curse upon the Labdacids to encourage the spectators to believe the chorus when they claim that the curse has been effective; yet the matter has little importance in the drama. Attempts to show Oedipus or Jocaste to be personally guilty have failed completely. If a spectator of the *Oedipus Tyrannus* asks why Oedipus is destroyed, he may remember the curse

---

[19] See Ch. 14.

upon the Labdacids; yet in the play the curse has no importance. In the *Electra* there is no disputing the guilt of Clytemnestra and Aegisthus, and the curse upon the house of Atreus supplies one of the play's themes. The final scene, which is not adequately explained in recent treatments, any more than it is in Reinhardt's own, seems to suggest that the working of the curse continues. Yet the curse upon the family and the guilt of the murderers are always kept subordinate; the stress is upon the nature of Electra and its violent extremes of love and hatred. In the *Philoctetes* the gods require the hero to sacrifice his individual feelings so as to further the accomplishment of their grand design. In the second play about Oedipus, we are told little about the reasons which have led the gods to ruin Oedipus and little about those which have led them to rehabilitate him.

Reinhardt notes all this, and remarks that we find in Aeschylus a very different attitude towards divine justice. Like a pupil of Wilamowitz and an heir of nineteenth-century historicism, he tries to explain the difference in terms of an historical development. The will of the gods in Sophocles, he says, 'is no longer an ever-present force which hovers over a character and makes itself felt in his deeds and in his life. On the contrary, it confronts him one day as something alien, incomprehensible ...' Yet Reinhardt himself clearly shows how the action of a Sophoclean play is rapidly swept onwards to its appointed conclusion by the force of what he calls the daimon. In speaking of the daimon, the word 'fate' is inappropriate; in Sophocles, the daimon is a god-directed force, and the gods control the action quite as firmly as they do in Homer or in Aeschylus. Because Sophocles does not encourage us to ask the question Aeschylus would have asked, how the gods have arrived at their decision, Reinhardt does not ask it either. But if we do ask it, we see that although in most cases the direct evidence is incomplete, in every instance the question would admit of being answered in purely Aeschylean terms. Sophocles as an artist is by no means as interested as Aeschylus in questions of divine justice, of guilt and of responsibility. But that does not mean that his religion was different, or that he was trying to express a different point of view. The difference is not ideological but artistic; it can scarcely be altogether unconnected with the passing of the fashion for writing trilogies on continuous themes, although this by itself cannot account for the poet's individual preference.

Sophocles, like Aeschylus, remained content with the traditional religion of early Greece. Both believed in the justice of the gods;[20] and

[20] In the fifth chapter of *The Justice of Zeus* (1971), I tried to show in what sense Sophocles believed in divine justice. I did not intend to suggest that the theme of divine justice had special importance in his works.

for both that justice meant not only that Zeus punished men or their descendants for their offences but that the gods maintained the order of the universe. The purposes of the gods involved the fates of innumerable men and cities and took into account chains of crime and punishment that reached back to the beginnings of human history, and were too complicated for any mortal to understand. Even when the gods deigned to impart knowledge through the medium of oracles and prophets, human intelligence seldom sufficed to interpret them correctly.

This religion recognised that great heroes were exposed, as ordinary men were not, to the danger of provoking the anger of the gods. That anger could be avoided by the practice of what Reinhardt called Sophoclean humility, by recognising the limitations of human capacity; but such humility came more easily to ordinary persons, like Ismene or Chrysothemis, the Odysseus of the *Ajax* or the Creon of the *Oedipus Tyrannus*, than to great heroes. In a grave crisis an Ajax or an Oedipus can give more effective protection than an Odysseus or a Creon; yet the hero is more prone to offend a god by seeming to refuse him honour than is an ordinary person. In the moment of the hero's catastrophe, when he is abandoned by the gods, the poet and his audience will not withdraw their sympathy; the modern scholar who wrote with reference to the Aeschylean Cassandra that 'it is difficult to sympathise with a mortal who has betrayed a god' was grotesquely dragging into Greek religion an attitude derived by Christianity from its Oriental element.

Greek *dikē* is not identical with modern justice, and the Greek poets were acutely conscious of the terrible aspect of the gods. An extreme example comes from a papyrus fragment certainly from Sophocles' *Niobe*, published in 1971;[21] Apollo is pointing out to his sister Artemis that one surviving daughter of Niobe is cowering behind a great jar. 'Shoot a swift arrow at her,' he cries, 'before she manages to hide!'; this is the ruthless Apollo of the Cassandra scene of the *Agamemnon* or the pediment at Olympia. At the same time the reader of Sophocles, most of all the reader of the two late plays, can hardly overcome the impression that the poet feels towards his own remote and awe-inspiring gods a strange piety and a strange affection. The second play about Oedipus displays as clearly as any document that we possess the simple sentiments which an early Greek felt towards his own locality and its divinities, a sentiment like those of the peasants who chanted, 'Rain, rain, dear Zeus'; it shows also in its

[21] This fragment, together with the other remains of Sophocles' *Niobe*, is admirably edited and explained by W.S. Barrett in Richard Carden, *The Papyrus Fragments of Sophocles* (Berlin 1974), 171ff.

most austere and complex form the reverent respect for the awful and inscrutable superhuman that marked the ancient religion at its sublimest level. In all the beauty and splendour of the world the early Greeks saw the working of the gods; they had to live with them, and could under certain conditions even be their friends; for the piety mingled with awe with which they regarded them was not conditional upon the gods' treating mankind or individual men with any special kindness.[22]

---

[22] See *The Justice of Zeus* (quoted in n.20 above), 33, with 173, n.34.

21

Eduard Fraenkel

Eduard David Mortier Fraenkel was born in Berlin on 17 March 1888, the night of the old Emperor's funeral.[1] His father, Julius, a wine-merchant, was a first cousin of Ludwig Traube and an uncle of Ernst Fraenkel; his mother, Edith, was a remarkable woman, devoted to good works, but also to culture, to whom her distinguished son never ceased to acknowledge his great debt. He was educated at the Askanisches Gymnasium, which at that time had on its staff a number of distinguished scholars. Fraenkel's two successive headmasters were Woldemar Ribbeck, a brother of Otto Ribbeck and the author of an edition of Aristophanes' *Acharnians*, and Adolf Busse, who edited a number of ancient commentators on Aristotle for the Berlin series; and the assistant masters included Georg Andresen, the editor of Tacitus, and Ernst Hambruch, the Aristotelian scholar. Hambruch, an inspiring teacher, was much admired by Fraenkel; but the master who most influenced him was Otto Gruppe, whose *Griechische*

---

* This obituary notice first appeared in *Gnomon* 43 (1971) 634f.

[1] I list the obituary notices of Fraenkel known to me. The obituary notice in *The Times* of 6 February 1970 (by R.G.M. Nisbet) was followed by a note of mine in *The Times* of 11 February; both are reprinted, together with Colin Macleod's obituary notice from the *Oxford Magazine* for 13 March 1970 (pp. 209-10) in *Pelican* (the magazine of Corpus Christi College), vol. I, no. 2 (1970), pp. 31-3. See also Scevola Mariotti, 'Ricordo di Fraenkel', in *La Nazione del Lunedi*, 25 May 1970; Heinz Haffter, 'Eduard Fraenkel zum Gedenken', in the *Neue Zürcher Zeitung*, 12 March 1970, 33; Silvia Rizzo, 'Ricordo di Eduard Fraenkel', in *Rassegna di Cultura e Vita Scolastica*, Anno XXIV, n. 4-5, aprile-maggio 1970, 13-4 (an excellent account of Fraenkel's Italian seminars by a participant); Arnaldo Momigliano, 'Eduard Fraenkel', in *Encounter*, February 1971, 55-6; Italo Mariotti, 'Per Eduard Fraenkel', *Belfagor*, Anno XXV, fsc. 6, 1970, 690-4; Carl Becker, *Jb. der Bayr. Akad. der Wiss.* (1970), 1-10. By far the best and most interesting account of him and his work is that of Sebastiano Timpanaro, 'Ricordo di Eduard Fraenkel', in *Atene e Roma*, n.s. XV, fasc. 2-3 (1970), 89-103. [Add now M. Puelma, *Information de l'Université de Friburg/Suisse, Communications* (1969), no. 12, 15 juin, 19f.; J. Delz, *Basler Nachrichten*, 9.3.70; G. Williams, *PBA* 56 (1975), 615f.]. I am indebted to L.E. Rossi and Colin Macleod for providing me with material which has greatly assisted the writing of this notice, and to Rudolf Kassel for advice.

Mythologie und Religionsgeschichte in I. von Müller's *Handbuch* and
Geschichte der klassischen Mythologie und Religionsgeschichte published as a
supplement to Roscher's *Lexikon* are still invaluable. Gruppe taught
Fraenkel not ancient literature, but ancient history, and his course
included a thorough introduction to Greek art. This writer of learned
books never seemed too busy to help his pupils, and his exceptionally
wide general culture made a deep impression upon Fraenkel.

In 1906 Fraenkel entered the University of Berlin as a student of
law. Gruppe had advised him to study classical philology, but at that
time an unbaptised Jew had little prospect of obtaining a professorship, and Fraenkel was unwilling to resign himself to the prospect of
teaching in a school. He learned much from Seckel's lectures on the
history of Roman law, and the grounding in Roman legal science
which he received at that time had an important effect upon his later
studies. But even as a schoolboy he had been fascinated by the famous
evening public lectures at the Victoria-Lyzeum given by Wilamowitz;
he heard the series which were afterwards made use of for *Staat und
Gesellschaft der Griechen* in the series 'Kultur der Gegenwart'.

Even as a first-year student of law, Fraenkel found time to spend
four hours a week in attending Wilamowitz's lectures on Thucydides;
and when after his Abiturium a rich aunt gave him a thousand marks
to spend the winter in Italy, he found the courage to approach
Wilamowitz for advice on how to employ this precious time.
Wilamowitz talked to this unknown student of law for two whole
hours, and left an impression that was to last for life.[2] That winter
Fraenkel travelled widely in Italy, forming at once the passion for that
country and its people which was never to leave him. He decided that
in order to spend his life as a student of classical philology he could
face even the dreaded prospect of being a schoolmaster, and on his
return enrolled as a student of classical philology.

Wilamowitz's lectures were all that Fraenkel had hoped for, and he
also learned much from Eduard Meyer, Diels and Norden. But Berlin
contained too many friends and offered too many distractions, and in
1909 Fraenkel decided to transfer to Göttingen. It was a decision he
did not regret. He owed to Wilamowitz, he said later, his enthusiasm
for the ancient world and his whole conception of 'Alter-

---

[2] Wilamowitz's advice was characteristic: 'Anyone who doesn't give himself a pain
in the neck craning up to look at the ceiling of the Sistine Chapel doesn't deserve to be
in Rome at all. Don't waste time looking at the dolls in the Vatican Museum! Don't
worry about the topography of the Palatine (no one understands it)! Spend as much
time as you can in the Campagna; you must hire a bicycle! [as Fraenkel did, so that
he nearly perished in an accident on the Appian Way]. For Florence, read
Machiavelli's history; for Rome, read Polybius!'

tumswissenschaft', but the man who really educated him – less by what he said than by what he was – was Friedrich Leo.[3] He was also deeply influenced by Jacob Wackernagel; it was Wackernagel, and not Leo, who aroused his interest in early Latin and in Plautus. In Göttingen began his lifelong friendship with Günther Jachmann, with Giorgio Pasquali, and with Peter Von der Mühll; and in Göttingen he met Hermann Fränkel, who became his brother-in-law, and Paul Jacobsthal, who was later to be his colleague at Oxford. Returning to Berlin for the winter of 1910-11, he attended the classes of Johannes Vahlen and of Wilhelm Schulze; in Schulze's seminar he was later to meet Ruth von Velsen, who became his wife.

After a thorough viva voce examination at Göttingen conducted by Leo and Wendland, Fraenkel obtained his doctorate in 1912 with a thesis entitled 'De media et nova comoedia quaestiones selectae' which showed great promise and contains much that is still valuable. After a further nine months in Italy, made possible by the award of the Sauppe-Stipendium, he joined the staff of the Thesaurus at Munich, where he had as trainer his Göttingen friend Jachmann. He spent two years in Munich, and from this period date his acute and learned articles on the meaning of *fides* and the gender of *dies*,[4] as well as several Thesaurus articles.

In 1917 Fraenkel habilitated in Berlin, and was appointed Privatdozent in that university; the next year the important article 'Lyrische Dactylen'[5] began the series of his contributions to metrical study. In 1920 he became Professor Extraordinarius, and two years later appeared perhaps the most remarkable of all his books, *Plautinisches im Plautus*,[6] a work which after fifty years has lost none of its freshness and little of its credibility. Since 1922 our knowledge of Menander has been much augmented, and the brief additions printed at the end of the 1960 Italian version of the book are perhaps its least satisfactory part. And yet the general picture of Plautus' method of handling his Greek originals has not in any serious way been modified; the largest single piece of evidence, the fragments of Menander's *Dis Exapaton* lately published by E.W. Handley, serve largely to confirm Fraenkel's conclusions.

A year later Fraenkel went as Professor Ordinarius to Kiel, where his Berlin friend Felix Jacoby wished to have him as his colleague.

[3] See his foreword to Leo's *Ausgewählte Kleine Schriften* (Rome 1961).
[4] Both are reprinted at the beginning of vol. I of *Kleine Beiträge zur klassischen Philologie* (Rome 1964).
[5] Op. cit., 165f.
[6] Berlin 1922; an Italian version by F. Munari, with additional notes, *Elementi Plautini in Plauto*, appeared at Rome in 1960.

During the winter of 1925-26 he spent a sabbatical term in Florence as the colleague of Pasquali; and in 1928 he published *Iktus und Akzent im Lateinischen Sprechvers*, a detailed investigation of these concepts and their relationship in Latin verse. The acute criticisms of Paul Maas[7] seriously undermined the conclusions of this work, and Fraenkel in his later years disowned it; but like all his productions it contains much valuable material. In 1928 Fraenkel left Kiel for Göttingen, where he had among his colleagues Richard Reitzenstein; while deputising for an absent professor at Basel, he was able to enjoy the company of Wackernagel and Von der Mühll.

In 1931 Fraenkel moved to Freiburg im Breisgau; during his time there appeared the important study entitled 'Kolon und Satz'[8] which embodies the most substantial products of his lifelong interest in the order of words. Then in 1933 the National Socialists came to power. During that summer Fraenkel was forbidden to teach, and the next year he left Germany.

He spent the summer term of 1934 in Oxford, where he was given rooms in Christ Church. Many people showed him kindness, which at the time he was not always quick to appreciate; later he spoke of the friendliness of Sir John Myres, and through his old friend Jacobsthal he became acquainted with Sir John Beazley. He had already begun work on his edition of the *Agamemnon*, and Beazley was among those who helped him by translating portions of his commentary.

After an autumn in Scandinavia, where he met A.B. Drachmann in Denmark and Einar Löfstedt in Sweden, Fraenkel returned to Oxford. But his connection with the place seemed likely to prove temporary, for he was elected, on Housman's advice, to a Bevan Fellowship at Trinity College, Cambridge, and began preparations to remove his family. However, in 1935 the Corpus Christi Chair of the Latin Language and Literature was vacated by the resignation of A.C. Clark; there happened to be no strong local candidate, and Fraenkel was appointed. Undoubtedly the chief factor in his election was the support of Housman, who despite his earlier polemical exchanges with the school of Bücheler and Leo had been impressed by Fraenkel's substantial review of his *Lucan*, and after the election wrote to a newspaper to silence an ignorant critic of the electors' choice.[9]

Anyone who had predicted at the beginning the enormous success

---

[7] DLZ 1929, 2244-7 = *Kl. Schr.* 588f.

[8] See *Kleine Beiträge* (cited above) i, 73-139; cf. SB Munich, Ph.-hist. Kl. (1965), Heft 2.

[9] *Sunday Times*, 23 December 1934; see A.E. Housman, *Selected Prose*, ed. John Carter, (Cambridge 1961), 129 = *The Letters of A.E. Housman*, ed. H. Maas, (1971), 366 = *The Classical Papers of A.E. Housman*, (1972), iii, 1277.

which Fraenkel was to enjoy as a professor in Oxford would have been treated with derision. But this would have been due to personal, not to academic considerations. Fraenkel lectured effectively, especially on Catullus, Virgil and Horace; but the powerful impact which his teaching made at the beginning was due to his famous seminars on the *Agamemnon*. Both dons and undergraduates attended these classes, which extended over many years; the play and its problems were discussed in great detail. The German tradition of the seminar, invented, it would seem, by Gesner, Heyne and Wolf, greatly developed by Ritschl, carried further by Usener and Bücheler, and perfected by the generation of Fraenkel's Berlin and Göttingen professors was in the Oxford of those days something wholly unfamiliar.[10] In 1950 Fraenkel published his edition of the *Agamemnon* in three volumes, containing prolegomena, a new text, and the most detailed commentary ever devoted to a Greek book. The difficulties presented by the text are such that no editor can expect his conclusions to command general assent. Many of Fraenkel's judgments are open to question, as the edition of Denniston and Page, published seven years after his, was soon to show. Even if one bears in mind that the translation makes no literary pretensions, one may still wish it had been made into the author's native language; and the vast number of references to secondary literature, invaluable as they are to professional scholars, make the book somewhat heavy reading. Still, any competent judge must acknowledge that it is indispensible for the serious study of the *Agamemnon* in particular and of Greek tragedy in general. It represents an amount of learned labour that would have sufficed for most men's entire lifetime.

In 1953 Fraenkel retired from his chair on reaching the age limit; but fortunately this made little difference to his activities. By this time, for reasons which will be given presently, he had become as acceptable in Oxford as he had formerly been uncongenial. As Corpus Christi Professor he had been a Fellow of Corpus Christi College and had occupied college rooms. The College now elected him to an Honorary Fellowship; and the President, W.F.R. Hardie, placed at his disposal a large room which had formed part of the presidential lodging, and which provided an ideal place for Fraenkel to work surrounded by his very considerable personal library. By a special arrangement of an unprecedented sort he was enabled to continue his famous seminars, which he had now devoted to many other authors besides Aeschylus, notably Horace, Aristophanes, Euripides,

---

[10] Mr A.H. Griffiths pointed out to me that Gesner held seminars in Leipzig in the 1730s (see Ruhnken, *Opusc. oratoria*, Leiden 1767, 465f). See also L.E. Rossi et al. (eds) *Due Seminari di Eduard Fraenkel* (*Sussidi Eruditi*, 28, Rome 1977).

Plautus and Sophocles, and to the study of metre, and which had now become an Oxford institution.

In 1957 Fraenkel brought out his *Horace*, written in admirably clear English – better than that of the *Agamemnon* – and offering detailed studies of many of the poems. Timpanaro has truly said that Fraenkel did not relish anything that savoured of decadence; and despite the partiality for Callimachus' epigrams acquired from Wilamowitz, this markedly affected his attitude to Hellenistic literature. Some features of Horace's work are more illuminated by the Hellenistic poets than by the great classics who were his formal models, and to this aspect of his author Fraenkel was not especially sensitive. A generation of readers familiar with the work of Syme was bound to feel surprise at Fraenkel's evident assumption that Augustus and his regime were in all ways admirable; the balance has been redressed by Fraenkel's pupils, R.G.M. Nisbet and Margaret Hubbard, in their commentary on the *Odes*. Fraenkel's *Horace* is more cautious in this respect than most earlier treatments, but like most modern studies of ancient lyric poets, it tends to exaggerate the value of Horace's poems as sources for their author's biography. But it remains true that Fraenkel's *Horace* is not only a learned, but a genial, humane and understanding book. Written after the extirpation of Hitlerism, it shows far less of the bitter side of its author's nature than the *Agamemnon*; and not only scholars, but many ordinary readers, have found it as delightful as it is informative.

After the war Fraenkel, to his great satisfaction, was able to resume contact with his continental colleagues. Many foreign scholars were attracted to Oxford by the presence of the learned exiles; and he could pay regular visits to his beloved Italy, where he taught at Florence, Urbino, Pisa, Bari and Rome, to the great satisfaction of both himself and his hearers. He several times went to Germany, where he much relished the atmosphere of the classical seminar of the Freie Universität in West Berlin, as it then was, and even travelled as far as Israel; he sincerely regretted that his health did not allow him to accept Wendell Clausen's invitation to fly to the United States and speak at Harvard.[11]

One of his closest friends in Italy was Don Giuseppe de Luca, whose publishing firm 'Edizioni di Storia e Letteratura' enabled him to realise several of his cherished projects.[12] It reprinted Schulze's *Graeca Latina*; it brought out Leo's *Ausgewählte Kleine Schriften* and F. Munari's Italian version of *Plautinisches im Plautus*; and it published the

---

[11] Even earlier E.A. Havelock had invited him to Yale.

[12] See Fraenkel's contribution to *Don Giuseppe de Luca: Ricordi e Testimonianze*, ed. M. Picchi (Rome 1963).

last three of Fraenkel's own books. In 1962 Fraenkel devoted a short book to the poet who had always been his favourite – *Beobachtungen zu Aristophanes*. Many textual problems are discussed, not always in such a manner as to silence doubt, but always with freshness and clarity as well as with great learning, and a delightful chapter on 'Die Parabasenlieder' shows what it was like to hear Fraenkel speak about this particularly congenial author. Two years later Fraenkel brought out a two-volume selection of his own shorter writings,[13] which gives an impressive picture of the variety of his interests and the massive solidity of his scholarship. In 1968 came his last book, *Leseproben aus Reden Ciceros und Catos*, a difficult but rewarding work which throws much light on the problems of word order and prose rhythm which had long occupied his mind. During his last years he was increasingly concerned with Sophocles, whose depiction of heroic natures in conflict with a hostile world strongly appealed to him.

His last years must have been some of the happiest of his long life. Finally, on the 5 February 1970, he chose not to survive his wife, who had sustained him with unbounded love and loyalty, and to whom he had always been devoted, but to end his life 'after the high Roman fashion'. Only a narrow sectarianism will presume to blame him for that action, which was in complete accordance with his own rules of life.

Fraenkel's complex, intense and dominating personality made a powerful impression upon all those who met him. From the first, a withered arm had set him apart from others; even in his early days in Germany, many had found him difficult to get on with; and this was markedly the case during his first years in Oxford. The persecution he had undergone at home had done little to mitigate his uncomfortable qualities,[14] and such a lover of tradition must have suffered deeply at the shock of sudden translation to unfamiliar surroundings and to what must have seemed at first an alien world. At first, and for long afterwards, he often treated people who were trying to be kind to him with startling rudeness and insensitivity; and at his classes he made little effort to conceal his horror at what seemed to him the amateurishness of English scholars of all ages. Countless stories are told of his tactlessness with colleagues and his severities towards his

[13] See n. 1 above.
[14] In 1934 a German scholar, who in his youth had done good work, wrote to Fraenkel, 'The time has come when we can no longer be friends'. After the war, when a time had come when they could be friends again, this person sent Fraenkel a book with a Latin inscription in which he professed himself 'memor' and received in reply the two words 'et ego'. (For the same person's relations with Rudolf Pfeiffer, see p. 265 below.)

pupils at this period; they are not all false. In the seminar he could be terrifying; a head of a college might be curtly commanded to fetch a book, a celebrated scholar might be told that his translation was correct, but expressed in poor *Englisch*, an innocent young lady might be reduced to Niobe-like weeping by a savage reprimand provoked by her ignorance of Aristotle's *De Caelo*. A number of his pupils were so scared by this treatment that they gave up the classes, or even the subject. But the tougher sort held out, grew tougher still in the course of stern battles with their formidable teacher, and gained enormously from being forced to try to satisfy his exacting standards.

As time passed, Fraenkel gradually acquired more sympathy with his environment. He found that not all Oxford tutors were amateurs; and he became aware that in some ways Oxford undergraduates were actually better subjects for his kind of teaching than his former pupils. They might be ignorant of important branches of the subject, as well as of modern languages, secondary literature, and the history of scholarship; but many had had a solid grounding in Greek and Latin grammar, and had closely studied and perhaps partly learned by heart at least a few works of ancient literature. What they lacked, Fraenkel was singularly well qualified to provide. His intimate knowledge of both Greek and Latin literature was combined with knowledge of linguistics, metric, Roman law, and with wide acquaintance with the monuments of ancient art, so that few scholars were better equipped to help them to enable themselves to use the tools and materials of modern scholarship.

But Fraenkel could not have persuaded his pupils to make the great effort which his conception of scholarship demanded without other gifts which do not always accompany great learning – boundless enthusiasm for the study of the ancient world, untiring eagerness to communicate that enthusiasm to others, and the imaginative sympathy that makes literature seem alive. His great qualities as a teacher had to be set against grave defects. He lacked the gift of divination, and in default sometimes overdid the search for interpolations after the fashion of his friend Jachmann. He was not quick on the uptake, and so tended to come to the seminar with his mind made up; colleagues who wanted his opinion were best advised to write to him, and if anyone at the seminar had a good idea, Fraenkel could not always be brought even if he listened to it, to understand it. He therefore lacked that ability to elicit good suggestions from his hearers which the famous exponents of the seminar tradition to which he belonged had notably possessed. He was slow to understand what other people were thinking and to assess their characters, and tended to extremes of blame or praise. To undergraduates he was, in his later years at least, kind and sympathetic; but he would come down upon young graduates with all the ferocity which Leo had shown to him and his contemporaries. Those who assumed, as he did, that because he was a great teacher and a great scholar he would know what was best for them were sometimes disappointed. But his profound learning and solid judgment gave him enormous advantages and his passionate keenness to assist anyone who had the slightest desire to learn something of the ancient world made a deep impression on his hearers. Hard as it might be for them to get him to discuss a problem with them, they were gripped by what he had to say; and though Oxford in his time contained several great and many distinguished scholars, several of whom, as he freely admitted, in various respects excelled him, not one of these did nearly as much as Fraenkel to inspire others with a love for learning.

During his later years, his life in Oxford became happier. The resumption of contact with the continent, and especially Italy, made a profound difference to his life; and in Oxford itself his relations with others became altered. He was now surrounded by younger colleagues whose attitude to their studies had been formed largely by his influence, and he never ceased to help them with support and counsel. He who had been the type of the unassimilated foreigner became part of the fabric of his own college, where his conversation was both instructive and entertaining. Fraenkel never became anglicised, even to the extent that he supposed he had been; for example, he never learned to appreciate the excellence of such characteristically English scholars as Jebb and Denniston. But his attitude to England changed greatly, and foreign visitors often amused us by reporting that he had lectured them on the superiority of this or that English practice. When he first arrived in Oxford, the old-fashioned insistence on the value of translation into Greek and Latin was much exaggerated; some tutors thought themselves justified in playing at this instead of practising scholarship. Now it has been to a great extent relaxed, and the practice is in danger of dying out. Fraenkel greatly regretted its decline, and strongly insisted on its educational value. Timpanaro says that Fraenkel found Italian students readier than the English to accept the legacy of the German school of which he was a member. Certainly Fraenkel did not found a school in Oxford in the sense of being surrounded by a group of reverent and imitative disciples. But his influence, more than any other factor, somehow created an amalgam of German 'Altertumswissenschaft' and English classical scholarship which combined much of what was best in both; and many scholars of different aims and interests and from different countries would agree that their conceptions of the subject had been much affected by his influence. As he grew older the milder aspect of his complicated character was always more in evidence. Fraenkel often said of Wilamowitz that for all the influence of his books and articles he was first and foremost a teacher. That applies equally to Fraenkel; and even those who had to endure, as young graduates, his sometimes alarming strictures, will guard his memory with deep gratitude and affection. For innumerable scholars, amateur and professional, in Germany, in Italy, in England and elsewhere, he personified the urge to learn from and enjoy the achievements of the ancient world, and he has left a gap that nobody can fill.

Fraenkel was a Fellow of the British Academy and a holder of its Kenyon Medal for Classical Studies, and a member of the academies of Bologna, Göttingen, Lund, Munich and Stockholm and of the Istituto Lombardo. He held honorary doctorates from the Freie Universität of Berlin, Urbino, St Andrews, Florence and Fribourg, and in his favour the University of Oxford waived its usual rule of not making such awards to its own resident members. Very appropriately Sarsina, the birthplace of Plautus, made him an honorary citizen.

22

Rudolf Pfeiffer

Rudolf Carl Franz Otto Pfeiffer was born on September 28, 1889, the son of Carl Pfeiffer and his wife Elizabeth, born Naegele. His family lived in Augsburg, a city which had played an important part in the cultural history both of medieval and Renaissance Bavaria. They occupied the house which had belonged to Conrad Peutinger, the Augsburg town chronicler and imperial councillor who studied in Italy and has a place among the noted humanists of his time. Peutinger gave his name to the medieval copy of an ancient map discovered by Conrad Celtis and finally published by Marcus Welser; and he had decorated the walls of the house with beautifully executed maps, which made a deep impression on Pfeiffer from his earliest years.

Pfeiffer received his early education in the Benedictine Abbey of St Stephan. Although a comparatively recent foundation, having originated in 1828 when Ludwig I was working to reestablish the Benedictine Order in Bavaria, this school belonged to a great tradition; its sister establishment, St Anna, went back to the sixteenth century, and had had as headmaster Hieronymus Wolf, the editor and translator of the Attic orators, and the neighbouring Abbey of St Ulrich had existed for eight centuries before its suppression during the Napoleonic period. In Pfeiffer's time St Stephan had a celebrated headmaster, Dom Beda Grundl, to whom Pfeiffer acknowledged a special debt of gratitude. In a speech delivered at St Stephan in 1953, Pfeiffer said that it inherited both the proud tradition of the Benedictine order and also the intellectual tradition transmitted from the ancient world; there was naturally a certain tension between them, but such tension might lead to a compromise that turned out fruitful. Throughout his life Pfeiffer remained faithful to both traditions, and his career certainly testifies to the fruitful nature of the compromise. He was a devout Catholic, but he was a Catholic after

* Following in *PBA* lxv, 1979. See the obituary notice of K. von Fritz, SB Bay. Akad. der Wiss., 1979 and the full account by W. Bühler in *Gnomon* 52 (1980), 402f.

the fashion of Erasmus, with nothing of the bitter partisanship of the Counter-Reformation. At the start of the nineteenth century Bavaria had a great cultural leeway to make up. Its Academy had been founded in 1759, and its University, which had begun in modest circumstances at Landshut, moved to the capital only in 1827. But under the direction of Friedrich Thiersch, a Thuringian educated at Schulpforta who had been a pupil of Hermann, Wolf and Heyne, classical studies there were set on the right path. Before the end of the century they were flourishing under the leadership of distinguished scholars like Karl Halm and Wilhelm Christ, and Munich had become the home of the great Thesaurus Linguae Latinae under the direction of Eduard Wölfflin. At the University of Munich, Pfeiffer was fortunate enough to be the pupil of Otto Crusius, a man of keen intelligence and wide culture and a lover of music as well as literature. Crusius had been taught at school in Hanover by H.L. Ahrens, the initiator of the modern study of the Greek dialects, editor of the Greek bucolic poets and notable authority on Aeschylus; Ahrens himself had been taught by Karl Otfried Müller, and had inherited his sympathy with German romanticism. Later, Crusius had been a pupil of the great Latinists Ritschl and Ribbeck at the University of Leipzig before succeeding Erwin Rohde first in Tübingen and then in Heidelberg before coming to Munich. Crusius did important work on Babrius and on Greek fables, on Herondas and the mime, and on Greek music; he laid the foundations of the study of the Greek collections of proverbs. He communicated an interest in this subject to Pfeiffer, who at one time thought of producing the edition of the Greek paroemiographers that Crusius had died without achieving, but in the end handed on the task to his gifted pupil, Winfried Bühler. Crusius' biography of Rohde is an important document for the history of the distinctively South German school, interested in Greek religion and early thought, to which both men belonged. Rohde had been an early friend of Nietzsche, and had defended his *Birth of Tragedy* against the ferocious onslaught of the young Ulrich von Wilamowitz-Moellendorff; his great book *Psyche* shows the influence of Nietzsche's distinctive contribution to the study of early Greek thinking, with its special stress upon the treatment of irrational elements. Crusius also strongly felt the influence of Nietzsche, and unlike most scholars took note of his warning that the scientific study of the ancient world as it developed in Germany during the second half of the nineteenth century had become incompatible with humanism. But Crusius believed that with proper care the modern scholarship of the time could be invested with a humanistic purpose; 'das Ideal des Neuhumanismus,' he wrote in 1910, 'ist durch das Läuterungsfeuer der Geschichtswissenschaft gegangen und hat standgehalten.' Crusius took a special interest in the influence of the classical tradition on succeeding ages; with Otto Immisch and the Polish scholar Thaddaeus Zielinski he edited the series 'Das Erbe der Alten', and in 1912 he added to the subtitle of the journal *Philologus* which he long edited, which had been 'Zeitschrift fur das Klassische Altertum', the words 'und sein Nachleben'. This learned and cultivated scholar had a profound influence upon Pfeiffer.

In 1913 Pfeiffer obtained his doctorate with a study of the Augsburg Meistersinger and translator of Homer, Johannes Spreng. It is significant that he began his career with a work inspired by local piety; but in Pfeiffer's case local piety involved allegiance to a universalist tradition. Then he obtained a post in the university library at Munich; his career was interrupted by the First World War. Pfeiffer was severely wounded, and at one time seemed unlikely to survive. But he was nursed back to health by the devoted care of his wife, born Mina Beer, whom he had married in 1913. Frau Pfeiffer was a gifted musician and a woman of great kindness of heart, and till her death in 1969 she and her husband remained a singularly devoted couple.

In 1918 Pfeiffer was appointed a Sub-Librarian in the library of the University of Munich. He was still occupied with Renaissance studies, but he found time for Greek poetry also. In 1920 he had a year's leave to continue his studies in Berlin, where like another student from a very different background from that of Prussia, Karl Reinhardt, he fell under the spell of Wilamowitz. The distance that separated the outlook of the Bavarian Catholic from those of the East Prussian nobleman, whose atheism retained a distinctly Lutheran cast, did not prevent Pfeiffer from being deeply impressed by the vast learning, keen intelligence and complete devotion to scholarship of Wilamowitz. Berlin provided him with something he could not have found at home, at least before Eduard Schwartz came to Munich from Strasburg in 1919. But his Berlin experience did nothing to weaken the links that bound him to his place of origin. Otto Schneider's edition of the hymns, epigrams and fragments of Callimachus had appeared as long ago as 1870, and though the hymns and epigrams had been edited by Wilamowitz, the publication of new papyri had created an urgent need for a collection of the new fragments. This Pfeiffer satisfied by editing *Callimachi Fragmenta nuper reperta* for the series of *Kleine Texte für Vorlesungen und Übungen* founded by Hans Lietzmann; the book appeared in 1921, and a second edition, rather misleadingly entitled an *editio maior*, superseded it in 1923. Meanwhile, in 1922, he had discussed some of the problems arising from the new discoveries in a small but brilliant pamphlet called *Kallimachosstudien*. These works were enough to prove that Pfeiffer was an editor of Greek poetry of the highest quality.

In 1921 Pfeiffer had become Privat-Dozent in the University of Munich; but in 1923 he returned to Berlin as Professor Extraordinarius, joining for a time the sessions of the famous 'Graeca', the private seminar held by Wilamowitz after his retirement from his Chair. Wilamowitz greatly appreciated Pfeiffer's scholarship, and later named him as one of the editors of his *Kleine Schriften*. Almost immediately, he was appointed to a full professorship in the then new university of Hamburg, which at that time was a centre of great intellectual activity, stimulated by the proximity of the Warburg Institute. Pfeiffer's publications at this time show that he was still occupied with Callimachus. In 1925 he reviewed Wilamowitz' great book on Hellenistic poetry together with a fourth edition of his text of the hymns and epigrams, and in 1928 he dealt with the newly published fragment of the prologue to the *Aitia* in a masterly article, which is still indispensable for the study of the poem.

Despite the attractions of Hamburg, Pfeiffer could not have remained in the north of Germany for ever, and in 1927 he accepted a call to Freiburg-im-Breisgau, inaugurating his tenure of the Chair with a fine lecture on 'Gottheit und Individuum in der frühgriechischen Lyrik' which he later offered to Wilamowitz on his eightieth birthday. Soon afterwards, in 1928, a vacancy occurred at Munich, and Pfeiffer could not resist the temptation to return to his Bavarian home.

He worked steadily away at Callimachus, in 1932 devoting to the important new fragment of the Lock of Berenice an article of the same high quality as that about the *Aitia* prologue, and in 1934 bringing out an important study of the newly-discovered summaries of Callimachean poems called the *Diegeseis*. He also wrote articles about important new papyrus texts of other authors, such as the *Skyrioi* and *Inachus* of Sophocles, the *Niobe* and *Diktyoulkoi* of Aeschylus, and new fragments of the pseudo-Hesiodic catalogue and the Homeric scholia; and he pursued his interest in the history of scholarship, publishing his first important study of Erasmus, notable studies of Goethe in relation to the Greeks and of Wilhelm von Humboldt, and (in 1938) a discussion of the historical relationship between classical scholarship and humanism which contains already the whole outline of the great *History of Classical Scholarship*, whose first volume was to appear thirty years later.

As early as 1926, Pfeiffer had alluded to 'a resistance to the principle of humanism that is deeply rooted in the German nature'.

When he left for Munich he had been succeeded in the Chair at Freiburg by a younger scholar of great ability, who soon after called on him in his new home to ask why he did not show more respect for 'die ehrenwürdige Gestalt des Führers'. Pfeiffer made no response to this enquiry, and soon afterwards reminded his visitor that he had a train to catch. Even if his wife had not been of Jewish origin, he could never have compromised with National Socialism, whose total incompatibility with his beliefs had been apparent to him from the beginning. In 1937 he resigned his Chair and went with his wife to England.

Arriving in Oxford virtually without means of support, the Pfeiffers were rescued by the great generosity and resourcefulness of Father Martin D'Arcy, S.J., Master of Campion Hall, the Jesuit house in Oxford. Pfeiffer's old Freiburg colleague, Eduard Fraenkel, had been established in Oxford as Corpus Christi Professor of Latin since 1935, and was able to explain the great intellectual distinction of the new arrival, and to introduce him to the congenial society of Corpus Christi College, whose last President had been P.S. Allen, the editor of the letters of Erasmus. But Pfeiffer's command of English was at that time and for some years after imperfect, and it was not found possible before 1946 to provide him with a university post. However, he was invited to lecture in the University, the *Odyssey* and the early lyric poets being the first topics that he chose. These first lectures were not easy for English undergraduates, used to a very different approach; but the exceptional gifts of the lecturer and his impressive character were apparent even to this audience. In their small house in Walton Well Road, he and his wife were kind and generous hosts to undergraduates.

Further support came from the Clarendon Press, which under the enlightened direction of Kenneth Sisam was quick to undertake to publish the edition of Callimachus at which Pfeiffer had so long been working. Everyone who met Pfeiffer at this time could see that he had been greatly stricken by his grievous experience, which must have been truly shattering for a man so devoted to his own part of the world and its traditions. But for the edition of Callimachus the exile turned out to be a blessing. The great collection of papyri excavated by Grenfell and Hunt at Oxyrhynchus at the turn of the century contained a number of so far unpublished manuscripts of Callimachus, which Edgar Lobel was engaged in editing with his unique skill. In 1939 another eminent Greek scholar, Paul Maas, arrived from Germany, and was appointed adviser to the Clarendon Press. Pfeiffer not only had the great advantage of being able to examine the new papyri at first hand, but of that of doing so together with Lobel and Maas, and of discussing with them the many problems which the new material posed. These three men were perhaps the three living persons best qualified for the task, and they discharged it with astonishing success. Further, the Bodleian Library had great attractions for any classical scholar, but for one with Pfeiffer's strong interest in the history of scholarship the advantage of being able to use it was especially great.

The first volume of the Callimachus, containing the fragments, appeared in 1949; it has a full apparatus criticus and a concise but exhaustive commentary in elegant Latin. Pfeiffer had complete command of the whole relevant literature, including the ancient grammarians; the fragments from papyri were handled with masterly paleographical skill; and the text of fragments preserved in quotations rested on an intimate acquaintance with the textual tradition of each author by whom a quotation had been preserved. Where no kind of certainty could be attained Pfeiffer was cautious; but he was capable of brilliant supplements and emendations, so that he did much to improve the quality of the text. It is hard to think of a critical edition of an ancient author that comes nearer to perfection.

Pfeiffer was not anxious to edit the hymns and epigrams; but the Press felt that the edition should be completed by a volume that contained them, and this duly appeared in 1953, together with the scholia on the hymns and with prolegomena and indexes to the whole work. The archetype of the hymns is reconstructed in masterly fashion, and the work in general is of high quality; but the small number of conjectures mentioned in the apparatus suggests that Pfeiffer did not give the work quite the same degree of critical attention that he had bestowed upon the fragments, and he effected fewer improvements in the text than might have been expected of such a scholar. He was already much occupied with his next great work, the *History of Classical Scholarship* which he had been planning for many years.

In 1946 Pfeiffer was appointed to a special University Lectureship in the History of Scholarship, in 1948 he was made Senior Lecturer, and in 1950 Reader. By now his spoken English was a great deal better, and his gentle charm and humorous modesty had made him many friends in Oxford. But in 1951 he accepted a pressing invitation to return to his old Chair in Munich. His wife missed her native country, and Pfeiffer himself felt a duty to return home and help in reestablishing the cultural traditions of his country which had been so brutally interrupted by the National Socialist interlude. For many years after his return Pfeiffer kept up his ties with England by returning each summer with his wife to work in the Bodleian, always finding time to renew relations with his English friends.

He was now free to concentrate upon his History of Scholarship, all the more after his retirement from his Chair in 1957. Sometimes he published articles about Greek poetry, usually when stimulated by a new papyrus; but from this time on most of his publications were related to the subject of this work. In 1955 he brought out an important study of Erasmus, based on a lecture given in England during the war, in 1957 a notable account of French humanism, and in 1961 a sketch of the history of philology from his own point of view. On his seventieth birthday in 1959 he was honoured by the printing of a selection from his shorter writings, with a complete list of his publications, admirably edited by Winfried Bühler.[1]

The first volume of the *History*, dealing with the period from the beginnings to the end of the Hellenistic age, appeared in 1968; it was published by the Clarendon Press, and by the author's own wish the language of the book was English. The first chapter treats of the period from the eighth to the fifth century BC, the second with the age of the sophists, and the third with that of Socrates, Plato and Aristotle. Part Two contains six chapters on Alexandrian scholarship, each of them, except the first, built around a leading figure (Zenodotus, Callimachus, Eratosthenes, Aristophanes, Aristarchus); then follow a chapter on the Pergamenes and another on the later scholars from Aristarchus to Didymus.

Pfeiffer's commitment to the thesis that philology in the proper sense begins with scholar poets, who are impelled by their love of poetry to preserve the poetry of the past, has led him somewhat to depreciate the progress towards scholarship made by the Greeks before the Hellenistic age. Soon after the book was published, the discovery of a papyrus at Derveni containing a fourth-century commentary on an early Orphic poem startlingly demonstrated that scholarly exegesis did not begin at Alexandria; and it may be argued that Aristotle and his school deserve more credit than they are given. But the work is one of immense learning, for the author's command over the great mass of primary and secondary literature seems virtually complete, and the innumerable details are never allowed to obscure the connecting themes or to blur the underlying humanistic purpose.

In 1969 Pfeiffer suffered the heavy blow of his wife's death; and from now his health gradually deteriorated, chiefly owing to the effects of the wound he had received during the First World War. His doctor recommended exercise, but he could walk only if supported on both sides; yet he bore these afflictions with unvarying cheerfulness

[1] See my *Discipline and Imagination* (1981), Ch. 5.

and patience. In 1970 he was saddened by the death of his old friend
and colleague Eduard Fraenkel, who had been unwilling to survive
the death of his beloved wife. To a friend who in an obituary notice
had defended Fraenkel's suicide as being wholly in accord with his
own rule of life, Pfeiffer wrote that while he would never presume to
blame Fraenkel for his action, he thought that sufferings must be
endured but not evaded. He lived on, still working, till 6 May 1979.
The learned world should be grateful to him; for though the second
volume of his *History* has by his high standards many defects, it is still
a work of very considerable value.[2]

Pfeiffer acted wisely in taking Fraenkel's advice and continuing
with the Renaissance period, leaving out the Middle Ages. He would
never have denied the importance of the period, and certain passages
of his writings suggest that his treatment of such figures as Clement,
Origen, Augustine and Cassiodorus would have been of great interest;
but his main concerns had never lain there, and if he had tried to write
about it he would have had wholly insufficient time for the later period
of which he had so great a knowledge; as it is, his second volume,
which appeared in 1976, is nowhere near as complete as he would
have wished. Part One deals with the Italian Renaissance, Part Two
with the Netherlands and Germany in the Renaissance period, Part
Three with the period between the French Renaissance and what
Pfeiffer calls 'German Neohellenism', and Part Four with German
Neohellenism in the eighteenth and nineteenth centuries, ending
somewhat abruptly in 1850.

Once more at the beginning of the work the insistence that
philology must begin with a scholar poet, in this case Petrarch, has
caused the author to be less than just to that poet's precursors; the
early humanists on whom Giuseppe Billanovich and his school have
thrown so much light in recent years, hardly receive their due. But by
far the least satisfactory part of the book is the last, dealing with the
great age of scholarship in Germany. The method of concentrating
attention on a few leading figures tends to obscure the links
connecting them, which often involve lesser scholars who find no place
here; the scholars are seldom considered in their social and historical
context; and towards the end the work becomes almost desultory,
such great figures as Lobeck and Meineke finding no mention. This
must have come about partly because this section of the work came
last; but it is clear that Pfeiffer felt less sympathy with the scholars of a
secular age than with their Christian predecessors. But when all this
has been said, the second volume has great merits. The treatment of

[2] See *Discipline and Imagination*, Ch. 2.

Petrarch and Politian is of high quality; and so is that of Erasmus and of Bentley, though the timidity and vacillation of Erasmus is hardly glanced at, and the importance of Christianity as an influence on Bentley may be found somewhat exaggerated.

Pfeiffer's distinctive conception of classical scholarship was developed in response to the general crisis of humanism in his time and in his country. The scholars of his generation were confronted by the recurring problem of the relationship between scholarship and humanism in a particularly acute form. Goethe and his contemporaries had been the first modern Europeans to make a serious attempt to see the Greeks directly, and not through Latin spectacles; in their time classical scholarship had a directly humanistic purpose. But as the new scientific study of the ancient world developed on a gigantic scale, classical philology became only one of the various disciplines that made up its totality, and literature was often judged by standards that took no account of literary values. From the point of view of the historian, it was an advantage that the Greeks were no longer idealised; from another viewpoint, it meant that the study of Greek literature and art was ceasing to be humanistic. The central issues became buried beneath vast heaps of facts; the classicism of the age of Goethe was derided as feeble sentimentalism. Nietzsche in his early work on the advantages and disadvantages of history was the first to warn of the impending crisis; but the time was not ripe for the German learned world to be alerted to its nature. By their ability and energy, Wilamowitz and his contemporaries were able to put off the day of reckoning, so far as the study of the ancient world was concerned; but after the First World War, German scholars were faced with a formidable dilemma. If they continued on the same path, their studies might become dry and technical beyond endurance; if they tried to return to the humanism of an earlier age, they would risk sacrificing honesty and exactitude for the sake of a facile and superficial substitute for the real thing.

During the late twenties and early thirties, Werner Jaeger tried to deal with the problem by institutionalising what he called a 'Third Humanism'. Like Karl Reinhardt and Bruno Snell, Pfeiffer showed no enthusiasm for this attempt, which in any case was destined to peter out miserably when the National Socialists came to power. For Pfeiffer the relations between humanism and philology were determined, in the last resort, by his religion. Clement and Origen had brought philology into the service of the Church by applying the critical methods of Aristarchus to the study of the Bible; and Erasmus had gone back to Origen, taking philology into the service of his *philosophia Christi*. Pfeiffer found it natural to adapt Leibniz's phrase '*philosophia perennis*' and entitle an account of the history of philology '*philologia perennis*'.

Even those who have no sympathy with Pfeiffer's Catholic faith must acknowledge that it lends a singular unity and simplicity to his conception of humanism and philology and the relationship between them. Also, the history of scholarship has seldom been written from a Catholic point of view, and Pfeiffer was able to correct several misapprehensions. In modern times it has been generally recognised that the Renaissance was very far from being a movement in the direction of paganism, and also that the Reformation was by no means altogether a movement in the direction of humanism and enlightenment; Pfeiffer's treatment does full justice to these undoubted truths. Again, his Erasmian Catholicism saves him from the element of Lutheran rusticity and provincialism that is present in the work even of some of the greatest German scholars; for him humanism is a European, even an ecumenical phenomenon. Marcello Gigante has rightly written that Pfeiffer does not reject the historicism of German philology, but renews it, purged of its excesses and its nationalistic element, by means of the sensibility of one who stands in the mainstream of a European culture. Even apart from his great achievement as a scholar and as a historian of scholarship, Pfeiffer has made a valuable contribution to the modern discussion of the fundamental purpose of the study of the ancient world. So long as that subject continued to be studied, Pfeiffer is likely to be remembered as one of the leading scholars of his time.

Pfeiffer was a member of the Bavarian Academy, to whose proceedings he made notable contributions, and became a Fellow of the British Academy in 1949. He was also an Honorary Member of the Austrian Academy, the Academy of Athens and the Académie des Inscriptions et Belles-Lettres. He held the Bavarian Order of Merit, the Greek Order of the Phoenix, and the Grand Cross of the Federal Republic of Germany. He was an Honorary Fellow of Corpus Christi College, Oxford.

23

Maurice Bowra

Sir Maurice Bowra has described the early part of his career in an autobiography which, though some complain that it lacks the salt of malice, is much better reading than most reminiscences of scholars (*Memories, 1898-1939*, London 1966). He is also to be the subject of a memorial volume of appreciations and reminiscences by various friends; this will include the full and admirable obituary notice published in *The Times* of 5 April 1971, the address delivered by Sir Isaiah Berlin at a memorial service held in the University Church at Oxford on 17 July 1971 and the appreciation by Mr Cyril Connolly printed in the *Sunday Times* for 29 August of that year. All these writings will be quoted in the following pages.

Cecil Maurice Bowra was born on 8 April 1898 at Kiukiang, in China, where his father, Cecil Arthur Verner Bowra, of a Kentish family, was working as an official in the Chinese Customs Service. His father was an intelligent and cultivated person, conservative in his opinions and somewhat austere in character, who combined loyalty to his own country with devotion to the interests of his Chinese employers. During his childhood Maurice Bowra was somewhat in awe of his father, but later they could talk without reserve. Maurice was clearly more like his father's father, Edward Charles Bowra, also a Chinese scholar and a member of the Customs Service, a dashing and imaginative person who unfortunately died young. Cecil Bowra was brought up by his mother, daughter of an East India Company official, Samuel Woodward, by a natural daughter of the Lord Cornwallis who was Viceroy. This is why Maurice Bowra was able to reply to an inquiry whether his family had any connection with the United States by saying, 'Not since my great-great-grandfather surrendered at Yorktown.' In childhood Maurice Bowra saw less of his father than of his mother, born Ethel Lovibond, the daughter of a brewer living in Fulham, who though a collateral descendant of John

* This chapter first appeared in *PBA* lviii (1972), and was reprinted in *Maurice Bowra: A Celebration* (1974), the book alluded to in its first paragraph.

Locke preferred to claim descent from the last man in England hanged for forgery. She was a gay and amusing person with a special gift for understanding others, even if their background was very different from her own.

Soon after Maurice Bowra's birth his father was transferred to Newchwang, in Manchuria, and he spent happy early years there before being brought to England in 1905. Living with his paternal grandmother and her second husband, the Revd. George Mackie, at Putney, he first had lessons from a governess – Ethel M. Dell's sister – and then went to an old-fashioned but good boarding school kept by two ladies. Here, with lessons from Cecil Botting, a master at St Paul's who collaborated with his High Master in the well-known Greek textbook known as 'Hillard and Botting', he began his classical education.

After an exciting visit to his parents, now at Mukden in Manchuria, in 1909-10, Bowra at the age of twelve entered Cheltenham College. The place and its headmaster, the Revd. Reginald Waterfield, were not free from the absurdities of the Victorian school, as Bowra was well able to appreciate. But it provided a sound training in Greek and Latin; G.F. Exton, a dry Cambridge scholar, gave a good grammatical grounding, and Leonard Butler, later a Fellow of St John's College, Oxford, gave Bowra a taste for writing Greek verse which he carried into later life. But Bowra found the school work boring, and used his last two years in the sixth form not to concentrate on classics, but to read widely. He learned French well enough to understand Verlaine and Baudelaire, tackled the Divine Comedy in a bilingual edition, and began to learn German. In 1916 he won the top scholarship to New College, Oxford.

Soon after this he returned to China by the Trans-Siberian Railway to spend the interval before joining the army in a visit to his parents. This journey, made at the most impressionable age, was of great importance in his life. He was deeply impressed by the marvels of Peking, where his father was now living as Chief Secretary of the Customs Service with an establishment of thirty servants and a cook who bore the title of 'Great Eating Professor'. On the way back he had the great good fortune to stay for some time in Petrograd. He made friends who were able to inform him about the interesting state of Russia at that time, and quickly acquired a working knowledge of the language. He was deeply fascinated by a brilliant and delightful Russian girl, who, he later wrote, 'had much fancy and humour, and unlike some Russians did not bother to talk about her soul or even mine'. This girl afterwards disappeared during the Revolution, and may have starved to death. To the end of his life Bowra wrote and spoke of her as he did of no other person, and it is clear that she filled a special place in his affection.

Bowra kept the Michaelmas Term of 1916 in a depleted Oxford; but early in 1917 he joined the Royal Field Artillery. He trained at an officer cadet school in Bloomsbury, and was much irritated by the 'spit and polish' on which his instructors insisted; but he made good friends, and managed to complete the course successfully. In September he was commissioned, and went to France in time to take part in the later stages of the Third Battle of Ypres. Later he was present at the successful action at Cambrai, and saw much heavy fighting during Ludendorff's offensive of March 1918 and the decisive counter-offensive of the month of August.

'Whatever you hear about the war,' Bowra later said to Cyril Connolly, 'remember it was inconceivably bloody – nobody who wasn't there can ever imagine what it was like.' But he carried out his duties with success, and seems to have developed at this time the ability to get on terms with very different people that he showed later. While in the trenches he read widely. He read a good deal of modern literature – during one leave he bought together Hardy's *Moments of Vision*, Yeats's *The Wild Swans at Coole*, and Eliot's *Prufrock*; but he read also Greek and Latin books, which now that he had left Cheltenham he took up with keen interest.

In April 1919, Bowra came into residence at New College, and from then until his death Oxford was his home. The cultural break occasioned by the First World War did not take effect immediately; it was not until the thirties, after the slump, that the wet blanket of collectivist thinking came down to stifle English intellectual life. The Oxford of the twenties contained many people who were not only intelligent but also gay and amusing, and in this society Bowra's quick wit and dominating personality made him conspicuous. Bowra's undergraduate friends in his own college included, to name only those who later became famous, Cyril Radcliffe, Roy Harrod, and Henry Price, and J.B.S. Haldane was a young don there; in other colleges he met Robert Boothby, L.P. Hartley, and Lord David Cecil; he frequented the *salons*, if that is the right word, of F.F. Urquhart and R.H. Dundas, and in Cambridge got to know G.H.W. Rylands.

At this time and for long afterwards Bowra presented a formidable as well as an engaging figure. 'I was not nearly so sure of myself as I should have liked,' he later wrote, 'and this made me present a brassy face to the world and pretend to be more hard-boiled than I was.' Like most people with the wit to think of them, he found it hard to resist the temptation to utter devastating remarks; and the temptation was strengthened by the extreme sensitivity which never left him. One can understand the rumour that the character of Markie Linkwater in his friend Elizabeth Bowen's novel *To the North* owed something to the impression made by the young Bowra.

New College at that time cannot be said to have offered the best classical tuition to be had in Oxford. The Mods tutor was the flaccid and unappealing H.L. Henderson, and the Greats historian, P.E. Matheson, was then well past a not very impressive best. One philosophy tutor was A.H. Smith, a cultivated and sympathetic person who did all he could to help Bowra and was to remain his friend for life; but Smith was scarcely the man to give him the intellectual training which he needed. The other tutor in philosophy was H.W.B. Joseph, who devoted great force of will and not inconsiderable ability to the rigorous enforcement of his own approach to philosophy upon his pupils. It is hard to imagine a tutor less congenial to Bowra than this chilly logician, who in Sir Isaiah Berlin's opinion 'undermined his faith in his own intellectual capacity'.

Fortunately not all the tuition Bowra received was from the fellows of his own college. Gilbert Murray had been Regius Professor of Greek since 1908, but still contrived to give some personal instruction to undergraduates, and this together with his lectures was far more important to Bowra than anything his other tutors could provide. Bowra wrote with special appreciation of Murray's famous classes in the translation into Greek of English verse and prose. Bowra was at all times a strong believer in the educational value of this now unfairly disparaged and neglected exercise, particularly in the hands of a scholar like Murray or J.D. Denniston. Bowra did not win any of the university scholarships and prizes given primarily for composition and in those days highly valued; but he obtained First Classes both in Mods and Greats.

In 1922 Bowra, with the support of Murray and his old friend A.S. Owen of Keble was elected to a tutorial fellowship at Wadham College, at that time, despite the beauty of its buildings and the eminence of some of its old members, a small, poor and not notably distinguished institution. In later years his tuition was sometimes a little hasty; but it was always exciting, and in his early years it was superb. Wadham did not provide Bowra with the most promising material, but he had among his pupils a future Secretary of the Cabinet in Norman Brook, a future historian of the Delphic Oracle in H.W. Parke, and a future Poet Laureate in Cecil Day Lewis. He also took an effective part in college business, being prominent among those who placed the finances of Wadham on a new footing by persuading the governing body to sell part of the Warden's garden to allow the building of Rhodes House. In 1930 he was elected to serve as Proctor, thus gaining the best possible introduction to the business of the university.

Bowra's social life as a young don was even more varied and exciting than it had been while he was an undergraduate. He more than anyone helped to launch into civilised life the brilliant generation that came up after the immediate postwar years, and aesthetes like Brian Howard and Harold Acton, scholars like Kenneth Clark, Isaiah Berlin, Roger Mynors, and John Sparrow, and men of letters like John Betjeman, Cyril Connolly, 'Henry Green', and Evelyn Waugh all owed much to his friendship and his influence. At that time several houses in the neighbourhood of Oxford were centres of intellectual activity, and Bowra was at home in all of them; he visited the Murrays on Boar's Hill, the Morrells at Garsington, and the Asquiths at Sutton Courtney, and made contact with other distinguished frequenters of these establishments.

Bowra spent part of his vacations in continental travel, and like other English intellectuals during the twenties and early thirties he found Weimar Germany a fascinating study. A visit on the way back from Yugoslavia with Hugh Gaitskell in 1927 was followed by a longer stay in 1932, when his friend Adrian Bishop was living in Berlin. He became intimate with several distinguished Germans, notably with the historian Ernst Kantorowicz, with the Curator of the University of Frankfurt, Kurt Riezler, and his wife, and with Baroness Lucy von Wangenheim. All these had some connection with the circle about Stefan George, of whom Bowra later wrote in *The Creative Experiment*: the classical scholar closest to this group was Karl Reinhardt, whom Bowra much admired. His visits to Germany enabled Bowra to form an early first-hand impression of the National Socialists, for whom, unlike many English people at that time, he conceived and expressed an instant disgust.

Even while his social life and college employments were at their height, Bowra was never idle. The habit of reading in bed, which he maintained throughout his life, ensured that he continued to extend his knowledge; and what he read he usually remembered. An article on 'Homeric words in Arcadian inscriptions', *Classical Quarterly* 20 (1926), 168f., followed up in 'Homeric words in Cyprus', *Journal of Hellenic Studies* 54 (1934), 54f., was a pioneer work; later the decipherment of Linear B was to lend special interest to these investigations of the two Greek dialects that conserved most Mycenaean features. In 1928 he published, in collaboration with his Wadham colleague H.T. Wade-Gery, a translation of Pindar's Pythian Odes into free verse, which was beautifully printed by the

Nonesuch Press. This was one of the first renderings of Greek verse –
certainly one of the first by academic persons – to throw off the worn-
out trappings of sub-Tennysonian traditionalist verse. It had a
deserved success, and later formed the basis of the translation of all
Pindar's epinician odes which Bowra published in the Penguin
Classics series in 1969. More good translations by Bowra have
appeared in *The Oxford Book of Greek Verse in Translation* (1938).

In 1930 Bowra published *Tradition and Design in the Iliad*, a well-
written and well-reasoned book which ranks high among his writings.
He was not the only scholar at that time to maintain that 'there was a
single poet called Homer, who gave the *Iliad* its final shape and artistic
unity, but who worked in a traditional style on traditional matter'.
But Bowra's book is wholly free from the nationalism and
sentimentality that disfigured other unitarian studies in the English
language. It gets to grips with the central problems of composition,
but is not afraid to describe and discuss the *Iliad* as we have it as a
poem with a plot and with its own kind of unity, and he never loses
himself in mists of archaeological and linguistic detail. Bowra was
acquainted with the work of Murko, though not yet with that of
Milman Parry, whose *L'Epithète traditionnelle* had appeared two years
before, and at one point considered whether the *Iliad* might not be an
oral poem. He concludes that Homer is likelier than not to have used
writing, but to have used it for his own use, not for the poem to be
read, but for it to be recited; we shall see presently how interesting it
is, in the light of current opinion, to find this in a book published as
long ago as 1930. The work has a freshness and liveliness that make it
after more than forty years still well worth reading.

During the thirties Bowra was mainly occupied with early Greek
lyric poetry. Papyrus publications had substantially increased the
small amount of material available, and elucidation was badly
needed. With Wade-Gery as his colleague in Wadham Bowra kept in
close touch with the latest developments in early Greek history,
archaeology, and art, and set out to use this to illuminate the poetry.

Bowra was not suited to be a textual critic. He lacked the accuracy
and caution expected of an editor, and he had been denied the gift of
textual divination. The presentation of the early lyric poems in *The
Oxford Book of Greek Verse* (1930), for which he was responsible, leaves
much to be desired; and his Oxford text of Pindar (1935), though its
apparatus criticus contains some useful matter, has not enough
positive merits to compensate for its numerous inaccuracies. In 1936
he brought out *Greek Lyric Poetry*, a large interpretative book which
devotes a chapter to each major figure; in 1938 it was followed by
Early Greek Elegists, a slighter volume which contained the Martin

Lectures delivered at Oberlin College in Ohio. In later years Bowra
was critical of the former book, which in 1961 he subjected to a radical
revision.

> I was too often carried away by my imagination [he wrote] and did not
> pay a sufficiently critical attention to views which I put forward because
> they fascinated me. Nor was I careful enough with some small details. I
> knew that they mattered and I enjoyed discoursing about them, but with
> them too enthusiasm was not enough. In trying to find solutions for all
> problems I went further than the fragmentary evidence allowed, and too
> many of my hypotheses were fragmentary and unsubstantiated.

That characteristically severe self-criticism is just; but the book's
failings are not only on the side of technical scholarship. The writing
slides far too easily into cliché; people who knew Bowra only from his
conversation must have been staggered to find him capable of writing
'Alcman well understood the Spartan girls who sang in his choirs and
entered completely into their happy dainty longings' or 'Over their
ripening desires Sappho presided'. Correspondingly, the critical
approach adopted to the authors is disappointingly conventional. Yet
with all its faults the book has attractive qualities, showing as it does
its author's wide knowledge and real love of literature. To a beginner
in scholarship at that time it seemed to offer a fascinating glimpse of
the picture of early Greek civilisation then being drawn, under the
influence of Beazley, by men like Payne and Blakeway, and to help the
reader to enjoy the precious fragments whose number the papyri had
excitingly increased.

In 1936 the Regius Chair of Greek at Oxford was to be vacated by
the retirement of Gilbert Murray, to whom Baldwin as Prime
Minister was known to have assigned the task of choosing his
successor. The most proficient Greek scholar teaching in Oxford at
that time was beyond question J.D. Denniston, whose famous book
The Greek Particles had appeared in 1934.[1] But Murray considered
particles a dull subject, and thought that Denniston lacked what he
used to call 'originality'. Bowra tells us in his *Memories* that he himself
was convinced that Denniston ought to be appointed, but that once he
became aware that Murray was unlikely to recommend Denniston, he
began to consider himself a candidate. When the choice fell upon E.R.
Dodds, at that time Professor of Greek at Birmingham, Bowra was
bitterly disappointed, and it cannot be said that he did much to make

[1] Bowra's obituary notice of Denniston in *PBA* 35 (1949), 219f. is one of his best
pieces of writing.

life easier for the new professor, with whom he was later on friendly terms, but only after many years had passed. But it was not long before Bowra became aware that Cyril Bailey's consoling remark that the apparent disaster might prove to be a blessing in disguise had been fully justified.

During the winter of 1936-37 Bowra was absent from Oxford as Visiting Professor at Harvard, where he stayed in Lowell House. He made a powerful impression on both colleagues and audiences, and as usual made good friends. Among the older people, he saw much of John Livingston Lowes, of Felix Frankfurter, and of William James, the son of William and nephew of Henry; among the younger, he made friends with Harry Levin, F.O. Matthiessen, and Ted Spencer. Among the classical scholars he had friendly contacts with Carl Jackson and with E.K. Rand; but the most significant of his friendships was with John Finley, who was later to be his colleague as Eastman Professor at Oxford. Before the end of his visit, Bowra was offered a permanent post at Harvard, and had to think hard before declining. He was surely right. Though he was anything but insular, Bowra was too English to have settled down anywhere outside England, perhaps too Oxonian to have settled down outside Oxford.

In 1938 the Warden of Wadham retired from office, and though only forty years of age Bowra was put forward for the succession by Wade-Gery together with Professor F.A. Lindemann, later Lord Cherwell. Considering the difference in their political opinions, it may seem strange to find Lindemann as one of Bowra's strongest advocates; but over the then all-important question of Chamberlain's policy of appeasing Hitler they were in close agreement.

Not surprisingly, the news of Bowra's election came as a shock to that section of opinion which he would have described as *bien pensant*. He was, as *The Times* obituary notice of him says, 'a free thinker, an epicure and an uninhibited advocate of pleasure'; worse still, many of his epigrams about respected persons and institutions had got about. Soon after his election at Wadham, some of his friends outside that college entertained him at a party held to celebrate his triumph; they ended by celebrating black mass in a college chapel – not his own – and were ejected by the verger. It was predicted that Bowra would be the greatest possible failure as the head of a college. In the event, he was generally acknowledged to have proved the greatest possible success.

Fortunately for Wadham College, though less fortunately for the common good, Bowra was never offered a government post during the war. If he had been, the result might have been remarkable. The powers that enabled Bowra to master the contents of innumerable books in a short time served him well in gaining a rapid grasp of business. His gift for understanding the working of other people's minds helped him to find the arguments that would convince them, and he was able to get through the agenda quickly without giving his colleagues the feeling that they had been hurried into acquiescence. His remarkable gift for discerning ability in others led to some wise choices in fellowship elections, and he maintained the friendliest relations with his colleagues, guiding and encouraging the younger ones without ever seeming to patronise them. Every undergraduate in the college got a vivid impression of the Warden's personality, and knew that he placed nothing before the education and welfare of the junior members of the university.

Bowra's *Sophoclean Tragedy* appeared in 1944; it had been written a good deal earlier, but its publication was delayed because of the war. Its distinguishing note is the contention that in Sophocles' work the justice of the gods is upheld. Although some psychological arguments that do not convince are used, and at times the nature of divine justice seems to be conceived in too uncomplicated a fashion, this makes the book a valuable contribution to the understanding of the poet.

As early as 1934, Bowra had written for his own amusement a study of Yeats. He had become friends with Yeats, who for some time lived in Oxford; he showed Yeats an early draft, and Yeats's comments on it are to be found in *Memories* (p. 240). Other essays about modern poets followed, and these finally appeared in the volume *The Heritage of Symbolism* (1943); besides Yeats, there are chapters on Valéry, Rilke, George, and Blok. This publication and that of *From Virgil to Milton* (1945) a valuable study of the secondary epic, made possible Bowra's election to the Oxford Chair of Poetry, a post held for five-year periods which he occupied from 1946 to 1951; the renewed interest in this chair and its occupants dates from the period of his tenure. By way of an inaugural lecture, he gave under the title of 'The background of modern poetry' a lucid and intelligent account of the aims and presuppositions of the modern movement. In 1949 he published *The Creative Experiment*, a kind of sequel to *The Heritage of Symbolism*, in which he discussed Cavafy, Apollinaire, Mayakovsky, Pasternak's early poetry, Eliot's *The Waste Land*, Lorca's *Romancero Gitano*, and Rafael Alberti's *Sobre los Angeles*. *The Romantic Imagination* (1950) contains lectures given when he was Charles Eliot Norton Professor at Harvard in 1948-9, staying at Eliot House under the auspices of his old friend John Finley. Many of the essays on modern and medieval poetry which he composed subsequently are reprinted in the volume *In General and Particular* (1964). Special mention may be made of *The Simplicity of Racine*, where his familiarity with certain of the poet's sources gave him an advantage over other Racinian critics, and his Taylorian Lecture of 1961 on 'Poetry and the First World War', a subject on which he was particularly well qualified to speak. In 1965 he gave the Wiles Lectures at the Queen's University, Belfast, which appeared the following year under the title *Poetry and Politics, 1900-1960*; the book contains interesting remarks about poets whom he knew, like Edith Sitwell, Quasimodo, Seferis, and Neruda.

'If we do not know what an author has tried to do,' Bowra once wrote, 'we cannot justly decide whether he has succeeded in doing it.' Much of his critical work was designed to answer just this question. He concentrates on an attempt to explain the author's artistic purpose and the method he has used in order to achieve it; he would have agreed with Carlyle that to read any author properly one must as far as possible enter into his mind and see with his eyes. The catholicity of his taste and the warmth of his enthusiasm for literature enabled Bowra to do this effectively in the case of many different writers; and at a time when some of the most influential literary critics were restricted in their interests and narrow in their sympathies, these qualities made his writings especially valuable. The merits of his critical writings are balanced by marked deficiencies. That very enthusiasm for authors which was one of his chief assets was a disadvantage in so far as it caused his approach to authors to be descriptive rather than critical. Too often his descriptions have a kind of cosiness, as though all were for the best in the best of possible worlds; and this effect is strengthened by the flatness of much of the writing. It is instructive to compare his work with that of another critic of comparably wide sympathies, Edmund Wilson. One cannot imagine a scholar like Bowra being as misguided as Wilson was over the *Philoctetes* of Sophocles or the Dead Sea Scrolls; yet by comparison Bowra's critical writings lack a cutting edge. Bowra is most successful with those modern poets who stand closest to the romantic tradition, particularly his friend Yeats; he is less at home with Eliot, as his careful but uninspired summary of *The Waste Land* shows. But even this essay is a far more valuable guide to someone not yet acquainted with the poet or his methods than many more penetrating critical studies would supply; and this is true of most of Bowra's criticism.

Bowra should by right have succeeded to the Vice-Chancellorship of Oxford in 1948, when an unforeseen accident removed the then incumbent; but he was at Harvard at the time, and so was enabled to serve out his term as Professor of Poetry and then be Vice-Chancellor from 1951 to 1954. His tenure of the post was the most memorable of modern times. The qualities that made him such a successful head of his own college stood him in good stead in this office also. He was an effective chairman of committees, able to master great masses of material with impressive speed and altogether free from the inability to decide which is such an infuriating characteristic of academic persons. His swiftness in repartee silenced antagonists; and his brilliant conversation, combined with a good nature remarkable in one so witty and always more in evidence as he grew older, made him countless friends. After he had ceased to be Vice-Chancellor Bowra was re-elected to the Hebdomadal Council by a number of votes far in excess of any previously recorded, and continued to serve on this body, on the General Board, the University Chest, and as a Delegate of the Clarendon Press, doing valuable service to all these bodies. He was much concerned to see that important posts, and also honorary degrees, should go to the best candidates, and his great power to recognise ability in others helped him to do the university specially valuable service in this respect. The prominence on university committees of a person of so much scholarly distinction and of such a cosmopolitan outlook did much to redeem Oxford from the reproach of parochialism, which in earlier times might justly have been levelled at it.

The British Academy also profited from Bowra's great administrative ability. He had become a Fellow in 1938 and was President from 1958 to 1962. In two matters in particular, that of the Treasury Grant and of the setting up of a British Institute in Teheran, he did the Academy great service.[2]

This public activity never diminished the flow of Bowra's writings, and his best written work, with the exception of his early book about the *Iliad*, belongs to the last part of his career. The later works dealing with modern poetry have already been described. *Heroic Poetry* (1952) shows an astonishing knowledge of primary epic literature in many languages, and presents its results in most attractive fashion; hardly any other scholar could have written this book. The same is true of *Primitive Song* (1962), which offers translations from the verse of those communities which may be thought to give a notion of the primitive way of life. Bowra's large contribution to the study of epic poetry was rounded off by a posthumously published book entitled *Homer*, written for Duckworth's 'Classical Life and Letters' series, and giving a clear and extremely up-to-date account of the Homeric poems. Here Bowra works out ideas already touched on in his Andrew Lang Lecture of 1955, 'Homer and his Forerunners'. While fully taking into account the work of Milman Parry, Bowra showed how its acceptance was perfectly consistent with a unitarianism, placing Homer at the end of

[2] See Sir Mortimer Wheeler's *The British Academy, 1949-68*.

a long poetic tradition, of the kind advocated in *Tradition and Design in the Iliad* forty-two years earlier.

Bowra meant his *Pindar* (1964) to be his main achievement in scholarship. Not everyone will think it was. Two years before its publication, Elroy L. Bundy had challenged the assumption that Pindar's odes of victory were full of personal and historical allusions, and had insisted that the main clue to their interpretation lay in the truth that the poet's primary purpose was to praise the victor he was celebrating. Bowra's book never questions the assumption of Wilamowitz that a study of Pindar can take the form of a biography. Unlike Wilamowitz, he did not give his book a biographical form, but to reject the analysis of individual poems in favour of chapters each devoted to some general topic was a still greater error. The mass of generalisations becomes tedious, and the style tends more than usually towards cliché. The *Pindar* is indeed a useful book. Bowra was familiar with the whole relevant literature; he took far more trouble over detail than he had in *Greek Lyric Poetry* in 1936; and his obvious affection for his subject lends the work a special attraction. But it breaks no new ground, and can hardly be compared with Bowra's work on Homer.

Some of Bowra's early articles were collected in the volume *Problems in Greek Poetry* (1954); articles of the later period are reprinted in *On Greek Margins* (1970). These articles, particularly the later ones, contain some of Bowra's best classical work. He would take an individual work, usually a poem, often one that had suffered neglect because of its isolation, and would explain its significance and relate it to its historical context.

Bowra was the successor of his teacher, Gilbert Murray, as the leading provider of works designed to explain Greek literature to the English-speaking general reader; and the *Times* obituary well says that if Murray's style was the more delicate instrument, Bowra was more direct and realistic. As early as 1935 he contributed to the Home University Library a small but useful book called *Ancient Greek Literature*. In 1957 he brought out *The Greek Experience*, a well-written and carefully considered book which is generally considered the best work of its kind now available in English. *Landmarks in Greek Literature* (1966) is another valuable survey; and *Periclean Athens* (1971) is not only full of information but reveals a gift for historical narrative that makes the reader wish Bowra had essayed it earlier.

Bowra would normally have vacated the Wardenship of Wadham in 1968, when he reached the age of seventy. But the Fellows honoured him by using their power to extend his tenure for two years; and when in 1970 that period expired, they granted him the unusual privilege of continuing to occupy rooms in college. Here he died suddenly, as he would have wished, on 4 July 1971. In spite of increasing deafness, he had retained all his powers to the last.

Bowra's achievement as a scholar and critic is, by any standards, considerable; his career as a university administrator is the most distinguished of modern English. Yet his most remarkable success lies in his influence on those who encountered him in Oxford. This influence was powerful throughout his career, but most of all in the early part of it; later it was more widely diffused but less highly concentrated.

An important element in this influence was the brilliance of his talk. *The Times* obituary notice speaks of 'the scintillating, shimmering and sometimes thunderous wit of his conversation'. 'His wit was verbal and cumulative,' writes Sir Isaiah Berlin. 'The words came in short, sharp bursts of precisely aimed, concentrated fire, as image, pun, metaphor, parody, seemed spontaneously to generate one another in a succession of marvellously imagined patterns, sometimes rising to high, wildly comical fantasy.'

But Bowra was far more than an amusing talker; he was, in Sir Isaiah's words, 'a major liberating influence'. In Bowra's early years in Oxford the constricting stuffiness of Victorian convention still lay heavily on much of English social life. Much of intellectual life was correspondingly inhibited; till well into the thirties most senior academics and schoolmasters reacted with sheer horror to any movement in literature and the arts that seemed to break away from the Victorian tradition. Against this tradition Bowra was an open rebel. He was ready, and had been since his early years, to lend an ear to innovations in art and literature. He had a kind of religion, like that of the early Greeks, but he did not believe in Christianity, and would have agreed with Keynes in finding it odd of so many earnest Victorian atheists to go on proving it to be false and wishing it were true. He enjoyed pleasure, and thought that on the whole what people liked tended to be good for them.

In politics, his sympathies, like those of many generous-minded members of his generation, were with the left rather than the right; but not all modern left-wingers could safely claim him as a kindred spirit. During the General Strike of 1926 his sympathies were with the strikers; he was a close friend of Hugh Gaitskell; and after the Papadopoulos government came to power in Greece, he gave up the Hellenic Cruises that had been one of his favourite recreations. During the thirties he campaigned actively against the policy of appeasing National Socialist Germany. Dislike of appeasement was by no means confined to left-wingers; but Bowra loathed everything that was associated with the predominance of men like Baldwin and Neville Chamberlain. Yet he was never a doctrinaire socialist; anyone in doubt on the matter should study the references in his *Memories* to the late Lord Lindsay of Birker, Master of Balliol. His left-wing sympathies arose from his desire for liberty, which in his youth was threatened chiefly by right-wing and conventionally religious authoritarians. He did not care for cant; and in his later years, when most cant was coming from the left, he did not allow ideological sympathies to blind him to its nature. One of his strongest terms of disapproval was 'cagey'; he detested the stuffy, cautious conventionality that is epitomised by his friend Anthony Powell's famous character, Kenneth Widmerpool. Bowra did what he could to block the advance of Oxford's Widmerpools, of whatever political colouring.

Unlike most people who talk a great deal, Bowra was uncannily observant of others and alive to their reactions. No one was more generous in giving encouragement to others, and in England, where reserve and the cult of good form so often damp enthusiasm, this quality was particularly precious. The number of people who acknowledge a debt to Bowra for having strengthened their self-confidence at a critical period is very great; the people in question are of very different kinds, and many exceptionally gifted. When Bowra had reached a position in which he could use his gift of discerning talent by promoting able people, he spared no pains to do so. During his last months he was in hospital suffering from a painful complaint when he was informed that a gifted young scholar, whose promise he had long before discerned, had been appointed to a high position. Bowra was so excited that he almost leaped out of bed in his delight.

Those who knew only Bowra's writings may find it hard to understand, but no person who knew him at all well can fail to be surprised that nothing that he ever wrote gives the faintest inkling of the impression which he made in conversation. He wrote indeed better than most scholars, and especially in the later part of his career he knew how to order his material with great skill. But even where he avoids cliché, what he wrote seems flat and pedestrian beside the brilliance of what he said. To this deficiency of style corresponds a deficiency of content. His work in technical scholarship is solid, sound, judicious, but it is never brilliant; his criticism is sane, lucid, sympathetic, but it lacks flair.

How can we explain this puzzling limitation? We have seen that he himself wrote of his lack of self-confidence in early life; and something of this uncertainty always remained with him. One sign of it was his extreme sensitivity to adverse criticism; at a hint of disloyalty he could become furious even with old friends. Sir Isaiah Berlin thinks that his self-confidence was undermined by the destructive criticism of Joseph; but the roots of his diffidence must lie further back. At school he had disliked the hard grammatical grind of the old-fashioned classical education; he came to love the ancient authors during the war, when he read them for pleasure, just as he read Anatole France, Verlaine, or Baudelaire. He read rapidly, and his quickly-moving brain tended to bypass difficulties; he seldom stopped to break his head over a knotty problem. At Oxford he became well aware of his deficiencies; he was aware of the difference between his scholarship and that of men like Housman or Lobel, and though he knew that he was capable of some achievements which they never attempted, the knowledge worried him. But by an act of will he gave himself the resolution necessary to carry through each plan; he tapped speedily away on his typewriter, seldom pausing for reflection, for too much reflection might weaken his determination. As in technical scholarship he made mistakes until he learned not to expose his weakest side, so in criticism he failed to come to grips with the chief critical problems; that very sympathy with the authors whom he studied that was one of his best qualities had also its reverse side. Cyril Connolly has said that he was a poet *manqué*. Certainly his talk was more like a creative writer's than like a scholar's, and if he had essayed creative writing perhaps he would have shed some of his inhibitions. Scholarship gave him a discipline he needed; and yet it may have promoted what Sir Isaiah calls 'a peculiar lack of faith in his original and splendid gifts'. His least inhibited writing was his occasional verse, and it is sad that little of this is likely to be published while those who can recognise its allusions are alive.

But his achievements are so considerable that the regret felt by his friends that he did not accomplish more is a striking tribute to the power of his personality. He was the most celebrated Oxford character since Jowett, whom he surpassed in scholarship and in warmth of character. His services to his college and his university were unique; so was his effect upon colleagues and undergraduates of all kinds, obscure as well as famous. But when all this has been said, it gives no notion of what it was like to talk with him, and still less of the affection and admiration felt for him, at least during his later years, by all who knew him.

Bowra was knighted in 1951, and in 1971 was made a Companion of Honour; he was a Commander of the Légion d'Honneur, a Knight-Commander of the Greek Order of the Phoenix and a holder of the German Order *Pour le Mérite*. He was a corresponding member of the American and Irish Academies, and held honorary doctorates from

Paris, St Andrews, Harvard, Aix-en-Provence, Columbia and Hull, and from Trinity College, Dublin. At Oxford he became Doctor of Letters in 1937 and Honorary Doctor of Civil Law in 1970, and was Honorary Fellow of New College and of Wadham College.

24

E.R. Dodds

Eric Robertson Dodds was born on 26 July 1893 at Banbridge, County Down in Northern Ireland, the son of Robert Dodds and his wife, born a Miss Allen. His father's family were northern Presbyterians, descended from Scotch immigrants; his mother's were Anglo-Irish, who had a dubious claim to aristocratic connections, but had also intermarried with the natives. His father was the head-master of a small grammar school, who came to grief because of drink and died when his son was seven years of age. Dodds thus became wholly dependent on his mother, who supported him by teaching, first at Bangor on Belfast Lough and later, from 1902 or 1903, in Dublin. She was a conscientious but possessive and unsympathetic parent, and though Dodds escaped religious indoctrination and from an early time was able to read widely, his childhood was by no means altogether happy. At St Andrew's College, Dublin, where his mother taught, and later at Campbell College, Belfast, he obtained a good grounding in the classics and in modern literature, particularly from the sixth-form master at the latter, Roby Davis, besides playing football well enough to be tolerated by the herd. Finally he was provoked by the tyrannical behaviour of a pompous headmaster into writing him an angry letter, and was expelled from Campbell College for 'gross, studied and sustained insolence'; a later headmaster apologised, and expunged this statement from the official records.

In 1912 Dodds entered University College, Oxford with a scholarship in classics. Coming from a different country and holding radical opinions, he did not find life in prewar Oxford altogether easy; but he made good friends among his contemporaries, and was successful in his studies. While working for Classical Moderations, the literary and linguistic part of the course, he had an excellent tutor in A.B. Poynton, who published little but later impressed Eduard Fraenkel as a learned man; and he was deeply influenced by the teaching of Gilbert Murray, who since 1908 had held the Regius

---

* This obituary notice first appeared in *Gnomon* 52 (1980), 78f.

Chair of Greek and who at this time lectured on the *Bacchae* and gave his famous class on the art of translation. In 1914 Dodds obtained a First Class in Moderations, and won the Ireland Scholarship, the most coveted of the university scholarships awarded mainly for translation into Greek and Latin and then greatly prized.

During that summer he spent a holiday in Germany, and only just got back in time. The university rapidly emptied, and for a time Dodds worked as a medical orderly in an army hospital in Serbia, but he returned to take his final examinations. He was a member of a small group of undergraduates, including Aldous Huxley and the future art critic T.W. Earp, who met weekly to read each other their poems; at a class on Plotinus given by J.A. Stewart he met an American graduate whom he invited to address this group, and who when he did so read them 'The Love Song of J. Alfred Prufrock', which he had just written. The head of Dodds' college objected to his support of the Easter Rebellion, and though not formally sent down he was asked to leave; many years afterwards, when it was put to him that in a year when England was fighting for her life and sustaining appalling casualties on the Somme, this was hardly surprising, he did not dissent. But he continued to work for Greats, the second part of the Oxford course, and duly obtained a First Class in 1916.

Returning to Ireland, Dodds spent some time teaching in a school. He much enjoyed the literary life of Dublin, where he got to know Yeats, A.E., Lennox Robinson and Stephen MacKenna, the translator of Plotinus, whose journals he later edited. But, as he once remarked he had the wrong religion for one part of Ireland and the wrong politics for the other, and from 1919 he lived in England.

In that year he was appointed to a lectureship in classics at the University of Reading where he had several interesting colleagues and a congenial head of the department in P.N. Ure. He studied Neoplatonism, at that time by no means a fashionable subject, with the enthusiasm of a believer in its doctrines; later after the belief had left him the interest would remain. In 1922 he published valuable notes on Plotinus, and followed them with the two small volumes, texts and translations with introduction, of *Select Passages Illustrative of Neoplatonism* (1923, 1924). At this time he married Miss Annie Powell, then a lecturer in English in the same university, a highly cultivated and intelligent lady whose somewhat formidable manner and appearance concealed a sensitive and understanding nature. Despite the not entirely easy temperaments of both partners, the marriage was wholly happy, down to the time of Mrs Dodds' death in 1973.

In 1924 Dodds was appointed to the Chair of Greek in the University of Birmingham, where he and his wife occupied a delightful house in which they spent what was probably the happiest period of their lives. They were at the centre of a lively circle of congenial friends; Dodds appointed to a lecturership the poet Louis MacNeice, and became intimate with him and with his friend and fellow-poet W.H. Auden, whose family then lived in Birmingham. Dodds later helped MacNeice with his brilliant translation of Aeschylus' *Agamemnon*, and after his death acted as his literary executor. In 1929 Dodds himself published *Thirty-two Poems*, some of which have found a place in various anthologies. Dodds had a genuine poetic gift, as those who heard him lecture might easily guess, and it is a pity that he gave up writing poetry.

In 1928 Dodds published in the *Hibbert Journal* (26, 1928, 459f.) a penetrating article on the *Confessions* of St Augustine which he called 'a study of spiritual maladjustment'. In the following year he brought out an article called 'Euripides the Irrationalist'.[1] No author had suffered more than Euripides from the perennial tendency of scholars to read modern attitudes into ancient writings, and this paper, reversing the title of a then popular work by the ingenious and insufferable Verrall, supplied a valuable corrective. In 1933 appeared his edition with commentary of the *Elements of Theology* of Proclus, the most useful summary of Neoplatonic metaphysics which has survived from antiquity; A.D. Nock, later a valued friend of Dodds, drew attention to the book's high quality (*Cl. Rev.* 48, 1934, 140).

In 1936 the Regius Chair of Greek at Oxford was due to be vacated by the retirement of Gilbert Murray, an incumbent of unique prestige. The Prime Minister, Stanley Baldwin, was content to leave the choice of a successor to Murray himself, thus presenting him with an awkward problem. The Oxford Hellenist who had most distinguished work to show was J.D. Denniston, who had brought out in 1933 his authoritative study *The Greek Particles*, and who was liked and admired by both colleagues and pupils as few Oxford tutors have ever been. But Murray felt that particles were too technical a subject, and did not think Denniston sufficiently 'original', an important word in his vocabulary. An energetic and colourful candidate for the Chair, eleven years younger than Denniston, was Maurice Bowra; but though Murray liked him he did not altogether approve of him, and doubted whether his scholarship was sound enough. So Murray compromised by recommending Dodds, who was not eager to leave Birmingham, but found it difficult to refuse.

For many years Dodds and his wife greatly regretted this decision. Virtually all members of the Oxford faculty had wanted either

---

[1] *Classical Review* 43 (1929), reprinted in *The Ancient Concept of Progress*, 78f.

Denniston or Bowra, and few of them knew enough of Neoplatonism to appreciate the main publications of Dodds up to that time; those who knew the articles about Augustine and Euripides must have been shocked by them. Dodds' rumoured support of Irish republicanism and Socialism did not add to his popularity, particularly in Christ Church, the college to which the Regius Professor of Greek automatically belongs. In his inaugural lecture (*Humanism and Technique in Greek Studies*, 1936) Dodds suggested that since we now had texts of most ancient authors adequate for understanding we would do well to devote less energy to textual criticism and more to general interpretation; a colleague greeted him in the street with the words, 'I see, Dodds, that you have decided to kill research.' A more outgoing character might have dealt more successfully with the distressing situation in which Dodds found himself; but Dodds did not quickly get on terms with new acquaintances, and his experiences intensified a natural tendency to be suspicious. It was many years before he really settled down among his Oxford colleagues.

Undergraduates, however, from the first greatly appreciated his teaching. A deep and impressive voice, in which he read poetry superbly, enhanced the appeal of lectures which combined scholarly exactitude with literary sensitivity to a remarkable degree. At this time Dodds was working on his edition of the *Bacchae*, and at the same time compiling the notes that were later to take shape as *The Greeks and the Irrational*; he delivered a memorable course of lectures on the *Oresteia*, whose main connecting argument was later developed in a famous article: 'Morals and politics in the *Oresteia*'.[2]

On the outbreak of war in 1939 Dodds volunteered for service. He travelled to China on a cultural mission, vividly described in his autobiography; he later visited the United States, and after the end of hostilities went to Germany to help with the rehabilitation of the educational system. In 1944 he published his edition of Euripides' *Bacchae*, with introduction and commentary, later revised in the edition of 1960. Despite the preference given to humanism over technique in his inaugural lecture, the constitution of the text and other technical matters are dealt with in masterly fashion; but an even more notable feature of the book is the imaginative sympathy, matching in quality its exact scholarship and profound learning, with which the Dionysiac religion and its antagonist are treated.

In 1949 Dodds travelled to Berkeley, California to give the Sather Lectures; this resulted in the publication two years later of *The Greeks and the Irrational*. Interest in the problems discussed went back to

---

[2] In *Proc. Cambr. Phil. Soc.* (1960) = *The Ancient Concept of Progress*, 45f.

Nietzsche and Rohde, if not to Creuzer, and the application of modern anthropology and psychology to their treatment was not new; Dodds' own teacher Gilbert Murray had been a pioneer in this respect. But by now these disciplines had acquired a new assurance and stability, and Dodds was able to employ them with a mastery of the material, ancient and modern, and a sound judgment combined with imaginative insight that enabled him to make a great stride forward in the understanding of the complicated subject.

It may be argued that the opening chapters underrate the ethical elements in Homeric religion, and ascribe to a mysteriously rapid growth in superstition after Homer certain irrational beliefs which are prominent in later literature but not in Homer, perhaps because Homer knew them but did not choose to dwell on them. But these chapters have the great merit of having shown that Homeric religion is real religion and not a mere divine apparatus. Dodds gives an excellent account of Greek beliefs about madness, which he classifies as Apolline, Dionysiac, or emanating from the Muses or from Eros and Aphrodite; and he analyses the distinctive patterns of Greek dreams, showing how often modern rationalism has taken genuine experience for fiction. The theory of the shamanistic origin of dualistic beliefs about the soul which he put forward may be disputed; more important is his sketch of the rise of these beliefs and their effect on Plato. Dodds' account of the rationalism of the fifth century and the reaction against it is somewhat conditioned, like those of other scholars, by an unconscious equation of the ancient with the modern 'enlightenment'; much fifth-century rationalising was only a working-out of what had been implicit in earlier belief, and the irrational forces thought to have been set in motion by it had been at work much earlier. Atheism when directed against Greek religion was in any case very different from atheism directed against a religion dependent on supernatural claims made on behalf of historical or allegedly historical personages. But he gives an admirable account of Plato's dealings with the problems of the irrational, supplemented by 'Plato and the irrational',[3] and it is a pity he did not go on to discuss that of Aristotle. He reproaches the great philosophers of the third century with having gone back behind Plato and Aristotle to the 'naive intellectualism of the fifth century', and regrets that the protest of Posidonius did not have more effect. At the end of a careful discussion of the reasons for the decline of Greek rationalism after that time, he gives most weight to 'the fear of freedom – the unconscious flight from the heavy burden of choice which an open society lays on its

[3] *JHS* 77 (1947) = *The Ancient Concept of Progress*, 106f.

members'. More people will accept this diagnosis than will share the
hope that psychology will help to cure this malady that Dodds
cautiously expresses in the concluding pages. The book is written with
a literary skill rare among learned men, and throughout uses
consummate erudition to throw light on problems of central
importance not only for the past but also for the present and the
future. Little noticed at its first appearance and for some time after, it
has now for many years exercised immense influence. Many readers
have found it the most illuminating contribution to classical studies in
our time, and it will be long before it loses its power over its readers.

After the war Dodds' life in Oxford, like that of his loyal supporter
Eduard Fraenkel, became much happier. Younger men who owed
much to his teaching and writing took their places on the faculty, and
gradually the great originality and importance of his work came to be
understood. He now exercised considerable influence, and in his later
years many of his colleagues would have agreed with Auden, who
called Dodds the wisest man he ever knew. After his retirement in
1960 he went on living in his house at Old Marston, on the outskirts of
Oxford, in which Cromwell is believed to have received the surrender
of the town, and never ceased to keep in touch with friends and
colleagues until his death on 8 April 1979.

In the late forties Dodds lectured on Homer, and produced the
useful summary of Homeric scholarship published in M. Platnauer's
Fifty Years of Classical Scholarship (1950).[4] In 1959 he brought out a new
text, with introduction and commentary, of Plato's *Gorgias*. He found
that a good deal of work upon the manuscripts was needed, and
though in theory he disapproved of devoting much time to textual
work that was not likely to yield results of great importance, in
practice his academic conscience was too delicate to let him shirk the
duty. Like his *Bacchae*, his *Gorgias* is excellent from the technical as
well as from the interpretative point of view; but he chose this
dialogue for its relevance to the modern situation, and the book fulfils
a humanistic purpose.

In 1963 Dodds delivered the Wiles Lectures at the Queen's
University, Belfast, which resulted in the publication two years later
of *Pagan and Christian in an Age of Anxiety*. The book deals with the
period between the accession of Marcus Aurelius and the conversion
of Constantine, but deals with much that happened both before and
after that time. The first chapter deals with the pessimistic picture of
the cosmos common to pagans and Christians at that time; the second
with the equally common belief in daemons and other supernatural

---

[4] New edition: *Fifty Years (and Twelve) of Classical Scholarship* (1962).

agencies; the third with mysticism; and the fourth with the dialogue between pagan and Christian. Dodds acknowledged that he could have improved the book if he could have brought himself to read more deeply in the Fathers, whom he did not find congenial; but he none the less throws much light on Christians as well as pagans, and clearly brings out their distressing resemblance to each other. In assessing the reasons for the triumph of Christianity, he gives full weight to its having offered to its adherents the advantages of belonging to a community which took care of its members.

In 1973 Dodds reprinted six of his articles, adding four that had not yet been published, in a volume called *The Ancient Concept of Progress*. In the paper that gives the book its name, which is the most important of the new pieces, he was considerably more sceptical about the diffusion in antiquity of 'the idea of progress' than his friend Ludwig Edelstein had been in the posthumously published book on the topic that had appeared in 1967. Dodds found that 'only during a limited period in the fifth century was the idea of progress widely accepted by the educated public at large', one may doubt whether even at that time people believed in the possibility of moral progress on the part of whole communities, and even more whether anyone thought progress automatic or inevitable. In the same year Dodds' eightieth birthday was marked by the dedication to him of a special number of the *Journal of Hellenic Studies*.

In 1977 Dodds published his autobiography, *Missing Persons*, whose title is explained by the remark of J.C. Powys, prefaced to the book, that 'the persons we have been are lost rather than fulfilled in what we become'. The book is beautifully written, and describes with modesty and candour a life-story more varied than that of most scholars; it had great success, and was awarded the Duff Cooper Prize. But the reader feels that something is being withheld; there was more to Dodds' complicated personality than the book reveals.

From his early youth Dodds was actively interested, like his predecessor Gilbert Murray, in psychical research; he served on the council of the Society for Psychical Research from 1927, and was President from 1961 to 1963. He found the evidence for telepathy convincing, but though retaining an open mind about the subject he was never persuaded by the alleged evidence for survival after death. A study of supernormal phenomena in antiquity which appeared in *Greek Poetry and Life*, the volume dedicated to Gilbert Murray on his retirement in 1936, was reissued in an expanded and corrected form in the *Proceedings* of the Society in 1971, and again in *The Ancient Concept of Progress*.

Dodds was never easy to get to know; his moods varied, like those of many sufferers from asthma, and at times he withdrew into himself. But in later life at least he would talk genially with anyone with whom he came in contact; and those who could get through his defences found him a good friend and an agreeable companion. His talk, like his writing, showed much wit and humour; he read widely, and ranged over many topics. Although his early radicalism became milder, even where organised religion was concerned, he never lost his sympathy with rebellion, and unlike most people understood that different generations need to rebel against different things. A noble, though to his colleagues somewhat awe-inspiring, feature of his conversation was that it showed no touch of pedantry, not even of the innocent sort which most scholars enjoy.

Dodds was a Corresponding Member of the Academia Sinica, the Bavarian Academy, the American Academy of Arts and Sciences, and the French Institut; he had honorary degrees from Manchester, Dublin, Edinburgh, Birmingham and Belfast. He became a Fellow of the British Academy in 1942, and received its Kenyon Medal in 1971. He was an Honorary Fellow of University College, Oxford and an Honorary Student of Christ Church.

25

Denys Page

Denys Lionel Page was born on 11 May 1908, the son of F.H.D. Page, a railway official, and his wife Elsie. For some time the family lived in South Wales, so that in the cricket county championship Page was a supporter of Glamorgan; but they moved to Berkshire early enough to enable him to go to Newbury Grammar School. The headmaster, the Rev. W.H. Sharwood-Smith, was an admirable teacher of the classics, who had been a Scholar of Jesus College, Cambridge, of which his distinguished pupil was later to be Master.

In 1926 Page won a scholarship at Christ Church, Oxford. It was a time when several gifted undergraduates were in residence there, Page's chief friends were the Hon. Quintin Hogg, now Lord Hailsham of Marylebone, and D.J. Allan, later Fellow of Balliol College and Professor of Greek at Edinburgh; but he had acquaintances also among socially-minded and sporting undergraduates. An early photograph shows a studious-looking young man looking out anxiously from behind large spectacles; the worried expression recalls that which Lely captured so successfully in the great portrait of another *novus homo*, Matthew Prior, which hangs in the Combination Room of Trinity College, Cambridge. But if Page had anxieties, he quickly overcame them as he adopted the prevailing ethos of the college, and threw himself into Oxford life, working hard but always allowing himself time for relaxation. He won his place in the Christ Church cricket team as a terrifying fast bowler. Already he had very definite views about most things and about most persons; those he disapproved of 'he castigated', in the words of a contemporary, Lord Gordon-Walker, 'with a kind of mock fury, but with no real malice'. He did not change in this respect.

Page can have learned little from the Christ Church Mods tutors, S.G. Owen and J.G. Barrington-Ward, except how to write elegant Latin. He was taught ancient history by R.H. Dundas and R.P. Longden, and philosophy by M.B. Foster and Gilbert Ryle; he did

* Following in *PBA* lxv, 1979.

well in these subjects, but from the start his main interest was in Greek literature. Gilbert Murray's lectures and classes inspired him, as they did many hearers; he admired the unique scholarship of J.D. Beazley, who made him aware of the importance of a knowledge of Greek art and archaeology for a literary scholar; and he had the great good fortune to be sent for special coaching in Greek composition to J.D. Denniston, who was then working on his famous book *The Greek Particles*. In Denniston's hands translation into Greek was not simply a scholastic exercise, for instead of vague impressions as to whether a particular usage was right or wrong, he was able to supply precise details. Like all Denniston's friends and pupils, Page was charmed by his genial ferocity and sympathetic strictness, and there came to be a close friendship between their families.

Page obtained First Classes both in Mods and Greats, and won Craven and De Paravicini Scholarships, the Chancellor's Prize for Latin Verse and the Gaisford Prize for Greek Verse. After taking his degree in 1930 he was elected to the Derby Scholarship, and would have liked to go to Berlin to hear Wilamowitz; but it was too late, for the great man was too old, and died in September of the following year. Instead Page spent a year in the more relaxed atmosphere of Vienna, where he attended the seminars of the cultivated and civilised Ludwig Radermacher, acquiring a command of German that was to prove useful in war as well as peace. In 1931 he was appointed a Lecturer at Christ Church, and after the probationary year that was then usual he became Student and Tutor of the House in 1932.

As Derby Scholar, Page had begun his study of *Actors' Interpolations in Greek Tragedy, with particular reference to Euripides' 'Iphigenia in Aulis'*, and the book appeared in 1934. New discoveries and researches had altered the situation since Wilamowitz had treated of the subject, and Page was able to make a positive contribution to the detection of interpolations and to the understanding of the process by which they came into being. Already his detailed knowledge and keen critical intelligence could be discerned, and well-qualified reviewers like Albin Lesky and Friedrich Solmsen recognised the book's high quality. Two years later he contributed a brilliant essay on the elegiac lament in Euripides' *Andromache* to *Greek Poetry and Life: Studies in Honour of Gilbert Murray*.

In 1938 Page contributed an edition of Euripides' *Medea* to the series of red-covered editions of Euripidean plays that was published by the Clarendon Press. The plan was that Gilbert Murray's Oxford text of each play should be reprinted, and that the editor should provide simply the introduction and the commentary; but Page insisted on supplying a new text of his own editing. Text and commentary made a striking contribution to the understanding of the play, not seriously marred by youthful dogmatism. The introduction has born the passage of time less well; its high-flown eloquence now seems as dated as the Shavian Euripides whom Page had unsuspectingly taken over from Gilbert Murray. It had not occurred to Page that he might learn something from the discussion of Euripides by E.R. Dodds, whose appointment to the Regius Chair of Greek in 1936 he had so much disapproved of that he for many years refused to speak to him.

From the beginning of his time as tutor Page applied himself to the study of the early Greek lyric poets. New papyrus discoveries had greatly increased the number of their fragments, and by his editions of Sappho (1925) and Alcaeus (1927) Edgar Lobel had set new standards of accuracy and learning in editing them. Other texts of these writers were markedly unsatisfactory, being disfigured by rash conjectures and supplements, which often violated language, dialect and metre. Page's first publications on Sappho and on Alcman date from this phase of his career; already the influence of Lobel on his work is easily perceptible.

Meanwhile the Loeb Classical Library invited Page to edit in a single volume all the Greek poetry on papyrus not contained in its volumes devoted to individual authors, apart from very small or unintelligible scraps; each text was to be accompanied by an introduction and a translation. Page embarked on this formidable task with his usual energy and confidence. Very often the texts were better edited or explained by him than by any previous editor; a vast amount of information was imparted; and the resulting book was not only a boon to readers, but a large contribution to knowledge. When it was published, in 1942, the entire stock was destroyed by enemy action, and it was long before it became generally available.

Page rapidly made his mark as tutor and lecturer, and proved highly congenial to his Christ Church colleagues and to most of those with whom he came in contact. As always, he had strong opinions one way or the other, and he did not see eye to eye with everybody. At first he was much stimulated and encouraged, like many others, by the friendship of Maurice Bowra; but later the two men drifted apart, perhaps because Page came to regard Bowra's scholarship as unsound. His earliest relations with Eduard Fraenkel, who had become Corpus Professor of Latin in 1935, were friendly, and Fraenkel's assistance is acknowledged in the preface to his *Medea*; but later the two became estranged. His relations, or lack of them, with E.R. Dodds have already been mentioned. But with most of his colleagues he was on good terms, Denniston and Lobel having most influence on his work.

In 1937 he became Junior Censor of Christ Church, and was a great success in that capacity; but a year later he resigned the Censorship and applied for a year's leave in order to get married. On a Hellenic Cruise he had met Katharine Elizabeth Dohan, of Pennsylvania, whose mother, Mrs Edith Hall Dohan, was a well-known archaeologist. In 1939 Page paid his first visit to the United States, giving the Dean West Lectures at Princeton; his marriage took place in Rome, not long before the outbreak of war in 1939. Page's married life was singularly happy, he and his wife being greatly devoted to each other; with their four beautiful daughters they made up an harmonious family.

Soon after his return to England, Page joined the department of the Foreign Office located at Bletchley Park which dealt with the branch of intelligence known as Ultra. He was assigned to the section which under the direction of Oliver Strachey dealt with the various hand ciphers used by our enemies, which came from divers sources. Page's great ability, combined with his command of German, enabled him to take an important part in this work, so much so that when Strachey retired in 1942 Page was chosen to succeed him. At the end of the war Page headed a special command mission to Lord Mountbatten's headquarters first at Kandy and later at Singapore, and did not return to Oxford until 1946.

He then resumed his teaching and research with all his usual vigour; he began to take part in University affairs by serving as Senior Proctor in 1948/9. But in 1950 the Regius Chair of Greek at Cambridge was due to be vacated by the retirement of D.S. Robertson, and though Page did not apply the electors offered him the post and he accepted. The alliance between Christ Church and Trinity College, as well as the traditional link of Trinity with the Regius Chairs, made it natural that Trinity should elect him to a Professorial Fellowship; and the Page family moved from 8 St Aldates to Strathaird, the large and comfortable house off the Madingley Road which had been the residence of J.D. Duff.

Page's early time in Oxford had been an exciting period in the history of Greek studies in that place, and of all the studies which are there classified as Literae Humaniores. The publication of new papyri, most of them from the Oxyrhynchus hoard, the presence of the learned refugees from Germany, the stimulus afforded by the work of Beazley, and the readiness of the younger ancient historians, impelled by Alan Blakeway, to use archaeological data to throw light on early Greek history helped to create an exhilarating atmosphere: so did the contact with a group of Roman historians which included Ronald Syme and with philosophers who were making an important contribution to their subject, most of them under the influence of J.L. Austin.

Cambridge at that time contained several classical scholars of very great distinction. But some of these were approaching retirement, and they cannot be said to have communicated with the undergraduates or with their junior colleagues as effectively as their counterparts in Oxford. The Tripos was badly in need of reform, and offered a training infinitely less stimulating than Greats did at that time. Housman, with his exaggerated insistence that the critical appreciation of literature was an emotional matter and had nothing to do with scholarship, had done harm in Cambridge education; and his opinion seemed to be confirmed by the activities of such opponents as Sir John Sheppard, Provost of King's College. The unkind remark that there was nothing in Cambridge between the high and dry of Trinity and the low and wet of King's was sadly not altogether without truth.

Page's arrival changed the atmosphere completely. Undergraduates were as fascinated as those of Oxford by his brilliant lectures, in which the necessary facts were set out with consummate learning and with crystal clarity, inferences from them deduced by cogent reasoning, and the whole performance, like that of a great advocate, rendered irresistible by the charm, liveliness and intelligence of the performer. One might easily not notice that these qualities had seldom been applied to the literary and artistic interpretation of the subject-matter, or that one had been admiring the lecturer rather than the poetry on which he lectured; and if one did, one had too much to be grateful for to think of complaining.

Not only undergraduates, but dons, especially the younger dons, benefited enormously from Page's presence. He was, as he continued to be throughout his life, princely in the generosity with which he sacrificed his precious time to help others in their work, and any colleague who applied to him found him both willing and able to assist him very greatly. In so large a college as Trinity it cannot be easy for a newcomer to arrive almost immediately at the centre of college life; but Page did so, and was very soon elected to the College Council.

The fruits of his prolonged and intensive study of the Greek lyric poets now began to appear in a series of important publications. In 1951 he brought out a book on Alcman's Louvre Partheneion, in 1953 an edition of Corinna, with commentary, and in 1955 his edition of the fragments of the Lesbian poets, made in collaboration with Edgar

Lobel, and his book *Sappho and Alcaeus*. The Alcman book contains a text of the riddling poem, with a careful diplomatic transcription of the papyrus, a commentary and full discussion. His theory about the general meaning of the poem cannot be called fully convincing, any more than any other theory that has been put forward; but the book remains indispensable for any serious study of the work. So is the text of Corinna with its accompanying expository matter. In *Lesbiorum Poetarum Fragmenta* Page added to Lobel's earlier editions of the Lesbian poets all the new material that had accrued, making naturally full use of Lobel's publication of most of it in the Oxyrhynchus series. By a kind of coquetry not uncommon among great scholars, Lobel had chosen to present the poems in a fashion whose austerity repels some readers; and it is possible to regret that Page took over this method. But the work is done in masterly fashion, and its contribution to the establishment of the texts is very great indeed.

Sappho and Alcaeus contains texts of the more considerable fragments, with detailed commentaries, set in the context of a general discussion of the authors and the many problems which their poetry and lives present. The commentaries on the text are of the highest quality; but the literary questions which these authors pose are less satisfactorily dealt with. Realising that some readers might expect a literary appreciation of the poets, Page dealt with the problem by copying out a long extract from John Addington Symonds, representative of the criticism of the nineties, but not calculated to satisfy all modern readers. Still, the two books devoted to the Lesbians are a magnificent achievement, which no living scholar could have equalled.

Two publications of the fifties that were more deeply affected by the weakness in handling literary questions manifested by the strange decision to make extensive use of Symonds were *The Homeric Odyssey* (1955) and *History and the Homeric Iliad* (1959). Both were based on lectures given in America, the former on Flexner Lectures delivered at Bryn Mawr in 1954 and the latter on Sather Lectures delivered at Berkeley in 1958; and the need to present the material in the form of arresting lectures aimed at a transatlantic audience allowed the rhetorical element to get somewhat out of hand. Both books display their author's usual comprehensive learning, clarity of thought and presentation, and penetrating logic. But they are marred by a displeasing dogmatism; the views of other scholars are often too brusquely brushed aside; and the assumption of multiple authorship is too readily used to account for features of the poems which might well be explained by other methods. The book about the *Iliad* displays remarkable knowledge of the relevant archaeological data, of the newly deciphered Linear B tablets, and of the oriental documents thought to have a bearing on the poem; and though arguments based on such material often lose their cogency in the light of fresh discovery and interpretation, much of this still retains its value. But in the appendix dealing with 'Multiple Authorship in the *Iliad*' some of the greatest poetry of the world is insensitively hacked about by a surgeon who hurries to operate without having paused to understand the nature of the case. This appendix, with much of the *Odyssey* book, occupies the same place in Page's work that the edition of Milton occupies in that of Bentley.

Denniston had long been working at an edition of the *Agamemnon* of Aeschylus on the scale of the red-covered Oxford editions of Euripides' plays, and he had meant to revise his draft in the light of Eduard Fraenkel's great commentary. But Denniston died in 1949, a year before the publication of Fraenkel's work, and it fell to Page to prepare the manuscript for publication. The work as it appeared seems to contain a good deal more of Page than of the original Denniston. Perhaps Page was too eager to differ from Fraenkel; yet the commentary is of great value, and did good service in showing that the vastly learned editor was not immune from error. The part of the work most open to criticism was the introduction, whose rhetoric recalls that of the Homeric books, and whose confident assumption that problems could be bypassed by taking it for granted that the poet's religion and outlook were crude and primitive has not gone unchallenged.

During the late fifties Page's life was altered by his wife's first serious illness. For a time he coped with the management of their large house almost single-handed; and though he carried on his work with great courage, the burden of anxiety must have been a heavy tax on even his resources. His wife recovered; and in 1959 their domestic problems were alleviated by his election to be Master of Jesus College. His vast energy enabled him to discharge the duties of this office with great thoroughness, while keeping up his rapid production of scholarly work of a high order. His wife was soon able to take an active part in social life, and Page threw himself into college affairs with characteristic enthusiasm. 'He was an active and sympathetic Master,' writes the author of an obituary notice in the annual report of Jesus College, 'always ready to listen to members of his College, even though some of them may not have realised that they were interrupting his work.'

After the fifties Page seldom returned to the parts of the field of Greek studies where his weaker side would have been exposed, preferring to concentrate on critical editions and commentaries. In 1962 he brought out *Poetae Melici Graeci*, a critical edition of the Greek lyric poets, other than the Lesbians. A minor edition of these poets appeared in 1968 as an Oxford Classical Text under the title of *Lyrica Graeca Selecta*, and a supplement containing new material, *Supplementum Lyricis Graecis*, followed in 1974. Page also edited large fragments of a papyrus containing an ancient work about lyric poetry, containing many quotations, which Lobel had long worked at before handing it over to him; this appeared as Part XXIX of the Oxyrhynchus Papyri in 1963. All these works are executed in masterly style, and the texts of the works they contain were notably improved by Page. His contribution to the editing and explanation of the texts of the Greek lyric poets would by itself suffice to make him one of the most distinguished Greek scholars of the twentieth century.

But now Page turned to the field of Hellenistic poetry, with results almost as remarkable. In 1965 his colleague at Trinity, A.S.F. Gow, followed up his great edition of Theocritus by publishing in two volumes *The Greek Anthology: Hellenistic Epigrams*, containing the text, with commentary, of those epigrams which must have formed part of the Garland of Meleager. To this work Page contributed the edition of Meleager himself; and when in 1968 the same partners brought out the two volumes of *The Greek Anthology: The Garland of Philip and some contemporary epigrams*, Gow was responsible for Antipater of Thessalonica, but Page for all the other authors. In 1975 Page brought out a minor edition of many of the poems published in these two volumes, which appeared as an Oxford Classical Text under the title of *Epigrammata Graeca*. To the end of his life Page continued to work at the Greek epigrams; his last book, published in the year of his death, was *The Epigrams of Rufinus*, containing text and commentary. He left almost ready for publication a further volume, containing all epigrams not included in the earlier volumes down to the year AD 50, together with certain others later than that year, this is to be published shortly. Page's work on epigrams shows his usual learning and acuteness, and makes a major contribution to the understanding of Hellenistic poetry.

In 1972 Page returned to the study of Greek tragedy by satisfying the acute need for a new Oxford Classical Text of Aeschylus. He used and supplemented the important investigation of the manuscripts by Dr R.D. Dawe in a book which had begun as a thesis which he supervised; and though the text of Aeschylus abounds with problems over whose solution agreement is unlikely ever to be reached, any competent person must agree that his edition has improved on all its predecessors.

Page often visited Greece, particularly Crete, and followed with keen interest the remarkable excavations on Thera directed by his friend Spyridon Marinatos. In his pamphlet *The Santorini Volcano and the Desolation of Minoan Crete* (1969), he warmly advocated the theory that Knossos was destroyed by the eruption of the Theran volcano, one that has now lost the favour of the vulcanologists. In 1972 he gave the Jackson Lectures at Harvard, making out of them the small and attractive book *Folktales in Homer's Odyssey*, which appeared the following year. In addition to his books, Page produced a whole series of valuable articles, notes and reviews, most of them concerned with lyric, tragedy or Hellenistic poetry; from the sixties on, many of them appeared in the *Proceedings of the Cambridge Philological Society*. A full bibliography of his writings may be found in the volume *Dionysiaca: Nine Studies in Greek Poetry by former pupils, presented to Sir Denys Page on his Seventieth Birthday* (1978).

Page's efficient conduct of business was evident in University as well as College matters, and many people believed that he would make an admirable Vice-Chancellor. But though the turn of his College to supply a holder of the office was long overdue, the safe men who sat on University Committees, who had then embarked on the policy of appeasing revolting students that was to find its natural consequence in the riot at the Garden House Hotel, decided against this. Their progressive orthodoxy was doubtless shocked by Page's forthright expression of conservative opinions, and by the crude attempts of undergraduate journalists to construe some of his remarks as a declaration of support for the regime of Papadopoulos; they need not have worried, for Page was by no means insensitive to public opinion, and as Vice-Chancellor would certainly have given general satisfaction.

Page could have retained his Chair until 1975 and the Mastership of Jesus until 1978; but in 1973 his wife's renewed illness led him to resign both offices and return to live quietly in Northumberland. After that time he rarely came south; but he continued to work hard, using the excellent classical library of the University of Newcastle. Early in 1978 lung cancer was diagnosed, and it was clear that he had not long to live; but he faced death with great courage and composure, and never ceased to work. Almost at the end of his life, he happened to learn from his eldest daughter that a young scholar who was her neighbour in Oxford was editing a collection of interesting inscriptions; Page asked to see the manuscript, and was able to improve it by a great many suggestions of which few living scholars would have been capable. He died on 6 July 1978, and Lady Page survived him by only a few weeks.

In the work of editing and explaining the remains of Greek poetry Page's achievement is very great; in our time only Edgar Lobel, whose aims and methods have been somewhat different, can be compared with him. Intimate acquaintance with the texts and mastery of grammar, syntax and metre, together with all relevant knowledge of the subject-matter, was brought to bear on editorial and interpretative problems, and keen critical acumen was constantly exerted to extend the bounds of knowledge. Like all human beings he had limitations, which others may remark in the awareness that his achievement far exceeds their own. He lacked the wide general culture and refined sensibility of his predecessor, Donald Robertson; he had little interest in philosophy, religion or the history of ideas; he did not easily appreciate qualities he did not share, and had no notion of what he might have learned from the writings of Karl Reinhardt or of E.R. Dodds. His tendency to see things and people in strong black and white made it hard for him to do full justice to the complexity of life.

But Page's charm and gaiety delighted most of those who met him, often surprising those who had known only the somewhat formidable personality revealed in what he wrote. His readiness to help pupils and colleagues was as great as his very considerable power to do so; and if his teaching had a fault, it was the generous fault of finding it easier to praise or to encourage than to warn or to reprove. He rendered great services to his two Universities and his three Colleges; and his place in the history of Greek studies is assured beyond dispute.

Page was elected Fellow of the British Academy in 1952, received its Kenyon Medal in 1969, and served as President from 1971 to 1974, doing it good service by his energetic conduct of its business. He was knighted in 1971; was a Doctor of Letters of Cambridge; held honorary doctorates from Oxford, Trinity College, Dublin, and the Universities of Newcastle, Hull and Bristol; and was a Corresponding Member of the Academy of Athens, the American Academy of Arts and Sciences, the American Philosophical Society and the Greek Humanistic Society. He was an Honorary Fellow of Trinity and Jesus Colleges and an Honorary Student of Christ Church.

Index